CHRIST THE TIGER

Paganism, Christianity, Romanticism and Sacrifice in the Poetry and Plays of T.S. Eliot

Hyam Maccoby
Edited by Deborah Maccoby

MAPLE
PUBLISHERS

CHRIST THE TIGER

Author: Hyam Maccoby

Copyright © Hyam Maccoby (2025)

The right of Hyam Maccoby to be identified as author of this work has been asserted by the author in accordance with section 77 and 78 of the Copyright, Designs and Patents Act 1988.

First Published in 2025

Front cover illustration: *Royal Tiger,* lithograph, 1829, by Eugène Delacroix (1798-1863), The Metropolitan Museum of Art, New York.

Back cover illustration: *Surprised!* 1891, by Henri Rousseau (1844-1910), The National Gallery, London.

ISBN 978-1-83538-381-0 (Paperback)
     978-1-83538-382-7 (Hardback)
     978-1-83538-383-4 (E-Book)

Book cover design and Book layout by:
    White Magic Studios
    www.whitemagicstudios.co.uk

Published by:
    Maple Publishers
    Fairbourne Drive, Atterbury,
    Milton Keynes,
    MK10 9RG, UK
    www.maplepublishers.com

A CIP catalogue record for this title is available from the British Library.

All rights reserved. No part of this book may be reproduced or translated by any form or by any means, electronic or mechanical, including photocopying, recording or by any information storage and retrieval system without written permission from the author.

The views expressed in this work are solely those of the author/editor and do not reflect the opinions of Publishers, and the Publisher hereby disclaims any responsibility for them.

TABLE OF CONTENTS

Editor's Preface 5

Editor's Memoir of Hyam Maccoby 17

Chapter 1: Christ the Tiger 41

Chapter 2: The Theme of Sexual Conflict in Eliot 64

Chapter 3: Eliot and Antisemitism 83

Chapter 4: Flowering Judas: A Study of the "jew" in "Gerontion" 100

Chapter 5: An Interpretation of "Mr. Eliot's Sunday Morning Service" 120

Chapter 6: Time and Eternity: A Commentary on "Burnt Norton" 133

Appendix 1: Two Notes on *Ash Wednesday* 174

Appendix 2: Two Notes on *Murder in the Cathedral* 180

Appendix 3: Difficulties in the Plot of *the Family Reunion* 187

Appendix 4: *The Family Reunion* and Kipling's "The House Surgeon" 200

Appendix 5; Review of *T. S. Eliot, Anti-Semitism and Literary Form*, by Anthony Julius 205

Appendix 6: Review of *Word Unheard: A Guide through Eliot's Four Quartets*, by Harry Blamires 207

Appendix 7: Three Letters: A) *TLS* Letter on Craig Raine on Eliot's Use of Cliches; B) *TLS* Letter on "Mr. Eliot's Sunday Morning Service"; C) *Jewish Chronicle* Letter on Eliot's Antisemitism 210

Appendix 8: An Examination, by The Editor, of "A Cooking Egg" 215

Appendix 9: The *Listener* Correspondence 236

Bibliography 242

Acknowledgements 250

About the Author and Editor 252

Index 253

"Yet the ancient pagan vision of the restoration of Nature to youth and vigour by sacrifice must not be lost. Even though this vision cannot, after all, be fulfilled in this world, even though the world cruelly disappoints it, the vision must be retained; otherwise, we should sink into worldliness and complacency, into the worst fate of all, satisfaction with the world as it is. This is the clue to all Eliot's poetry; the refusal to give up the vision of youth, combined with the conviction that this world can never satisfy the vision. This explains the extraordinary combination that we find in Eliot's poetry of the sensual and the meditative -- a combination of the voluptuary and the ascetic. And this emotional complex (which is not a contradiction but a fusion into a convincing whole of apparently contrary attitudes) is worked out at every possible level; from purely personal terms to a generalized theory of the history of human culture, and even (in the *Quartets*) as far as a highly abstract philosophical theory of Time and Eternity." (From Chapter 1.)

This book is dedicated to my mother, Cynthia Maccoby (1927-2016),

who began the work that I have completed.

Zichronah livracha (may her memory be for a blessing).

EDITOR'S PREFACE

In the 1980s, according to a September 2022 review in the *London Review of Books*, "Eliot emerged from reverence and then rejection to become a figure of primarily biographical interest".[1] The reviewer, Helen Thaventhiran, was writing about *Eliot After The Waste Land,* Volume Two of a major new biography of T. S. Eliot, by Robert Crawford. This second volume includes an examination of the recently released letters sent by Eliot to the love of his youth, Emily Hale (letters kept under embargo until 2020). But *Eliot After The Waste Land* came out in 2022 to mark a hundred years since the publication of *The Waste Land.* If this centenary is publicly recognized as a date that is important to commemorate, doesn't this mean that Eliot is far more than "a figure of primarily biographical interest"? The time has surely come to return, as a matter of primary interest, to the poetry and to understanding and appreciation of its greatness.

The essays collected in *Christ the Tiger* were written in the late 1960s and early 1970s -- a time when Eliot's poetic reputation and the primary critical focus on his poetry[2] were still very strong, though starting to decline from their pre-eminence in the 1950s and early 1960s; and these essays focus on the poetry, even while they acknowledge its indissoluble connection with the life. As the author of this book, Hyam Maccoby, puts it in Chapter 1:

The poetry is an expression of Eliot's personal dilemma, but he has

---

1 "Things Ill-Done and Undone", *London Review of Books*, September 8, 2022. This is, of course, an exaggeration; but it is an exaggeration of a truth. Many academic books and articles have been published in recent years on Eliot's poetry, but they tend to belong to specialist academic enclaves and to concentrate on social and cultural issues rather than primarily on the poetry (see next footnote on postmodernist academic studies of Eliot). Recent books written about Eliot in a style intended for the general reader do tend to be biographical, rather than about the poetry. Four books came out to mark the 2022 anniversary, all biographical: the Robert Crawford biography; Lyndall Gordon, *The Hyacinth Girl*; Mary Trevelyan and Erica Wagner, *Mary and Mr. Eliot*; and Matthew Hollis, *The Waste Land: A Biography of a Poem* (all London, 2022).

2 In the late 1960s and early 1970s, the dominant fashion in literary criticism was "The New Criticism", which focused on textual analysis and could go to the extreme of excluding other considerations altogether. A postmodernist and cultural critical reaction against "The New Criticism", concentrating on social issues, often to the detriment of textual analysis and appreciation, set in later; but, in recent years, the wheel seems to be turning full circle, and a sense of the need to focus on the poetry seems to be returning; see a fairly recent feminist critic, Cassandra Laity: "For purist New Critics ... social issues and biographical particularities encroached upon aesthetic creativity, while for many postmodernists and cultural critics formalist aesthetics merely camouflaged social prejudice.... However, cultural and postmodern critics are increasingly concluding that a text's association with a socially prejudiced author need not contaminate its value as an aesthetic object or negate its attendant poetics." (*Gender, Desire and Sexuality in T. S. Eliot*, edited by Cassandra Laity and Nancy K. Gish, Cambridge, 2004, pp. 9-10.)

achieved the feat of standing outside his personal dilemma to such an extent as to see it as representative of the human condition itself. (One is at liberty, of course, to see this as a feat of projection rather than of impersonality. At this level, the extremes of the subjective and the objective come together.)[3]

Hyam Maccoby (1924-2004), my father, is known as a Jewish historian who wrote on New Testament studies, Jewish/Christian relations and Jewish and Christian theology. But he graduated from Oxford University in English Language and Literature and taught English for many years in secondary schools. Before he began writing his first published book, *Revolution in Judaea: Jesus and the Jewish Resistance*[4], the first edition of which appeared in 1973, he was working on a book entitled *Flowering Judas*[5]: *The Christian Image of the Jew*: a projected comprehensive survey of antisemitism in English literature, from Chaucer's "The Prioress's Tale" to the poetry of Ezra Pound and T. S. Eliot. Even though *Flowering Judas* was never completed, my father, before he abandoned it, had drafted many chapters that eventually became separate essays, most of which he published in various magazines. Most of the chapters in *Christ the Tiger* originate from his unfinished book *Flowering Judas*. His work on Eliot was at first only a part – though the culminating part – of this wide-ranging project; but my father developed a particular interest in Eliot, as is shown by the shorter pieces on specific points in relation to his writings that my father contributed to the scholarly journal *Notes and Queries* (one of these pieces – "The Fourth Tempter – Devil or Angel?" -- was republished in the 1971 book *Twentieth Century Interpretations of Murder in the Cathedral*[6]).

These shorter articles are mostly reproduced here in the Appendices; but, between 1968 and 1970, my father published in *Notes and Queries* a series of line-by-line analyses of the five parts of "Burnt Norton", the first of the *Four Quartets*. I have put these analyses together to form the final chapter of *Christ the Tiger*.

To return to the Appendices: I have also included letters and reviews written by my father in relation to Eliot. In addition: there is no mention in my father's essays of one of Eliot's most-debated poems, "A Cooking Egg" (which is, in my view, one of his antisemitic

---

3   P. 58. Eliot himself wrote, in a famous quotation: "the more perfect the artist, the more completely separate in him will be the man who suffers and the mind which creates; the more perfectly will the mind digest and transmute the passions which are its material". ("Tradition and the Individual Talent", *The Sacred Wood*, 1920: London, 1932, p. 54.)

4   New York, 1980.

5   This title, like *Christ the Tiger*, is taken from Eliot's poem "Gerontion".

6   David R. Clarke (ed.), *Twentieth Century Interpretations of Murder in the Cathedral*, New Jersey, 1971, pp. 93-96. See Appendix 2(a).

poems). This omission seems to me to be a lacuna in the book; so I have ventured to write my own analysis of "A Cooking Egg" based on the lines of interpretation put forward in *Christ the Tiger* -- lines that seem to me to shed a great deal of light on the poem. I have included my analysis as Appendix 8.

The structure of *Christ the Tiger* is based on this paragraph in Chapter 1 (p. 58):

> Yet the ancient pagan vision of the restoration of Nature to youth and vigour by sacrifice must not be lost. Even though this vision cannot, after all, be fulfilled in this world, even though the world cruelly disappoints it, the vision must be retained; otherwise we should sink into worldliness and complacency, into the worst fate of all, satisfaction with the world as it is. This is the clue to all Eliot's poetry; the refusal to give up the vision of youth, combined with the conviction that this world can never satisfy the vision.... And this emotional complex (which is not a contradiction but a fusion into a convincing whole of apparently contrary attitudes) is worked out at every possible level; from purely personal terms to a generalized theory of the history of human culture, and even (in the *Quartets*) as far as a highly abstract philosophical theory of Time and Eternity.

Chapter 1, the title essay, sets out the main themes of the book: Paganism, Christianity, Romanticism and Sacrifice in Eliot's poetry and plays. My father places Eliot's work in the context of the Romantic movement and emphasizes his preoccupation with the continuity between Christianity and the late pagan mystery-religions that centred around dying-and-resurrected Young Gods such as Adonis, Attis and Osiris. These mystery religions were spiritualized cults that were based upon ancient pagan fertility rites that at times had involved actual human sacrifice. My father writes (p. 57): "In Eliot's poetry ... it is the mystery-cult inheritance of Christianity that is really significant."

Chapter 2 – "The Theme of Sexual Conflict in Eliot" -- includes a discussion of "a generalized theory of the history of human culture", in relation to Eliot's study of anthropological theories of an ancient cultural battle between matriarchy and patriarchy – a battle reflected in Eliot's poetry in the dysfunctional relationship between the sexes in the modern Waste Land (a relationship based on his own personal problems but universalized). Special consideration is given to "Sweeney Among the Nightingales" and *The Family Reunion*. Eliot's vision of the sex-war is also discussed in terms of "The Romantic Agony", as seen in the work of late-Romantic writers such as Baudelaire or Flaubert (in his novel *Salammbo*). I also point out in a footnote (pp. 80-81, footnote 173) that, in an essay published in another collection of my father's articles, he defines Romanticism as a "secret attachment to matriarchy, in a patriarchal context".[7]

Chapter 6 is concerned with Eliot's "highly abstract philosophical theory of Time and Eternity", as worked out in the first of the *Four Quartets*, "Burnt Norton". One of the purposes of these essays is to place Eliot's poetry within the context of the ferment of ideas of his time (a period of revolutionary theories about the development of human culture and about the nature of Time[8]). The 1960s and '70s harked back to these modernist ideas of the 1920s. I will explain later how Chapters 3, 4 and 5 fit in.

In an unpublished (and unfinished) draft essay that was to have been one of the concluding chapters in *Flowering Judas*, my father considers "the question whether what I have been doing in this book can be called literary criticism". He refers to *The Merchant of Venice*, but his comments are very relevant to his study of Eliot and are worth quoting at length, to make clear the main perspective from which *Christ the Tiger* is written:

> Have I been considering these Christian works in order to understand and appreciate them or simply to use them as evidence for a thesis about Christianity? If the latter, then their literary merit does not come into the enquiry; I might just as well have used works of no literary merit. If the former, what does it matter what light these works throw on religious issues, since the enquiry is purely aesthetic? This dichotomy, in my view, is a false one. Aesthetic considerations can never be separated from religious considerations. I prefer to think that what I have been engaged in is the literary criticism of religion. A religion is an imaginative creation; its meaning is to be found not in works of theology, but in its myth. It reaches its fullest expression in works of art, such as the Book of Job or *The Merchant of Venice*. To understand and appreciate a religion, a historico-scientific enquiry is always inadequate. The religion must be approached at its moment of white heat, where it achieves formulation in

---

[7] See Hyam Maccoby, "The Delectable Daughter", *Midstream*, September 1970. This article was republished in edited form in the posthumously published book *Antisemitism and Modernity: Innovation and Continuity*, London, 2006. See p. 88 of *Antisemitism and Modernity* for the quotation.

[8] See Appendix 6, where, in a review of Harry Blamires' book *Word Unheard: A Guide through Eliot's Four Quartets*, 1969: London, 2016, my father, criticizing Blamires' non-philosophical approach, describes *Four Quartets* as "a philosophical poem, produced in the midst of ideas (philosophical and scientific) about Time".

the mind of a great artist. We can think either that *The Merchant of Venice* throws light on Christianity, or that Christianity throws light on *The Merchant of Venice.* If the first, we are thinking religiously; if the second, aesthetically; but both points of view are essential in order to find the truth either religiously or aesthetically. For these two points of view are simply two different ways of looking at the same total truth. For a great artist is always religious, and a powerful religion will always find expression in great art.

This fusion of religious and aesthetic considerations resulted in a brilliantly illuminating interpretation (in my view) by my father of *The Merchant of Venice.* In his essay "The Figure of Shylock", published in the American Zionist magazine *Midstream* in 1970, my father argued that those critics (many of them Jewish) who – rightly pointing out the worthlessness of most of the Christians in the play – argue that Shakespeare is sympathetic towards Shylock[9] obscure the greatness of the play:

> *The Merchant of Venice* is a great play, not in spite of its anti-Semitism, but because of it. The sentimental reading, by which Shakespeare is on Shylock's side, spoils the great theme of the play – the clash between two theologies. It is this which gives a grandeur to the character of Shylock which commentators have labored in vain to explain. Though every anti-Semitic charge is made against Shylock (he is mean, a money-grubber, cruel, heartless, self-righteous), yet the grandeur is there. He is a man who dares to look God in the face and say: "I deserve such-and-such." This, according to Christian theory, is what is wrong with him; but, according to Judaism, it is what is right with him. Shakespeare has found the nub.[10]

---

9   See, for instance, Howard Jacobson: "It's said that finally, as he readies himself to take out Antonio's heart, he is the Jew of pitiless legality, the moral opposite of love as represented by the Christians. Were Shakespeare interested in pursuing this opposition to the detriment of the Jews, he wouldn't have allowed the Christians to show as quite so squalid." ("Villain or Victim, Shakespeare's Shylock is a character to celebrate", The *Guardian*, February 5, 2016.)

10 *Midstream*, February 1970. This essay appears in revised form in my father's posthumously published book *Antisemitism and Modernity, op. cit.* under the chapter title "Shakespeare and Shylock". It often happens that, when authors revise in later years writings from decades earlier, they do so for the worse; and this seems to me to be the case here. In the second version, my father took out the comment on Shylock's grandeur. I prefer the earlier version.

Shakespeare, my father argues, is making a theological point about Original Sin – a doctrine that, my father emphasizes, is alien to Judaism, which has an essentially optimistic view of human nature and its capacity to deal with sin; Judaism does not need the sacrifice of a human/divine Saviour in order to save mankind from eternal damnation, because in Judaism, human beings are not damned in the first place. As my father puts it in the essay: "The Jews did not stand so much in need of a doctrine of Mercy, because they believed that God was merciful enough to give them a chance from the start."[11] In *The Merchant of Venice*, the Christians, recognising their own worthlessness, throw themselves upon the mercy of God; in contrast, the Jew, Shylock, insists on justice, grossly distorted by Shakespeare into cruel legalism (the pound of flesh). Shylock says in the trial scene: "My deeds upon my head! I crave the law" (Act IV, Scene 1, l. 207), "I stand for judgment" (*ibid.,* l. 103); and "I stand here for law" (*ibid.,* l. 142). In this crucial trial scene, in her famous speech beginning "The quality of mercy is not strained", Portia (here representing the Virgin Mary, while Antonio is a Christ-figure, ready to die to pay the debt of sinful mankind, represented by his friend Bassanio) makes explicit the play's basic conflict (as conceived by Shakespeare) between Christian Mercy and Jewish Justice, saying to Shylock:

> Therefore, Jew,
> Though justice be thy plea, consider this,
> That, in the course of justice, none of us
> Should see salvation (*ibid.,* ll. 198-201.)

To return to Eliot: of course, all literary critics of his work have mentioned his Christianity; but, on the whole, his poetry has been treated aesthetically, with the religious dimension underplayed. An exception is a book -- *"Anglo-Catholic in Religion": T. S. Eliot and Christianity* -- by Barry Spurr, which was published in 2010 (though based on a doctoral thesis he had written in the late 1970s at Oxford University, under the supervision of Helen Gardner, whom he calls "the *doyenne* of Eliot scholars"[12]). Spurr writes in his Preface that Eliot's "widow, Mrs. Valerie Eliot [who died in 2012], has told me that 'her husband's religious side has been neglected by most writers, and a major book is badly needed'".[13]

"Anglo-Catholic in Religion" is indeed a major book; and I recommend it to readers who want to know in detail about Eliot's personal religious development. I have also found the book very helpful in its explanation of the differences between, on the one hand, Anglo-Catholicism and Roman Catholicism, and, on the other hand, between Anglo-Catholicism

---

11   *Midstream*. February 1970.
12   Barry Spurr, *"Anglo-Catholic in Religion": T. S. Eliot and Christianity,* Cambridge, 2010, p. ix.
13   *Ibid.,* p. xii.

and mainstream Anglicanism. But again, the book is primarily biographical. Nonetheless, Spurr emphasizes elements in the poetry that also figure prominently in *Christ the Tiger*; in particular, the central importance to Eliot of the Incarnation – a doctrine that, Spurr writes, "is at the very heart" of Anglo-Catholicism:

> what Eliot was searching for was the philosophy of the Incarnation (the Word of God being made flesh, in the birth of Christ), which is at the very heart of Anglo-Catholic doctrine and spirituality and the sacraments which are derived from it, Catholic teaching affirming that the entire sacramental system, central to the faith, in an extension of the Incarnation.[14]

Yet, despite his book's focus on Eliot's Anglo-Catholicism, Spurr recognizes the continuing hold that Eliot's deep-rooted Puritan heritage had on his poetry -- a hold that is strongly emphasized in *Christ the Tiger*. Spurr tells us about Eliot's ancestor

> Andrew Eliot, a cordwainer (or shoemaker), who set out from East Coker[15] in 1668, after the Restoration of the monarchy and episcopacy, for the Massachusetts Bay Colony in New England. This was a Puritan theocracy where his Calvinistic Christianity would be free from persecution. (Similarly, on Eliot's mother's side, the Stearns, one of her ancestors had been amongst the original settlers of the Bay colony.)

Spurr points out: "The original Calvinism of those religious emigrants was theologically diluted by their descendants over the centuries into Unitarianism, while elements of the original Puritan spirit, in matters of moral principle and temperament, were retained." Eliot, Spurr continues, rejected the "diluted" Unitarianism in which he had been brought up, in favour of the doctrines and rituals of Anglo-Catholicism: "Eliot was highly critical of a religious system which had jettisoned theology and prioritised morality, which could not survive (he believed) in a vacuum." But Spurr also concedes that "the degree to which Eliot negated and disposed of the legacy of New England Puritanism (to the extent that it was preserved in his family's Unitarianism) is questionable".[16] My father regarded Eliot as essentially a Calvinist, and thus fundamentally a Romantic – see Chapter 1 (pp. 60-61) of *Christ the Tiger*:

> Calvinism is the best label for him; and a Calvinist is really a Romantic at

---

14 *Ibid.*, p. 21.
15 The village in Somerset that gives its name to the title of the second of *Four Quartets*.
16 Spurr, *op. cit.*, pp. 1-3.

heart -- one whose Romantic dream is so strong that it has made the world into a Desert, which however he is determined to struggle through with courage, and in which he hopes to build a fortress against the evils of the Desert.

Spurr also stresses the continuity between the poetry written *before* Eliot's formal conversion to Anglo-Catholicism in 1927[17] and the poems written *after* that date; Spurr emphasizes that Eliot's was no sudden conversion but the culmination of a long religious process.[18] The same point is made in *Christ the Tiger*: "Eliot's conversion was a real step in his life, but it was not a break; it was the inevitable step towards which his previous thinking had led him." (Chapter 1, p. 45.)

Yet, despite this recognition of continuity, Spurr agrees with the view, held by almost all critics, that the poems in Eliot's third volume -- published in 1920 in New York under the title *Poems* and in London under the title *Ara Vos Prec*[19] – are "satirical". My father, however, argues that the 1920 poems are – though ironic in expression – essentially serious Christian poems. He writes, at the end of his analysis of one of the 1920 poems, "Mr. Eliot's Sunday Morning Service" (Chapter 5, p. 132):

> I am sorry if I have destroyed the satirical attack on the clergy that is so beloved of people who prefer those of Eliot's poems that were written before his "defection" to religion. I am afraid that close inquiry would produce similar results in the case of the other "satirical" poems of this period.[20]

---

17   He became a naturalized British citizen in the same year.

18   See *ibid.*, pp. 112-113: "The term 'conversion', in Eliot's case tends to diminish the importance of all the diverse elements that led up to his baptism and confirmation over so many years, and, by implying certitude and finality, contradicts Eliot's conception of the individual Christian experience ... as a much more complex phenomenon, shot through with doubts and backslidings."

19   B. C. Southam, *A Student's Guide to the Selected Poems of T. S. Eliot*, London, 1968, p.12. Peter Ackroyd, *T. S. Eliot*, London, 1985, pp. 98-99. Surely the very title *Ara Vos Prec* indicates that these are religious poems – but I suppose the proponents of the "satirical" Eliot must argue that the title is itself satirical. It is taken from Dante's *Purgatorio*, at the end of Canto XXVI, where the French troubadour Arnaut Daniel, suffering the flames of Purgatory as punishment for the sin of lust, speaks to Dante: "'Ara vos prec, per aquella valor/que vos guida al som de l'escalina,/ sovegna vos a temps de ma dolor.'/Poi s'ascose nel foco che gli affina." ("'Now I pray you, by that Goodness which guides you to the summit of the stairway, be mindful in due time of my pain.' Then he hid himself in the fire which refines them.")

20   One reason that I wrote Appendix 8 – "An Examination, by the Editor, of 'A Cooking Egg'" – was to test out this statement.

In particular, my father argues (pp. 59-60) that the *Ara Vos Prec* poem "The Hippopotamus" is

> really about the deification of the body, which, in all its apparent bulkiness and ridiculousness (as symbolized by the Hippopotamus), is the substance of the Incarnate God and of the Church, which is called the Body of Christ.

Almost all critics call this poem "satirical".

It seems to me that the underlying reason for Spurr's interpretation of the *Ara Vos Prec* volume as "satirical" is that Eliot's published antisemitic poetry (which includes some of his greatest poems, such as "Gerontion", "Sweeney Among the Nightingales" and "Burbank with a Baedeker, Bleistein with a Cigar") is almost exclusively confined to *Ara Vos Prec* -- and Spurr does not want to acknowledge Eliot's antisemitism. In an Appendix that denies that Eliot was antisemitic, Spurr passionately attacks Anthony Julius's 1995 book *T. S. Eliot, Anti-Semitism and Literary Form*, calling it "so misleading as to be vicious".[21] Spurr argues that the antisemitic parts of "Gerontion" are "spoken by a character created by the poet, not necessarily representative of the poet himself".[22] Spurr goes on to give a "satirical" interpretation of the lines in "Gerontion"

> My house is a decayed house
> And the jew squats on the window-sill, the owner,
> Spawned in some estaminet of Antwerp,
> Blistered in Brussels, patched and peeled in London.[23]

Spurr (who spells "jew" as "Jew"; but the capital letter was only inserted by Eliot in 1963[24] and doesn't really make much difference to these lines) writes: "this is satirical poetry as much ridiculing the speaker, the 'little old man'[25] synonymous with decaying European culture after the First World War, as the subjects of his disdain".[26] For my father's detailed interpretation of "Gerontion" as a serious religious poem in which the "jew" is central, see Chapter 4 of *Christ The Tiger*. Chapter 3 explores Eliot's antisemitism in general,

---

21 *Ibid.*, p. 265.
22 *Ibid.*, p. 259.
23 T. S. Eliot, *Selected Poems*, London 1961, p. 31.
24 In T. S. Eliot, *Collected Poems, 1909-62*, London, 1963.
25 The meaning of the word "Gerontion".
26 Spurr, *op. cit.*, pp. 259-260.

though with special emphasis on "Burbank with a Baedeker, Bleistein with a Cigar" and the discarded draft poem "Dirge".

"Mr. Eliot's Sunday Morning Service", another of the *Ara Vos Prec* poems, has been mentioned earlier. Spurr goes along with the usual critical interpretation of it as a "satirical" attack on the Christian clergy.[27] In his book *T. S. Eliot, Anti-Semitism and Literary Form*, Anthony Julius (despite his focus on Eliot's antisemitism) also accepts the general view of this poem. Julius criticizes my father for interpreting "Mr. Eliot's Sunday Morning Service" as a serious Christian sermon that goes through a history of religion: Judaism (seen in the first verse as over-materialistic), Hellenism, Christianity and secularism. Julius, agreeing with the generally accepted view that the first verse is an attack on the Christian clergy, concludes: "the poem is not about Jews. Maccoby seeks offence where none is given."[28] Julius's book was widely reviewed (partly because he had been the divorce lawyer of Diana, Princess of Wales); and almost every review I have read of his book mentions these comments; all the reviewers who refer to these remarks agree with Julius.[29] Undeterred, I have included my father's line-by-line interpretation of "Mr. Eliot's Sunday Morning Service" as Chapter 5 of this book, so readers can judge for themselves (I have added a footnote in response to Julius's detailed comments on the meaning of "sutlers" in the first verse).[30]

My father agrees with Julius that, as he puts it, Eliot "was able to place his anti-Semitism at the service of his art"[31], i.e., that he made art out of antisemitism. But, as my father points out in a review – published in the London *Evening Standard* in September, 1995 -- of Julius's book (see Appendix 5), he almost entirely leaves out the anthropological/pagan dimension of Eliot's work. Julius never explains how Eliot's antisemitism fits into his artistic philosophy because Julius never explains what that philosophy is. My father also commented on Julius's book in a 1996 letter in the *Jewish Chronicle* (see Appendix 7): a contribution to a heated correspondence that had arisen in response to a review[32] in the

---

27 *Ibid.*, p. 46: "'Mr. Eliot's Sunday Morning Service' (1917) savages the Church for failing to preserve the knowledge of salvation in the incarnate Word."

28 Anthony Julius, *T. S. Eliot, Anti-Semitism and Literary Form: New Edition, with a Preface and a Response to the Critics*, 1995: London, 2003, pp. 6-7.

29 For my father's reply to one of these reviews – by Stephen Medcalf in the *TLS* -- see Appendix 7(b).

30 My father concedes that the poem is anti-Judaism rather than antisemitic but argues: "the distinction is generally hard to maintain. Eliot's undoubted antisemitism is rooted in traditional Christian anti-Judaism and is thus ultimately theological rather than racialist." See Appendix 7(b).

31 Julius, *op. cit.*, p. 11. See also Appendix 5, where, agreeing with Julius, my father writes: "Eliot made poetry out of antisemitism; a fact that has repercussions in the general theory of what poetry is and does."

32 October 6, 1995. Josipovici wrote in this review, with reference to Eliot's poem "Sweeney Among the Nightingales": "Eliot, along with Kafka and Proust, made writing possible for me, and so helped me to develop as a man and a Jew. I would be happy to trade the whole of that impeccable philo-Semite, Joyce (the darling of the politically correct), for just that one Sweeney poem of Eliot's." On August 30, 1996, Julius's response to his critics, including Josipovici,

Jewish Chronicle of Julius's book by Gabriel Josipovici, who argued that he derived so much pleasure from Eliot's poetry that it could not be antisemitic. My father wrote that Julius "fails to distinguish between vulgar and philosophical antisemitism, and therefore cannot explain how Eliot's antisemitism is compatible with great poetry. He thus lays himself open to Professor Josipovici's criticism."[33]

In his own review of Julius's book, my father sums up his view of the role of antisemitism in Eliot's work:

> Eliot (in the light of his reading of anthropology) saw and accepted the kinship between the Cross and the dying-and-resurrected young gods of ancient mystery religions; and he connected these themes with the Romantic cult of youth. All this entered into his contempt for the Jews as opponents of the Young God and as un-Romantic devotees of earthbound values and "liberalism".... Unawareness of these dimensions vitiates Julius's attempt to analyse Eliot's greatest antisemitic poem, "'Gerontion".[34]

And it seems to me that, illuminating and fascinating though Barry Spurr's book is, he misses out the same vital aspect of Eliot's Christianity: a dimension that in this book is called "Christ the Tiger" -- the quotation from "Gerontion" that forms the title of this book. The title of Spurr's book comes from Eliot's famous description of himself: "classicist in literature, royalist in politics, and anglo-catholic in religion".[35] And to Spurr, Eliot's Christianity is ordered and classicist. Spurr leaves out its dimension of Romanticism, paganism, and violence – which are precisely the subject of my father's book. The big lacuna in Spurr's otherwise illuminating account of Eliot's journey from Unitarianism to Anglo-Catholicism is the omission of any reference to Eliot's anthropological studies.[36]

---

appeared in the *Jewish Chronicle's* Literary Supplement. Josipovici responded (in a letter printed in the Jewish Chronicle on September 20, 1996): "at the heart of our disagreement, of course, is the fact that I respond with pleasure to a poem like 'Sweeney Among the Nightingales' and he does not". For my father's analysis of "Sweeney Among the Nightingales" (a poem to which my father responded with great pleasure; and Julius too seems to admire the poem as a work of art – see *op. cit.,* p. 86: "an anti-Semitic, Modernist work of considerable complexity and interest"), see Chapter 2.

33 The *Jewish Chronicle*, October 11, 1996.
34 The London *Evening Standard*, September 18, 1995. See Appendix 5.
35 T. S. Eliot, *For Lancelot Andrewes: Essays on Style and Order,* London, 1928, p. ix.
36 A much older book that examines Eliot's poetry from a religious perspective is Genesius Jones, O. F. M. [Order of Friars Minor], *Approach to the Purpose: A Study of the Poetry of T. S. Eliot,* London, 1964. Fr. Jones was a Franciscan Friar; and his book is written very much from an orthodox Roman Catholic outlook. It is significant that the

Although the issue of Eliot's antisemitism features very prominently in this book, I have not included the word "antisemitism" in the sub-title, because it seems to me that, in the view presented in this book, Eliot's antisemitism, though central to his work, is, as my father puts it at the beginning of Chapter 3, a "natural concomitant" to Eliot's Christian/pagan, Romantic vision of Sacrifice: "antisemitism is a natural concomitant of the sacrificial view of life that was Eliot's inspiration from the time of his earliest writings" (just as Eliot's view of the relationship between the sexes, the subject of Chapter 2 of this book, is both central and a "natural concomitant" to this vision).

As I have said above, Spurr provides an illuminating (even though in one crucial aspect incomplete) biographical account of Eliot's religious journey from Unitarianism to Anglo-Catholicism. But what about my father's own religious development? What was his attitude to religion at the time he wrote these essays? Answering these questions requires a look at his life up to the late 1960s and early 1970s.

---

copyright, publisher and date page carries a *Nihil obstat* and an *Imprimatur* from Roman Catholic censors; we are told in a note that *"the* Nihil obstat *and* Imprimatur *are a declaration that a book or pamphlet is considered to be free from doctrinal or moral error"*. (Italics in original.) The book has many far-fetched interpretations but can also be very interesting and illuminating. In contrast to Spurr, Fr. Jones does include mention of Eliot's anthropological studies and their relation to his Christianity. But, in my view, Fr. Jones tends to underplay the savagery of Eliot's vision. Fr. Jones has a tendency to refer to the totem and mystery-religion eating of the sacrificed animal or god as merely "food rituals" that he sees in terms of *Agape*, the Greek term for family or community love, which he distinguishes from *Eros*, meaning sexual love, and *Charis*, the love of God. See *ibid.*, p. 89: "By Agape I mean to represent the emotions and feelings of love which have as their base a sense of communal, brotherly or family sharing. It is symbolised in Mr. Eliot's poetry by food-ritual…. the most primitive food-rituals are associated with the sacrifice and resurrection of a god; it is his body that is eaten in the Vegetation Cults of *The Golden Bough*…. Agape is, as it were, a point of intersection where all the aspects of love meet. It is distinguished from the other two, however, by its quality of brotherhood or family union." He associates these "food rituals" with the Christian "Eucharist food ritual" (*ibid.*, p. 135); he continues here, quoting two lines from "East Coker" IV: "our sustenance is to be found in that food which hangs at the heart of the Cross … in that food which in the fullest sense constitutes Agape: *The dripping blood our only drink/The bloody flesh our only food"*. (Italics in original.) Fr. Jones seems unable to perceive the deliberate savagery of these lines. Again in contrast to Spurr, Fr. Jones interprets "Gerontion" as a serious religious poem and makes some illuminating comments about it (see my footnotes in Chapter 4); but he sees "Christ the Tiger" as an intermediate stage in Gerontion's (and therefore presumably Eliot's) journey towards Christianity, not (as is argued by my father) as the core of Eliot's Christian vision. See *ibid.*, p. 101, where Fr. Jones writes that Gerontion, "while he has not yet accepted the Christian position and still looks on Christ resentfully as a devouring tiger, is nonetheless looking towards the Christian position honestly".

EDITOR'S MEMOIR OF HYAM MACCOBY

Hyam Maccoby was born in Sunderland, on the north-east coast of England (a town which at that time had a large and close-knit Jewish community), into a deeply Orthodox Jewish family. Both his grandfathers were illustrious Rabbis from what was then White Russia (now Belarus). As my father told Ron Rosenbaum in a long interview published in 1998: "My family are all part of that Russian Jewry which moved to Western Europe and America as a result of the [turn-of-the-century] pogroms."[37]

My father's paternal grandfather was a Rabbi and Maggid (preacher) who was so illustrious that he was given a special title of his own: "The Kamenitzer Maggid", after his birthplace, Kamenitz-Litovsk in White Russia. The Kamenitzer Maggid (Chaim Zundel Maccoby) emigrated with his family to England in 1890.[38] My grandfather, Ephraim Meyer Maccoby, was born in Whitechapel, in the East End of London, in 1892, and attended the Central Free School there, where he was a star pupil; he was a brilliant mathematician who gained a scholarship to Cambridge and became what is known as a "Senior Wrangler" – i.e., he came top of the whole Finals examination. According to my uncle, my grandfather was offered professorships in mathematics in Canada and Australia, but turned them down, because he feared that the glittering academic career that beckoned him would not allow him enough time for the Talmudic studies that he regarded it as a religious duty to pursue.

---

37   Ron Rosenbaum, *Explaining Hitler: The Search for the Origins of his Evil*, London, 1998, p. 322 (square brackets in original).

38   In his book *British Jewry Since Emancipation*, Buckingham, 2014, Geoffrey Alderman mentions (p. 159) "the renowned *Maggid* of Kamenitsk (1858-1916), who had fled from Russia following the prohibition of his lecturing activities on behalf of the *Chovevi Zion* ["Lovers of Zion"] movement in the Pale of Settlement". The Kamenitzer Maggid supported the establishment of small religious Jewish agricultural colonies in Palestine; he was bitterly opposed to Herzl's political aim of a secular Jewish State. The Maggid was the first full-time preacher for *Chovevei Zion*; he travelled round the Pale of Settlement, speaking to crowds of thousands in Yiddish (so popular were his speeches that the Tsarist authorities feared he was preaching revolution, which was why he was forbidden to preach and had to flee to England with his family). In London, his sermons, which could last up to five hours, also attracted thousands. Sir Samuel Montagu, the wealthy Jewish Liberal MP for Whitechapel and founder of the Federation of Synagogues (an umbrella organisation for hundreds of small ultra-devout East End synagogues, attended by Eastern European Jews who regarded the mainstream Orthodox United Synagogue, which was modelled on the Church of England, as too lax and English), was alarmed by the growing influence upon the Jewish community of the atheism, Anarchism and Socialism of the radical left. Seeing in the Kamenitzer Maggid a means of keeping the Jewish masses within the fold of Orthodoxy, Montagu appointed him, in 1894, as the Maggid of the Federation (see *ibid*.). For biographical studies of the Kamenitzer Maggid, see Julius Jung. *Champions of Orthodoxy*, London, 1974, Chapter 2, and an entry on the Kamenitzer Maggid, written by Geoffrey Alderman, in the *Oxford Dictionary of National Biography*, edited by Lawrence Goldman, Oxford, 2004 (or online at https://www.oxforddnb.com/).

Instead, he became Head of Mathematics at the Bede Grammar School for Boys in Sunderland, where he had settled after marrying my grandmother, the daughter of another illustrious Rabbi, David Rabinowitz, who had also emigrated from White Russia to the East End of London but had later become a Rabbi in Sunderland. My grandmother (who was born in Mogilev, in White Russia), was descended from a long line of Rabbis, of which ancestry she was extremely proud ((I once had a flatmate whose mother was descended from ancient French nobility; when my flatmate described to me the aristocratic snobbishness of his maternal grandmother, I instantly understood, because I had seen the same qualities in my own paternal grandmother). She was a strange mixture of a simple, uneducated Russian peasant woman (in her family all the education, Jewish and secular, went on the boys) and a kind of Jewish dynastic Princess.[39]

But my father took little interest in his "roots"; I remember him complaining to me that, after he had delivered a lecture, among those who would come up to him afterwards to ask questions would always be someone who, instead of talking about the ideas my father had put forward, would claim to be a distant relative and insist on going into the family tree.

I have no memories of my paternal grandfather, because he died of a heart attack when I was four. But everything I have learned about him from relatives indicates a man who, despite his mathematical brilliance, was narrow-minded, chauvinist and authoritarian. My mother told me that her father-in-law once remarked to her that he thought Sir Walter Scott was a great writer; but added the proviso: "Of course, in so far as a *goy* can be called a great writer." I am not sure what he made of Shakespeare and Eliot.

My father was born on March 20, 1924, after the births of three daughters. As was to be expected in an Orthodox Jewish family, in which boys are always valued above girls, he was celebrated and spoilt like a little prince. His mother was warned by doctors not to have any more children; otherwise, she ran the danger of becoming deaf. Nonetheless, less than a year later, on March 6, 1925, my uncle David was born -- and the doctors' warning turned out to be correct; my grandmother did indeed become deaf; from then on, she had to wear hearing aids. My uncle suffered all his life from a sense of having been rejected by his father on account of his mother's deafness. So my father's position as his own father's ally and favourite was sealed.

---

39 She often told the story of how, as a young girl, she had had two suitors: one was the son of a rich Jewish businessman; the other was my grandfather. She was given a free choice by her father (this was not always the case for Orthodox Jewish girls at that time). She told me she actually preferred the businessman's son personally, but she felt her duty, as the descendant of so many Rabbis, was to continue the Rabbinical line; she could not turn down my grandfather, a student of the Talmud who was the son of the Kamenitzer Maggid. I always admired my grandmother's indifference to money, but I could not help thinking, when she told me this story, that she had made the wrong choice.

My grandfather taught his two sons Hebrew and the Talmud from the age of four. My father took to Hebrew like the proverbial duck to water; in great contrast to my uncle, who complained bitterly in later years about his father's main teaching method towards him, which was to whack him on the head every time he made a mistake. My uncle also found the convoluted logical arguments of the Talmud tedious and incomprehensible, whereas my father loved them. My uncle David became an atheist and a Communist at the age of 14 and grew up to be a bohemian Abstract Expressionist artist. He was the rebel son; up until his mid-20s, my father was the dutiful son, in league with his father in what might be dubbed a two-man Society for the Preservation and Glorification of Orthodox Judaism.

My grandfather, and my father up till his mid-20s, believed, fervently and completely, in the literal truth of the first five books of the Hebrew Bible – that is to say, they believed that these five books (known as the Torah) had been dictated to Moses by God on Mount Sinai. But to them this was not a matter of blind faith, but of reason and logic. My grandfather (who studied science as well as mathematics) was presented in his youth with a problem faced by anyone who is both a modern intellectual and a believer in the literal truth of the Bible: how to reconcile the scientific evidence of evolution with the account of Creation, put forward in the Book of Genesis, that states that the world was created by God in six days, approximately six thousand years ago.

This problem had been resolved in the 19th century, in a logically ingenious way, in a book called *Omphalos*, by the naturalist Philip Gosse, who was a member of the fundamentalist Calvinist sect known as the Plymouth Brethren. The word "omphalos" is Greek for "navel". Philip Gosse's basic argument was that, just as Adam must have had a navel, even though he had been created fully-grown by God and therefore had not gone through the normal process of being born, so the Earth -- even though it had been created by God in six days approximately six thousand years ago – must necessarily have been created with an evolutionary past, even though no such past had in fact existed.

In his brilliant memoir *Father and Son* (which is one of my favourite books), Philip Gosse's son, the literary critic, poet and man of letters Edmund Gosse, writes:

> Never was a book cast upon the waters with greater anticipation of success than was this curious, this obstinate, this fanatical volume…. He offered it, with a glowing gesture, to atheists and Christians alike. This was to be the universal panacea; this, the system of intellectual therapeutics which could not but heal all the maladies of the age. But alas! atheists and Christians alike looked at it and laughed and threw it away.[40]

---

40 Edmund Gosse, *Father and Son*, 1907: Oxford, 2004, p. 64.

It would surely have consoled Philip Gosse, in his heartbreak over the dismissive reception of his book, if he had known that, in the 20th century, his theory would be taken up enthusiastically by my grandfather – as a means of reconciling the two conflicting sides of himself, the Cambridge Senior Wrangler and the Orthodox Jewish believer – and, up till his mid-20s, by my father as well. By the time my father explained Philip Gosse's argument to me, when I was about twelve, my father had stopped needing it, because he no longer believed in the literal truth of the Book of Genesis; but I could tell, from the way he set out the Omphalos Theory to me, that he was still impressed by its irrefutable logic.

At the Bede Grammar School for Boys in Sunderland, my father was a star pupil (just as his father had been at the Central Free School in London). My father focused on Latin and Greek (subjects very useful in relation to his study of Eliot) and, at the early age of 17, won a coveted Domus Exhibition in Classics to Balliol College, Oxford. I once asked him why he had not chosen to specialize in Hebrew and Jewish studies at school and university; he replied that these subjects were so dear to his heart that he could not bear to spoil them by turning them into academic studies. Indeed, they were not "subjects" to him, but were interwoven with his inmost being.

I think my father spent two terms at Balliol in late 1941 and early 1942; but, when he turned 18 in March of 1942, he joined the British Army for service in the Second World War. He was allocated to the Royal Signals and sent to Bletchley Park, where he worked as a radio operator, intercepting and passing on coded messages. It was typical of my father that, having sworn an oath of secrecy, he told his family almost nothing about his time at Bletchley. All he ever told us was that he once received a special commendation, after, unknown to him, an inspector had been concealed on the premises watching him work; and he was also told that some of the messages he intercepted were vital in the War effort.

There was, however, one story he told his family that had nothing to do with Bletchley; it took place before he was sent there, while he was undergoing army training. All the new recruits were required to attend what was billed as an "ecumenical" religious service. But it turned out to be nothing of the sort; all the way through, there were references to Jesus. Furious, my father sent an official complaint to his immediate commanding officer, demanding an interview. When he obtained it, the commanding officer said with surprise, after my father had explained his objection to the service: "But doesn't everyone believe in Jesus?" My father insisted that Jews do not believe in the divinity of Jesus. He was received with incomprehension. So he took the case higher and higher up the chain of command – all the time encountering the same baffled reaction --- until he finally achieved an interview with the General of the Regiment.

As my father entered the General's office, he heard an aide announce him in a loud whisper: "Sir, it's the Jew-boy!" The General asked my father to explain his grievance. Once again, he went through the topic of the so-called "ecumenical" service and its references to Jesus as divine. Just like the other officers, the General responded: "But doesn't everyone believe that Jesus is God?" My father once again replied: "No, Jews do not believe that Jesus is God." "Well, why don't they?" the General asked. To which my father responded: "Because one Jew-boy doesn't believe that another Jew-boy can be God." Thus, at the age of 18, my father articulated his opposition to the doctrine of the Incarnation that is central to the poetry of T. S. Eliot.

At the end of the War, my father was taken away from Bletchley and sent to an army base in Scotland to guard some munitions that were supposed to be stored there. However, it turned out, as the result of some complicated administrative mix-up, that the "weapons stores" were non-existent. My father said neither he nor his fellow-soldiers attempted to disabuse the authorities; like the others, he turned up every day for his hours of guard duty of stores that weren't there; and spent the rest of the time (and even the hours of guard duty) writing a book (he said the other soldiers were also working on books or private hobbies). This book, written by my father at the age of 21, has never been published; but his parents (especially his father) were so proud of it that they had it printed and bound. I found it recently among my father's books. It is an extraordinary work, written by a young man who is extremely intelligent but also a religious fundamentalist -- but one who seeks to justify his literal faith by means of reason and logic.

The book, called *The Heretic and the Tradition: An Inquiry into the Meaning of Religious Belief* and written under the penname "Chaim Zundel", is very lucidly and wittily written, in a style modelled on that of the Roman Catholic writer G. K. Chesterton, whose work my father greatly admired (despite Chesterton's antisemitism). The book begins by arguing that the only rational and logical religions are the three Orthodox "Judaic" religions: Judaism, Roman Catholicism and Islam (my father knew the first two religions far more deeply than he knew Islam).

In Chapter 2, entitled "The Church of the Prophet Simpkins", my father very entertainingly (but sadly very briefly) illustrates his explanations of the development of a religion by imagining a bank clerk called Mr. Percy Simpkins, who one day receives a Revelation of a religion of thirteen gods: six male, six female and – the greatest god of them all -- one of neutral sex. Simpkins writes a Holy Book, converts his family, gathers disciples; and, after long decades of persecution, Simpkinsianism triumphs and becomes the State Religion of the United Kingdom. St. Paul's Cathedral is converted into the Temple of the Thirteenth God. (I can't help wishing my father had turned this idea, which only takes up a few pages of his youthful book, into a fantasy novel in the style of G. K. Chesterton; the concept even seems prophetic of our current debates about transsexualism.)

To return, somewhat reluctantly, from Simpkinsianism to Judaism, Christianity and Islam: these three religions, argues "Chaim Zundel", rely on what he believes to be the three requisites for a rational religion: Revelation, Tradition and Church. The kind of religion with which the book is dealing begins, he argues, with a divine Revelation, written down in a Holy Book. The Holy Book contains Laws, which are holy and immutable, but usually vague and difficult to understand. So an interpretative, authoritative Tradition of religious Law forms that claims to go back to the founders of the religion; thus the Popes, the guardians of Roman Catholic Law, claim an unbroken chain of succession from St. Peter; the Caliphs, historically the guardians of Islamic Law, claimed an unbroken chain of succession from Mohammed; and the Jewish Oral Law (which was codified and written down in the first centuries CE to form part of the Talmud) is historically claimed to go back to Moses, passed down from generation after generation of religious leaders. The Church is the organization that forms to apply the religion in everyday life.

When new developments arise that require further interpretation, which cannot be found in either the Holy Book or the Tradition, a religion must find a means of issuing a definitive ruling on these issues. In Roman Catholicism, this problem is solved by the dogma of the Infallibility of the Pope: a doctrine that "Chaim Zundel" defends as logical and rational. In Islam, the problem of issuing a definitive ruling has historically been solved by the decision of the Caliph, the head of the Islamic Church – again this method is seen by "Chaim Zundel" as logical and rational. In Judaism, the Oral Tradition has historically laid it down that newly-arising problems must be solved by a majority decision of the Sanhedrin of Rabbis – decisions that are recorded in the Talmud. This majority decision is regarded as human, fallible and subject to change; but the law that decisions must be made by a majority decision of the rabbis is a divine law; so the majority decision, however fallible, is regarded as ultimately of divine origin, part of the continuous chain of Tradition that leads back to the divine Revelation. To "Chaim Zundel", the method adopted by Judaism is the most rational and logical; so that, by a process of elimination, he reaches the conclusion that Judaism must be the only true religion (since he argues that only one religion can be true).

I have mentioned that, unlike his mother, my father showed very little interest in his family tree, with all its generations of Rabbis. His emphasis in this very early book upon the continuous chain helps to explain why. A narrow family tree, even if were to go back many centuries, was nothing at all to him in comparison with the glorious line of spiritual and intellectual descent that stretched back three thousand, five hundred years or so to the earth-shattering Revelation on Mount Sinai -- a Revelation in which my father, at this time of his life, had complete, literal faith. Even after he had lost his literal faith in the Revelation – in which the Mission of the Jews, as the Chosen People who at Mount Sinai entered into a Covenant with God, was revealed to them -- still to him everything in Judaism went back to it.

As the title *The Heretic and the Tradition* makes clear, the book's focus of attack is what the author regards as heresy – in particular, the trends of Protestantism and religious liberalism. "Chaim Zundel" attacks Protestantism – the rebellion against Orthodoxy – because it jettisons the interpretative Tradition and the Church, seeking to return to the original purity of the Book (which means that Protestantism tends to be far more severe than Orthodoxy).[41] And his criticism of liberal and reform religious movements is that, once one decides that a Revelation is only partial, it is up to the individual liberal theologian to decide which parts of it are inspired and which aren't.[42] But, "Chaim Zundel" argues, the whole point of the Revelation is that it is entirely of divine origin; there cannot, logically and rationally, be a partial Revelation. He adopts an all-or-nothing approach: "If it seems to you to be impossible to believe that a religion is true in every respect, great or small, then you are logically entitled to reject it altogether. In fact, you must do so."

There is little in this book about the actual content of the three religions; the young author is so concerned with the common factors that unite the "Judaic" religions, especially the centrality of Law, and is so intent on justifying the reason and logic of Orthodox faith, in all three religions, and attacking heresy that there is not much scope for a discussion of what the religions are about and how they differ from one another.

The most notable aspect of *The Heretic and the Tradition* is "Chaim Zundel"'s insistence that his faith is based on logical reasoning. The final part of the book is devoted to a discussion of whether faith is rational: the author concludes:

> The fact is that [religious] faith is not only not irrational but is of all forms
> of belief the most rational. At least, the religious believer should think so.
> He should feel that everything in him which is reasonable and logical
> urges him to believe in the religion.

One cannot help fearing what will happen to this young man if, in the course of time, the very intellectual power – the reason and the logic – that he has invested so deeply and sincerely in his religious beliefs should cause him to lose his faith.

---

41 "Chaim Zundel" points out that there is a Jewish form of Protestantism, citing as an example the Sadducees of the time of Jesus. In contrast to the Pharisees, the Sadducees disdained the interpretative Oral Tradition, relying on the literal words of the Book.

42 Ironically, in the mid-1970s my father became Scholar-Librarian at the Leo Baeck College in London, a college that trains Reform Rabbis. But, having gone back at this time to attending synagogue services, he always went to an Orthodox synagogue; he told me that intellectually he supported Reform Judaism, but emotionally he preferred the Orthodox services of his childhood and youth.

And this is precisely what happened. After the War, in 1946, my father resumed his Classics studies at Balliol College, Oxford (as part of his course, he studied both ancient and modern philosophy, in which he remained very interested, and which again proved very relevant to his work on Eliot; see Chapter 6 of *Christ the Tiger*). But, sometime during his second year, he experienced the most shattering event of his life: his loss of religious faith. I have dwelt at some length on his youthful book *The Heretic and the Tradition*, because it is only through this book that one can understand what such a loss of the deep literal belief that he had held all his life must have meant. His life had been given meaning, purpose and fascination by faith – backed by the whole of his remarkable logical and reasoning faculties – in an omnipotent God who had chosen the Jewish People to whom to reveal His message to mankind: a Revelation that my father had been utterly convinced had happened three thousand, five hundred years ago, and to which he had felt himself linked by an over-three-millennia-long chain of Jewish Prophets, Sages and Rabbis. He did not talk to me about the catastrophic effect his loss of faith had upon him; but I learnt some details from my mother and my uncle. It seems he was profoundly affected both mentally and physically. In accordance with the all-or-nothing approach that is so evident in his youthful book, his loss of faith caused him to adopt a position of complete atheism. But this meant that he felt there was no purpose or meaning in life. In mental terms, he seems to have suffered a nervous breakdown; in physical terms he began to suffer from headaches and eye troubles – a feeling of pressure behind the eyes from which he never fully recovered, and which seems to have been the physical expression of a loss of spiritual vision.

According to my mother, what triggered this catastrophic loss of faith was my father's encounter at Oxford with the "Form Criticism" of the Bible that showed conclusively that different authors had composed the Books of the Torah at different times, centuries after the events were supposed to have happened. But, in *The Heretic and the Tradition*, my father already mentions "Form Criticism", which he loftily dismisses, writing that the Talmud had already taken it into account and found arguments to refute it. But it could be that the wider intellectual outlook that my father experienced at Oxford made him understand the deficiencies in the reasoning of the Talmudic rabbis of the early centuries CE.

It seems that, following his nervous breakdown, my father spent a period of recovery at home and then returned to Oxford. He decided to switch from Classics to English Language and Literature, because he thought this would be less taxing on his eyes, which continued to give him great trouble. Towards the end of his third year, he met my mother (who was studying PPE [Politics, Philosophy and Economics]), through friends whom they had in common – friends who thought, rightly, that they would be well-suited. They became engaged two weeks after their first meeting. They had both wanted academic careers; but they failed to get Firsts (my father ascribed this to his nervous breakdown, from which he had still not really recovered; and my mother blamed the distraction caused by the whirlwind engagement). Soon after graduating, they married and went to live in my mother's birthplace and hometown, Llanelli, in South Wales. My mother's maiden name was Cynthia Davies (originally Davidov, but when her grandfather arrived in Wales, he found most people there were called Davis or Davies, so changed his name -- though, if he was attempting to hide his Jewishness, this didn't work, since it seems he was known locally as "Davies the Jew"). My mother's family (on both sides; her parents were first cousins) was also "part of that Russian Jewry which moved to Western Europe and America as a result of the [turn-of-the-century] pogroms". My mother's father was born in Nezhin[43], near Kiev, in what was then called "the Ukraine" (now Ukraine). My mother's family belonged to what my father's family called the *proster yiden*"[44] – the unlearned (i.e., unlearned in the Talmud), ordinary Jews (*prost* is Yiddish for "common" or "vulgar"). My father's rabbinical family were so arrogant that they despised not only the benighted *goyim* but also the "*proster yiden*" over whom the Rabbis had ruled in the Russian ghettoes. My maternal grandfather ran a scrap metal business in Llanelli[45]; he offered my father a job as manager of the scrap metal business – an offer that he accepted.

I think the main reason my father took a job that seems so unsuited to him was the rarefied intellectual and spiritual atmosphere in which he had been brought up under his father's domination – which was followed by the very different but still rarefied intellectual atmosphere of Oxford. In contrast, dealing with scrap metal brought him right down to earth. Another element of the job that attracted my father was that he was working with Gypsies; there was a well-hidden Romantic side to him (despite his critique of Eliot's Romanticism); and he was fascinated by the Gypsies; at this time, he learned to speak some Romany. In his spare time, he exercised his considerable creative talents by embarking on a part-time career as a songwriter. The high points of this career were: one song was sung by Petula Clark; and another was included in *Beat Girl*, a 1960s cult-film. My father also wrote songs

---

43 Even though my maternal grandfather lived in Nezhin till he was 18, he never set foot in Kiev, because Jews were not allowed into the big cities in the Russian Empire without permits.

44 I should point out that my mother came from a very musical family (and was very musical herself); one of her sisters, Naomi Davidov (she changed her name back to Davidov), became a concert pianist, well-known in her day for performances at the Queen Elizabeth Hall and the Purcell Room in London (Davidov is of course a much more suitable name for a concert pianist than Davies); and my mother's two other sisters became music teachers. One of my mother's uncles – S. Harry Davies – became a Professor of Philosophy at Swansea University.

45 I learned from a great-aunt that her father (my mother's grandfather), after arriving in Liverpool with his family, found a job in a furniture factory, but developed incipient TB as a result of inhaling wood dust. A doctor advised him that he could only recover if he got a job in the open air. He moved with his family to Swansea to work for some friends who had set up a rag and bone business there. They gave him a wheelbarrow, with which he went round the streets collecting unwanted items. He was later promoted to a horse and cart and managed eventually to buy his own horse and cart and set up his own family rag and bone business, which branched out into scrap metal (this proved very lucrative during the two World Wars; my mother grew up in some luxury).

and librettos for a projected musical about the Gypsies that was to have been called *Romany Rye* (after a novel about Gypsies by George Borrow), and another based on Defoe's novel about a picaresque adventuress, *Moll Flanders*; sadly, neither of these musicals was ever performed. Despite all these activities, my father's eye troubles continued; and, according to my mother, he also suffered from periodic depressions, during which he would say to her: "Judaism is finished, which means that everything is finished." It seems that nothing could make up for the void -- his own "Waste Land" -- caused by his loss of the faith that had given meaning and purpose to his life.

In these years in Llanelli, I and my brother and sister were born. After seven years in the scrap metal business, (during which time, my father once ruefully told me, he never managed to make a profit), he had had enough; and he applied for a job at Britain's only Jewish public school (i. e. expensive, fee-paying private school), Carmel College, which had a vacancy for an English teacher. He got the job; and, when I was five, we moved to England.

Carmel College (which was a boarding school modelled on Eton, but Orthodox Jewish) was situated deep in the English countryside, in Berkshire; to be near the school, we too settled deep in the English countryside, in Marlow, in the nearby county of Buckinghamshire. This period, at the end of the 1950s, was long before the advent of "multicultural Britain"; there had been a small Jewish community in Llanelli, of which my mother's family had been part (a number of Jews from Eastern Europe, after arriving in Liverpool -- where my mother's mother was born -- had, like my mother's family, gone southwards down the coast to South Wales); but here in Marlow, the population was homogeneously English. We were the only Jewish family on the estate where we lived and probably the only Jews in the whole of Marlow. At the state primary school that we attended, my brother and sister and I were the only Jewish children. I don't remember any antisemitism or even xenophobia[46] – we were warmly welcomed by our local community and treated as exotic. But my father began to fear that we would grow up without any sense of Jewish identity. He was especially perturbed because, religious education being compulsory, we attended classes in Christianity at our state primary school. My father had wanted us to be exempted, on the grounds of our being Jewish; but my mother thought it would be too difficult to explain to young children why they were being singled out in this way. After a dispute between my parents, my father gave in, and we attended the classes. But he countered by explaining to us that we were Jewish, teaching us what it meant to be Jewish and expounding on the differences between Judaism

---

[46] I vividly remember a little girl who came up to me every day on the school bus and asked me: "Are you English?" But I don't remember this as a hostile question; it was a kind of wide-eyed wonderment that a child should be on her school bus who wasn't English. Because of my father's "monologues" (see below) I would reply proudly: "No, I'm Jewish." (I would not deny nowadays being English as well as Jewish -- even though I was born in Wales.) Since she had no idea what this meant, she always retired in bafflement to her seat. It became a kind of ritual between us.

and Christianity. We didn't know any Jews, nor at that time did we carry out Jewish rituals or celebrate Jewish festivals; so my Jewish education consisted of long disquisitions by my father on the essential meaning of Judaism, in distinction from Christianity – long lectures usually delivered at mealtimes. Of course, as children of five, six or seven, these discourses went over our heads (they became clearer as we got older); and I regret to say that we laughed at them, calling them "Daddy's monologues" (unlike his own father, my father was not authoritarian, except on very rare occasions; he enjoyed being teased by his children). But my father had the last laugh, because, in later years, he turned "Daddy's monologues" into the books that made his reputation. And I personally believe that these "monologues", even in my very early years, sank into and had a profound effect on me. I didn't derive my Jewish identity and education from a Jewish community, Jewish rituals or a Jewish school; I got them straight from the horse's mouth, as it were, from a father who had the deepest knowledge and understanding of both Judaism and Christianity. On the other hand, it could also be said that these long lectures from very early years by a brilliant father -- who, despite all our teasing, was regarded by us as the fount of all knowledge and wisdom -- tended to make it difficult for us to form opinions of our own; which I think is probably true as well.

My father was gradually finding his way back to Judaism, on a different, humanist level. Instead of believing in the Torah as literal truth, faith in which he endeavoured to justify rationally and logically, he approached the Torah as myth – the essential principles of which he set out to understand, in distinction from those of the Christian myth. I think his need to teach his children about Judaism was a contributing factor in this development; but it was not the whole reason. My father was in contact with Orthodox Judaism again in Carmel College (he taught Hebrew to the boys as well as English, and must have discussed Judaism with them), which must have been an added impetus to this return to the study of Judaism and Christianity. But he had also been consulting doctors in London about his continuing headaches and eye problems. No physical cause could be found for them; and eventually a doctor, deciding the cause must be psychological, recommended him to a brilliant Viennese Jewish psychotherapist, practising in London, called George Frankl[47] (he had escaped from Austria during the Holocaust, after being imprisoned in Dachau; both his parents and most of his relatives died in the Holocaust). According to my mother, Mr. Frankl (who became a close friend of my parents) encouraged my father to abandon his all-or-nothing atheism (it

---

47   He was also the author of many books, including *The Failure of the Sexual Revolution*, London, 1974, *The Social History of the Unconscious*, London, 1989, and *Foundations of Morality*, London, 2000. A reviewer on Amazon writes of him: "He was a truly remarkable man with an extraordinary insight. It's only now he's gone that I realise how remarkable he was. I grieve for his loss. I'm not the only one. We take people like him for granted when they are there. It's only when they are not any more...."

https://www.amazon.co.uk/gp/customer-reviews/R1GRIG8DOPRCMM/ref=cm_cr_dp_d_rvw_ttl?ie=UTF8&ASIN=1871871050

seems he was for a time as fanatical an atheist as he had been a believer) and find his way back to Judaism in this new, humanist way.

Instead of his previous literal belief in God, my father now saw God as a fictional character – a construct of the human mind. But he argued (in the unfinished concluding essay to his projected book *Flowering Judas: The Christian Image of the Jew,* from which I quoted at the beginning of my Editor's Preface) that this does not mean at all that the image of God can be dismissed as unimportant:

> As if fictional characters are not the most powerful of all historical forces! Even a novel-hero can exert more power for good or evil than any actual individual. How much more, then, the Hero of that most tremendous imaginative construction, a religion! Such Heroes do not die easily. Their deaths have long reverberations. These Heroes are continually being resurrected in unexpected forms, especially in the minds of those who are most firmly convinced of their irrevocable deaths.

It was this attitude that led him to analyse great works of literature such as *The Merchant of Venice* and the poetry of T. S. Eliot, since, he argued, the inner meaning of Christianity was revealed most of all in the poetic insights of great Christian artists. And the antisemitism of these great poets seemed to him to reveal an antisemitism at the core of Christianity (or at least of one form of Christianity). To return to and examine more closely the passage from his *Midstream* article "The Figure of Shylock" that I quoted at the beginning of my Editor's Preface:

> *The Merchant of Venice* is a great play, not in spite of its anti-Semitism, but because of it. The sentimental reading, by which Shakespeare is on Shylock's side, spoils the great theme of the play – the clash between two theologies. It is this which gives a grandeur to the character of Shylock which commentators have labored in vain to explain. Though every anti-Semitic charge is made against Shylock (he is mean, a money-grubber, cruel, heartless, self-righteous), yet the grandeur is there. He is a man who dares to look God in the face and say: 'I deserve such-and-such'. This, according to Christian theory, is what is wrong with him; but, according to Judaism, it is what is right with him. Shakespeare has found the nub.

There are two important points here that I did not mention at the beginning, where I merely cited this quotation for the illuminating light that I believe it sheds on the play. First, my father does not place ultimate blame[48] on Shakespeare and Eliot for their antisemitism; his real critique is of Christian theology, into the inner core of which, he argues, these great poets have penetrated; they are revealing a truth about Christianity (or at least of one form of Christianity). And my father is also arguing that, in a distorted way, the antisemitism of Shakespeare and Eliot is correct: they have given expression to a truth about Judaism. In Chapter 3 of *Christ the Tiger* ("Eliot and Antisemitism"), my father writes (p. 100):

> By inspiring humanistic movements (democracy, socialism, industrialism), by insisting on justice, by embracing this world instead of regarding it as a waiting-period for the next, by embracing adulthood and maturity (what Eliot calls "old age") as positive values, and thus abandoning the beatific vision of childhood (here Eliot joins the tradition of Romanticism to that of Christianity), the Jew, in his view, is the enemy of the whole concept of Sacrifice, substituting for it the concept of progress and the perfectibility of man....

> Whether Eliot and his French forerunners are right in giving this important historical role to the Jews is a matter for serious consideration. Certainly, Judaism is the religion that, more than any other, gives the lie to the doctrine of Sacrifice, by refusing to allow any place for the dying-and-resurrected god.

My father abandoned his projected work *Flowering Judas: The Christian Image of the Jew* in favour of an analysis of the first antisemitic literature of Christianity: the Gospels. In

---

48   I say "ultimate blame" because of course my father does blame Eliot for using as a symbol of human degradation the image of the Jew, who suffered so much for centuries from Christian persecution. As my father writes in Chapter 3 of this book (p. 98): "[Eliot] was guilty of an antisemitism of a very subtle and pernicious kind. To regard the Jew as a symbol of humanity is one thing; James Joyce did that in an unobjectionable way in *Ulysses*. But to take the Jew as a symbol of fallen, unregenerate humanity is an entirely different thing. The last thing for a modern author to take as such a symbol, after what has happened in Christendom, should be the Jew." Nonetheless, the main theme of these essays is that Eliot penetrated to deep insights about both Christianity and Judaism. Anthony Julius writes (and my father agrees with him on this): "the opportunity that these poems offer for the study of anti-Semitism, and of the capacities of poetry, and of Eliot's own resourcefulness, outweigh the damage they can do. One can teach anti-Semitism from such texts; one can also teach poetry." (Julius, *op. cit.*, p. 305.) My father's main disagreement with Julius is that he shows insufficient awareness of the Christian/anthropological dimension --- the "Christ the tiger" dimension -- and so does not explain why Eliot's antisemitic poetry often rises to great poetry.

Revolution in Judaea: Jesus and the Jewish Resistance[49], he drew on the work of Paul Winter and S. G. F. Brandon to form his own reconstruction of the historical truth of the life of Jesus, who, my father argued, was a political-religious Messiah-figure and claimant to the Jewish throne who had been tried and executed by the Romans for political reasons, as a rebel against Rome; Jesus had not been secretly condemned to death by the Sanhedrin as a blasphemer against Judaism. In his next book, *The Mythmaker: Paul and the Invention of Christianity*[50], my father went on to reconstruct the life of St. Paul, who he argues, created Christianity as an amalgam of Judaism and late Hellenistic mystery-religions of the dying-and-resurrected god, into which Paul turned the human, Jewish Messiah-figure of Jesus. The rest of my father's writings were on similar historical, anthropological and theological themes. These essays on Eliot are not only part of the wider literary-theological inquiry that was the subject of the unfinished book *Flowering Judas*; they should also be seen as part of my father's whole life work. In a way, he was always the "Jew-boy", challenging Christian society to understand and appreciate the Judaism that it had rejected, misunderstood, and persecuted; this was why he interrogated Christianity's greatest pre-modern poet in English, William Shakespeare, and Christianity's greatest modern poet in English: T. S. Eliot.

My father's one play, *The Disputation* -- a dramatization of the medieval Barcelona Disputation (1263), in which the famous Jewish rabbi and scholar Nachmanides disputed with the Jewish convert to Christianity Pablo Christiani the respective cases for Judaism and Christianity --- was written as a kind of answer to *The Merchant of Venice*. As a work of art, *The Disputation* cannot be compared with *The Merchant of Venice* – my father was a great interpreter of creative art, not a great creative artist himself. Nonetheless, *The Disputation* seems to me to be a fine play that, in reply to Shakespeare's dramatization of the conflict between Christianity and Judaism from a Christian point of view, dramatizes the same conflict from the perspective of a Jew. In the Barcelona Disputation, in contrast to all other medieval disputations between Jews and Christians, Nachmanides was permitted freedom of speech by the King of Aragon, so that a real debate was possible.[51] My father refused to be self-censored by conventions of "good taste" or "ecumenicalism" in his critique of Christianity; he believed that freedom of speech means exactly that – freedom for everyone to make their case. In a crucial passage in *The Disputation* (an exchange taken almost word-for-word from Nachmanides's own account), the Rabbi points out: "if I am to represent the case for Judaism adequately, I cannot undertake to avoid remarks which to a Christian might appear blasphemous". The King grants the Rabbi "complete liberty

---

49 1973: New York, 1980.

50 New York, 1986.

51 See Hyam Maccoby, *The Disputation*, London, 2001. The play was made into a Channel 4 film and was also performed as a play in London and in the United States. See also my father's scholarly book on the medieval Jewish/Christian Disputations: *Judaism on Trial*, New Jersey, 1982.

of speech", prompting the King's confessor, the Dominican friar Raymond de Penaforte, to say in alarm to Nachmanides: "You must not avail yourself of this liberty to revile and blaspheme Christianity." To which Nachmanides replies: "I am aware of the rules of common courtesy."[52] My father always knew the difference between gratuitous offensiveness and critique that, however trenchant, is founded on respect, knowledge and understanding.[53]

In the long interview with Ron Rosenbaum referred to earlier, my father describes an argument with the American Jewish ecumenicist Rabbi Marc Tannenbaum:

> "[Tannenbaum] was very much against my whole line of approach. He was involved in Jewish-Christian relations in a very big way. And he was involved particularly in talks with the Pope to try to get the Pope to recognize Israel. And he felt that the line I was taking was counterproductive. But I reject that line of thought.... It's what I call pusillanimous. Here we are – for the first time in many centuries, we're able to speak out. Now, supposedly, we mustn't speak out because it's bad taste to speak out. One way or another, there's some gag on us. I said: if we don't speak out now, when are we going to speak out? We can't speak out in times of persecution, because we'll be persecuted. But, in times when we're not being persecuted, we mustn't speak out because that would show lack of gratitude to people for not persecuting us? So when do we speak out? Never?"

---

52 *The Disputation, op. cit.,* pp. 33-34.

53 See my father's letter to The *Times*, April 9, 1993, in relation to *Sorry, Judas*, a television programme, produced by Howard Jacobson, that aired on Channel 4 on April 6, 1993, and that claimed (in the credits) to be based on my father's book *Judas Iscariot and the Myth of Jewish Evil*, London, 1992. The Catholic journalist and author Daniel Johnson wrote a review (The *Times*, April 7, 1993) that expressed surprise "that proper scholars ... gave their blessings to this tasteless travesty". Johnson also commented that "Maccoby's polemics against Christianity are serious and sincere", adding: "I wish that the same could be said for last night's programme". Johnson concluded: "Only Christians are expected not to mind when things that they hold sacred are ridiculed on television during the most solemn week in their calendar." In response, my father wrote, in his April 9 letter: "I was engaged as a consultant.... During the first stages, I offered much advice which, however, was rejected. In particular, I warned against gratuitous offensiveness to Christians. After a certain point, I was excluded from consultation. I saw a tape of the programme in its developed form only a few days ago, when I expressed to the producer my anger both at the programme and at my virtual exclusion from it." In an article published in The *Independent* on January 21, 2006, Jacobson wrote: "Mr. Maccoby turned out to be disappointed by the programme, for which I continue to be sorry. I think he would have liked it to be more sober and more scholarly, which is not what television does." https://www.independent.co.uk/voices/commentators/howard-jacobson/howard-jacobson-nothing-like-an-unimaginative-scientist-to-get-nonbelievers-running-back-to-god-6111102.html

My father was a Zionist (a topic I will soon touch on); but there was absolutely no way he would have toned down his critique of Christianity in order to try to persuade the Pope to recognize Israel. He goes on to deny that he's calling for the end of Christianity:

> "I'm supporting a certain *strand* of Christianity against official Christianity. I'm saying that throughout the centuries there have been Christians who have actually protested against Christianity. People like Pelagius, who protested against Augustine. People who believed in the humanity of Jesus, not the divinity of Jesus."[54]

Even though he strongly disliked "ecumenicalism", my father became very much involved in and made his own significant contribution to the Jewish-Christian dialogue that has gone deeply and seriously into the Christian history of antisemitism. For instance, in 1980, my father gave the Cardinal Bea Memorial Lecture in Westminster Cathedral. My father disliked "ecumenicalism" precisely because it precludes genuine dialogue. He very much admired the courage of the many Christians who have faced up to the Christian historical record of antisemitism that laid the ground for the Holocaust; and he acknowledged the major shift in Christian attitudes that has taken place in the decades since the Holocaust: a return to the Jewish roots of Christianity; a new respect for Judaism as a religion in its own right, not just a fossilized forerunner of Christianity; and an emphasis on Jesus's life and teachings rather than his death.[55] It should be pointed out that the essays in *Christ the Tiger* were written at a time when this Jewish-Christian dialogue – which has resulted in real reconciliation between Jews and Christians -- was still in its early stages.

These essays, and my father's life work as a whole, seem to me to be so impressive that I hesitate to bring in my own criticisms. In relation to *Christ the Tiger*, most of my criticisms apply to one chapter: Chapter 4: "'Flowering Judas': A Study of the 'jew" in 'Gerontion'". This essay was published in the *Jewish Quarterly* in 1969, two years after the Six-Day War. The essay argues, convincingly in my view, that the antisemitism in "Gerontion" is not confined to the overt lines about the "jew" squatting on the windowsill; the image of the "jew", as the representative of old age and the materialistic values of this world, pervades the poem; and the poem itself "can be read as an introduction to everything Eliot subsequently wrote, including the *Quartets*" (pp. 116-117). My father also points out the incongruity between Eliot's concept of the "jew" and the actual Jew, who is the opposite of the "rootless cosmopolitan" depicted in "Gerontion" – indeed, my father argues (p. 111) that "one would

---

54 Rosenbaum, *op. cit.*, p. 324 (emphasis in original).

55 My father always spoke admiringly of the liberation theology movements that based themselves on the revolutionary, anti-Empire teachings of Jesus.

have thought that Eliot, with his views on the importance of Tradition and a sense of history, would have fixed on the Jew as the embodiment of his principles. But no; he fixes on the Jew as the embodiment of the very opposite: a soulless materialism rooted only in the present, grubbing about in unrelated particulars." My father explains (p. 112) Eliot's distorted view of the "jew" – a view that is perfectly compatible with Eliot's penetration into fundamental truths about Judaism -- in terms of Christian supremacism, which claims that "the Jews, 2000 years ago, missed the boat. They made the greatest error in all history by rejecting Jesus Christ; and therefore all their development after that point is not of the slightest interest or importance."

My father's protest against Christian supremacism is, in my view, entirely justified. But it is deeply ironic, that, in this very same essay, and almost in the same breath, in which my father makes this impassioned and convincing attack on Christian attitudes of triumphalism and supremacism over Judaism and Jews, he himself gives expression to Jewish attitudes of triumphalism and supremacism over "the Arabs".[56] Pointing out towards the end of the essay the connections between Christianity, Romanticism, Fascism ("the bastard child of the great Romantic movement") and violence, my father writes (p. 118):

> The Jew, however, has always been an anti-Romantic, denying the need for violence and setting up peace as his ideal. The Jew is the only person in the world who can stand the strain of peace, and is not continually longing for the excitement of violence. He never fights unless he is forced to; the Jews have never, in their long history, had a professional army, and all their military triumphs against the Greeks, the Romans and the Arabs, were won with amateur, civilian armies, gathered together for an emergency.

---

[56] As I have said above, my father admired the courage of the many Christians who have faced up to the record of Christian antisemitism that laid the ground for the Holocaust. But my father never managed to apply this admiration for Christian courage to the need for Jews to face up in their turn to the history of Israeli oppression of the Palestinians. This correlation is one of the main themes in the writings of the American Jewish theologian Marc Ellis: see my review in The *Jewish Quarterly*, Spring, 2003, of his book *Israel and Palestine: Out of the Ashes – The Search for Jewish Identity in the Twenty-First Century*, London, 2003: http://www.one-state.org/books/info/maccoby.htm

See also my review on Amazon of his book *Judaism Does Not Equal Israel*, New York, 2009: https://www.amazon.co.uk/gp/customer-reviews/R2MOMVUUWK89VZ/ref=cm_cr_arp_d_rvw_ttl?ie=UTF8&ASIN=1595584250

When I asked my father in his later years what he thought of the writings of Marc Ellis, he replied that he considered him to be "a very interesting thinker, but too idealistic".

The discrepancy between the idealized image of modern Israel contained in this passage and the reality of the actual militarized State of Israel, is breath-taking. Some may argue that this passage is simply out of date, written before we witnessed the depths of barbaric violence into which Israel has descended into recent years, particularly in its massacres of defenceless Gazan civilians in 2008-9 and 2014 – and (after I had finished writing this Memoir), the genocidal onslaught on Gaza perpetrated by Israel in 2023-2025. But this is still to look at Israel through rose-coloured spectacles, ignoring the ethnic cleansing of 1948 and the oppression of Palestinians even before the 1967 Occupation.[57] In relation to the 1967 Six-Day War, the myth that Israel was defending its existence against the Arab world has been exposed by scholars, in particular Norman Finkelstein, who, in Chapter 5 of his book *Image and Reality of the Israel-Palestine Conflict*, brings out convincingly, in my view, "Israel's provocation of Nasser and its responsibility for the failed diplomacy".[58] In footnotes to Chapter 4 of *Christ the Tiger*, I have commented further on my father's political references to modern Israel – references that were typical of Jewish intellectuals at that time, but not for that reason excusable (and sadly he never really changed his view of Israel).[59]

My father carefully explained to us children that the concept of the "Chosen People" does not mean that Jews are better than other people; in the Hebrew Bible the concept is of a "nation of priests" who are chosen to set a higher standard. Indeed, the Hebrew Bible is largely a record of failure; the fulminations of the Prophets are mostly not against the enemies of the Israelites/Jews, but against the Israelites/Jews themselves, for their inability to live up to God's demands and expectations. Nonetheless, this concept all too often shades into the view that Jews are in fact better – and the persecution and isolation to which my father's forebears had been subjected for generations in the Russian ghettos inculcated a compensatory attitude of arrogant superiority to the *goyim*. My father was not a Jewish chauvinist on the level of his own father; but he could not escape the inherited chauvinist attitudes. Between the ages of five and nine, before we moved to London, I didn't know any Jews, but was continually told by my father what wonderful people these unknown Jews were. As a result, when I first read *The Merchant of Venice*, at the age of twelve, I remember thinking that Shylock's "Hath not a Jew eyes?" speech meant that Jews are not *super*human but are human beings like everyone else (a salutary lesson, it seemed to me); I was very surprised to find out that Shakespeare meant that Jews are not *sub*human. My father formed an idealized dream-picture of Israel (which he never visited until he was in his 70s, and

---

[57] See Benny Morris, *The Birth of the Palestinian Refugee Problem Revisited*, Cambridge, 2004; Norman Finkelstein, *Image and Reality of the Israel-Palestine Conflict*, New York, 2003, Chapter 3; David Hirst, *The Gun and the Olive Branch: The Roots of Violence in the Middle East*, London, 2003, pp. 309-319.

[58] Norman Finkelstein, *Image and Reality of the Israel-Palestine Conflict*, op. cit., p. 124.

[59] I should point out that he supported a two-state solution and at one time advocated a confederal solution.

then only for a few occasions, staying in the bubble of a writers' colony in West Jerusalem) that he never allowed to be tarnished by reality. Far too late in my life, I abandoned Zionism and joined the Palestinian solidarity movement – an activism that led to conflict with my father; yet I always felt I was remaining loyal to his teachings in my early childhood about the ideals of justice, freedom and equality expressed by the Hebrew Prophets.

I also have problems with parts of the last paragraph of Chapter 4 (p. 119):

> My main object here, however, has been to discuss the "jew", and to argue that he is neither peripheral nor an aberration either in this poem or in Eliot's thought generally; that he is a central figure. Eliot ceased to make antisemitic references in his later poetry (or made them in a heavily disguised form); but that does not prove that his attitude towards the Jews changed fundamentally. He was shocked by the practical results in Germany of the Maurras-Barrès anti-Dreyfusard doctrine that appealed to him so much in his youth.[60] He did not subscribe to the "final solution". He was one of those "good" Christians

---

60 I think this requires qualification. Michael Curtis, in *Three Against the Third Republic: Sorel, Barrès and Maurras*, 1959: Princeton 2015 (a book to which my father refers in Chapter 3), writes (pp. 8-9): "It is abundantly clear that the attitude of Maurras, Barrès and Sorel to the society of their own day and the solutions they proposed, were remarkably prophetic of those to be adopted by later totalitarian regimes. The need for dictatorship, or the strong man, the stress on action, even purposeless action, the cult of energy, the concept of the elite, the denial of the realism, or the possibility, of political equality, the bitter anti-Semitism, even the idea of national socialism – all are to be found in the works of the three writers. It is unfair and unrealistic to juxtapose these ideas and theses with those of totalitarian regimes and thus to regard Barrès, Maurras and Sorel as embryonic Fascists, Nazis or Communists. Many of the ideas and activities of the later political movements would have been anathema to the writers, but their significant anticipations and relationships cannot be wholly discounted." Curtis's book covers the years between 1885 and 1914; he writes (p. 7): "The study ends in 1914 because the three writers had by this time made their original contributions to the thought of the country, if not their total political impact." To call the Holocaust "the practical results in Germany of the Maurras-Barrès anti-Dreyfusard doctrine that had appealed to [Eliot] so much in his youth" seems a leap too far.

Moreover, my father himself emphasizes, in an essay on the antisemitism of Ezra Pound, that, in contrast to the antisemitism of Pound, Eliot's form of antisemitism was not eliminationist ((even though, of course, "significant anticipations and relationships", as Curtis puts it, with the Nazi genocide of the Jews "cannot be wholly discounted"): "Eliot was influenced by Maurras to see the Jew as the archetypal enemy of Christendom, the rat gnawing at the Body of Christ. Eliot thus sees the Jew as a representative of Satan and therefore as an inevitable factor in life.... Pound is essentially an optimist, a 'fixer', whose frame of reference in this world. There is nothing mystical to Pound about the Jews. They are simply another obstacle to the good life, like phoney patrons, dishonest publishers or bad economists. Consequently, it was possible for Pound to attach himself to the Nazis, who regarded the Jews as a virus in the blood of humanity, to be eliminated by whatever disinfectant method might be available.... To Eliot, such a view would be a vulgarism ... the Jews were too important to be got rid of so easily. Another way of putting this is to say that to Eliot the Jew is symbolic of humanity itself; in criticizing the Jew, he was criticizing himself: the part of himself that he most disliked." (*Antisemitism and Modernity, op. cit.*, pp. 122-123.)

who believe that it is a commendable thing not to persecute the Jews, in spite of everything. These indeed are the Christians who have often protected Jews from the worst effects of persecution; and such Christians are certainly to be preferred to the active persecutors, torturers and murderers (even though Christian forgiveness is often very hard to bear). But one must protest when these worthy people are cited, as they often are, as vindicating the Christian record. To teach that the Jews are the arch-traitors of history and then to hold up one's hands in sorrow when simple-minded people take one's teaching literally is hardly admirable. There is something seriously wrong with a civilisation in which the Jews' only protection is the principle that one ought to be kind even to the Devil.

In relation to the first sentence: in my view, as I have said, my father makes his case about the poem brilliantly and convincingly. But in relation to the rest of the paragraph: as well as arrogant chauvinism, another legacy from centuries of persecution in the Russian ghettos is paranoia – understandable, but irrational and again divorced from reality. I agree that the appalling Christian record against the Jews is not vindicated by those Christians who rescued and protected Jews during times of persecution; but surely most of these Christians did so, not because they were acting on "the principle that one ought to be kind even to the Devil", but in accordance with simple human decency.[61] And surely there is something seriously wrong with the implication that, at the time of the Holocaust, the "only protection" that the Jews had was the Christian "principle that one ought to be kind even to the Devil". This ignores the anti-Nazi Socialist and Communist movements at the time – movements in which Jews were very prominent. There is also a very problematic elision in this paragraph between Christian persecution of Jews and the Nazi Holocaust. Of course,

---

61 This is not to deny that, in the case of Eliot, he *did* see Jews in general as having something of the Devil about them; this is corroborated by the most recently published material. See Eliot's letter of April 27, 1934 (written a year after Hitler had taken power) to Emily Hale (a letter mentioned in Robert Crawford, *op. cit.*, p. 223), in which Eliot refers to a German-Jewish dancer, whom he had gone to watch "purely out of benevolence", as "a rather second-rate Jewess mimic, very ugly, mildly satanic (as Jewish comedians are – why are they – why is there something diabolic about so many Jews?) rather pathetic, and with no knowledge whatever of dancing".
https://tseliot.com/the-eliot-hale-letters/letters/l297
Eliot's patronisingly superior "benevolence" towards the "mildly satanic" German-Jewish dancer does seem to chime to some extent with the Author's comments. But to jump from this, and even from "Gerontion", deeply antisemitic though the poem is, to the conclusion that Eliot's only reason for not supporting the Holocaust was the Christian principle that "one ought to be kind even to the Devil" is, in my view, a leap too far. See also previous footnote. And simple human decency must also have played its part.

Hitler revived medieval Christian antisemitism that was dormant in the European folk-memory; but my father writes as though medieval Christian antisemitism morphed straight into the Holocaust, with no Renaissance, Enlightenment or Emancipation in between.[62] By using the present tense – "is" – the last sentence also implies that even nowadays, in 1969, the date of this article, the Jews' "only protection" is the Christian principle "that one ought to be kind even to the Devil".

I was tempted, as the Editor, to edit out these passages that I find objectionable; but rather than censor them, I have left the essay intact and recorded my personal criticisms (with which others are sure to disagree) here and in footnotes. Both my father and Eliot insisted, in their very different ways, that all human beings, by virtue of being human, suffer from flaws, weaknesses and sins. It would be untrue – and untrue to my father's own teachings – to leave out what seem to me to be his own flaws, weaknesses and sins.

But, in relation to *Christ the Tiger*, my criticisms apply almost exclusively to parts of the chapter on "Gerontion"; and, as I've said, my father's interpretation of the poem itself is, in my view, illuminating and convincing. This book seems to me to be a meeting -- even though the encounter is "a clash of two theologies" -- of the minds of two brilliant men, one a great poet, the other a great interpreter of poetry – two men who were very different, from very different backgrounds, but who were also curiously similar. Both were very erudite and intellectually very precise. The attitude of both towards religion was characterized by great emotional depth, seriousness, and sincerity. Both were very much drawn towards religious ritual.[63] Both, as we have seen, placed great value upon Tradition (even though Eliot, as my father complains in Chapter 4, never understood or appreciated the Jewish tradition). In this passage (pp. 169-170) in Chapter 6 of this book, on "Burnt Norton" V, I feel my father is really talking about his own attitude towards the Jewish tradition:

---

62 I am not denying the continuity of medieval Christian antisemitic attitudes into later times – *The Merchant of Venice* is a case in point – but it is a question of emphasis. In my view, my father tended to over-emphasize the continuity of medieval Christian antisemitism and underestimate the progress in European treatment of Jews since the Middle Ages. In his posthumously-published last work, *Antisemitism and Modernity*, op. cit., he writes: "One of the aims of this book ... is to study the strange fusion that has taken place between antisemitism and advanced concepts of liberty" (p. 151) – a fusion that "for someone of left-wing orientation, such as myself ... is a painful feature of left-wing history" (p. 153). Here he seems to me to be influenced by the concept of the "New Antisemitism", which is aimed at left-wing criticisms of Israel, seeking to protect Israel from left-wing criticism by portraying the Jewish State as "the Jew among the nations". And there is something of this approach even in the 1969 essay, written two years after the Six-Day War and the start of the Occupation. For illuminating critiques of the concept of the "New Antisemitism", see Norman Finkelstein, *Beyond Chutzpah: On the Misuse of Anti-Semitism and the Abuse of History*, New York, 2008, and Antony Lerman, *Whatever Happened to Antisemitism? Redefinition and the Myth of the 'Collective Jew'*, London, 2022.

63 See Spurr, *op. cit.*, Chapter 5, pp. 121-147, for Eliot's meticulous observance of Anglo-Catholic ritual, fasting, confession and prayer. In his later years, my father went back more and more to the Orthodox Jewish rituals of his childhood and youth.

A work of art, just *because* it is so individual, extends the meaning of a whole culture; it is the realization of a possibility inherent in that culture. Similarly, in the realm of biology, all the strange and individual varieties of species are realizations of the inherent possibilities of life. Such varieties of individuality are impossible without a background of meaning, which is being worked out in infinite ways. It is through the concept of *tradition* that Eliot mediates the paradox of the finite and the infinite, as far as human culture is concerned. He sees tradition not as an inhibiting force, but as a releasing force, enabling infinite variety to take place, because it provides a background of meaning and possibility. A piece of wood, sawn off from a plank, never achieves the isolation of a work of art; on the other hand, it never achieves such connectedness either, even before it is sawn off. Isolation and connectedness do not contradict each other; they even imply each other. That is why Eliot is able to recommend "solitude" and yet to value the community (e. g. in "East Coker" V).

Eliot also resembled my father in harbouring an intense dislike of "ecumenicalism"[64], insisting on a real, basic difference between religions. Both men, despite their erudition, were very interested in popular culture.[65] And – just as, under the persona of the prim and precise "Mr. Eliot", Eliot, as my father emphasizes, concealed a far fiercer and more colourful nature – so my father, under the persona of the sedate New Testament scholar, had a far more vivid and picaresque life, as scrap metal merchant and '60s song writer, than most people knew. As stated earlier, he also had a well-hidden Romantic side, which, despite all his criticisms of Eliot's Christian Romanticism, helped him to understand it. My father too was always searching for the lost vision of his childhood and youth – a vision that he never really regained. And he emphasizes throughout this book that the power of Eliot's poetry derives from its penetration into and articulation of deep impulses that exist in all of us. Above all, my father had the deepest possible admiration for Eliot as a poet.

---

64 See *ibid.*, p. 6 for Eliot's view of ecumenicalism: "He scorned 'universalists' 'who maintain that the ultimate and esoteric truth is one ... that it is a matter of indifference to which of the great religions we adhere'. Ecumenism meant 'substituting a vague Christianity which the modern mind despises, for a precise Christianity which it may hate but must respect'. As David Edwards writes, with authority and finality, Eliot 'was no ecumenist.'"

65 See David E. Chinitz, *T. S Eliot and the Cultural Divide,* Chicago, 2003, for a fascinating book-length exploration of Eliot's life-long engagement with popular culture – a book that refutes the widespread belief that Eliot's poetry is only for the elite; a misconception that has played a large part in the eclipse of his poetic reputation.

There is a famous story, told by Stephen Spender, about an undergraduate who asked Eliot, at a meeting of the Oxford Poetry Club: "Please, sir, what do you mean by the line: 'Lady, three white leopards sat under a juniper tree'?" Eliot replied: "I mean: 'Lady, three white leopards sat under a juniper tree'."[66] Of course, Eliot was right; in a poem, words and meaning are indissoluble; the full meaning of a poem is the poem itself, to which no paraphrase can do complete justice. Yet, as my father puts it in Chapter 1 (p. 42):

> Eliot, like Dante, took ideas very seriously, and regarded them as the highest matter of poetry. Of course, this does not mean that we should expect to be able to formulate a complete prose paraphrase of *The Waste Land*; the medium (poetry) is, to some extent, the message. But this only means that ideas, in the deepest sense, do not go into prose (which slices them into successive abstractions).

For my father's complex and original interpretation of "Lady, three white leopards sat under a juniper tree" see Chapter 1 (pp. 44-46) and (in more detail) the second part of Appendix 1, including my footnote (p. 177, footnote 409) explaining the meaning of "the three stages of renunciation". For Eliot's own explanations of the leopards, in letters to various correspondents – explanations that, in my view, on the whole support my father's interpretation – again see my footnote in Appendix 1(b).

It is only through gaining some understanding of the ideas underlying Eliot's poetry that we can appreciate its rich and complex verbal texture, which my father analyses in the closest detail, even down to Eliot's subtle use of punctuation (see Chapter 5 and the analysis of "Burnt Norton" II in Chapter 6).

Eliot himself wrote in his essay on Dante: "in good allegory, like Dante's, it is not necessary to understand the meaning first to enjoy the poetry, but ... our enjoyment of the poetry makes us want to understand the meaning".[67] We respond to Eliot's symbolist poetry – which has an allegorical quality -- with our guts, because he evokes deep emotional human impulses; but, if we can gain some intellectual understanding of the poetry as well, we return to it with enhanced enjoyment, in a union of emotion and reason, flesh and spirit – whether or not this is a foreshadowing, in Eliot's Christian view, of the Incarnation in Heaven, or, in my father's Jewish view, of the Messianic Age on Earth.

---

[66] Stephen Spender, *Eliot*, Glasgow, 1975, p. 129.
[67] T. S. Eliot, *Dante*, 1929: London, 1965, p. 51.

EDITORIAL NOTE:

All quotations from Eliot's poetry are taken from *The Complete Poems and Plays of T. S. Eliot,* London, 1969, unless otherwise stated.[68]

---

[68] The "Collected Poems 1909-1962" (as chosen by Eliot himself) in this 1969 edition are reproduced in Volume 1 of *The Poems of T. S. Eliot*, edited by Christopher Ricks and Jim McCue, London, 2015 – an edition that includes many previously uncollected poems.

Chapter 1: Christ the Tiger[69]

I propose to trace through Eliot's creative work a certain thread of meaning; a theme or motif that can be summed up as: the continuity of paganism and Christianity, and the affinity of both to the literary movement or literary attitude known as Romanticism. I hope to show, in other words, that it was important to Eliot, as a poet, and as a Christian poet, to feel that Christianity contained within itself the insights of pagan religion; that Christianity was not so much the rejection of paganism as its natural flowering and development; and that the basic notion common to both paganism and Christianity was the notion of Sacrifice, not in the sense of mere abnegation, but in a more violent sense. In fact, I wish to argue that Eliot was a far more barbaric writer than he is normally taken to be; that his view of religion was a great deal fiercer and more colourful than can be discovered from the prevalent image of him as a decorous churchwarden, the prim and pedantic Mr. Eliot (an image that he himself rather tended to foster as a kind of disguise). And, further, that Eliot's religious vision has much in common with that of Romanticism in its later so-called decadent phase, the phase of Baudelaire and the "Romantic agony".

Eliot's progress to Christian faith has two features that mark it as striking and original. First, it is a movement from paganism (experienced through the study of anthropology) to Christianity. Eliot moved from the study of Frazer and Jane Harrison towards Christianity just *because* he discerned in Christianity those pagan elements that he thought were lacking in the modem secularized world (in contradiction to the commoner view that regarded the affinity demonstrated by anthropologists between paganism and Christianity as the refutation of Christian claims). Second, it is a movement from the late Romantic literary sensibility to Christianity, finding in this sensibility -- even, or especially, in the diabolism of Baudelaire -- essential Christian elements, or elements pointing towards Christianity rather than away from it.

I shall spend little time on the objection that it is inadmissible to extract a meaning from Eliot's poetry at all. It has become somewhat fashionable to assert the primacy of "pattern" in Eliot, and the unimportance of ideas except as counters in a kind of poetic game.[70] The

---

69 Editor's footnote: Previously unpublished. Probably written in the early 1970s.

70 Author's footnote: e. g. Donald Davie, "Pound and Eliot: a distinction", in *Eliot in Perspective*, ed. Graham Martin, London 1970.

   Editor's footnote: For a recent expression of a similar outlook, see "Radical Innovation and Pervasive Influence: *The Waste Land*", by James Longenbach, in *A Companion to T. S. Eliot*, edited by David. E, Chinitz, 2009: Chichester,

heroic course has even been taken of denying that *Four Quartets* is a philosophical poem[71]; further than this aestheticism cannot go. That *The Waste Land* could have been stimulated by the reading of books on anthropology seems horrifying to a certain kind of critic. Eliot must have been joking about being influenced by Frazer and Jessie Weston.[72] My own view is that Eliot, like Dante, took ideas very seriously, and regarded them as the highest matter of poetry. Of course, this does not mean that we should expect to be able to formulate a complete prose paraphrase of *The Waste Land*; the medium (poetry) is, to some extent, the message. But this only means that ideas, in the deepest sense, do not go into prose (which slices them into successive abstractions). Frazer and Jessie Weston are the stimulus, but what they stimulate is a poetic exploration on multiple levels.

It is necessary, first, to give a straightforward demonstration of the existence in the poetry of the theme under discussion. In the Notes to *The Waste Land*, Eliot expresses a special debt to Jessie L. Weston's book *From Ritual to Romance*, which, he says, "will elucidate the difficulties of the poem much better than my notes can do". The book is concerned with the continuity between paganism and Christianity. Weston argues that the essential elements of the Grail tradition that underlies the medieval Christian romances of the Holy Grail tell a story of a mysterious Vessel that has to be found in order to save the life of the wounded Fisher King and restore the fertility of the Waste Land; that this legend has at

---

2014. Like Davie (*op. cit.*, p. 64), Longenbach takes issue with Cleanth Brooks (*op. cit.*, p. 456). (For Brooks's -- in my view – brilliant line-by-line analysis, which brings out the unified, coherent meaning underlying *The Waste Land*, see his 1939 essay "*The Waste Land*: Critique of the Myth", reproduced in *T. S. Eliot: The Waste Land: A Selection of Critical Essays*, edited by C. B. Cox and Arnold P. Hinchliffe, London, 1968.) Longenbach calls *The Waste Land* "a delicate interplay of disembodied tones" (*op. cit.*, p. 453) and "built from the interplay of parts rather than a synoptic vision of the whole" (*ibid.*, p. 457). Quoting Roland Barthes on the "'syntagmatic' imagination", Longenbach sums up *The Waste Land* as "a poem 'whose fabrication, by arrangement of discontinuous and mobile elements, constitutes the spectacle itself'" (*ibid.*, p. 450).

71 Editor's footnote: See Donald Davie, *op. cit.*, p. 64: "*Four Quartets* is generally misread as a philosophical disquisition".

72 Editor's footnote: See, for example, Hugh Kenner, *The Invisible Poet: T. S. Eliot*, 1960: London, 1965, p. 129: "We shall do well to discard the notes as much as possible." Kenner refers to Eliot's typically self-deprecating and obfuscating "pleasantry, twenty-four years later, about [his own] 'bogus scholarship'" in the Notes to *The Waste Land* (*ibid.*, p.130). (For the "bogus scholarship" quote, see Eliot's essay "The Frontiers of Criticism" in *On Poetry and Poets*, 1943: New York, 2009, p.121.)

For a recent expression of Kenner's view, see Lawrence Rainey in *The New Cambridge Companion to T. S. Eliot*, edited by Jason Harding, Cambridge, 2017, p. 75: "*The Waste Land* has as much to do with Grail legends and vegetation rituals as *Ulysses* has to do with the notorious schema that Joyce concocted as he neared the end of his masterpiece ... (Vladimir Nabokov famously thought the entire schema was devised tongue in cheek).... Both writers, as publication approached, worried that their works might seem too disordered, too lacking in structure for contemporary readers, and each responded by hinting that his work was governed by an arcane logic that could be readily reconstructed by anyone willing to look for it. But the core of *The Waste Land* is not to be found in the speculations of Arthurian scholar Jessie Weston or in the pseudo-arcana of vegetation rituals."

its root an ancient Ritual, practised in the British Isles and surviving secretly in remote parts of Britain after the triumph of orthodox, mainstream Christianity; that this Ritual is part of the whole worldwide complex of ancient pagan religion that is concerned largely with fertility and that involves the death and rebirth of a god or king; and that, in its later spiritualized, mystery form, the Ritual merges the dying and resurrected gods of the pagan mystery-religions with Christ: "I firmly believe that it is only in the recognition of this one-time claim of essential kinship between Christianity and the Pagan mysteries that we shall find the key to the Secret of the Grail."[73]

Weston was strongly influenced by the work of Sir James Frazer.[74] The best-known examples of such dying and resurrected mystery-religion god-kings are the Near-Eastern cult-figures Attis, Adonis and Osiris[75]; and one of the most striking aspects of Frazer's treatment of these figures in *The Golden Bough* was the analogy that he too drew between them and the Christian dying and resurrected god, Jesus.[76] This analogy is one of the main insights on which *The Waste Land* is built, for it interweaves the figures of the Fisher King, the Hanged Man and Jesus in a poem about a Waste Land that is yearning for renewal -- i.e., modem civilization. *The Waste Land* is also about the decaying relations between the sexes; so the theme of lack of fertility is both a personal and a social one; as indeed it was

---

73 Editor's footnote: Jessie Weston, *From Ritual to Romance*, 1920: New York, 1957, p.149. Weston sums up her "general hypothesis" as follows: "The Grail story is not *du fond en comble* ['from top to bottom'] the product of imagination, literary or popular. At its root lies the record, more or less distorted, of an ancient Ritual, having for its ultimate object the initiation into the secret of the sources of Life, physical and spiritual. This ritual, in its lower, exoteric form, as affecting the processes of Nature, and physical life, survives to this day, and can be traced all over the world, in Folk ceremonies.... In its esoteric 'Mystery' form, it was freely utilized for the imparting of high spiritual teaching concerning the relation of Man to the Divine Source of his being, and the possibility of a sensible union between Man, and God.... when Christianity came upon the scene, it did not hesitate to utilize the already existing medium of instruction, but boldly identified the Deity of Vegetation, regarded as Life Principle, with the God of the Christian Faith. Thus, to some of the early Christians, Attis was but an earlier manifestation of the Logos, Whom they held identical with Christ." (*Ibid.*, pp. 203-4.)

74 Editor's footnote: "I owe to Sir J. G. Frazer the initial inspiration which set me, as I may truly say, on the road to the Grail Castle". (*Ibid.*, p. vii.)

75 Editor's footnote: See Eliot's "Notes on the Waste Land": "To another work of anthropology I am indebted in general, one which has influenced our generation profoundly; I mean *The Golden Bough*; I have used especially the two volumes *Adonis, Attis, Osiris.*"

76 Editor's footnote: See Sir James Frazer, *The Golden Bough: A Study in Magic and Religion, Abridged Edition*, 1922: London, 1950, p. 345: "we may surmise that the Easter celebration of the dead and risen Christ was grafted upon a similar celebration of the dead and risen Adonis, which ... was celebrated in Syria at the same season". See also *ibid.*, pp. 360-361, on the resemblance between the rites of Attis and Christ: for instance, "the death of the Saviour was ... made to fall upon the very day on which, according to a widespread belief, the world had been created. But the resurrection of Attis, who combined in himself the characters of the divine Father and the divine Son, was officially celebrated in Rome on the same day." See also *ibid.*, pp. 367-368 on the similarity between Osiris and Christ: "[Osiris's] tomb ... would seem to have been to the Egyptians what the Church of the Holy Sepulchre is to Christians in Jerusalem.... the tomb of their dead and risen Lord".

in ancient pagan religion, in which the fertility of the fields and of the sexes were regarded as linked.

An earlier appearance of the same theme -- the link between the basic myth of Christianity and the myths of paganism -- is in "Gerontion" (which Eliot at one time wanted to include in *The Waste Land* as a kind of prologue, till he was dissuaded by Ezra Pound[77]):

> In the juvescence of the year
> Came Christ the tiger
>
> In depraved May, dogwood and chestnut, flowering judas,
> To be eaten, to be divided, to be drunk
> Among whispers

Here Christ is presented as a sacrificial victim, but, surprisingly and somewhat shockingly, not as the usual sacrificial lamb, but as a tiger. Eliot is going back even further than Attis, Adonis and Osiris (who came relatively late in pagan religion) to the prehistoric religion of totemism, in which the totem-animal of the tribe, normally taboo, is eaten at a great annual totem-feast, in which the tribe absorbs the *mana* or life-force of the animal by eating him and so becoming one with him. Eliot is employing the parallel, also to be found in the work of Frazer and other anthropologists, between the Christian Eucharist, in which the body and blood of Christ are eaten, and this ancient totem-feast.[78] Notice also the seasonal reference - "in the juvescence of the year" -- which points to the significance of the fact that the death and resurrection of Christ took place in the spring, a time for the renewal of fertility by magical rites.

Eliot's next book-length poem after *The Waste Land* was *Ash Wednesday*, which is a meditation on the meaning of Christian sacrifice. *Ash Wednesday* is Eliot's conversion poem, the work which celebrates (if such a sad poem can be said to celebrate) his decision to enter

---

77 Editor's footnote: See Chapter 4, p. 116, footnote 269.

78 Editor's footnote: See Sigmund Freud, *Totem and Taboo*, (1913), in *The Penguin Freud Library, Vol. 13, The Origins of Religion*, London 1990, p. 217, quoting Frazer (from Part V of the unabridged *The Golden Bough: Spirits of the Corn and of the Wild, Volume 2*, London 1912, p. 51): "we can trace through the ages the identity of the totem meal with animal sacrifice, with theanthropic human sacrifice and with the Christian Eucharist.... We can see the full justice of Frazer's pronouncement that 'the Christian Communion has absorbed within itself a sacrament which is doubtless far older than Christianity'." For Freud's influence on Eliot, see A. David Moody, *Thomas Stearns Eliot Poet*, 1979: Cambridge, 1994, p. 289: "Eliot was thoroughly acquainted with Freud's work". Moody adds in a footnote: "TSE considered Freud's work complementary to that of Frazer in throwing light upon the complexities of the human soul – see 'Lettre d'Angleterre', *Nouvelle Revue Française* XXI.122 (1 November 1923), pp. 622-3" and argues that *The Interpretation of Dreams* (1900) and *Totem and Taboo* (1913) "must surely have contributed to *The Waste Land* as least as much as *The Golden Bough*". (Ibid., p. 372.)

the Christian Church. We might expect, then, if Eliot's conversion meant a conviction of the uniqueness of Christianity and its non-continuity with paganism, that the Frazerian links between the two would be broken; that Eliot would show repentance for his pre-conversion endorsement of Frazer. *Ash Wednesday*, on the contrary, confirms the link between pagan and Christian doctrines of sacrifice. Eliot's conversion was a real step in his life, but it was not a break; it was the inevitable step towards which his previous thinking had led him.

I am referring to the extraordinary passage in *Ash Wednesday* II that begins:

Lady, three white leopards sat under a juniper tree
In the cool of the day, having fed to satiety
On my legs my heart my liver and that which had been
contained
In the hollow round of my skull.

When one reads the whole passage carefully, one sees that it is really about Christian sacrifice. The Lady with her three leopards symbolizes the Church, which requires its members to sacrifice their desires (symbolized by the soft parts of the body, the heart, liver and brain; the "legs" are a euphemism for the genitals, as, in my view, can be seen by reference to the source-poem, Baudelaire's "Un Voyage à Cythère"[79]), so that the Church itself can "shine with brightness".[80] But why does Eliot adopt such bizarre, violent, bloodthirsty imagery? Why the ferocity of the image of the leopards feeding on the poet's innards? There

---

79   Editor's footnote: I have not found this source mentioned in the work of any other critic. The editors of the 2015 *Poems* do not mention it in their Commentary on this passage (*Vol. I, op. cit.*, pp. 741-745). But the Baudelaire poem's features of: a desert landscape; a three-pronged gallows; birds of prey "gorgés" (satiated) with the intestines and genitals of the Hanged Man; while, below the gallows, which is compared to a cypress tree (possibly one origin of the juniper tree, which is in the cypress family), quadruped beasts of prey prowl; while at the end of the poem the poet recalls the "black panthers" who "formerly loved so much to tear my flesh"; all these features – together with the well-known very strong influence of Baudelaire over Eliot – point, in my view, to a close resemblance, disturbing though it is. The novelist Charles Williams wrote to Eliot to ask him if there were any literary allusions in connection with the leopards or the unicorns (in Part IV) "that one would perhaps be happier for recognizing". Eliot replied, with typical self-disparagement and obfuscation: "no bibliography is going to help you, and I'm damned if I will – or rather if I would-if-I-could.... But if one can explain *obscurus* by *obscurior*, and the less by the greater, the *Vita Nuova* may help. But if the three leopards or the unicorn contain any allusions literary, I don't know what they are. Can't I sometimes invent nonsense, instead of always being supposed to borrow it?" (*The Letters of T. S. Eliot, Volume 5*, edited by Valerie Eliot and John Haffenden, London 2014, p. 197.) As many critics have pointed out, the unicorns derive from Dante's *Purgatorio*, XXIX, ll. 106-108; see the Commentary to the 2015 *Poems, Vol. I, op. cit.*, p. 750.

80   Author's footnote: See my "Two Notes on Ash Wednesday", *Notes and Queries*, November 1966.

Editor's footnote: See Appendix 1(b), where this article is reproduced. See also in Appendix 1(b) my footnotes 409 and 410.

is of course a certain modish surrealism about the picture -- one can imagine the scene painted by Salvador Dali -- and there is even a certain grotesque humour about the passage. But there is also the relating of the theme of sacrifice to its origins in the remote history of the race, to the long history of the concept of sacrifice from its most primitive origins in the totem-feast and the human-sacrificial cults.

After *Ash Wednesday*, Eliot turned to verse-drama; and here too the theme of pagan and Christian sacrifice is prominent. In *Murder in the Cathedral*, Thomas is a sacrificial figure, one of the martyrs who die, like Jesus, to atone for the sins of mankind, so that the burden of the world's guilt may be washed away periodically by blood. The pagan aspects of martyrdom are present in the play. For example, as in *The Waste Land*, the concept of fertility is linked with a strong feeling of the passage of the seasons. The Chorus says:

> war among men defiles this world, but death in the Lord renews it,
> And the world must be cleaned in the winter, or we shall have only
> A sour spring, a parched summer, an empty harvest.[81]

Thomas is a winter sacrifice; and it is hinted that there is at least an affinity between the Christian martyrs and the pagan martyrs who were killed in very ancient times in winter, in order that their lives should enter into the waning life of nature and thus give the Universe a new charge of energy. Frazer stresses this aspect of the human-sacrificial cults:

> If the crops did not answer to the expectation of the husbandman, this
> would be attributed to some failure in the generative powers of the god
> whose function it was to produce the fruits of the earth. It might be
> thought that he was under a spell or was growing old and feeble.
> Accordingly, he was slain in the person of his representative ... in order
> that, born young again, he might infuse his own youthful vigour into the
> stagnant energies of nature".[82]

The death of Christian martyrs does not exactly renew the godhead itself, but it does renew nature in the sense that it removes from her the stain of sin. The Chorus cry at one point, when oppressed by the sense of sin:

> Clear the air! clean the sky! wash the wind! take stone

---

81 Editor's footnote: T. S. Eliot, *Murder in the Cathedral*, ed. Nevill Coghill, London, 1965, p. 61, ll. 15-17.
82 Editor's footnote: J. G. Frazer, *The Golden Bough: A Study in Magic and Religion*, Part VI, *The Scapegoat*, Third Edition, London, 1913, p. 256.

from stone and wash them.
The land is foul, the water is foul, our beasts and ourselves
defiled with blood....
How how can I ever return, to the soft quiet seasons?[83]

There is a paradox here, in that the main sin, apparently, that the martyr expiates by his death is -- the murder of the martyr! Yet, says Thomas, in his Sermon, "A martyrdom is always the design of God"[84]. Does this mean that God designs the sin of those who murder the martyr? Thomas says:

This is the sign of the Church always
The sign of blood. Blood for blood.
His blood given to buy my life,
My blood given to pay for his death,
My death for His death.[85]

It seems as if Christian sacrifice is involved in a kind of vicious circle: every sacrifice atones for sin but is itself a sin that requires further atonement -- in fact, is the *chief* sin that requires atonement. This difficulty is certainly not unknown in pagan sacrifice but assumed new dimensions in Christianity.

Leaving this point aside for the moment, we see that the effect of sacrifice in both paganism and Christianity is the restoration of nature to energy and innocence. The final Chorus of *Murder in the Cathedral* expresses this sense of restoration:

We praise thee, 0 God, for thy glory displayed in all the
creatures of the earth,
In the snow, in the rain, in the wind, in the storm, in all of
Thy creatures, both the hunters and the hunted....
all things affirm Thee in living;
the bird in the air, both the hawk and the finch; the
beast on the earth, both the wolf and the lamb; the
worm in the soil and the worm in the belly.[86]

---

83 Editor's footnote: Coghill, *op. cit.*, p. 82, ll. 397-398, l. 401.
84 Editor's footnote: *Ibid.*, p. 57, l. 65.
85 Editor's footnote: *Ibid.*, pp. 80-81, ll. 371-375.
86 Editor's footnote: *Ibid.*, p. 90, ll. 618-619 and l. 623.

Notice that even the cruelty of Nature, the ceaseless violence of "the hunters and the hunted" -- the hawk hunting and eating the finch, the wolf hunting and eating the lamb, the worm parasitic on the human belly -- has been cleansed of sin (by the martyrdom of Thomas) and made good and natural; though in a previous very powerful Chorus this aspect of nature has been described with horror ("I have smelt them, the deathbringers"[87]). In a world reconciled with God, even the violence by which one creature eats another is good, because it is all part of the great totem-feast in which God's worshippers eat God. Somehow, violence has to be admitted into the world-picture and sanctified.

In *Murder in the Cathedral*, Eliot uses the technique of Greek tragedy; and this stylistic similarity is symptomatic of a similarity of content. Greek tragedy arose out of a ritual of sacrifice -- probably human sacrifice originally[88], but later (possibly) that of a goat[89] -- and is basically concerned with the death and resurrection of the god Dionysus.[90] The echoes of Greek tragedy in Eliot's dramatic work (showing a conscious relating of Christian and pagan notions of sacrifice) are even plainer in his second play, *The Family Reunion.* The Eumenides appear; and the plot is based on an actual Greek tragedy: the *Oresteia* of Aeschylus. Harry, the protagonist, is based on Orestes; but he is also a Christ-figure. He is not so much a martyr as a scapegoat, who takes the sins of the community (the Family) on his head and is driven out to wander in the desert. In *The Family Reunion*, the subject of sacrifice and expiation is so strong and the relation between the pagan and Christian attitudes so pervasive that this relationship can be regarded as the major theme of the play.[91]

---

87 Editor's footnote: *Ibid.*, p. 74, l. 233.

88 Editor's footnote: See Frazer, *The Golden Bough, Abridged Edition, op. cit.*, p. 392: "a tradition of human sacrifice may sometimes have been a mere misinterpretation of a sacrificial ritual in which an animal victim was treated as a human being. For example, at Tenedos, a new-born calf sacrificed to Dionysus was shod in buskins.... Yet on the other hand, it is equally possible, and perhaps more probable, that these curious rites were themselves mitigations of an older and ruder custom of sacrificing human beings.... This interpretation is supported by many undoubted cases in which animals have been substituted for human victims."

89 Editor's footnote: See Jane Harrison, *Prolegomena to the Study of Greek Religion*, 1903: London 1962, p. 420. Harrison disagrees with the commonly accepted scholarly view (see next footnote) that "tragedy" means "goat-song": "Tragedy I believe to be not the 'goat-song' but the 'harvest-song' of the ... form of spelt known as 'the goat'." Harrison goes on to argue that "when the god of the cereal, Bromios-Braites-Sabazios [titles of Dionysus] became the god of the vine" a "fusion and confusion" took place between the word *tragodia*, the "spelt-song", and the word *trugodia*, the "song of the wine-lees" (*ibid.*). Harrison identifies Dionysus more with the bull than the goat (*ibid.*, pp. 431-436). She does not dispute, however, that drama arose from the sacrificial rites of Dionysus: "from the religion of Dionysus sprang the drama" (*ibid.*, p. 567).

90 Editor's footnote: See Gilbert Murray, *Aeschylus: The Creator of Tragedy*, Oxford, 1940, p. 1: "Greek tragedy ... was, in literal meaning, a 'Goat-song', i. e. a *molpe* (dance and song combined), performed at the altar of Dionysus over the sacrifice of a dismembered goat, which, by a form of symbolism common in ancient religion, represented the god himself."

91 Editor's footnote: For a more detailed analysis of *The Family Reunion*, see Chapter 2.

I have now mentioned cursorily the main areas of Eliot's work in which the theme under discussion is present in a prominent way. In his later work, the theme of sacrifice certainly appears (especially in *The Cocktail Party*), but it gives way in importance to the related theme of Vocation. But there are many relevant passages in these later plays, in *Four Quartets* and in the minor poems. Eliot's early anthropological studies permanently coloured his thought. A paper that he wrote as a young man for a seminar at Harvard shows a deep acquaintance with the anthropological research of the time; he had read Durkheim, Lévy-Bruhl, Jane Harrison, Max Müller, Tylor, and Lang[92], as well as Frazer and Jessie Weston. We may even say that Eliot's interest in this subject (an interest that is also shown by his editorial policy in The *Criterion*) was one of the main stimuli for his move from poetry to poetic drama. The theme of expiation or sacrifice has been, from the earliest times, one of the main sources of the dramatic impulse; in fact, drama began as *ritual,* in which expiatory myth was acted out.[93]

With the material that we now have before us, we can begin to ask some rather more basic questions. Why was Eliot so fascinated by primitive myths of sacrifice? What was the precise relation, for him, between paganism and Christianity? From a more literary point of view, what is the relevance of all this to what Eliot was doing as a poet, and particularly to his attempt to develop the poetic mode of late-Romanticism in a new direction? Finally, we may return to the question of how Eliot used the pagan-Christian theme in his attempt to renew the poetic drama.

The basic myth of Christianity is that of the death and resurrection of Christ, and the atoning and saving power of this sacrifice. Even in very early times, a strong similarity was noticed between this myth and those of Adonis (Tammuz), Attis and Osiris, gods who died young and were resurrected, and whose sacrifice saved their worshippers from death and gave them immortality. The similarity was pointed out again and again by early opponents

---

92 Author's footnote: *Josiah Royce's Seminar, 1913-1914: as recorded in the Notebooks of Harry T. Costello,* ed. Grover Smith, New Brunswick, 1963. One of Eliot's contributions to this seminar was a paper on explanation and description in anthropology. He criticized "evolutionist" doctrines in anthropology, gave his approval to Durkheim's method and criticized Lévy-Bruhl on the ground that he "draws the line between the crude mentality of primitive [man] and his own [mentality] too sharply" (p. 74; square brackets in original). The editor, Grover Smith, in a valuable note (p. 73) relates Eliot's views on interpretation in this seminar to his later views on tradition as continual re-creation of the past and on religious ethics as a "redeeming" of the past.

93 Editor's footnote: See Sigmund Freud, *Totem and Taboo,* (1913), in *The Penguin Freud Library, Vol. 13, The Origins of Religion, op. cit.,* pp. 218-219: "Why had the Hero of tragedy to suffer? And what was the meaning of his 'tragic guilt'? I will cut the discussion short and give a quick reply. He had to suffer because he was the primal father [Freud's theory of the primal father killed by the primal horde has been discredited by later scholarship, but this does not affect his general "Oedipus complex" theory of the guilt aroused by unconscious fantasies of father-murder in patriarchal culture; see George Frankl, *Foundations of Morality, op. cit.,* p. 112 and p. 139] ... the tragic guilt was the guilt he had to take on himself to relieve the Chorus from theirs."

of Christianity, who concluded that the central Christian myth was derived from the Near-Eastern mystery-cults, which of course preceded Christianity in time. The Early Fathers were worried by this form of attack and did not attempt to deny the similarity. Justin Martyr was reduced to answering that it was a trick of Satan, who, knowing the form the Christian religion would take, had deliberately brought about base imitations in advance, with the object of discrediting Christianity when it eventually arrived.[94]

Modern Christian apologists, however, have tended to take the very different line that the similarities between Christianity and the mystery-cults show the universality of Christianity, which is the crown and culmination of all previous religions, and contains in itself the religious insights imperfectly and tentatively expressed in paganism. This line involves a much higher estimate of pagan religion than was usual among early Christian writers. Instead of being inventions of the devil, pagan cults become adumbrations of Christianity, striving towards the light. (As a matter of fact, this view was held in ancient times by the heretical Gnostic sect the Naasenes, who regarded the mystery-cults as valid forms of religion, leading up to the final Saviour, Jesus Christ.)[95]

In modern times, a powerful stimulus towards an increased respect for paganism has been the misery and sense of alienation arising from the scientific and industrial revolutions. In a world which was becoming more and more cold and impersonal, people began to yearn for the old gods, who had given the course of nature qualities of imagination and warmth. The Romantic movement of the 19th century is, in one important aspect, a revulsion from the impersonality of the scientific point of view, a demand for the restitution of a personal link with nature. So we find Wordsworth, in a poem deploring the modern industrial world, crying

> Great God! I'd rather be
> A Pagan suckled in a creed outworn.[96]

We find Keats and Shelley displaying a new interest in pagan mythology; an interest which was not the 18th-century love of elegant and learned Classical allusions, but a passionate involvement in the emotional reality of the Greek myths. Eliot's *The Waste Land*, depicting the modern city as the infertile Waste from which the gods have departed, and which requires to be redeemed by some renewal of pagan ritual, is firmly in this tradition of the Romantic Movement.

---

94 Author's footnote: *First Apology*, Ch. liv; *Dialogue with Trypho*, Chs. lxix-lxx.
95 Editor's footnote: See Jessie Weston, *op. cit.*, Chapter XI: "The Secret of the Grail (2): The Naasene Document" (pp. 149-163).
96 Editor's footnote: From the sonnet beginning "The world is too much with us".

The difference is that, between the time of Wordsworth and the time of Eliot, a great deal more had been discovered about Greek mythology. Anthropologists like Frazer, Jane Harrison and Durkheim had related it to mythologies of other parts of the world and to the myths of primitive tribes surviving into modern times. It had been discovered that Greek myths were in large part disguised and smoothed-up versions of much more savage myths; and, even more important, that myths were very often disguised versions, in story form, of what was originally tribal ritual. (Keats moved intuitively in this direction when he preferred the older, more rugged breed of gods, the Titans, to the smooth Olympians.)[97] The prehistoric worldwide religion of totemism was discovered; and links were found between this ancient religion and the more civilized forms of later paganism. This deeper, more scientific investigation lies in the background of Eliot's poetic use of paganism.

The great difference between the new 20th-century view of pagan religion and the old 19th-century Romantic view is that paganism was now revealed to be much crueller, much less charming than had been thought. Wordsworth paints a pretty picture of the solaces of pagan religions:

> So might I, standing on this pleasant lea,
> Have glimpses that would make me less forlorn;
> Have sight of Proteus rising from the sea;
> Or hear old Triton blow his wreathed horn.[98]

Keats too gives a delightful picture:

> Who are these coming to the sacrifice?
> To what green altar, O mysterious priest,
> Leadst thou that heifer lowing at the skies
> And all her silken flanks with garlands drest?[99]

Reading this, it does not occur to one to feel sorry for the heifer, much less to consider the darker background of the sacrificial cult. One is aware of the feeling of oneness with nature in the spring festival, and the sense of oneness within the human community. What does not appear is the fear of nature; the profound sense of insecurity that lies behind pagan rituals, and that led to their frequently savage cruelty. Eliot refers explicitly to this in *Four Quartets* ("The Dry Salvages" II):

---

97 Editor's footnote: See "Hyperion".
98 Editor's footnote: From the sonnet beginning "The world is too much with us".
99 Editor's footnote: From "Ode to a Grecian Urn."

> The backward look behind the assurance
> Of recorded history, the backward half-look
> Over the shoulder, towards the primitive terror.

Wordsworth calls for a renewal of man's sense of kinship with nature; but, when he thinks of nature, he has in mind majestic mountains and peaceful lakes, not earthquakes, famines, floods, sharks or crocodiles. Nature to primitive man was terrifying as well as beautiful. There is a powerful passage in Gilbert Murray's *Five Stages of Greek Religion* about this:

> The extraordinary security of our modern life in times of peace makes it hard for us to realize, except by a definite effort of the imagination, the constant precariousness, the frightful proximity of death that was usual in these weak ancient communities. They were in fear of wild beasts; they were helpless against floods, helpless against pestilences. Their food depended on the crops of one tiny plot of ground: and if the Saviour was not reborn with the spring, they slowly and miserably died. And all the while they knew almost nothing of the real causes that made crops succeed or fail. They only felt sure it was somehow a matter of pollution, of unexpiated defilement. It is this state of things that explains the curious cruelty of early agricultural doings, the human sacrifices, the scapegoats, the tearing in pieces of living animals, and perhaps of living men, the steeping of the fields in blood.[100]

Even the earlier Romantics were not entirely unaware of nature's darker side. The later Romantics, however, were much more aware of it. Tennyson speaks of "Nature red in tooth and claw".[101] Mario Praz, in his *The Romantic Agony*,[102] shows how the Romantic cult of nature degenerated into a cult of sadism and masochism, a development foreshadowed by the Marquis de Sade himself.

The early Romantics, on the whole, regard nature as kind and comforting, a refuge from the anxieties of industrial civilization. This trustful reliance on the comforting qualities of

---

100 Author's footnote: Gilbert Murray, *Five Stages of Greek Religion*, 1925: London, 1935, pp. 34-5.
101 Editor's footnote: *In Memoriam*, LV.
102 Author's footnote: See *The Romantic Agony* (first published in English 1933), translated from the Italian by Angus Davidson, Second Edition, Oxford 1970, pp. 97 ff.

nature is allied to an optimistic human psychology; a belief in the ultimate goodness and kindness of human nature, especially when a link and a union have been effected with external nature. The later Romantics have become convinced that nature, both internal and external, is cruel; but, in many cases, they persuade themselves that they like this cruelty; they attach their libido to the cruelty and become sadists or masochists, power maniacs or willing victims, whether in imagination or reality. Eliot, however, goes on from there. The recovery of the pagan vision is for him a recovery of the pagan terror, a recovery of a sense of horror and of insecurity. The vision of hell must be recovered before we can recover the vision of heaven. The sense of alienation from nature is the essential precondition for reconciliation with nature and with what is beyond nature. The enemy is the kind of security exemplified by modem city life, with its complacency, aimlessness and neurasthenic anxieties arising from the disappearance of real fear. The total exposure to the cruelty of nature that is the lot of the martyr is what redeems mankind. This is one of the meanings attached to the Desert or Waste Land. In his religious pageant "The Rock" (an inferior work, which, however, in its explicitness sometimes throws light on his major poems) Eliot says, reproving modem man:

> you neglect and belittle the desert. ("The Rock" I)

This is the Desert in its meaning of the inhospitable universe, hostile to man; the Desert that convinces man of his essential insecurity and need for God; the "primitive terror" that is the motive force behind religion and self-surrender. But of course, as always in Eliot, the Desert has other meanings too. It can mean the comfortable Waste Land of civilization, a Desert not because it lacks security but because it lacks meaning and spiritual fertility. It can also mean another kind of Desert; the Desert of the spiritual quest, of asceticism voluntarily sought for the sake of renewal - the Desert in which the children of Israel wandered for their 40 years of preparation, or which Jesus entered for 40 days of meditation and trial. The Desert is a good example of the kind of shifting symbol that Eliot uses; the shifts of meaning that are quite natural to the unconscious mind and that enrich the symbol with a nimbus of related reference, but that have led some people to suppose that he intends no meaning at all.

What became of the "primitive terror"? What role did it play in the development of religion and in the transition from paganism to Christianity? These questions are worth pursuing, since they provide a key to much of Eliot's thought.

The pagan method of dealing with the "primitive terror" was what might be called a cyclical theory of Nature; the fact that rebirth is impossible without a death. Thus paganism is very aware of the cyclical processes of Nature; the "primitive terror" returns only when this cyclical process is somehow interrupted, e.g. by eclipses or catastrophes, when the cyclical process has to be re-activated by sacrifices; and to a lesser extent at crucial turning-points in the cycle, such as the winter and spring solstices, when a sacrifice seems indicated, just in case Nature's energies of renewal need jogging along a little. In its more confident and attractive phases,[103] paganism shows itself as a loving symbiosis with Nature, a sensitive adaptation to the rhythms of the seasons and to the corresponding rhythms of human life: youth, middle age and death. It is this aspect of paganism that Eliot celebrates in "East Coker" I:

> Keeping time,
> Keeping the rhythm in their dancing
> As in their living in the living seasons
> The time of the seasons and the constellations
> The time of milking and the time of harvest
> The time of the coupling of man and woman
> And that of beasts. Feet rising and falling.
> Eating and drinking. Dung and death.

Eliot praised the "pagan ... insight" that he saw in the work of Rudyard Kipling (especially the later stories, echoes of which appear in *Four Quartets* and *The Family Reunion*).[104] The townspeople's loss of the rhythms of cyclical renewal Eliot regarded as a disaster. At the beginning of *The Waste Land*, he depicts the restless cosmopolitan Marie, who says:

> I read, much of the night, and go south in the winter.

The same point is made in *The Family Reunion*, where Amy, the country matriarch, custodian of the pieties of the countryside, is described as repudiating the idea that she should coddle her old age by going south in the winter, and so avoid contact with the cycle of the seasons – "That's not Amy's style at all."[105]

However, the pagan solution to the problem of "the primitive terror" could be too successful. The regularity of the rhythms of nature could become a great bore. The rhythmic cycle of birth, death and rebirth could be regarded as the inescapable treadmill of earthly existence. The beauty of the regular rites of the pagan year could turn into a nightmare of mechanical duties, to which the "primitive terror" itself would be preferable. This is how

---
103 Editor's footnote: i.e., the humanistic periods.
104 Editor's footnote: See *A Choice of Kipling's Verse: selected with an essay on Rudyard Kipling by T. S. Eliot*, 1941: London, 1963, p. 33. See also Appendix 4.
105 Editor's footnote: T. S. Eliot, *The Family Reunion*, 1939: London, 1963, p.12. See also Chapter 2.

the matter often appears in Eliot's poetry. Consider, for example, the conclusion of the lines quoted above from "East Coker":

> Feet rising and falling.
> Eating and drinking. Dung and death.

Even in these lines, in a passage celebrating the pagan vision, a note of slight disgust and ennui can be felt. But in a passage of *The Family Reunion*, the image of rising and falling feet, symbolising cyclic recurrence, acquires a nightmare quality:

> Over and under
> Echo and noise of feet.
> I was only the feet, and the eye
> Seeing the feet: the unwinking eye
> Fixing the movement. Over and under.[106]

The image of the Circle is one of Eliot's shifting, ambivalent symbols, sometimes symbolizing peace, reconciliation, harmonizing pattern; and sometimes symbolizing imprisonment, boredom, eternal meaningless recurrence, as in *The Waste Land* I:

> I see crowds of people, walking round in a ring.

-- a reminiscence of the circles of Dante's Hell. In fact, this vision of boredom becomes a source of panic in itself, a re-emergence of the "primitive terror" in a different form.

Christianity derives not from paganism in its joyous periods, when religion made man feel in harmony with the processes of animal and seasonal nature, but from later paganism, when this feeling of harmony had been lost. Christianity's roots are in the mystery-cults of the dying and resurrected Saviour-gods, particularly Attis and Adonis. These cults arose out of a feeling of alienation from nature; yet they took their leading ideas from the religion of nature. It no longer made sense to think of man and nature renewing themselves cyclically by a process of death and rebirth; because it was now felt that nature, or life in this world, was not enough. There was something fundamentally wrong with this world, which no amount of rebirth or renewal could cure. The process of rebirth was still the solution, but it was not a rebirth into this world, a world refreshed and renewed, but into another world. The cyclical processes of nature had come to seem an inexorable Wheel; and rebirth now meant *escape* from the cycle of earthly rebirth, escape from the Wheel of existence, into an

---

[106] Editor's footnote: *The Family Reunion, op. cit.*, p. 100.

eternal state where there was no time and therefore no death. Rebirth was no longer to be recurrent, but final; and along with this came a narrowing-down of the subject of rebirth to the individual rather than the race or tribe (for religion was no longer concerned with the survival of the species on earth).

This is the phase of religion which Gilbert Murray called "the failure of nerve"[107], but which can also be regarded (if you prefer) as a higher phase of religion, in which spirituality and individuality came into their own. Yet this later phase of paganism was not a break from the earlier paganism, but a re-interpretation of it, in which new meanings were given to all the old pagan ideas such as sacrifice, rebirth; even the Wheel of nature became now not the ultimate aim and ground of religion, but a symbol of the eternal reality behind appearance (as Vaughan uses it when he speaks of "a great ring of pure and endless light",[108] or as Eliot uses it in the *Quartets* in his phrase (in "Burnt Norton" II) "the still point of the turning world"). So there is in fact a continuity from the earliest forms of pagan religion to the latest and to Christianity.[109]

There is of course another thread in Christianity, apart from that derived from the mystery-cults -- the thread of Judaism. This too is an escape from the Wheel of nature but not into another world. It is an escape into a linear picture of history. By its Messianic doctrine, the idea of a Kingdom of God to be established one day on earth, Judaism gives a linear direction to history. Thus Judaism gives rise to a humanism which escapes from the static eternal recurrence of early-pagan humanism; and significance remains attached to the human race rather than to the individual. In so far as Christianity has at times given up its longing for the other world, and developed humanism, sense of progress and community and the idea of the kingdom of God on earth, it has been cultivating its Jewish heritage.

---

107 Author's footnote: *Five Stages of Greek Religion*, op. cit., Chapter 4.

Editor's footnote: See also Murray's summing up, in his introductory chapter, of this period (*ibid.*, p. 4): "It not only had behind it the failure of the Olympian theology and of the free city-state, now crushed by semi-barbarous military monarchies; it lived through the gradual realization of two other failures – the failure of human government, even when backed by the power of Rome or the wealth of Egypt, to achieve a good life for man; and lastly the failure of the great propaganda of Hellenism.... This sense of failure threw the later Greek back upon his own soul ... upon the comparative neglect of this transitory and imperfect world for the sake of some dream-world far off, which shall subsist without sin or corruption, the same yesterday, today and for ever."

108 Editor's footnote: Henry Vaughan, "The World", which begins: "I saw Eternity the other night,/Like a great ring of pure and endless light".

109 Editor's footnote: And Jane Harrison argues that the ultimate mystery-religion, Orphism, was a revival, on a spiritual level, of the early matriarchal, savage pre-Olympian religion, the religion of the "primitive terror", not the joyous, confident, humanistic and harmonious religion of Olympus: "The Eros of the Orphics was a mystery-being, a *daimon* rather than a *theos*, a potency wholly alien to the clear-cut humanities of Olympus.... Orphism was the last word of Greek religion, and the ritual of Orphism was but the revival of ancient practices with a new significance." (*Prolegomena*, op. cit., p. xii; emphases in original.)

In Eliot's poetry (though not always in his prose[110]) it is the mystery-cult inheritance of Christianity that is really significant. For Eliot, the bloom has left the world, which cannot be restored to its original innocence and freshness. All that one can do is to make the best of a fallen world and prepare for re-birth into a better one. It is not a question of restoring the world to full freshness, but of "shor[ing] against my ruins" (see *The Waste Land*, V), fighting against the corruption of time in order to stay in the same place:

There is only the fight to recover what has been lost.
And found and lost again and again ("East Coker" V).

This is the basis of his reactionary attitudes; he defends the Church and the Establishment like someone defending a fortress. The Church and the Tradition (both religious and literary) are for him an oasis won from the Desert, which is constantly threatening to take back what has been so painfully won from it. So the sacrifices of the faithful do not restore the whole world to its youth (as in early pagan religions); they merely prevent the total victory of old age and death. They defend the border of the sown against the encroachments of the Desert. The real rebirth is not in this world at all.

---

110 Editor's footnote: See, for instance, the Appendix, consisting of the English text of three broadcast radio talks that Eliot had given to the people of Germany in 1946, that Eliot added to *Notes towards the Definition of Culture*, London, 1948. Amid the need for "shor[ing] against my ruins" (*The Waste Land*, V) Eliot demonstrates a genuinely "Classical" sense of the need to preserve the legacy of the humanistic Christian European culture. He concludes with an acknowledgement that Christian Europe has its roots not only in the ancient civilisations of Greece and Rome, but also in that of the ancient People of Israel (pp. 123-124): "my last appeal is to the men of letters of Europe.... we can at least try to save something of those goods of which we are the common trustees: the legacy of Greece, Rome and Israel, and the legacy of Europe throughout the last 2,000 years". (It is true that he omits the continuing Jewish contribution to European culture --see Julius, *op. cit.,* p. 198 -- and of course the role of European Christian antisemitism in preparing the ground for the Holocaust; see George Steiner, quoted below, p. 236.) Even in the earlier essay "Wordsworth and Coleridge" (1932-1933), Eliot shows great sympathy with the passion for social justice that informs the *Lyrical Ballads*: "I believe that you will understand a great poem like *Resolution and Independence* better if you understand the purposes and social passions which animated its author; and unless you understand these you will misread Wordsworth's literary criticism altogether.... it is Wordsworth's social interest that inspires his own novelty of form in verse" (*The Use of Poetry and the Use of Criticism*, 1933: London, 1964, pp.73-74; italics in original). In an even earlier essay, "Second Thoughts on Humanism" (1928), Eliot, after defining what he means by "true Humanism", concludes: "There is no opposition between the religious and the *pure* humanistic attitude; they are necessary to each other." (*Selected Essays*, 1932: London, 1999, pp. 488-491; italics in original.) See also Roger Kojecky, *T. S. Eliot's Social Criticism*, London, 1971. Even though Kojecky, in my view, underplays Eliot's reactionary tendencies -- for instance, Kojecky denies Eliot's antisemitism (pp. 12-13) --- the book, which deals mainly with Eliot's prose writings, nonetheless brings out the depth, complexity and development of his concern with social issues. For a much more recent summing-up of Eliot's social theories, see John Xiros Cooper's illuminating chapter "T. S. Eliot's Social Criticism", in Jason Harding (ed.), *The New Cambridge Companion to T. S. Eliot, op. cit.*, pp. 145-161. Eliot himself summed up the difference between his prose and his verse as follows: "I should say that in one's prose reflections one may be legitimately occupied with ideals, whereas in the writing of verse one can only deal with actuality." (*After Strange Gods*, 1934: reprinted Athens, 2020, p. 28.) In other words: in prose, a writer can express his or her conscious and moral aspirations; in poetry, a writer can only articulate the actuality of his or her subconscious ideas and impulses.

Yet the ancient pagan vision of the restoration of Nature to youth and vigour by sacrifice must not be lost. Even though this vision cannot, after all, be fulfilled in this world, even though the world cruelly disappoints it, the vision must be retained; otherwise, we should sink into worldliness and complacency, into the worst fate of all, satisfaction with the world as it is. This is the clue to all Eliot's poetry; the refusal to give up the vision of youth, combined with the conviction that this world can never satisfy the vision. This explains the extraordinary combination that we find in Eliot's poetry of the sensual and the meditative - a combination of the voluptuary and the ascetic. And this emotional complex (which is not a contradiction but a fusion into a convincing whole of apparently contrary attitudes) is worked out at every possible level; from purely personal terms to a generalized theory of the history of human culture, and even (in the *Quartets*) as far as a highly abstract philosophical theory of Time and Eternity. The poetry is an expression of Eliot's personal dilemma, but he has achieved the feat of standing outside his personal dilemma to such an extent as to see it as representative of the human condition itself. (One is at liberty, of course, to see this as a feat of projection rather than of impersonality. At this level, the extremes of the subjective and the objective come together.)

We can now trace the constant pattern in Eliot's poetry; a pattern that, on the personal level, concerns itself with the hopes of youth and the disappointments of age; and, on the cultural and religious level, concerns itself with the development of early paganism into late paganism and finally into Christianity. The pattern goes like this: a dazzling early vision of sensual beauty, followed by the corruption of the vision into routine, boredom, and despair, followed by the realization that the real task of life is to cope with the boredom and despair without ever losing the memory of the early vision, even though it is mainly this very memory that makes the later deterioration so hard to bear. On the personal level, this means that nearly all Eliot's poems are about the problem of coping with old age. In his essay on Dante, Eliot suggests that old age sets in about the age of seven[111] -- in other words, old age is the human condition. Gerontion, the old man, thinking of his early vision of the Christ Child and "waiting for rain", is not just an old man - he is a symbol of what it means to be human. But it is a great mistake to think, as some commentators have said, that his boredom and despair show that he is damned; on the contrary, if he were *not* bored and despairing, then he would be damned, like the other old man in the poem, the "jew". Gerontion's very boredom and despair show that he has not lost the vision of his youth.[112]

The sexual component of this attitude is very interesting. Several critics have detected an aspect of misogyny in Eliot's work. It is certainly possible to collect much evidence to

---

[111] Editor's footnote: T. S. Eliot, *Dante, op. cit.*, p.58.
[112] Editor's footnote: See Chapter 4.

support this (the manuscript of *The Waste Land* has given further substance to the charge[113]). However, this kind of approach gives little indication of the subtlety of Eliot's attitude towards women and towards the relation between the sexes.[114] The youthful sexual drive is for Eliot the divine vision itself, as it was for Dante; the tragedy of life is the deterioration and corruption of this vision into the sexuality of adulthood. Everywhere in Eliot's poetry, we find Woman portrayed as the beatific vision, from the Hyacinth Girl in *The Waste Land* (and even earlier the little girl loved by the waiter in "Dans le Restaurant") to the Lady in *Ash Wednesday* and the *Quartets*. The image of Woman is interwoven with the pagan vision of the cycle of the seasons - for example, Amy and Mary in *The Family Reunion*.[115] But Woman is also associated with the deterioration of the pagan vision into convention and routine; and the hero of *The Family Reunion* has to rebel against Woman and even kill his mother, like Orestes, in order to break through to the Christian order. At the same time, Woman is the terrifying Chaos itself from which religion is man's refuge; and, in the last resort, this Chaos (the "primitive terror") turns out to be identical with the beatific vision ("And the fire and the rose are one"[116]). The adult, un-visionary relationship of the sexes is shown by Edward and Lavinia in *The Cocktail Party*, making the best of a bad job, stoically enduring the purgatory of adult life in the hope of eventual rebirth after death.

Early humanistic paganism was the youth of the human race, its glimpse of perfection. Later paganism degenerated into routine; and the mystery-cults, rebelling in horror against this, repudiated the body and sought salvation and rebirth outside the world altogether. Christianity, however, in Eliot's view, while deriving its world-weariness from the mystery cults, did not really reject the body. In fact (in Eliot's view), Christianity deified and apotheosized the body in the doctrine of the Incarnation, a doctrine central in all Eliot's thought, and thus recovered in idea the original humanistic pagan vision. The beauty and blessedness of the body could not be realized on earth, but it should be realized after death. This is the meaning of Eliot's profound early poem "The Hippopotamus", which has been misread as a satire[117] on the Church, but is really about the deification of the body, which,

---

113 Editor's footnote: See T. S. Eliot, *The Waste Land: A Facsimile and Transcript of the Original Drafts, including the Annotations of Ezra Pound*, edited by Valerie Eliot, London, 1971, pp. 39-40 for Eliot's misogynistic discarded draft parody of Pope's "The Rape of the Lock": "Odours, concocted by the cunning French/Disguise the good old hearty female stench." (*Ibid.*, p. 39.) Just as the discarded antisemitic draft parody "Dirge" is an artistic failure, so is this parody. It seems that physical disgust in relation to both Jews and women overcame the artistic quality of both drafts.

114 Editor's footnote: See Chapter 2.

115 Editor's footnote: See Chapter 2.

116 Editor's footnote: The last line of the last part (Part V) of "Little Gidding", the last of the *Four Quartets*; so this line ends the whole poem.

117 Editor's footnote: See my Editor's Preface (p. 13).

in all its apparent bulkiness and ridiculousness (as symbolized by the Hippopotamus), is the substance of the Incarnate God and of the Church, which is called the Body of Christ.[118]

We can now see something of Eliot's relationship to the Romantics. Like them, he deifies the values of youth and deplores old age; but, unlike the Romantics, he sees value in the deliberate sacrifice of the hopes of youth and in the acceptance of compromise with age. There is a grim purposefulness about this that derives from Eliot's Calvinist background. Eliot, in his revulsion from what he considered to be the unrealistic Romantic dream, thought of himself as promoting a new Classicism.[119] But he acknowledged that the temper of his mind remained Romantic.[120] Calvinism is the best label for him; and a Calvinist is really a Romantic at heart -- one whose Romantic dream is so strong that it has made the world into a Desert, which however he is determined to struggle through with courage, and in which he hopes to build a fortress against the evils of the Desert. Meanwhile, even for the Calvinist, there is still room in the world for the true Romantics who refuse to compromise

---

118 Editor's footnote: See also the mention of "The Hippopotamus" (plus my footnote) in Chapter 5 (pp. 128-129), in connection with "Mr. Eliot's Sunday Morning Service". See also Appendix 8 (p. 229), where I relate the Author's interpretation of "The Hippopotamus" to "A Cooking Egg".

119 Editor's footnote: See Eliot's 1916 Oxford University Extension Lecture syllabus: "Syllabus of a Course of Six Lectures on Modern French Literature", reproduced in A. David Moody, *Thomas Stearns Eliot Poet, op. cit.*, pp. 41-49: "Romanticism stands for *excess* in any direction. It splits up into two directions: escape from the world of fact, and devotion to brute fact. The two great currents of the nineteenth century – vague emotionality and the apotheosis of science (realism) alike spring from Rousseau.... The beginning of the twentieth century has witnessed a return to the ideals of classicism. These may roughly be characterized as *form* and *restraint* in art, *discipline* and *authority* in religion, *centralization* in government (either as socialism or monarchy). The classicist point of view has been defined as essentially a belief in Original Sin – the necessity for austere discipline." (*Ibid.*, pp. 43-44; emphases in original.) Also see Chapter 4 of *Christ the Tiger*, pp. 100-101, footnote 219, quoting Kenneth Asher, who suggests that the reactionary writers by whom Eliot was influenced, who considered themselves to be "classical", were in fact Romantics.

120 Editor's footnote: For Eliot's recognition that he was by temperament a Puritan, see his description of himself as combining "a Catholic cast of mind, a Calvinistic heritage, and a Puritanical temperament" (T. S. Eliot, "Goethe as the Sage", *On Poetry and Poets, op. cit.,* p. 43). See also Eliot's description of himself as "by temperament but not in doctrine, an old-style hellfire calvinist" (Robert Crawford, *Eliot After the Waste Land, op. cit.,* p. 222). For the link between Calvinism and Romanticism, see Eliot's comment on Byron's Romantic diabolism: "It could come only from the religious background of a people steeped in Calvinistic theology." (T. S. Eliot, *On Poetry and Poets, op. cit.,* p. 225.) Grover Smith (in *T. S Eliot's Poetry and Plays: A Study in Sources and Meaning,* 1956: Chicago, 1960), writes of the similarity between Byron and Eliot (p. 1): "Characters in Eliot's own poems are seldom heroic, but they share with the heroes of Byron's Eastern romances a characteristic burden of blight and guilt, attributable, it may be, to a common Adam's curse of Calvinism." Eliot must have recognized this link himself. Grover Smith also writes of Eliot: "Some critics, catching at his techniques of style, have called him a classicist; they have been less precise than Eliot himself, for, as he has acutely said, 'a poet in a romantic age cannot be a "classical" poet except by tendency'.... he was temperamentally a romantic, abhorring the gap between the actual and the ideal" (*ibid.*). For the Eliot quotation, see his essay on Baudelaire (*T. S. Eliot: Selected Prose,* edited by John Hayward, London, 1953, p. 190). For more on Eliot's recognition of his own Romanticism, see his fragmentary early lines asking God to forgive his "romantic irritations" and promising to overcome them with his "classical convictions" (T. S. Eliot, *Inventions of the March Hare, Poems 1909-1917,* edited by Christopher Ricks, New York, 1996, p. 83).

with life at all; but these are the martyrs, who die young, remain eternally young. Eliot gives a special place to the martyrs who keep alive the original pagan vision, people like Thomas and Celia, but he sees himself as Edward of *The Cocktail Party,* facing the purgatory of life with resignation, remembering his early vision with mingled pain and ecstasy, but not allowing it to disturb the duties of the Desert.

In Eliot, the concept of sacrifice really takes two forms: the sacrifice of the martyr, who dies; and the sacrifice, which is in some ways even harder, of the man who lives on and slowly petrifies, but accepts and comes to terms with this process and offers up his suffering to God, as an acceptable oblation which goes to sustain and nourish the body of the Church. The sacrifice of the martyr is the subject of tragedy; it is the story of the man who, by his very nature, attracts down to himself, like a lightning-rod, the forces of evil.[121] But the story of the man who lives on is the subject matter of comedy. In Eliot's plays, as his interest shifts from the man who dies to the man who lives on, from the theme of Sacrifice to the theme of Vocation, the drama itself shifts from tragedy to comedy. The first play in which this shift is made is *The Cocktail Party,* which is subtitled "A Comedy"; and this play and the next, *The Confidential Clerk*, are, despite their frequent bitterness and pain, subtle adaptations of Greek comedies.[122] Most people feel this shift of Eliot's to be an anti-climax, and there is no

---

[121] Author's footnote: This is the solution of the paradox mentioned earlier. The martyrdom is both the expiation of the crime and the main crime itself, since it acts as a focal point for the forces of evil, which discharge and expend themselves upon the martyr, thus leaving the world clean for a while. Actual human sacrifice is thus avoided, and the responsibility for the sacrifice (now a "martyrdom") is shifted to some figure of evil who is sent into the desert or otherwise ostracized.

[122] Editor's footnote: *The Cocktail Party* (1949) and *The Confidential Clerk* (1953) are based, respectively, on the *Alcestis* and *Ion* of Euripides; see David Jones, *The Plays of T. S. Eliot*, London, 1963, Chapters 5 and 6. Eliot's last play, *The Elder Statesman* (1958) written seven years before his death, is based on a Greek tragedy, Sophocles' *Oedipus at Colonus* (though this play, the last play of Sophocles, is so serene and reconciliatory at the end that it resembles the last plays of Shakespeare rather than true tragedy; and *The Elder Statesman* too has something of this quality, despite its deficiencies as a work of art; Eliot's personal emotions of happiness seem to overwhelm his impersonal artistry; yet the way in which Eliot, the consummate poet, is at a loss for words because of his experience of love renders the play strangely moving). The Elder Statesman of Eliot's title, Lord Claverton, is the man who "lives on and slowly petrifies". He has constructed an artificial, pretentious outward shell that conceals from the world, from his daughter and even from himself his inner sense of guilt in relation to two buried memories. His inner demons rise up, like the Eumenides, in the form of two people from his past who confront him. In the end, he faces up to his demons and his guilt and confesses his sins to his daughter. He then finds that he has regained his real self and is able at last genuinely to love his daughter; and she (who had idolized the illusory persona he had created) is able at last genuinely to love the real man that he has become. Now that he is able to love and to be loved, he is ready to die (and has a serene off-stage death similar to that of Oedipus); but, as Moody points out, Lord Claverton is reborn in the form of his daughter's fiancé: "The 'daughter', by a reversal of the mode of sublimation practised in *Marina* and *Ash Wednesday*, becomes his beloved; and the man she loves is himself, his 'real self' brought into being by love." (*Thomas Stearns Eliot Poet, op. cit.*, p. 283.) *The Elder Statesman* reflects Eliot's marriage to his secretary, Valerie Fletcher, at the age of 68 (she was 30); a marriage that took place during the writing of the play. Lord Claverton says: "I see myself emerging/From my spectral existence into something like reality./.... I've been freed from the self that pretends to be someone;/And in becoming no-one, I begin to live./

doubt that the later comedies lack the poetic qualities of *Murder in the Cathedral* and *The Family Reunion.* Yet the shift was a movement from death to life; and there are signs in his latest work that Eliot was beginning to overcome his grim Puritanism and achieve the true Classical love of limitation and form as the delineation and structuring of the infinite.[123]

Nevertheless, there is no doubt that, at the height of his poetic powers, Eliot was more interested in the martyr than in the man who copes with life by living on. To Eliot, the Christian martyr is the successor of the pagan voluntary human sacrifice; and, in so far as the martyr is central to the Christian *Weltanschauung* (which he or she undoubtedly is, since the central object of Christian piety and contemplation is the Crucifixion), Christianity shares with paganism the mystery of violence -- the feeling that salvation, ultimately, is through the shedding of blood. The fascination with violence, the conviction that only through violence and in violence is ultimate reality met, that through violence the stagnating universe is jolted into new life, permeates Eliot's best poetry.[124] In "Gerontion", for example,

---

It is worthwhile dying, to find out what life is./.... I am only a beginner in the practice of loving." (*Complete Poems and Plays, op. cit.,* pp. 569-582.)

[123] Editor's footnote: This is most apparent in *The Confidential Clerk* (1949), in the personality of Eggerson (the real "Confidential Clerk" of the title and thus the real hero of the play). Colby believes his biological father to be the successful businessman Sir Claude Mulhammer (for whom he is working as Eggerson's successor Confidential Clerk after Eggerson's retirement) but discovers at the end that his biological father is the second-rate organist Mr. Guzzard. But at the end of the play, it becomes clear that Colby's "real" father is Eggerson, who points him towards his true Vocation: taking Holy Orders in the service of God, Colby's ultimate Father. Eggerson makes a satisfying whole of what is apparently a very narrow life, working in the City of London, then going back in the evenings to Mrs. Eggerson and his garden in the outer suburb of Joshua Park: "'All the travel *I* want is up to the City/And back to Joshua Park in the evening,/And once a year our holiday at Dawlish.'" (*Complete Poems and Plays, op. cit.,* p. 456; emphasis in original.) Colby, after being advised by Sir Claude to keep a "secret garden" -- an inner artistic (in Colby's case musical) life completely separate from his outer life in the City -- muses on the real garden created by Eggerson: "If you have two lives/Which have nothing whatever to do with each other --/Well, they're both unreal. But for Eggerson/His garden is part of one single world." Colby goes on: "If I were religious, God would walk in my garden/And that would make the world outside it real/And acceptable, I think." (*Ibid.,* pp. 473-474.)

[124] Editor's footnote: Genesius Jones (*op. cit.,* p. 317) also comments on the violence that pervades Eliot's poetry; but Fr. Jones argues that Eliot evokes violence in order to criticize it. To Fr. Jones, Eliot is an anti-Romantic poet who associates violence with "Personalities", while he himself approves of non-violent, mature "Persons". Referring to Eliot's essay "Tradition and the Individual Talent", Fr. Jones writes: "Mr. Eliot's flat denial of the Romantic theory of the Personality in poetry stands at the head of his critical work." (*Ibid.,* p. 315.) It seems to me that Fr. Jones takes Eliot's camouflage disguise of "Mr. Eliot" far too much at face-value. This view of Eliot leads Fr. Jones into what seems to me to be a complete misreading of the lines in "The Hollow Men" in which the "hollow men" say that they will be remembered "not as lost/Violent souls/But as the hollow men/The stuffed men". Fr. Jones writes: "The hollow men who have emptied themselves of Personality, in the hope of becoming Persons, declare that they will be remembered *not as lost/Violent souls.* The violent are the type of the irresponsible Personality." (*Ibid.,* pp. 317-318; italics in original). On the contrary, the "hollow men", as Grover Smith points out (*Poetry and Plays, op. cit.,* p. 105), resemble the people in Canto III of Dante's Inferno who "lived without blame and without praise" and so are not damned but exist in a kind of vague twilight world, like the people in "Burnt Norton" III. The "hollow men" are not "empty"; they are "stuffed" with rubbish (see the Author's comment, in his Commentary on "Burnt Norton" III in Chapter 6 (p. 164), on the line "Tumid apathy with no concentration"; he compares "tumid" with

the old man begins by regretting that his youth had no share in the violence of the ancient world ("hot gates" i.e. Thermopylae) nor of the Renaissance world ("cutlass"). The poem finally resolves the old man's sense of stagnation by an explosion in which he, together with representative figures of the modern world ("De Bailhache, Fresca, Mrs. Cammel"), is blown to pieces and carried away by the destroying and revivifying wind. A similar explosion of violence resolves the stagnation in "Animula". Even in *The Cocktail Party*, when Eliot was beginning to lean towards comedy and life, the figure of the martyr appears, as the only character who comes face to face with reality. Celia is made to suffer a horrifying death, eaten alive by ants. To eat and be eaten -- this is the reality behind the facade of civilization, a reality sanctified by the Communion service itself, in which the worshipper eats God and is eaten by Him. "Christ the tiger" is, after all, Eliot's deepest religious insight.

> The dripping blood our only drink
> The bloody flesh our only food. ("East Coker" IV)

The thesis that Eliot thought of Christian martyrdoms (including the Crucifixion) as logically continuous with pagan human sacrifices is one that would probably shock the average churchgoer. Eliot came to Christianity by a circuitous route and after an encounter with the "primitive terror"; and Christianity seemed to him the creed that most took into account the native horror of existence.

I have tried to show that Eliot's poetry is a great deal more agonized, savage, even paranoid, than it is usually thought to be, either by those who bowdlerize his thought, or by those who emasculate him by turning him into a mere aesthete, interested only in non-referential "symbolism" or poetic "patterns". The motivations behind the poetry may seem at times shockingly primitive, but Eliot himself thought that it was part of the function of a poet to be primitive: "The artist, I believe, is more *primitive*, as well as more civilized, than his contemporaries."[125] That a primitive poetic insight was developed in response to the academic study of anthropology is typical of the complexity and unexpectedness of Eliot's mind.

"stuffed" in "The Hollow Men"). If the "hollow men" could become "lost/Violent souls", i.e., damned, they would have a chance of being saved. As Grover Smith points out (*Poetry and Plays, op. cit.*, pp. 105-106), at the end of the poem they do join the damned on the shores of the river leading to hell; and a hope is held out that they can now become "empty men" who can catch a glimpse of the "multifoliate rose", "The hope only/Of empty men". "Empty", which is like the emptiness of darkness and deprivation that is advocated in "Burnt Norton" III, is contrasted with "hollow" (there is a typical Eliotic ambiguity here; the lines mean "the only hope of empty men" and "a hope that can only be obtained by empty men"). As Grover Smith puts it (*ibid.*, p. 106): "having plunged into hell, the hollow men may find paradise".

125 Editor's footnote: from Eliot's review of Wyndham Lewis's novel *Tarr* (The *Egoist* 5, September 1918, pp. 105-106).

Chapter 2: THE THEME OF SEXUAL CONFLICT IN ELIOT[126]

It has been noted that *The Waste Land* can be read as a portrayal of the unsatisfactory nature of modern sexual relations; this would seem to indicate a positive, reformist attitude towards sex on Eliot's part, and a desire to offer remedies and prescriptions in the manner of D. H. Lawrence. On the other hand, a certain personal disgust with sex, amounting even to a hatred of women, has also been detected in Eliot's work.[127] I wish to argue that he did have a *message* to convey about sex: that the sexual predicament, especially that of the modern world, was central to his thought. Eliot's "thought" is a pervasive presence, if not quite an ingredient, in his poetry. And though his poetry often arises from personal suffering or neurosis, there is a degree of generalization by which the suffering attains universal significance and thus impersonality.

---

126 Editor's footnote: Previously unpublished. Probably written about 1970.

127 Editor's footnote: See, for example, Ian Hamilton, "The Waste Land" in *Eliot in Perspective*, op. cit., p.108: "No-one in *The Waste Land* ... actually enjoys sex. It is not even granted to be a pleasurable, exciting evil. It is seen throughout as a kind of enervated reflex." Grover Smith (in *T. S. Eliot's Poetry and Plays*, op. cit., pp. 37-38), is one of the few early critics to comment on the *Ara Vos Prec* poem "Ode", which Eliot never allowed to be reprinted; it describes a bride, on the morning after her wedding night, as "Succuba eviscerate". (For the poem, see *Inventions of the March Hare*, op. cit., p. 383.) See also the misogynistic discarded draft parody in T. S. Eliot, *The Waste Land: A Facsimile and Transcript of the Original Drafts*, op. cit., pp. 39-40 (already mentioned in Chapter 1) and the artistically successful lines in "Sweeney Erect" about the "nameless epileptic" (Grover Smith, *Poetry and Plays, op. cit.*, p. 47) woman: "This withered root of knots of hair/Slitted below and gashed with eyes,/This oval O cropped out with teeth:/The sickle motion from the thighs/Jackknifes upward at the knees/... clawing at the pillow slip." In the 1970s, the feminist critique of Eliot was just beginning. For a recent helpful summary of changing feminist attitudes towards Eliot's poetry, see Gail McDonald, "Gender and Sexuality" in *The New Cambridge Companion to T. S. Eliot, op. cit*. McDonald writes that, in the 1970s and '80s, "in general, the view of Eliot placed him firmly in the conservative-patriarchal-repressive camp" (p. 171); but she comments a little earlier (p. 169): "More recently, as the performativity of gender and the recognition of fluidity in sexual desire have been more thoroughly explored, the emphasis has fallen more heavily on the meanings of sexuality more broadly defined – and this shift in focus has raised other sorts of questions, about transgressive desires, queer perspectives, and the cultural constructedness of gender and sexuality." Unfortunately, much of this recent criticism, being located within esoteric academic enclaves of "gender studies" and "cultural studies", tends to be permeated with post-structuralist literary theory and academic jargon and is largely inaccessible to the general reader. For example, the phrase "the performativity of gender" is included in the title of Cyrena Pondrom's article "T. S. Eliot: The Performativity of Gender in *The Waste Land*", *Modernism/Modernity* 12, no. 3 (2005): "Eliot and his contemporaries recognized the performativity of gender as a source of ontological instability of the self long before it became a touchstone of post-structuralist theorizing."

We may find some light on the subject by studying a poem which may seem at first irrelevant: "Sweeney Among the Nightingales". This poem has been generally recognized as one of Eliot's most powerful; but it is hard to understand the source of this power until one notices the underlying sexual themes.

The usual interpretation of the poem is that it contrasts the tawdriness of modern life (as displayed in Sweeney's party) with the nobility of the Homeric past, as displayed by the tragedy of Agamemnon's death.[128] The sonorous "lift" of the end of the poem is one of the most familiar effects in English poetry:

> The host with someone indistinct
> Converses at the door apart,
> The nightingales are singing near
> The Convent of the Sacred Heart,
>
> And sang within the bloody wood
> Where Agamemnon cried aloud
> And let their liquid siftings fall
> To stain the stiff dishonoured shroud.

This certainly *sounds* as if it means something very important, and no-one can read it without feeling moved, but what does it mean? That "And sang", ringing out so musically -- are we to take it that the nightingales at least, are the same as they ever were; that nature retains her grandeur even if men become petty? Or that the nightingales are indifferent to the fate of mankind; that "it is equally significant or insignificant whether it is Agamemnon who is betrayed and murdered or Sweeney, and there is no more relevance in the nightingales' lovely song than in their casual droppings"?[129] Is the contrast between Sweeney and Agamemnon evoked only to be dismissed? Certainly, the actual content of the Agamemnon episode hardly seems to sort with the heroic rhythms employed; for what, after all, is so uplifting about the spectacle of birds excreting over the corpse of a man treacherously murdered by his adulterous wife? But if the heroic/sordid contrast of ancient/modern times is so precarious, what is the point of the poem? And why indeed should the poem be held to have any point even if the contrast is upheld? Surely Eliot has

---

128 Editor's footnote: See, for example, Edmund Wilson, in *T. S. Eliot: A Selected Critique*, edited by Leonard Unger, New York, 1948, pp. 174-175, on "the inferiority of the present to the past" (p. 174). See also Elizabeth Drew, *T. S. Eliot: The Design of his Poetry*, New York, 1949, p. 42: "the emphasis is ... upon the distinction between two atmospheres, two attitudes towards reality".

129 Author's footnote: Helen Gardner, *The Art of T. S. Eliot*, 1949: London, 1968, p. 83.

more to say than to express a sentimental nostalgia for a supposed heroic past? All this is difficult enough without even the mention of pettier puzzlements such as the question of how the body of Agamemnon came to be excreted on by birds in a wood, though he died in his bath, and how Agamemnon's body came to be in a shroud, with no perceptible interval, after emitting his death-cry.

The power of the poem is a *datum;* and the power does have *something* to do with the evocation of a heroic past. After the ironic quatrains describing the seedy goings-on at the party, the final six lines give a terrifying yet vitalizing awareness of a deeper dimension of life. It is as if the trivial carousing has been interrupted by a serious accident, or rather a savage crime, shocking the participants into silence broken only by the sound of the nightingales' singing. Yet the crime occurred on a different time-plane.

Eliot once said that all he was trying to do in "Sweeney Among the Nightingales" was "to create a sense of foreboding".[130] In order to reconcile this characteristically deprecatory statement with his view expressed elsewhere that "the poem is intensely serious and among the best I have ever done",[131] one would have to regard the creation of a sense of foreboding as more than a literary exercise. Otherwise, it should be given as much (or as little) weight as Eliot's remark that *The Waste Land* was "just a piece of rhythmical grumbling".[132] If there is a sense of foreboding in the poem, it is not in the polished anti-climaxes of the second and third verses, nor in the studied triviality of the conspiracy against the "man in brown", but in the sudden opening of an abyss of horror at the end by which the conspiracy acquires retrospectively a new dimension.

If we apply three Eliotian words -- "boredom"; "horror" and "glory"[133] -- we shall get to the heart of the poem; and also approach an understanding of Eliot's orientation towards sex. In Eliot, the movement is always an escape from boredom through horror, which then gives a glimpse of glory. The immediate point of the Agamemnon incident is not some "heroic" archaic nobility, but its revelation of a primitive horror; and the horror thus revealed is the battle of the sexes. From the bored, debilitated manoeuvres which represent the sex-war at Sweeney's party, we suddenly move to an episode of archetypal horror showing the sex-war at its most savage. The effect is like that of a dream in which some humdrum

---

130 Editor's footnote: F. O. Matthiessen, *The Achievement of T. S. Eliot*, 1935: Second Edition, New York, 1947, p. 129.
131 Editor's footnote: Valerie Eliot (ed.), *The Letters of T. S. Eliot, Volume 1, 1898-1922*, New York, 1988, p. 363.
132 Editor's footnote: T. S. Eliot, *The Waste Land: A Facsimile and Transcript of the Original Drafts, op. cit.*, p. 1.
133 Editor's footnote: T. S. Eliot, *The Use of Poetry and the Use of Criticism*, 1933: London, 1964, p. 106 (essay on Matthew Arnold): "It is an advantage to mankind in general to live in a beautiful world; that no one can doubt. But for the poet is it so important? We mean all sorts of things, I know, by Beauty. But the essential advantage for a poet is not, to have a beautiful world with which to deal: it is to be able to see beneath both beauty and ugliness; to see the boredom, and the horror, and the glory."

scene suddenly turns into a nightmare, bringing out the emotional reality against which the boredom was a defence-mechanism.

The death of Agamemnon is a central incident in a bloodthirsty saga of the sex-war. Not only was Agamemnon murdered by his wife, but Orestes, his son, retaliated with matricide. Eliot read these stories (to which he returned again and again in his work) in the light of the anthropological work of Frazer and Jane Harrison, by which the prettifications of Greek myth were stripped away, and the archaic sadism and violence revealed. We may note how many allusions to intra-sexual violence are woven into the economical last six lines of the poem. The "bloody wood" in which the nightingales sing is the wood of the Furies, those terrifying, hag-like women who avenge wrongs committed against the female sex[134] (Agamemnon suffers because of his murder of his daughter Iphigenia). The nightingales themselves are not merely melodious birds. Eliot's original epigraph[135] to the poem alluded to the Philomela myth, in which the nightingale represents the wrongs of rape and mutilation committed against a woman, and her subsequent terrible revenge on the male. The nightingales are themselves the Furies, and show their exultant contempt for the dead Agamemnon, whom they have hounded to death through their agent Clytemnestra, by excreting on his corpse (this shows not indifference, but revengefulness and triumph). Part of the effect of the potent word 'sang' is this sense of exultation. Yet the word "nightingale" is also a slang expression for prostitute;[136] and the prostitutes who are treated with such off-hand contempt by Sweeney earlier in the poem and suffer from the boring modern way of ill-treating women by depriving them of mystique and significance, become transformed in the end into nightingale-Furies who exact due revenge from Sweeney/Agamemnon. Eliot was no doubt aware of the sexual perversion in which a masochistic male receives satisfaction from being excreted on by a dominant female. We see now why Agamemnon utters his death-cry in a wood, not in his bath; for, by a telescoping of images, his death-place (wherever it may literally have been) is the sacred stronghold of the Furies where the female principle triumphs.

---

134 Author's footnote: See Grover Smith, *Poetry and Plays, op. cit.*, p. 45.

    Editor's footnote: Smith writes: "The nightingales ... migrated into Eliot's concluding stanzas from the grove of the Furies ('bloody wood') in Sophocles' *Oedipus at Colonus*." See Antigone's words in *Oedipus at Colonus*: "Here, where we are,/There is a kind of sacred precinct, overgrown/With laurel bushes, olive, and wild vine; And it is full of the voices of many nightingales." (Sophocles, *The Theban Plays: King Oedipus, Oedipus at Colonus, Antigone*, Translated by E. F. Watling, London, 1947, p. 72.) See also the words of the Chorus: "None of us/Would venture into the sacred close./The implacable goddesses – Hush!/Take not their name in vain." (*Ibid.*, p. 75.)

135 Editor's footnote: see Grover Smith, *Poetry and Plays, op. cit.*, p. 45.: "The epigraph, in Greek, 'Alas, I have been struck deep a deadly wound', echoes Agamemnon's cry when Clytemnestra smites him.... Another epigraph, from the anonymous *Raigne of King Edward the Third* (Act II, scene 1, lines 109-10), was prefixed to the poem as published in *Ara Vos Prec*; it alludes to the Philomel myth: 'Why should I speak of the nightingale? The nightingale sings of adulterous wrong.'"

136 Author's footnote: *Ibid.*, p. 46.

When the nightingales are first introduced, they are "singing near/The Convent of the Sacred Heart". The nuns in this convent, devoting their compassionate thoughts to the bleeding heart of the crucified Jesus, are, anthropologically speaking, the linear descendants of the women who mourned annually for the dead Adonis or Attis. The song of the nightingales (who symbolize these nuns as well as later the Furies) is a song of mourning as well as a song of triumph. For Eliot derived from his study of Frazer the knowledge that it was as a sacrifice to the Mother Goddess or the female principle that the Young God always died;[137] she demanded his death, even though her acolyte-women made reparation to him by their rites of mourning.[138] Even the nuns in the Convent of the Sacred Heart testify to the savagery of the conflict between the sexes in the history of religion. And through this association, we are led to think of the death of Agamemnon as no mere palace squabble, but as an incident of religious significance; he is one more sacrifice to the goddess, on whose behalf Clytemnestra performs a priestess function. The "bloody wood" in which he dies is also the "Sacred Wood",[139] and the presiding Furies, from another aspect, are the Muses,

---

137 Editor's footnote: This should perhaps be qualified a little. Adonis and Attis were both said to have been killed by boars (Frazer, *The Golden Bough, Abridged Edition, op. cit.*, respectively p. 327 and p. 347). But Frazer points out later that the boars were probably originally Adonis and Attis themselves (*ibid.*, p. 471); so it does seem that they both indeed died as a sacrifice to the Mother Goddess. Another story about the death of Attis is that "he unmanned himself under a pine tree and bled to death on the spot" (*ibid.*, p. 347) for the sake of the cruel Goddess Cybele. But Osiris is said to have been killed by his evil brother Set (*ibid.*, p. 363). See Maccoby, *The Sacred Executioner, Human Sacrifice and the Legacy of Guilt*, New York, 1982, p. 109, where Maccoby points out a major contrast between the mystery-religions and Christianity (despite the continuity between them). Conceding that in the mystery-religions -- which he sees as a reappearance of matriarchy – there was an emergence of "a dark male figure of evil as antagonist and slayer of the god", Maccoby goes on: "but there was no grim father-god demanding the sacrifice of the young god on patriarchal grounds, as there was in Christianity – which thus provides a unique amalgam of patriarchal and matriarchal motifs". *See* discussion below in this chapter about *The Family Reunion*.

138 Editor's footnote: Frazer draws attention to the resemblance between ancient Greek statues of Aphrodite with the dying Adonis in her arms and Michelangelo's *Pieta*: "The type, created by Greek artists, of the sorrowful goddess with her dying lover in her arms, resembles and may have been the model of the *Pieta* of Christian art, the Virgin with the dead body of her divine Son in her lap, of which the most celebrated example is the one by Michelangelo in St. Peter's. That noble group, in which the living sorrow of the mother contrasts so wonderfully with the languor of death in the son, is one of the finest compositions in marble. Ancient Greek art has bequeathed to us few works so beautiful, and none so pathetic." (*The Golden Bough, Abridged Edition, op. cit.*, pp. 345-346.) On a visit to Rome in 1926, a year before his conversion, Eliot "surprised his relatives by falling to his knees in front of Michelangelo's *Pieta*". (Ackroyd, *T. S. Eliot, op. cit.*, p.159.) Eliot may have had this passage from Frazer in his mind at the time.

139 Editor's footnote: The title that Eliot gave to his 1920 collection of essays on poetry and criticism. In "Ode" (*Inventions of the March Hare, op. cit.*, p. 383), Eliot, describing his lack of poetic inspiration, writes of "silence from the sacred wood". Grover Smith points out (*Poetry and Plays, op. cit.*, p. 37) a probable source of the phrase in Laforgue's poem "Cythère", with its reference to "un bois trop sacré". For the ultimate origin of the term – and this must also be a direct source of Eliot's use of the phrase -- see the second century CE Greek traveller and geographer Pausanias, *Description of Greece, Books 8.22-10, with an English translation by W. H. S. Jones*, Harvard, 1935, p. 295: "On Helicon, on the left as you go to the grove of the Muses, is the spring Aganippe" (Book 9: 29: 5) and the subsequent account of the sacred grove of the Muses on Mount Helicon. Pausanias also describes a statue of Orpheus in this grove, writing: "They say that the women of the Thracians plotted his death.... The Thracians

the thrice triune goddess who demands the death of her male devotee and at the same time gives him the sweet song of her nightingales. So, in six lines, Eliot has expressed many aspects of the conflict between the sexes in mythology and religion. The rather late and sordid story of the bloody death of Agamemnon (though more inspiriting in its violence than the frozen, inhibited antagonisms of modern life), is given greater significance by being traced, through the mediation of the Christian myth, to origins in the pagan rituals of sacrifice by which the cosmic polarity of the sexes was expressed.

It may be as well to give at this point a brief conspectus of the importance of the conflict between the sexes in Eliot's work generally. It will be seen that this is far more than the distaste for women of which Eliot has been accused; for the dangerousness and, at times, distastefulness of women are amply balanced by the dangerousness and distastefulness of men. What Eliot is concerned with is the situation in which one half of the human race yearns for the other half, yet these two halves, in their relations with each other, are hostile, suspicious, treacherous and murderous -- two enemy camps perpetually at war. And this is a situation that for Eliot is of utmost significance in terms of religion, politics and human destiny, quite apart from the purely personal unhappiness that was the immediate source of his meditation.

Among the treacherous, insensitive males portrayed by Eliot are the "house-agent's clerk" of *The Waste Land* III, casually and contemptuously seducing the typist, and the other seducer in the "narrow canoe" in the same part of the same poem; and, as background music or counterpoint in this poem, there is the legend of Philomela, violated and mutilated by Tereus. Sweeney, in "Sweeney Erect", is another contemptuous male, and this time the background legend is that of the cold betrayal of Ariadne by Theseus. The hostility of the male to the female develops into actual murderousness in "Sweeney Agonistes" ("Any man might do a girl in/ Any man has to, needs to, wants to /Once in a lifetime, do a girl in")[140] -- though the title recalls the female treachery of Delilah. The murderer of the female becomes the protagonist in *The Family Reunion.*

Corresponding to the theme of ill-treatment is the theme of hysteria, dissatisfaction and sense of degradation in the female. There is the neurotic upper-class woman in *The Waste Land* II, desperately trying to communicate with the male; and in the same part of the poem there is the pathetic, down-trodden working-class Lil, ill, over-worked and on the point of

---

say that such nightingales as nest on the grave of Orpheus sing more sweetly and louder than others." (*Ibid.*, pp. 301-303; Book 9, 30: 5-6.) Elizabeth Drew (*op. cit.*, p. 43), claims that the term "The Sacred Wood" derives from the first chapter of Frazer's *The Golden Bough* (*Abridged Edition, op. cit.*), about the wood at Nemi, sacred to Diana, where in ancient times a King-Priest would be slain by a younger challenger who would take his place. There may be an association here; but surely the primary reference is to the Sacred Grove of the Muses on Mount Helicon.

140 Editor's footnote: from part 2 of "Sweeney Agonistes": "Fragment of an Agon".

betrayal and desertion by her husband. Another reaction is that of the prostitute, turning her degradation and dependence into a weapon of exploitation; and there is a remarkable bevy of prostitutes in Eliot's poetry – in "Sweeney Erect", "Sweeney Agonistes", "Sweeney Among the Nightingales" – and of semi-prostitutes like the narrator of the Lil episode.

The female, however, has her own positive capacity for aggression against the male. Grishkin ("Whispers of Immortality") is likened to a jaguar. Rachel ("Sweeney Among the Nightingales") has "murderous paws"; and Clytemnestra actually performs a murder of the male in the same poem. In *The Family Reunion*, the Eumenides embody the angry Female, avenging her wrongs; while the "Lady" in *Ash Wednesday* is accompanied by three white leopards who feed on the poet's body (evoking Baudelaire's "Un Voyage à Cythère", with its savage male sacrifice to the love-goddess).[141]

Finally, the female may have defects of insensitiveness, incomprehension or overdominance that reflect unfavourably on the male. Amy, the matriarch of *'The Family Reunion*, casts a blight on the family, and especially on her son Harry. In the early Laforguian poems ("Prufrock'", "Conversation Galante"), the male, searching for a mysterious ideal of femininity, is repelled by the common-place incomprehension and complacency of actual women.

Despite all these hostile, stifling, uncomprehending or resentful women and brutal, insensitive, over-sensitive or condescending men, the picture of sexual relations is not all negative. There is an ideal of sexual bliss, expressed mainly in isolated moments of revelation, such as the incident of the hyacinth girl in *The Waste Land*, the sensual moment experienced by the waiter in "Dans Le Restaurant", or the Beatrice/Mary figure of *Ash Wednesday*. In *The Family Reunion*, Harry rejects his mother Amy, and even his childhood sweetheart Mary, but finds a new mother-figure in Agatha. There is even a picture of a working marriage-relation in *The Cocktail Party*, though this is something of an armed truce. In "East Coker" I, we have the mention of "The association of man and woman/In daunsinge, signifying matrimonie -- /A dignified and commodious sacrament". But this is a later development[142]; in the earlier poetry, the glimpses of sexual bliss serve only to increase the poignancy of sexual disillusionment. Prufrock's vision of the "sea-girls" makes him all the more aware of the inadequacies of society ladies. The conflict between the sexes arises from the clash between the reality and the ideal and can be resolved only by compromise or resignation to disappointment.

---

141 Editor's footnote: See Chapter 1 and Appendix 1(b).

142 Editor's footnote: There is also, in *The Confidential Clerk*, the happy marriage of Mr. and Mrs. Eggerson; and there are also the happy engaged couples Lucasta/B. Kaghan and Monica/Charles in, respectively, *The Confidential Clerk* and *The Elder Statesman*. But by the time of these final plays, Eliot had shifted "from death to life" (see Chapter 1).

The question is whether the sexual conflicts in Eliot really amount to a sex-war. Here we need some definitions. To say that there is a sex-war is to say that there is a basic antagonism between the sexes, a permanent state of hostilities (lasting, at any rate, until the sexual millennium, just as the class-war lasts until the economic millennium). Strindberg, for example, held that such a war exists, and so, in rather different ways, did D. H. Lawrence and George Bernard Shaw, not to mention James Thurber, who (I believe) actually coined the phrase "sex-war".[143] It means that there is a permanent struggle for dominance between the sexes; and it usually means that each sex stands for some principle or orientation towards life that it tries to impose on the other. There may be different *valuations* of the sex-war; one may be pro-male, or pro-female; or one may think that the struggle is terminable and evil, or that it is interminable and good, or that it can be transmuted into a polarity by which its cruelty can become fruitful interchange.

The concept of a sex-war began with the late-Romantic writers, but the concept was deepened in an unexpected way by the work of anthropologists who believed that they had discovered a male/female dominance pattern in pre-history in the form of matriarchal and patriarchal epochs. There was thus, according to this view, a literal sex-war of huge dimensions covering a span of thousands of years. The growth of agriculture had been the key factor in the eventual victory of the male sex,[144] but this victory was insecure and partial. Eliot was aware of early 20th century developments in anthropology, especially as they affected the interpretation of myths, and his mind and work were deeply influenced.[145] There were thus two independent channels through which the concept of the sex-war came

---

143 Editor's footnote: The famous cartoonist James Thurber (1894-1961) drew a sequence of sketches entitled "The War Between Men and Women", included in *The Seal in the Bedroom and Other Predicaments*, New York, 1932. His 1942 short story "The Catbird Seat" was made into a 1959 film called *The Battle of the Sexes*. The Author's appreciation of Thurber was typical of the Author's strong interest in popular culture (an interest shared by Eliot – see my Editor's Memoir of Hyam Maccoby).

144 Editor's footnote: Frazer and Jane Harrison portray early agriculture as centring around worship of the Earth as the dominant Mother Goddess (see Frazer, *Abridged Edition, op. cit.*, Chapters XLV and XLVI, on the Corn-Mother; and Harrison, *Prolegomena, op. cit.*, p. 272: "To the modern mind it is surprising to find the processes of agriculture conducted in the main by women, and mirroring themselves in the figures of women-goddesses.") But George Frankl argues that the onset of organized agriculture marked the beginning of patriarchy: "we would do well to consider that in agriculture it is the seed, man's particular contribution to life, which assumes central significance, becomes the active and causative principle; it is the man who inspires and fecundates the Earth-Mother; he makes her dependent upon him for the realisation of her life-giving potentials" (*The Social History of the Unconscious, op. cit.*, p. 134). This viewpoint is generally accepted nowadays by anthropologists; see, for instance, Yuval Noah Harari, *Sapiens: A Brief History of Humankind*, London, 2014, p. 152: "At least since the Agricultural Revolution, most human societies have been patriarchal societies that valued men more highly than women."

145 Author's footnote: Eliot's reading in anthropology was wide: see Richard Wollheim in Graham Martin (editor), *Eliot in Perspective, op. cit.*, p. 171.
Editor's footnote: see also Chapter 1 above.

to Eliot: the late-Romantics and the anthropologists. I propose to show how these channels flowed together to produce the frame of mind in which Eliot composed his masterwork of the sex-war: *The Family Reunion*.

A key-work of the late-Romantics, in this respect, is Flaubert's *Salammbo*. This work had more influence on Eliot than is perhaps realized (it is doubtful, for example, whether Phlebas would have been a Phoenician without it). *Salammbo* is the real origin of Eliot's "Sweeney Among the Nightingales", for in this novel Flaubert evoked a "heroic" past which was full of seediness and baseness but was redeemed by the violence and bloody conflict of "mighty opposites"[146]. And the basic conflict in *Salammbo,* as in "Sweeney Among the Nightingales", is that between the sexes. Carthage is dominated by two figures, the male god, Moloch, and the goddess, Tanit. They are enemies, and yet consorts. Moloch's human representative, Matho, is loved by Tanit's representative, Salammbo, who nevertheless inflicts on him a cruel death at the climax of the book. The two sexes are polar opposites, and therefore must be enemies; yet they yearn for completion in each other but can achieve it only in violence and blood. The Romantic revolt against the surface tranquillity of liberal, bourgeois society leads to the concept of the sex-war, just as it led to the concepts of the race-war and the class-war. There is excitement in the idea of war; and the clash of opposing forces is a kind of love, since it breaks down the bourgeois atomism and brings back the flow of the universe by the shedding of blood.

It is doubtful whether Flaubert goes beyond the sado-masochistic thrill of the sex-war to the concept of a sexual millennium, in which the sex-war is resolved and brought to peace without sacrifice of polarity and without sinking into bourgeois compromise. The great champion of this concept is D. H. Lawrence. His optimism and humanism are foreign to Eliot, who cannot see the solution to basic human problems as achievable in this world. The resolution of the sex-war for Eliot is in another world; and in this world the "coping" or armed truce achieved by Edward and Lavinia in *The Cocktail Party* is the best that can be hoped for. Meanwhile, he is still a Romantic in refusing to accept the assumptions of bourgeois domesticity and in seeing the sexes as fundamentally at war. In this world, as Heraclitus had said, "War is the father of all and king of all"[147]; and it is only from the point of view of eternity that the "fire" of sex is seen to be identical with the "rose".

The research work of the anthropologists enabled Eliot to see that the sex-war was an integral part of the meaning of religion. The development of ancient religion, as revealed in myths and rituals, was a struggle between the old goddesses and the new gods, between

---

146 Editor's footnote: *Hamlet*, Act 5, Scene 2, l. 62.
147 Editor's footnote: fr. 44 (Author's translation), Ingram Bywater, *Heracliti Ephesii Reliquiae by Heraclitus, of Ephesus*, Oxford, 1877 (henceforth, "Bywater"). See Chapter 6, discussion of the lyrical passage that opens "Burnt Norton" II.

female and male. Frazer and others had used their knowledge to discredit Christianity by revealing its affinities with paganism, but with Eliot the argument worked the other way; the affinities with paganism validated Christianity as an organic growth. The question was: at what particular stage of the sex-struggle had Christianity emerged? Was it the religion of the Male or of the Female, or, if of both, by what kind of synthesis or orientation?

Here we must turn to Eliot's *The Family Reunion* -- a work that has not received the appreciation it deserves.[148] The protagonist Harry is the man from "Sweeney Agonistes" who has "done a girl in"; the play is the elaboration in dramatic terms of the state of mind of the ultimate sex-warrior, the wife-murderer (who, for good measure, also brings about the death of his mother). And this theme is explored with the depth afforded by connections with the *Oresteia* of Aeschylus and with the underlying Greek myth of the terrifying Erinyes, or female Furies, who stand guard over the female principle and avenge the encroachments of the male.

Unfortunately, the importance of the link with the *Oresteia* has been played down even by Eliot's most perceptive critics. Grover Smith says: "Eliot's debt to the *Oresteia* of Aeschylus is less even than most critics have conceded."[149] This judgment is understandable, because Harry's crime (or fancied crime) is not matricide, as in the case of Orestes, but wife-murder; and though Harry does, at the end of the play, in a sense kill his mother, he does so casually, almost absent-mindedly, after the agonies and tribulations of the play have been resolved. Helen Gardner even seems to think this mother-killing to be an attempt to work up some interest in the last act; it cannot, she says, be regarded as central in the play.[150] That the very casualness of the matricide, the off-handedness of the evocation of the *Oresteia*, might have some intentional artistic point seems to have escaped critical enquiry; as has the fact that the ending of the play (far from being an afterthought) has been carefully prepared in the very first speech of the first scene, when Amy says, "And clocks could be trusted, tomorrow assured/ And time would not stop in the dark!"[151]

Harry's conflict with his mother is undoubtedly central in the play, and like Orestes, Harry has a murdered father to avenge. His mother has not indeed physically killed his father; but she has killed his influence on Harry and the rest of the family; she has deprived

---

148 Editor's footnote: See, however, Moody, *Thomas Stearns Eliot Poet, op. cit.*, p. 172: "*The Family Reunion* is far and away the most interesting of Eliot's plays, and this has much to do with its being a true development of his poetry." But Moody's book came out in 1979, i.e. after the writing of this essay. Nowadays, like Eliot's poetry and plays in general, *The Family Reunion* is unfairly neglected.,

149 Author's footnote: *T. S. Eliot's Poetry and Plays op. cit.*, p. 201.

Editor's footnote: See again, however, Moody, *Thomas Stearns Eliot Poet, op. cit.*, p. 180: "The obvious relation with the *Oresteia* is of great importance." Again, Moody's book came out in 1979, after the writing of this essay.

150 Author's footnote: *The Art of T. S. Eliot, op. cit.*, p. 155.

151 Editor's footnote: *op. cit.*, p. 11. See also p. 15: "I do not want the clock to stop in the dark."

Harry of a father, for whom he is searching (this theme of the search for the lost father is continued in Eliot's later plays[152]). Harry's remorse is for the killing (or imagined killing) of his wife; but the woman who looms in his mind throughout is his mother, and his attempts to rid himself of her are the subject of the play. He married an unsuitable wife in a vain attempt to escape from his mother; and his hatred of his wife is fed from the store of misogyny built up in him by his strained relation with his mother, so that the guilt – imagined or not – of his wife-murder is assuaged only by the resolution of the basic mother-relationship – a resolution that can then be followed by a guilt-free elimination of the mother herself. (A very similar psychological progression can be seen in *Hamlet*, where the hero's agonized hate-love relationship with his mother, by which he barely avoids murdering her, is resolved, only to be followed by his elimination of her by accident.)

Harry is not only Orestes; he is also Aegisthus, Clytemnestra's lover. Harry's hatred of the world and sense of disgust arise from the fact that his mother, as he feels, has rejected his father in order to monopolise *him.* Harry must kill not only his mother, but also the lover of his mother, that is, himself. He must break his attachment to his mother so that he can grow up and follow his father. This theme involves the task of the Hero, and the quest of religion, and it reflects anthropological insights about the development of society, through unimaginable torments and bloody struggles, from the mother-centred community to the father-centred community. Like Jesus to his mother, Harry is saying to Amy, "Wist ye not that I must be about my Father's business?"[153] The *Oresteia*[154] itself has this anthropological dimension; for the Eumenides or Erinyes who pursued Orestes were originally the triple form of the archaic Aegean Goddess; and the *Oresteia* tells how they were tamed into submission to the patriarchal Olympian gods.[155]

---

152 Editor's footnote: See, in particular, *The Confidential Clerk.*
153 Editor's footnote: Luke 2: 49.
154 Editor's footnote: dated to 458 BCE; see Gilbert Murray, *Aeschylus, op. cit.,* p. 11.
155 Editor's footnote: I think this requires a lot of correction, qualification and clarification. Jane Harrison comments, in relation to the *Eumenides,* on "the real *agon* [conflict]of the play, the conflict between the new order and the old, the daimones of Earth, the Erinyes, and the *theoi* [gods] of Olympus, Apollo and his father Zeus, and further necessarily and inherently the conflict of the two social orders of which these daimones and *theoi* are in part the projections – matriarchy or, as it is better called, the matrilinear system and patriarchy". (*Themis: A Study of the Social Origins of Greek Religion,* 1912, revised 1927: London, 1963, pp. 385-386.) But Harrison makes a very clear distinction between the Erinyes and the Eumenides. In her earlier book *Prolegomena to the Study of Greek Religion, op. cit.,* pp. 217-256, she points out that, at the end of the play, Aeschylus (who contributed to the shaping of the myth) transforms the Erinyes, "The Angry Ones", or Furies -- whom she describes as hideous, animal-like (often snake-like) figures, originally of indeterminate number and deriving from a primitive, cruel period of Greek matriarchy, before the emergence of anthropomorphic goddesses and hero-daimons -- into the benign, dignified local Underworld Triple-Goddesses of Athens, the *Semnae Theai,* "The Venerable Goddesses". (Harrison explains that the Semnae are called Eumenides --"The Kindly Ones" -- in the play's title – the word "Eumenides" only appears in the title, not in the play's text, where Orestes' pursuers are only called the Erinyes -- because the Eumenides, who were identical to the Semnae, were Underworld Triple-Goddesses who were worshipped at

A full consideration of *The Family Reunion* would take us too far afield; it would have to start with Grover Smith's remark that "by the quasi-redemptive sacrifice of Harry as the family's Isaac, will occur the true birthday and the true family reunion".[156] I shall content myself here with some further consideration of the character of Harry's mother Amy, whom Eliot regarded as the most successful character in the play.

Amy is a complex character - so much so that Eliot could say that "we are left in a divided frame of mind, not knowing whether to consider the play the tragedy of the mother or the salvation of the son".[157] She is not just a conventional, organizing mother. She is especially associated, true, with the regular revolutions of time -- with the "clock" -- but she is associated also with the seasons, which are also a kind of clock. Regularity can be a sign of artificiality and tameness, but it can also be a sign of oneness with the regular rhythms of nature; this ambiguity is part of Amy's character, and an essential element in femininity. (Woman has her regular cycles of menstruation and pregnancy; she is thus magical and mysterious, pulsing with the phases of the moon and the tides, but she is also conservative and time-bound -- see the ambiguous moon-imagery throughout the play.)

Argos, where the *Oresteia* trilogy takes place -- see *ibid.*, p. 255.) Aeschylus's Semnae/Eumenides accept at the end of the play the new patriarchal order and the acquittal of Orestes, in return for being honoured: "The Erinyes, in the play of Aeschylus, are transformed into Semnae, into the local goddesses of Athens.... Athenian though he is, it is not the glorification of a local cult that inspires Aeschylus; it is the reconciliation of the old order of vengeance with the new law of mercy." (*Ibid.*, p. 252.) The Author is clearly correct to say that the Semnae/Eumenides "were originally the triple form of the archaic Aegean Goddess". But Jane Harrison warns against identifying the Semnae/Eumenides with the Erinyes: see *ibid.*, pp. 241-242: "After the time of Aeschylus, classical writers ... begin to accept the fusion and use the names Erinyes, Eumenides and Semnae as interchangeable terms. A like laxity unhappily obtains among modern commentators." Moreover, Harrison points out Aeschylus's emphasis on "reconciliation", rather than "submission" (the Author's word) of the old matriarchal order to the new patriarchal dispensation. In my view, the reason that the Author fuses the Erinyes with the Semnae/Eumenides is his own deep adherence to Judaism -- an even more patriarchal system than that of the classical, Olympian-worshipping Greeks and one that discarded goddesses altogether; as a result, the Author tends towards over-emphasis of the fearsome side of the "archaic Aegean Goddess", who seems to have had many beneficent aspects. See Jane Harrison, *ibid.*, p. 256, where she writes that the Eumenides and the Semnae "are gentle, staid, matronly figures, bearing in their left hands, for tokens of fertility, flowers and fruit, and in their right, snakes as the symbols not of terror and torture, but merely of that source of wealth, the underworld". It may be argued that the goddesses had been "tamed", but they surely reflect genuine positive qualities of the "archaic Aegean Goddess". See the whole of Harrison's Chapter VI in the *Prolegomena*, "The Making of a Goddess". Summing up the message of the *Oresteia*, George Frankl makes it clear that the Erinyes came to represent not the Goddess herself, but the anger of the Goddess against the transgressor of her laws: "the good and benevolent mother goddess can turn into a ruthless Fury if the law of the blood is offended against. The benign and kindly Demeter turns into the Furies, the Erinyes, personifying the rage of the mother against the transgressor of her laws.... In the 'Oresteia', Aeschylus shows how the rule of revenge becomes a ruthless and inescapable fate that haunts society, and he sets out to show a way by which the ancient concept of justice and its chain of violence can be replaced by a higher code of law and morality, governed by reason and persuasion, by intellect rather than the blind forces of instinct."(*The Social History of the Unconscious, op. cit.*, pp. 30-31.)

156 Author's footnote: Grover Smith, *T. S. Eliot's Poetry and Plays op. cit.*, p. 211.
157 Author's footnote: T. S. Eliot, *Poetry and Drama*, London, 1951, p. 31.

When Ivy tries to persuade Amy to "go south in the winter", Amy does not even reply, and Charles says: "That's not Amy's style at all."[158] This little exchange is an echo of *The Waste Land* I: "I read, much of the night, and go south in the winter", where the speaker, Marie, a rootless cosmopolitan like Harry's wife, shows that she is out of touch with the rhythms of day and night and of summer and winter.

In his essay on Kipling, Eliot, referring to Kipling's short stories "A Habitation Enforced" and "My Son's Wife", comments:

> What is most important in these stories, and in *The Wish House* and in *Friendly Brook*, is Kipling's vision of the people of the soil. It is not a Christian vision, but it is at least a pagan vision -- a contradiction of the materialistic view: it is the insight into a harmony with nature which must be re-established if the truly Christian imagination is to be recovered by Christians.[159]

It is a useful simplification to regard Amy in *The Family Reunion* as representing the pagan vision, while Harry and Agatha represent the Christian vision. The two visions are portrayed in conflict with each other; and Amy is thus given a less sympathetic treatment than she might otherwise have received. For a sympathetic expression of the pagan vision, we may turn to "East Coker" I:

> Earth feet, loam feet, lifted in country mirth,
> Mirth of those long since under earth
> Nourishing the corn. Keeping time,
> Keeping the rhythm in their dancing
> As in their living in the living seasons
> The time of the seasons and the constellations
> The time of milking and the time of harvest
> The time of the coupling of man and woman
> And that of beasts. Feet rising and falling.
> Eating and drinking. Dung and death.

This pagan vision is one of regularity and rhythm; it is a vision that sees man as one of the animals. The Christian visionary, as conceived by Eliot, must at some point reject with

---

158 Editor's footnote: *op. cit.*, p.12.
159 Editor's footnote: *A Choice of Kipling's Verse, op. cit.*, p. 33.

disgust and loathing the elements of the pagan vision, in order to rise to a transcendent view that can then embrace and include the pagan vision. The peaceful image of "feet rising and falling" in "East Coker" I has its analogue in Agatha's vision of horrified boredom:

> Only feet walking
> And sharp heels scraping. Over and under
> Echo and noise of feet.
> I was only the feet, and the eye
> Seeing the feet: the unwinking eye
> Fixing the movement. Over and under.[160]

"Dung and death" is a formulation that has its place in *The Family Reunion* too, but not as a summary of the rural cycle of growth by which even death is a form of manuring the ground for further growth, but in Harry's scatological vision of reality as an underground sewer.[161] The Christian vision includes the pagan vision, but only by sharply rejecting it, in order to regain it at a higher level. The pagan vision is calm and measured; it overcomes death by locating life and immortality in the community. The Christian vision is agonized; it rejects the world and the community and all their rhythms and regularities, not in order to overcome death but to face it in lone terror. And it is Woman, in particular, who is the guardian of the pagan vision. Kipling, in one of the stories that so impressed Eliot ("An Habitation Enforced"), instinctively makes the "deity" of his country community a woman, the matriarchal Lady Conant. ("'Who is she?' 'God -- A local deity, then.'")[162]

There is much in common between Amy and Mary, who, at the beginning of the second scene, also shows a sympathy with the rhythms of nature:

> I had rather wait for our windblown blossoms
> Such as they are, than have these greenhouse flowers
> Which do not belong here, which do not know
> The wind and rain, as I know them.[163]

---

160 Editor's footnote: *op. cit.*, p. 100. See Chapter 1, pp. 53-55. The Christian regains the earlier pagan "primitive terror".

161 Editor's footnote: See: "The noxious smell untraceable in the drains/Inaccessible to the plumbers," *ibid.*, p. 27. See also next footnote and Appendix 4.

162 Author's footnote: For further connections between *The Family Reunion* and Kipling, see my "The Family Reunion and Kipling's The House Surgeon", *Notes and Queries*, Feb. 1968.

Editor's footnote: See Appendix 4, where this essay is reproduced. For the quotation from "An Habitation Enforced", see Rudyard Kipling, *Actions and Reactions*, London, 1909, p. 23.

163 Editor's footnote: *op. cit.*, p. 45.

It is not just domestic tyranny that makes Amy design a marriage between Harry and Mary; she recognizes Mary as the kind of wife she wants for her son. Here she makes a mistake, the same mistake she made in her own marriage; but Amy's development into a domestic tyrant is hardly her own fault; it is her tragedy, the warped development of a thoroughly womanly woman married to a man who does not fit into Woman's view of the universe; yet Amy is still trying vainly to fit her son into the same pattern. Mary is more intelligent than Amy; Mary is able to give fuller verbal expression to the feminine pagan vision in her dialogue with Harry: "I believe that the season of birth/Is the season of sacrifice/For the tree and the beast,/and the fish/ Thrashing itself upstream."[164] But she is also intelligent enough to realize that Harry is a special soul who cannot be made to serve Woman's biological purposes; and she gives him up.[165] He is one who stands outside the recurrent cycle of birth and death represented by the fish thrashing blindly towards the female, like a spermatozoon towards the ovum; the cycle represented in religion by the Young God myths of Attis and Adonis. He is the servant not of the Goddess, but of God.[166] He is to be a sacrificial victim, but not of the pagan type.

The first crude impression one gets from the play (and this is, even in the final analysis, the most reliable clue to the play's meaning) is one of strong fear and hatred of women. The hero has murdered, or at least wanted to murder, his wife; and it turns out that his father too has wanted to murder his wife. The hero is haunted by women in a repulsive supernatural form. The most powerfully presented character in the play is the formidable Amy, from whose influence the hero is struggling to free himself. As has been shown by Grover Smith[167], the Eumenides are projections of the hero's mother, and reflect his feelings towards her. The sympathetic female figures Mary and Agatha are denied and unattainable to the hero and his father respectively, who are condemned to marry women they hate.

---

164 Editor's footnote: *Ibid.*, p. 56.

165 Editor's footnote: This statement should, I think, be qualified a little. Before she sees the Eumenides, Mary believes them to be a figment of Harry's imagination and imagines she can fight them; after she sees them, she accepts defeat and gives Harry up, but she still thinks he is in terrible danger from them and should stay at Wishwood and not follow them. Agatha has to reassure her that they are not demons but divine guides (*ibid.*, p. 112). See Appendix 3, footnote 462.

166 Editor's footnote: In their early stages, Adonis and Attis represented the cycle of birth and death (see Maccoby, *Revolution in Judaea*, op. cit., p. 87: "In their original form [the mystery-religions] were cults of human sacrifice"). Even in their later mystery-religion forms, Adonis and Attis were still sacrificed to the Goddess. See also above in this chapter, footnote 137 on Maccoby's argument about the contrast between the mystery-religions and Christianity.

167 Author's footnote: *T. S. Eliot's Poetry and Plays*, op. cit., p. 206.

Editor's footnote: Smith writes here: "Harry's inner restraint, the power of his mother, having haunted him through the miseries preventing tranquillity in his marriage, is reinforced by its alliance with the now tripled and externalized *imago* of that same power." (Emphasis in original.) Smith also argues (*ibid.*) that the Eumenides later, in their benevolent form, become "a projection of Agatha rather than of Amy".

Even Mary is tangentially identified with the Eumenides, when Harry hurls the same accusation of stupidity against her and against them.[168] Harry, in setting himself against the female principle, has unleashed a primitive force of fury. Woman, by her sympathy with the rhythms of the universe, is the protector of man, but, when he sets himself against her, he sets himself against the universe itself and faces chaos.

Yet the goal of all yearning, represented by Agatha and the image of the rose-garden, is also Woman. The woman whom Harry loves is the woman whom his father loved too, but, like his father, he must separate from her. She is reserved for another world, where she will appear as the eternal Rose, the Queen of Heaven. Even the Eumenides at the climax of the play lose their aspect of horror and become "bright angels"[169].

C. L. Barber[170] charged *The Family Reunion* with emotional immaturity and amorality because the view of sexuality expressed in it is one of despair, or at best Puritan resignation, as far as this world is concerned. The gravamen of these charges applies not so much to Eliot as to Christianity itself. In the last analysis, I am sympathetic to this kind of attack on Christianity; but the last analysis is rather a long way off. Meanwhile, the cry of horror that is Eliot's deepest reaction to sex is preferable to a bourgeois "maturity" based on repression - the kind of maturity shown by the uncles and aunts of the play.[171]

Eliot sees Woman as at once the trap of respectability or pagan monotony, the furious vortex of chaos, and the goal of all yearning. Christianity, then, to Eliot, is the religion in which man frees himself from the leading strings of Nature, but at the cost of alienation from the world and from Woman; Christianity, to Eliot, is an adventure that turns the world into a Waste Land but preserves the sensual vision of childhood from developing into "mature" compromise and complacency. By estranging man from woman, Christianity, to Eliot, preserves the vision of the Queen of Heaven. The theme of sexual conflict in Eliot is a strange and compelling fusion of late Romantic sado-masochistic literary attitudes and the traditional Romanticism of Christianity and the mystery-religions.

---

168 Editor's footnote: *op. cit.*, p. 58

169 Editor's footnote: *op. cit.*, p. 107.

170 Author's footnote: C. L. Barber, in Unger (ed.), *op. cit.*

  Editor's footnote: C. L. Barber writes here, *ibid.*, pp. 416-426: "To assert 'the necessity' of Christianity, the dramatist presents his hero in the grip of the irrational dread and horror of life which naturalistic thought regards as characteristic of neurotic maladjustment ... the writer has failed to keep an objective attitude towards his hero. Instead he slips over into identifying himself with Harry's point of view, affirming Harry's values instead of dramatizing Harry's state of mind."

171 Author's footnote: "[Baudelaire] was at least able to understand that the sexual act as evil is more dignified, less boring, than as the natural, 'life-giving', cheery automatism of the modern world". (Originally from Eliot's Introduction to Baudelaire's *Intimate Journals*, 1930; T. S. Eliot, *Selected Prose, op. cit.*, p. 194.)

ADDENDUM NOTE TO CHAPTER 2

We may now ask: is there a connection between Eliot's deep awareness of sexual conflict and his antisemitism? In general, Eliot sees the Jews as a force of disintegration in modern life. (Like many Christians throughout the ages, he is prepared to make an exception of the strictly Orthodox Jew, who is regarded as a kind of fossilized Old Testament Jew, waiting for the Second Coming of Christ, when the Orthodox Jew will awake from his long sleep and join Christendom.)[172] The Jews, for Eliot, are, indeed, representative of modernism itself, with its anti-heroic, trivializing stance, and its acceptance of "boredom" as life itself; they themselves, consequently, are not bored, but adapt with bright-eyed enthusiasm (like the "rats" in "Burbank") to conditions of degeneration and seediness. Thus, in the focal poem "Sweeney Among the Nightingales", the "boredom" stage of the poem (as opposed to the later stages of "horror" and "glory") is especially identified with Jews. The dreary, modern, trivial version of the sex-war is enacted, on both sides, by Jews: by Rachel (*neé* Rabinovitch), a Jewish prostitute, who is plotting in some way against the "man in mocha brown", whose Jewishness is shown by his "heavy eyes", his "golden grin" (i.e. gold teeth) -- characteristics he shares with Bleistein – and, by "leaning in" through the window, a feature he shares with the "jew" of "Gerontion".

The Jewish prostitute is a figure of some importance in French pornography. She is the last degenerate representative in literature of the "beautiful Jewess" story of the medieval *exempla*. Eliot's Rachel is not only a symbol of Jewish degeneration, but also contains a hint of the frightening quality of female sexuality in the original myth of which she is the pitiable remnant. She "tears at the grapes with murderous paws", and so recalls the murderous Jewess of the medieval ballad of St. Hugh. She has about her just one hint of the "horror" that lies behind the fascination of the legend of the Jew's Beautiful Daughter.[173] Yet, in her

---

172 Editor's footnote: See the notorious passage in *After Strange Gods* on the need to impose a quota on "free-thinking Jews" (see footnote 181 in next chapter).

173 Editor's footnote: See Hyam Maccoby, "The Delectable Daughter", *Midstream*, September 1970. Republished in edited form in the posthumously published book *Antisemitism and Modernity: Innovation and Continuity, op. cit.* This essay addresses the recurrent legend of the mean old Jew who has a beautiful, good-hearted daughter who falls in love with a Christian -- for instance, Shylock and Jessica, or Isaac of York and Rebecca in Scott's *Ivanhoe*. The Author points out, in "The Delectable Daughter", that, in some medieval variations of the legend (for instance, the ballad of St Hugh), there is "a malevolent Jew's Daughter" (*ibid.*, p. 88). In the same essay, the Author writes that the legend (which he links to similar Greek legends, such as the legend of Jason and Medea, and even the Biblical legend of Jacob, Rachel and Laban) is characteristic of "the kind of society which may be named uneasy Patriarchalism, a society in which fear of the Father is too great to allow the Son to grow up and become a responsible adult, taking his father's place, and in which, consequently, the tendency of religion is to set up a secret matriarchy within the patriarchal system as a form of shelter against responsibility. Another name for this

sordidness, she presents a polar contrast to the females of the later part of the poem: to the destroying Furies, to the avenging Clytemnestra, and finally to the nuns of the Convent of the Sacred Heart, representatives of the Christian solution to the problem of intra-sexual violence: the solution of chastity and virginity, so much at odds with the Jewish acceptance of sex as part of ordinary living, rather than as a painful and insoluble mystery pointing to another world.

The "dirtiness" of the Jews, in opposing the bright radiance of the Virgin Mary in the medieval ballads,[174] has its echo in the colour of the clothing of the Jew in the "sordid" part of the poem. His excremental clothing echoes the constant medieval connection of Jews with excrement.

At the same time, the Jews' acceptance of sex makes them sexually abhorrent and frightening. They do not beget, but "spawn", as in "Gerontion", and they are likened to swarming creatures like rats (see also their characterization as "'polyphiloprogenitive'" in "Mr. Eliot's Sunday Morning Service").[175] Relevant here is the Nazis' fear of Jewish sexuality and their fear of contamination of the Aryan stock and of the "corruption" of German womanhood (the real fear here is of the sexual awakening of German women, schooled to docility of domesticity and childbearing). This is a feature shared by antisemitism and hatred of black people; the animal sexual power projected on to the hated race is a displacement of the frustrated sexual yearnings of the haters, and a fear that the system of defences may be breached. But it is transfigured into a loathing of what is considered to be an insult to womanhood and to the nobility of true sexual relations.[176] There are thus

---

secret attachment to matriarchy, in a patriarchal context, is Romanticism: the conspiracy of the Mother with the Son against the Father, the sweet, secret and doomed rebellion of the Son." (*Ibid.*)

174 Editor's footnote: One of the essays in the Author's unfinished book *Flowering Judas* (see my Preface) is on Chaucer's "The Prioress's Tale", a poem in which the Jews are seen in terms of excrement and are very much portrayed as the enemies of the Virgin Mary. This essay is unpublished, but the Author (summing up his unpublished essay) discusses "The Prioress's Tale" in his book *The Sacred Executioner: Human Sacrifice and the Legacy of Guilt, op. cit.*, pp. 156-162.

175 Editor's footnote: See Chapter 5 below.

176 Editor's footnote: It is interesting, however, to consider in this context Eliot's scatological and pornographic "blue" verses, which project his fantasies (the fantasies of a sexually repressed man who clearly had deep doubts about his own masculinity) on to Black people, Jews, and women. Thus Eliot celebrates the black King Bolo's bodyguard, who each had "a pair of great big hairy balls/And a big black knotty penis" and were "an innocent and playful lot/But most disgusting dirty./King Bolo lay down in the shade/His royal breast uncovering/They mounted in a banyan tree/And shat upon their sovereign." (*The Inventions of the March Hare, op. cit.*, p. 316; for more of Eliot's "blue" verses, see the 2015 *Poems, Vol. II, op. cit.*) In these verses, forbidden impulses are temporarily liberated but are regarded as "dirty" and "disgusting" and celebrated in their very dirtiness and disgustingness. In contrast to his portrayal of Black people in terms of the temporarily liberated Freudian Id, Eliot, in a 1921 letter to Ezra Pound, portrays Jews, in one aspect, as bourgeois, repressive, life-denying representatives of the Freudian Superego: "Bolo's big black bastard queen/Was *so* obscene/She shocked the folk of Golder's Green." (*Inventions of the March Hare, op. cit.*, p. 320; emphasis in original.) However, Eliot also has a verse about a Jewish doctor, a

multiple connections, as one might expect, between Eliot's conception of sexual polarity and conflict and his antisemitic imagery.[177]

"bastard jew called Benny", who fills the "prick" of "Columbo" (Christopher Columbus) with "Muriatic Acid" -- the "jew" as a Devil-like Father-figure who both inflates Columbo's "prick" (thus being responsible for his forbidden sexual impulses) and castrates and kills him; he dies, but is resurrected by Queen Isabella of Spain, "That famous Spanish whore" (*ibid.*, p. 315). See Bryan Cheyette, "Eliot and 'Race': Jews, Irish and Blacks", in *A Companion to T. S. Eliot, op. cit.*, p. 346: "Once again the 'jew' is foundational ('underneath the lot')." David Chinitz points out that the "Benny" verse is (like several other examples of Eliot's "blue" verses) taken almost word for word from a folk ballad: "The Benny stanza has been cited as further evidence of the poet's anti-Semitism, and I do not wish to imply that Eliot's debt to an earlier source exonerates him of such charges. But there is some relief, perhaps, in the discovery that this instance of vulgar Jew-baiting originated in the imagination of another." ("T. S. Eliot's Blue Verses and their Sources in the Folk Tradition", *Journal of Modern Literature*, 23.2, Winter 1999-2000.) But Eliot's debt to a racist, antisemitic, and sexist folk tradition only shows that he taps into a general social phenomenon that is the result of society's repressive attitudes. Nonetheless, the "blue" verses express the primitive energy of repressed and forbidden impulses, and are the result of Eliot's fascination with popular culture and exploration of verse at *all* levels, even the "foul rag and bone shop of the heart" that is the raw material of his serious, "proper" poetry: "Now that my ladder's gone/I must lie down where all the ladders start/In the foul rag and bone shop of the heart." (Yeats: "The Circus Animals' Desertion".) Eliot's widow, Valerie Eliot, clearly trying to save her husband's reputation, wrote of the "blue" verses (in a letter published in the *TLS*, Feb. 17, 1984): "Almost all were written during his Harvard days and none later than 1916." But the editors of the 2015 *Poems* point out that, when Eliot was asked in a 1959 interview "Do you write anything now in the vein of *Old Possum's Book of Practical Cats* or *King Bolo*?", he replied "Oh yes, one wants to keep one's hand in, you know, in every type of poem, serious and frivolous and proper and improper. One doesn't want to lose one's skill." (2015 *Poems, Vol. II, op. cit.*, p. 249.) It is clear from this interview and from Eliot's letters (see *ibid.*, pp. 250-269) that the "blue" verses continued throughout his poetic career. It may seem surprising or shocking that Eliot could write them at the same time as he composed the complex, sublimated beauty of, for instance, *Ash Wednesday;* but Bolo's "big black Queen", who "was extremely lecherous" (*ibid.*, p. 279) is only the other side of the coin of the pure, Beatrice and Virgin Mary-like "Lady" of *Ash Wednesday*; the two must necessarily coexist. The "big black Queen" in her own way represents a Romantic "secret attachment to matriarchy, in a patriarchal context" (see footnote 173 in this chapter); she embodies the primitive "fire" at its most primitive. It is only in Heaven that "the fire and the rose are one" (the last line of the *Quartets*); as the Author writes earlier in this chapter (p. 72): "it is only from the point of view of eternity that the 'fire' of sex is seen to be identical with the 'rose'". So the "blue" verses, crude though they are—indeed, in their very crudity -- are an integral part of the Romantic "Christ the tiger" dimension of Eliot's poetry.

177 Editor's footnote: Antisemitic imagery that will be explored in the next chapter.

Another aspect of Eliot's view of women is that of treachery and deception, which connects his perception of women with his antisemitism – see the lines in "Gerontion" in which History is personified as a woman who "deceives with whispering ambitions/Guides us by vanities" (this seems to be linked to the "jew" in the first stanza). Eliot also sees women, in one aspect, as associated, like Jews, with the Devil, witches dabbling -- even though in a charlatan-like way, which is part of their seediness and sordidness -- in the occult and satanic; this is apparent in the characters of Mesdames Sosostris, Blavatsky and de Tornquist (see my Appendix 8). And both Jews and charlatan witches are seen as degenerate remnants of once noble ancient traditions.

Chapter 3: ELIOT AND ANTISEMITISM[178]

Eliot's antisemitism has been a source of much embarrassment. Hard-core devotees continue to deny that he was antisemitic at all.[179] Others admit, and even exaggerate, his antisemitism, but regard it as of no significance, a mere pathological aberration of an otherwise great writer. The *Times* obituarist of Ezra Pound, for example, referred to Eliot's "almost insane physical nausea" about Jews, contrasting this unfavourably with Pound's "anti-Jewishness", which was "simplistic and ideological".[180] A close study of Eliot's antisemitism, however, shows that it was even more ideological than Pound's, being derived from the cultural and religious tradition of Christendom, as mediated, in particular, by Henry Adams and Charles Maurras. We shall see, moreover, that antisemitism is a natural concomitant of the sacrificial view of life that was Eliot's inspiration from the time of his earliest writings.

The volume of Eliot's antisemitic writing is very small, compared with Pound's outpourings; and the theme disappears in Eliot's work altogether after the early 1930s, when Eliot, no doubt, became dismayed by the direction antisemitism was taking in Germany. Nevertheless, it is impossible to ignore this thread in Eliot's writing, both because of the virulence and emotional intensity of the antisemitic passages embedded at the core of some of Eliot's best work, and because of the seriousness with which he himself regarded the matter (as is shown by his proposal in *After Strange Gods* to impose a quota on Jewish residents of the United States).[181]

---

178 Editor's footnote: Originally published as "The Antisemitism of T. S. Eliot" in *Midstream*, Volume 19, Number 5, May 1973. Republished in edited form in Hyam Maccoby's posthumously published work *Antisemitism and Modernity: Innovation and Continuity, op. cit.* Hyam Maccoby edited the article for a series of lectures he delivered in 1998. I have reproduced the original 1973 *Midstream* text. Reprinted by kind permission of Mr Herbert Block, Executive Director of the American Zionist Movement. See Acknowledgements.

179 Editor's footnote: This continues even in recent times. See Chapter 4, p. 100, footnote 217.

180 Author's footnote: The *Times*, November 2, 1972.

181 Author's footnote: T. S. Eliot, *After Strange Gods, op. cit.*, pp. 19-20.

Editor's footnote: The crucial quotation is: "the population should be homogeneous; where two or more cultures exist in the same place they are likely either to be fiercely self-conscious or both to become adulterate. What is still more important is unity of religious background; and reasons of race and religion combine to make any large number of free-thinking Jews undesirable." For attempts (unconvincing, in my view) to exculpate this passage from the charge of antisemitism, see, for example: Craig Raine, *T. S. Eliot*, Oxford 2006, pp. 157-160; Jewel Spears Brooker, in *T. S. Eliot and Our Turning World*, edited by Jewel Spears Brooker, New York, 2001, pp.162-163; and David M. Thompson, *ibid.*, pp. 172-3.

Moreover, Eliot never disowned the passages in question, and continued to allow their re-publication, with very minor alterations of punctuation (e. g. "Jew" for "jew") that rendered them slightly less offensive. The exception was *After Strange Gods*, which he did not allow to be re-published; and, though it seems probable that this was because of the antisemitic passage, he never offered this as the reason.[182] He is reported to have told a friend: "'I am not an antisemite and never have been…. It is a terrible slander on a man.'"[183]

---

182 Editor's footnote: In 1952, Eliot wrote to Isaiah Berlin, who had challenged him about this passage: "the sentence of which you complain (with justice) would never have appeared at all at that time, if I had been aware of what was going to happen, indeed had begun to happen, in Germany". He also wrote that he could "not understand why the word 'race' occurs in the sentence, because my emphasis was on the adjective 'free-thinking'". (Quoted in Crawford, *op. cit.*, pp. 206-207.) But on April 28, 1964, Eliot wrote to Patricia Gruber of *Fact Magazine*, New York: "I did make the statement which you quote, but I have ever since regretted making it in that form, for it was not intended to be anti-semitic. What I had in mind was that I hoped there would be more co-operation between practising Christians and practising Jews, but I agree that the statement as it stands is regrettable." (*The Letters of T. S. Eliot, Volume 9: 1939-1941*, edited by Valerie Eliot and John Haffenden, London, 2021, p. 518, footnote 1.) Eliot's replies to correspondents about his work were often inconsistent. The response to Isaiah Berlin is the only quotation from Eliot that I have found in which he admits the "justice" of the accusation that this passage is antisemitic. But even here he does not make it clear whether this was the reason that he refused to allow the book to be republished, nor does he do so in his reply to Patricia Gruber. See discussion on this question (of whether this was the reason) in Julius, *op. cit.*, pp. 193-194. Julius concludes convincingly that Eliot never made the issue clear.

183 Author's footnote: William Turner Levy and Victor Scherle, *Affectionately, T. S. Eliot*, London, 1969, p. 81.

Editor's footnote: Despite Eliot's denials and the efforts of his apologists, the most recently published material supports the claim that he was an antisemite. See Eliot's letter of 12 September 1941 to J. H. Oldham, published in *The Letters of T. S. Eliot, Volume 9, op. cit.*, pp. 914-915. In this letter, Eliot criticizes an article by the Rev. Dr. James Parkes (who was one of the pioneers of Christian acknowledgement that centuries of Christian antisemitism had laid the ground for the Holocaust). Parkes's essay, which argued that "the Jewish problem" did not exist, eventually appeared in The *Christian News-Letter* (Eliot was on its Advisory Committee), but Eliot objected to its inclusion (see Crawford, *op. cit.*, pp. 352-353). Eliot's remarks in his letter to Oldham on 12 September 1941 bear out many of the Author's comments on Eliot's antisemitism: "Dr Parkes does not strike me as succeeding either in explaining the problem or in offering a way out. He merely explains it away, which is quite a different thing: it may please some of those who have no taint of antisemitism in them, but will not alter the feelings of those who have." Here Eliot seems almost to admit that he has in himself a "taint of antisemitism". He goes on (and in the process explains why he advocated a quota on "free-thinking Jews"; see my two previous footnotes) to complain that Parkes "does not discuss the religious problem proper. This, in my view, is not the problem of those Jews who maintain their religion – the problem of the true Jews – but that of the half-Europeanised Jews who have lost their faith without adopting any other. Some of this class are, of course, among our finest citizens; but it [is] surely from among this class also that come the irresponsible Jews – capitalist or revolutionary as the circumstances dictate. This is primarily a religious, not a racial problem." (*Letters, Vol. 9, op. cit.*, p. 914; square brackets in original.) He sees Jews as "half-Europeanised" – i.e., outside European culture – and holds "free-thinking" Jews responsible for both Capitalism and Communism. (He also makes it clear that his antisemitism is religious, not racial; a point stressed by the Author.) Eliot ends this letter with a most egregious paragraph, which appears to involve a travesty of Parkes's comment "No man knows what Jewish casualties as a result of the Nazi occupation of Europe may have risen to be before the domination is destroyed." (Crawford, *op. cit.*, p. 353.) Eliot's concluding paragraph is: "To suggest that the Jewish problem may be simplified because so many will have been killed off is trifling; a few generations of security and they will be as numerous as ever." (*Letters, Vol. 9, op. cit.*, p. 915.) It is impossible, in my view, to see how anyone can read this sentence -- which is quoted by Crawford (*op. cit.*, p.

However, he never offered any public defence; and it was hardly a matter on which he was entitled to stand on his dignity, once the facts of the Holocaust became known. It seems, then, that, like many antisemites, he had some private definition of antisemitism by which he felt himself justified in disclaiming this label; what this definition may have been will be discussed shortly. It seems probable that his attitude towards the Jews did not change fundamentally, despite his decision to refrain from mentioning them in his later work.

Heroic efforts have been made to deny that there is any antisemitism in the well-known passages in Eliot's early work where Jews are portrayed. It has been argued, for example, that the "jew" (in "Gerontion") and Bleistein (in "Burbank with a Baedeker, Bleistein with a Cigar") are simply unpleasant people who happen to be Jews, and that no slur is intended on Jews as a whole. A characteristic expression of this view is by Anne Ridler: "Is a poet to be labelled 'antisemitic' because he describes unpleasant people who are Jews? As well say that the 'young man carbuncular' of *The Waste Land* implies that the poet could have no friend with a spotty face."[184] It is curious that Anne Ridler did not notice that her own argument is mildly antisemitic. She is saying that, as a tolerant man, Eliot was prepared to *forgive* Jews their Jewishness, just as he would generously overlook, in a friend, the blemish of being spotty. However, this mild kind of antisemitism (by which being a Jew is regarded as a slight disfigurement, for which other qualities may compensate) does not begin to be an adequate description of Eliot's attitude towards the Jewishness of his characters. The Jewishness is not something *separate* from the unpleasantness, but intimately connected with it.

Take this passage, for example, from one of Eliot's finest poems, "Gerontion":

My house is a decayed house,
And the jew squats on the window sill, the owner,
Spawned in some estaminet of Antwerp,
Blistered in Brussels, patched and peeled in London.

---

353) and also by Helen Thaventhiren in her *LRB* review of Crawford's book; see beginning of my Editor's Preface -- and deny that Eliot was an antisemite. To quote Crawford on this sentence: "He revealed that underneath his arguments there remained, despite denials, a deep-seated antisemitism he had harboured since childhood." (*Op. cit.*, p. 353.)

184 Author's footnote: Letter in The *Listener*, May 13, 1971.

Editor's footnote: See Appendix 9. For other and more recent "heroic efforts" to deny the antisemitism in Eliot's early work, see Chapter 4, p. 100, footnote 217.

Is the "jew", as has been suggested, merely a historical "type"[185], not intended to be representative of the Jews as a whole? One would have to be very innocent, and very ignorant of antisemitic literature and of the history of antisemitism, to believe this. The passage is full of allusions to the stock accusations against the Jews, to be found in profusion at the time in productions ranging from popular fiction to "scientific" works of antisemitic theory. The points continually hammered home in these productions were that the Jews were a disintegrative force in Western culture, that they had no loyalties or roots, that they were animal-like and menacing in their fertility, that they were without cultural ideals, that they sought power over Gentiles, that they congregated in cities and had no feeling for the land. All these points are to be found in this passage from "Gerontion". The "jew" is associated with decay and dilapidation; he is a rootless, restless cosmopolitan, moving from city to city, born on the move in a lodging-house; he is "spawned" in frightening and disgusting proliferation, like an insect or a frog, and "squats" like an animal; he owns the house of the Gentile, but remains an unassimilated onlooker or voyeur outside it; he is a creature of the crowded city, not of the organic unity of the countryside. There is the typical antisemitic paradox of the Jew as an agent of disintegration and death, who yet manifests an evil, enviable energy and reproductive faculty; the energy of the bacillus, or of the "spider" and "weevil" mentioned later in the poem; an energy that contrasts with the lethargy and self-distrust of the forces making for life. The similarities in all this to the standard antisemitic charges preclude the possibility that Eliot is presenting a portrait of a single unrepresentative Jew or even an unrepresentative *type* of Jew.

However, there is a valid point to make here that leads into a more subtle kind of defence of Eliot against the charge of antisemitism. The "jew" in "Gerontion" is, after all, not really a *dramatis persona*; Eliot is not here portraying a "character", such as one might find in a novel. The "jew" is a symbol or metaphor, a kind of hieroglyph for the forces of disintegration in life, for the closing-in of "the world" as Gerontion stiffens into old age and travels farther from his youthful vision of the Christ-child. This is a poem, not a factual treatise; in a poem, the poetical counters and devices should not be scrutinized with the literalness one gives to a sociological tract. If a poet uses, say, the image of a bat to convey a sense of the sinister, this is not because the poet detests bats in real life; the poet may know that they are in fact harmless and useful creatures, whose sinister aura is the result of a series of fortuitous historical, literary and psychological circumstances; yet those circumstances may have made the bat the indispensable symbol at that point in the poem. Similarly, the function of the "jew" in Eliot's poem is not to embody the poet's view on the Jewish question, but (because of the associations of the word "jew") to evoke the appropriate aura of seediness,

---

185 Editor's footnote: Murray Biggs, letter in The *Listener*, June 3, 1971. Biggs writes of the "jew" in "Gerontion": "this Jew is ... as much a historical type as the Christian type of hypocrite. To disapprove a type of Christian or Jew, however, is not to disapprove all, or even most, of their lineage." See Appendix 9.

menace and alienation that belongs to the situation of the only character with whom the poem is really concerned: Gerontion.

This approach to the question seems very plausible and is probably present in some form in the minds of those who feel impatient when the matter is raised. Here, for example, is a typical formulation (from an article on *The Waste Land*):

> these remarks, like the tedious many of late which go on about Eliot's alleged antisemitism, assume that this poem and others by him direct our attention on to the world that we experience in our daily encounters, in which every voice we hear is spoken by some person, that person socially conditioned and with some design upon us. But the voice of Countess Marie Larisch (who was a niece of the Empress of Austria and hence in fact a cousin of the Archduke[186]) is a voice that sounds not in society, not even "in the poet's head", but specifically in a *poem*, and in a poem which is haughtily indifferent to any society at all, whether that of London in 1920 or of Vienna before 1914.[187]

Plausible as this argument sounds, it rests on a very simple fallacy. It assumes that a person's responsibilities as a poet can be neatly cordoned off and separated from his or her responsibilities as a moral being. Actually, the argument defeats itself; for, if taken seriously, it makes Eliot into a far more immoral person than he would appear to be made by the original charge of antisemitism. To be an antisemite is bad enough; but to be the kind of person who uses an antisemitic stereotype in which he or she does not believe, merely to give impact to his or her verse, is to be thoroughly despicable. It is far more creditable to Eliot to say that he was a sincere antisemite than to say that he used the word "jew" as a conscious artist, in the awareness that its historical and literary overtones would so arouse atavistic fears and prejudices in his readers as to create a poetical atmosphere, mood or pattern at which he was aiming. This, if artistically successful, would indeed be what William James called the philosophy of George Santayana: "a perfection of rottenness"[188].

Fortunately, there is no need to suppose that Eliot was quite so corrupt. If the passage in "Gerontion" were all we had to go by, we might perhaps conclude that Eliot was, on this

---

186 Editor's footnote: See *The Waste Land* I.
187 Author's footnote: Donald Davie, "T. S. Eliot and the 'out there'", The *Times Literary Supplement*, December 10, 1971 (emphasis in original).
188 Editor's footnote: *The Letters of William James*, Vol. II, edited by Henry James, Boston, 1920: Alpha Editions reprint, Athens, 2020, p.122.

one occasion, tempted to utilize the emotive power of the antisemitic image, derived from popular literature and the *Protocols of the Elders of Zion*, in order to intensify Gerontion's sense of plight. But other passages, now to be considered, are numerous and weighty enough to rule out such an interpretation, unless we are to think of Eliot as a cynically wicked person, prepared to make repeated use of the misery of a slandered people as a poetical device. Eliot used antisemitism because he sincerely believed in it; and this is not to say that "Gerontion" is a poem about antisemitism, in the same sense that Drumont's *La France juive devant l'opinion*[189] was a book about antisemitism. "Gerontion" is a poem about Gerontion; or rather, it is a poem about growing old, about compromise with the world, about the dissatisfaction and lethargy which are the price of retaining the vision of youth and the hope of renewal. It is quite true that the "jew" is not a character in the poem, but a symbol. He symbolizes the forces of this world, which conspire to obliterate the vision of youth; but the reason that the "jew" has this symbolic force is not simply that Eliot calculated that his readers would react to the word "jew" in this way, but because he reacted in this way himself, because that is what the Jews meant to him. A poem is not propaganda for any particular views; but in its imagery and symbolism, it draws on everything that the poet sincerely feels and believes about the world; and, if there is no background of such sincerity, the imagery will be either lifeless or enlivened by mere malevolence.

Other ways of defending Eliot from the charge of antisemitism have been tried, but, before discussing these, we had better have more of the evidence before us. Even more blatant than the passage in "Gerontion" is the poem "Burbank with a Baedeker: Bleistein with a Cigar", which contains the following stanza:

> But this or such was Bleistein's way:
> A saggy bending of the knees
> And elbows, with the palms turned out,
> Chicago Semite Viennese.[190]

Bleistein, like the "jew" in "Gerontion", is a rootless cosmopolitan, "Chicago Semite Viennese" – echoing "Antwerp ... Brussels ... London". The mention of "Chicago" is particularly revealing, as has been pointed out by Gabriel Pearson.[191] Eliot came from St Louis, the

---

189 Editor's footnote: Eduoard Drumont, Paris, 1886.
190 Editor's footnote: T. S. Eliot, *Selected Poems*, op. cit., p. 34
191 Author's footnote: Gabriel Pearson, "Eliot: An American Use of Symbolism", in *Eliot in Perspective*, ed. Graham Martin, London 1970, p. 98.

Editor's footnote: Pearson writes (*ibid.*, pp. 97-98): "Eliot's grandfather, William Greenleaf Eliot, a Unitarian minister, had left Boston in the early 1830s to establish himself in a role that was to be central in the development of St Louis and the State of Missouri.... W. G. Eliot's whole being, and with it that of his family, was invested in the destiny of the city.... the formation of Eliot's basic social attitudes coincided with a period of intense disillusionment

importance of which as a cultural and industrial centre declined during his childhood because of the expansion of nearby Chicago, largely owing to the influx of European immigrants, many of them Jews fleeing from persecution in Europe. Eliot's antisemitism, quite apart from its wider implications, had a specifically American origin in the distaste felt by patricians like Henry Adams or even Henry James at this influx. (Of course, these exact feelings were experienced by patricians in the other countries affected, including England.) These immigrants seemed to people like Henry Adams to be barbarous alien hordes, devoid of all culture, but with a lust for money and success that was both loathsome and enviable. Adams writes of himself:

> Not a Polish Jew fresh from Warsaw or Cracow – not a furtive Yaccob or Ysaac still reeking of the Ghetto, snarling a weird Yiddish to the officers of the customs – but had a keener instinct, an intenser energy and a freer hand than he – American of Americans, with Heaven knew how many Puritans and Patriots behind him, and an education that had cost a civil war.[192]

Adams did not know, or wish to know, that this "weird Yiddish" was a language with a longer history than the English language. He did not know that the "furtive" Jew, who (he wrote in a letter) "makes me creep"[193], brought with him from the "reeking" Ghetto a cultural tradition in both Yiddish and Hebrew in comparison with which the acquisitions of the patrician Adams were parvenu. He did not in the least consider that these Jews were the victims of persecution, or that the Ghetto with which he taunted them was the symbol and location of their sufferings. And similarly, Eliot (whose poems, particularly "Gerontion", are much influenced, even to the extent of verbal quotation[194], by his reading of Adams) shows not the slightest human feeling for or understanding of Bleistein, or rather of the people of whom Bleistein is a caricature.

"Chicago Semite Viennese". We have seen some of the associations of "Chicago", and it may be interesting to pursue the associations of the other two words. The word "Semite" is evidently not intended to make Bleistein any more attractive. In the popular thrillers of the

---

with St Louis as the ascendant city of mid-America. Eight years before his birth the census of 1880 had brutally revealed that Chicago's population had outstripped St Louis's. (Hence perhaps the sneer in 'Chicago, Semite, Viennese'.)"

192 Editor's footnote: Henry Adams, *The Education of Henry Adams*, 1918: Oxford 2008, p. 202.

193 Editor's footnote: Worthington Chauncey Ford (ed.), *Letters of Henry Adams (1892-1918)*, Volume 2, Boston, 1938, p. 338.

194 Editor's footnote: see Chapter 4 on the line "In depraved May, dogwood and chestnut, flowering judas", which is taken almost word for word from a passage in *The Education of Henry Adams, op. cit.*, p. 226.

time, such as those of John Buchan, the villain was inevitably described as having a "Semitic" look. This, strangely, did not mean that he was an Arab, for Arabs, in such fiction, were generally rather dashing and noble. The word "antisemitism", from its inception to the time of Hitler (who was very friendly with that pure-blooded Semite, the Mufti of Jerusalem), never really meant anything except Jew-phobia, and "Semite" was a pseudo-scientific euphemism for "Jew". This shifty procedure of hiding Jew-phobia behind an insincerely held "scientific" theory of "race" derives from the 19th century. It is disappointing to find Eliot subscribing to this procedure, for, in general, his antisemitism belongs to the tradition of Christianity, a tradition in which racialism, or the pretence of it, plays no official part.

The word "Viennese", too, repays some reflection. Bleistein is, in origin, a Viennese Jew; and this description evidently carries for Eliot connotations of grossness and lack of culture. The next stanza (plus one word) is:

> A lustreless protrusive eye
> Stares from the protozoic slime
> At a perspective of Canaletto.
> The smoky candle end of time
>
> Declines.[195]

Bleistein stares at the Canaletto with complete incomprehension. Such "protozoic" Viennese Jews as Arthur Schnitzler, Sigmund Freud, Ludwig Wittgenstein, Moritz Schlick, Arnold Schoenberg, Gustav Mahler, Stefan Zweig, and Max Reinhardt played no part in Eliot's concept of a Viennese Jew, though Vienna was at this very time the centre of a great efflorescence of Jewish culture. It is ironic that one of the greatest experts on Italian Renaissance art in the 20th century was Bernard Berenson, a Jew with a background very similar to that of Bleistein. Eliot's selection of a Viennese Jew as the representative of modern philistinism is a gaffe comparable to that of Shakespeare when he made his Jewish prototype, Shylock, a hater of music. Yet, to the true antisemite, this would be no argument; for to Henry Adams, for example, a cultured Jew was even more hateful than an uncultured one.[196] The idea found in Maurras, Barrès and Adams that "Christian" culture is debased by the participation of Jews and other aliens is included in Eliot's "Gerontion" in the figures of Mr. Silvero and Hakagawa, "bowing among the Titians".

---

195 Editor's footnote: T. S. Eliot, *Selected Poems, op. cit.*, p. 35.
196 Editor's footnote: Henry Adams, *The Education of Henry Adams, op. cit.*, p. 71: "The derisive Jew laughter of Heine ran through the university and everything else in Berlin."

Yet, in the line "Chicago Semite Viennese", the gravamen of the charge against Bleistein does not lie in the words taken separately, but in their combination. The point is not so much that Bleistein is uncultured, as that he belongs to no particular culture; he is an unsavoury mixture. He represents the disintegration of Western culture, and the approach of barbarism. He represents, in fact, the new America, gawking uncomprehendingly at Europe.

To continue the quotation:

On the Rialto once.
The rats are underneath the piles.
The jew is underneath the lot.
Money in furs. The boatman smiles,

Princess Volupine extends
A meagre, blue-nailed, phthisic hand
To climb the waterstair. Lights, lights,
She entertains Sir Ferdinand

Klein.[197]

The other Jew in the poem, "Sir Ferdinand/Klein", represents the infiltrating Jew, who corrupts European culture by participating in it and by financing it, and who is welcomed by Princess Volupine, the representative of that culture in decline. (The separation of "Sir Ferdinand" from "Klein" by line and stanza heightens the irony of his infiltration; and "Klein" at the beginning of a stanza echoes "Declines" at the beginning of a previous stanza.) Burbank represents the older America, admiring and imitating European culture from afar, and, with Baedeker in hand, unable to save it from Sir Ferdinand, just as he is unable to preserve his American cultural tradition from the philistinism of Bleistein. In the background ("On the Rialto once") lies the shadow of a third Jew, Shylock, who plotted to overthrow the ideal Christian, Antonio, by financial manipulation and usury. There is no reason to suppose that Eliot shared the well-meaning liberal-Romantic misconception of Shylock as a sympathetic character.[198]

---

197 Editor's footnote: T. S. Eliot, *Selected Poems, op. cit.*, p. 35.
198 Editor's footnote: see my Editor's Preface for the Author's view of Shylock. Genesius Jones, who clearly shares Eliot's antisemitism (even though *Approach to the Purpose* is informed by the ideas of the German-Jewish philosopher Ernst Cassirer, whose writings Fr. Jones evidently regards with great admiration), gives an accurate interpretation of Eliot's intentions: "The appalling Bleistein ... is the Jew, symbolised by the water rat which embodies 'Money

The whole poem thus contains a fairly complete antisemitic system and can best be understood in the light of this system. This is not to say that the poem is about antisemitism; it is about the situation of a cultivated young American vis-à-vis European culture, and about his sense of helplessness in the face of the various threats to a civilisation to which he feels himself deeply, though peripherally, attached -- rather like the situation of say, a Rome-educated British chieftain at the time of the barbarian invasions. But the symbol of the threat is the Jew, in his two manifestations of open philistinism and insidious infiltration. As a symbolist poet, Eliot required, as the "objective correlative" of his sense of culture decay, an image or symbol that would strike at the recesses of his own and his readers' unconscious mind -- and the archetypal image of the Jew was singularly fitted to do just this. It is an interesting reflection that the symbolist method, which is supposed to produce the "music" of poetry, can in practice lead to surrender to atavistic social prejudices -- for poetry does not distinguish between genuinely psychological archetypal images and those that have been socially induced by centuries-long indoctrination. To Eliot, the "jew" image, at this time, must have seemed as right and inevitable as his other symbols, such as the rat, the geranium, the crab, the fog or the mermaids. It has taken Hitler's Holocaust to shake the hold of this image on the European imagination.

As stated above, the theme of the poem is not antisemitism; but it is an important element in the total theme; and the poem cannot be understood at all if the antisemitism is regarded as incidental, or as a mere outburst of personal spleen. This is a systematic or philosophical type of antisemitism of the American-Bostonian type exemplified by Henry Adams, deriving, at one remove, from right-wing French religious anti-Judaism (Drumont, Maurras and the anti-Dreyfusards) and ultimately from the anti-Judaism of medieval Catholicism.[199] This kind of antisemitism is in fact far more poisonous and dangerous to the Jews than the kind of "gut-antisemitism" that is merely a xenophobic reaction similar to colour-prejudice. But the American-Bostonian type of antisemitism is not racialistic and is capable of making many individual exceptions among Jews, without abandoning the Jew-concept as a social and cultural category. At the same time, despite its theoretical, philosophical tone, this kind of antisemitism includes the "gut-reaction" as an ingredient and can be venomous enough in expression. In this poem, the lines "The rats are underneath the piles./The jew

---

in furs'. Where Burbank had sought the erotic past of Venice, Bleistein looks back to its commercial past. And so a scientific dimension is added to the historical perspective. Bleistein's prototype, moreover, is Shylock: 'On the Rialto once'. It is his lustreless protrusive eye (or Shylock's; in fact, every rat's eye) which stares from the protozoic slime under the piles at the beauty which Canaletto captures on canvas – and reflects only on the profit and the loss. There can be no resurrection for this water vermin." (*Op. cit.*, p. 298.)

[199] Author's footnote: John Harrison, *The Reactionaries*, London, 1966, pp. 149-152. See also M. Curtis, *Three Against the Third Republic, op. cit.*

is underneath the lot" express such venom that even Eliot's most dedicated white-washers prefer to ignore them altogether.

Even more embarrassing has been the bringing to light of another poem about Bleistein in the first draft of *"The Waste Land"*:

Full fathom five your Bleistein lies
Under the flatfish and the squids.
Graves' Disease in a dead jew's eyes!
When the crabs have eat the lids.
Lower than the wharf rats dive
    Though he suffer a sea-change
    Still expensive rich and strange

That is lace that was his nose
  See upon his back he lies
(Bones peep through the ragged toes)
  With a stare of dull surprise
    Flood tide and ebb tide
    Roll him gently side to side
    See the lips unfold unfold
    From the teeth, gold in gold
Lobsters hourly keep close watch
Hark! now I hear them   scratch   scratch   scratch.[200]

This poem, written after "Burbank", is of a much cruder type. The parody of Shakespeare's *The Tempest* song is feeble, and the sneer at Bleistein's nose is on a schoolboy level of antisemitism. The sheer aggression of this picture of Bleistein being eaten up by sea-creatures might lead us into thinking that the poem is an antisemitic lampoon of no more than pathological interest. This would be a mistake, for the poem, though artistically a failure, is serious in intention. We may note, first of all, parallels with "Burbank" and other Eliot poems. Bleistein's "protusive eye" now turns out to be the effect of "Graves' Disease". Instead of being under the rats, who are undermining the piles (i.e., a King Rat attacking the foundations of society), Bleistein is lying dead "lower than the wharf rats dive". The lustreless stare at the Canaletto has become "a stare of dull surprise" at his own death.

---

200 Author's footnote: T. S. Eliot, *The Waste Land: A Facsimile and Transcript, op. cit.*, p. 121.

His teeth, "gold in gold" (i. e. yellow with gold fillings; the first version had "black, yellow and gold") are paralleled by the "golden grin" of "the man with heavy eyes" (again the protuberant eyes) who appears along with "Rachel née Rabinovitch" in "Sweeney Among the Nightingales". (John Harrison's conjecture that "the man with heavy eyes" is a Jew[201] is thus confirmed; note too that he is "Outside the window, leaning in ", just as the "jew" in "Gerontion" "squats on the window sill".)

"Dirge" thus represents the defeat and death of Bleistein, who, in "Burbank", was triumphant. His protuberant eyes, which stared through a window or through the glass of an art-gallery at things that they ought not to see, are now staring in death. But the poem is not just a paean of victory, or hoped-for victory, over Bleistein. Savage though it is, "Dirge" is also a representation of the *purgation* of Bleistein. The poem shows many connections with the theme of purgation expressed throughout *The Waste Land*. The very form of "Dirge", as a parody of "Full fathom five", connects with the *Tempest* associations that pervade "The Waste Land" (e. g. "those are pearls that were his eyes" in Section II) and that evoke the theme of regeneration through "death by water", or baptism. There are strong connections (despite a complete difference in mood) between "Dirge" and Section IV of *The Waste Land*, entitled "Death by Water".[202] Phlebas the Phoenician is a muted and idealized version of Bleistein.[203] Just as the crabs have eaten the lids of Bleistein's eyes, so the bones of the dead Phlebas have been "picked" by the current. Just as the tides roll Bleistein "gently side to side", so the drowned Phlebas "rose and fell". Even the fact that Phlebas is a Phoenician is a muted version of Bleistein's Jewishness; for the Phoenicians were a trading, Hebrew-speaking nation, who had been treated in Flaubert's *Salammbo* as the ancient analogues of the modern Jewish bourgeoisie. (Carthage, it should be remembered, was a Phoenician colony.)

It is possible, then, that "Death by Water" actually takes the place in *The Waste Land* vacated by the rejected "Dirge". Why should this substitution have taken place? It would be comforting to think that Eliot repented the savage antisemitism of "Dirge", and for that reason substituted the sweetly elegiac "Death by Water". However, there are considerations that make this hypothesis untenable. Eliot, from the first, had a dual method of approaching the theme of purgation: a "sweet" method, and a "sordid" method. This may be explained by the simple fact that, while purgation implies cleanliness, it also implies dirtiness (as in *The Water-Babies*, when Tom in Ellie's bedroom thinks that whoever needs so much washing-apparatus "must be a very dirty lady"[204]). Or, to put the matter more theologically,

---

201 Editor's footnote: John Harrison, *op. cit.*, p. 150.
202 Editor's footnote: See also Madame Sosostris's warning in Section I: "Fear death by water".
203 Editor's footnote: See Chapter 4.
204 Editor's footnote: Charles Kingsley, *The Water-Babies*, 1863: New York, 2008, p. 13.

it is only when we realize how sinful we are that we are on the road to becoming virtuous. "Death by Water" is derived from "Dans le Restaurant" (written in French by Eliot), a poem in which the two methods are combined. A dirty waiter (who has told of a moment of sexual ecstasy in his boyhood) is given money by the poet to go and have a bath; the scene suddenly changes to where the drowned body of "Phlébas, le Phénician" is being cleansed by an undersea current (the French 'l'emporta' has the double meaning of "cleansed" and "carried"). Following "Dirge" in the manuscript is a fragment, also rejected, which treats the theme in the "sweet" manner:

> Those are pearls that were his eyes. See!
>
> And the crab clambers through his stomach, the eel grows big
>
> And the torn algae drift above him,
>
> And the sea-colander.
>
> Still and quiet brother are you still and quiet[205]

Why were these attractive lines rejected? I suggest that Eliot wanted to combine the "sweet" and "sordid" modes, but, having rightly rejected "Dirge" on artistic grounds, decided to fall back on his original treatment in "Dans le Restaurant", with some slight alterations in the direction of the sordid or grotesque (e. g., "picked his bones"). "Death by Water" remains decidedly on the "sweet" side; but the counterpoise is provided in "The Waste Land" by the figure of Mr. Eugenides, the seedy Levantine who is the modern version of Phlebas. The only remnant of Bleistein after this revision is the phrase "Gentile or Jew" (not contained in "Dans le Restaurant").

This analysis suggests a defence of Eliot's Jewish passages that his supporters have overlooked. It appears that even such a virulently antisemitic poem as "Dirge" is not merely an instance of an "almost insane physical nausea about Jews" (to quote again from the *Times* obituary of Ezra Pound). There is a theological point in the poem. Bleistein is undergoing a painful purgatory by water, just as Gerontion does, in imagination, in "the Gulf", and just as Newman's Gerontius does, in the poem from which Eliot derived the title and some of the ideas of "Gerontion".[206] Can it not be that Bleistein the Jew represents humanity itself, with its encrustation of sin and its need for purgation?

This is the most plausible defence of Eliot so far, and it deserves serious consideration. We should remember the connection between water-purification and *baptism*, which involves death and rebirth:

---

205 Author's footnote: T. S. Eliot, *The Waste Land: A Facsimile and Transcript, op. cit.*, p. 123.
206 Editor's footnote: See Chapter 4 below.

> Know ye not, that so many of us as were baptized into Jesus Christ were baptized into his death?
> Therefore we are buried with him by baptism into death: that like as Christ was raised up from the dead by the glory of the Father, even so we also should walk in newness of life....
> our old man is crucified with *him*[207]

The connection between "death by water" and baptism is reinforced by "Mr. Eliot's Sunday Morning Service", where we find the same alternation of "sweet" and "sordid" as we have already noted in "Death by Water", but this time related to baptism, in the contrast between the Baptism of Christ and Sweeney having his bath.[208] It is surely part of the meaning of "Dirge" that Bleistein is undergoing baptism. The cruel imagery of being eaten by sea-creatures arises from the relation between baptism and crucifixion. It is an image of *sacrifice*, of which baptism is one form or symbol; and the cruelty of the imagery is no more to be taken literally than the imagery of *Ash Wednesday*, in which the poet is eaten alive by leopards, and which relates to the sacrifice of bodily desires involved in membership of the Church.[209] Moreover, the imagery of "being eaten" is a basic religious symbol, derived, it is true, from prehistoric totem feasts, but in Christianity related to self-surrender and incorporation in the Divine.

Bleistein, seen in this light, is a sacrificial figure, his very grotesqueness and diseased fleshiness evoking the "old man", or humanity, which needs to be purged away. The title of the poem, "Dirge", is not, after all, ironical but a reference to the dirge sung for Adonis, images of whom (in some versions of the rite) were thrown into water.[210] The fact that Bleistein, Phlebas, Mr. Eugenides and Gerontion are all merchants, involved in "the profit and the loss" (*The Waste Land* IV), means merely that they are all ordinary human beings, soiled by the calculations of everyday living, as opposed to the martyrs, who do not survive into old age, and do not count the profit and the loss. If Bleistein has been chosen as a symbol of soiled humanity, so have others who are not Jews: Sweeney, for example, Phlebas, Mr. Eugenides, and Gerontion himself.

---

207 Author's footnote: Romans 6: 3-6, Authorized Version..

    Editor's footnote: See Genesius Jones, *op. cit.*, p. 101, on the symbolism of the "old man": "Gerontion, the little old man, whatever else he may be, is, in the religious perspective, 'the old man' of Pauline theology, who is to be transformed into the new."

208 Editor's footnote: See Chapter 5.

209 Editor's footnote: See Chapter 1 above and Appendix 1(b) below.

210 Editor's footnote: See Frazer, *Abridged Edition, op. cit.*, p. 335: "At Alexandria.... women attired as mourners ... bore the image of the dead Adonis to the sea-shore and committed it to the waves".

Yet I am afraid that even this will not serve to defend Eliot against the charge of antisemitism; though I have a strong feeling that this is the defence that he himself would have raised if he had ever deigned to defend himself. Christians often adopt a very similar argument nowadays to explain the antisemitism of the Gospels. They say that the Jews are not represented as especially wicked in killing Christ; they are simply the representatives of humanity; they may even (in one variant) have a God-given role in this respect, a kind of martyrdom. "We are all guilty" – but the Jews were chosen to bear the blame; to suffer damnation for mankind, just as Jesus suffered the physical doom that was due to humanity. On this view, the Jews become a kind of black Christ – the objectification of the doctrine by which Christ took upon himself the sins of humanity, and thus, in effect, became the arch-sinner himself. Or the matter may be put more metaphorically: humanity should look at the Jews in order to see the image of itself; they are like a nightmare image seen in a mirror. Here is a summary – by the German ex-pastor and writer on Christianity Joachim Kahl -- of a modern German defence of The Gospel According to St. John, the most anti-Jewish of the Gospels:

> Erich Grasser, New Testament professor at the university of Bochum, has made a detailed analysis of the anti-Jewish polemics in the gospel according to John. He has come to the conclusion that the passages in which the Jews are referred to contain "no antisemitism of any origin whatever". The '"Jews"' are not a historical people in the Fourth Gospel, Grasser claims, but "stylized types" exemplifying and embodying the world's lack of faith. John's intention was not to vilify real Jews – his polemics were "purely the result of theological reflection", "the product of a compellingly logical way of thinking" and "one of the earliest attempts to give a firm theological basis to the absolute claims of Christianity".

On this, Kahl comments:

Has any form of antisemitism ever had anything essentially to do with the Jews as a historical people? Whether they are defamed as the children of the devil or whether they are branded as an inferior race of people is really beside the point. Both these attitudes are mythological and both are the result of the same need to have an enemy.[211]

If Eliot, as seems likely, conceived that he was treating his Jewish characters in some such mythological way, then he was guilty of an antisemitism of a very subtle and pernicious kind. To regard the Jew as a symbol of humanity is one thing; James Joyce did that in an unobjectionable way in *Ulysses*. But to take the Jew as a symbol of fallen, unregenerate humanity is an entirely different thing. Whatever may be true about St John's Gospel, the last person for a modern author to take as such a symbol, after what has happened in Christendom, should be the Jew. For the historical effect of the Jew-myth has been the direct opposite of the effect claimed for it by modern apologists; it has not served to heighten people's sense of responsibility, but very much to lessen it -- to make them shelve their guilt and load it on to the Jew. True, Eliot had other symbols for unregenerate humanity; but only one of them, Sweeney, is not an echo and disguise of Bleistein; and Sweeney is not so much an image of guilt as of Caliban-like unshapen, ignorant humanity, of the body as yet unredeemed by the soul, rather than the traitor who consciously betrays the highest.

"Dirge" is an artistic failure, probably because, in this poem, Eliot allowed personal distaste to predominate over artistry in his use of antisemitic symbolism. But "Burbank" is not an artistic failure; in purely artistic terms, it is a triumph. In a poem of 32 lines, in a highly original idiom marked by wit, elegance and an astonishingly dexterous handling of literary allusions, Eliot has expressed a whole conspectus of the cultural plight of the modern world. It is not surprising that Eliot himself was very pleased with it. He called it, together with "Sweeney Among the Nightingales", "intensely serious" and "among the best that I have ever done".[212] It should not be a matter for surprise that antisemitism can inspire literary excellence. It has done so many times before. Chaucer's "The Prioress's Tale" and Shakespeare's *The Merchant of Venice* are obvious examples. For antisemitism is not a superficial thing; it has deep roots in mythology and in the history of religion.

The reason that great art can be inspired by antisemitism is that it is based on a permanent tendency of human nature. The Jew himself, as a symbol of evil, has been given this role by a culturally determined process; but the need for such a symbol is part of the human psyche. Early pagan religion solved the problem of guilt by sacrifice, i.e., by the restitution of life to the dying god (dying because of the tribe's guilt and pollution) through the death of their own best man. But there was always the dark figure of the Sacrificer, representing the guilt of the salvation-bringing Sacrifice itself. The Sacrificer (Cain, the

---

[211] Author's footnote: Joachim Kahl, *The Misery of Christianity or A Plea for Humanity Without God* (English translation of *Das Elend Das Christentums*), London 1971, pp. 53-54.

[212] Author's footnote: T. S. Eliot, *The Waste Land: A Facsimile and Transcript, op. cit.* p. xviii.
Editor's footnote: See also *The Letters of T. S. Eliot, Volume 1, op. cit.*, p. 363.

Scapegoat, Typhon, Mot, Hother) has to be driven into the desert, where he bears the sign of murder, though he never quite loses his priest-like function. This is the role assigned to the Jew in Christianity, a role that the Jews always refused to accept, though the legend of the Wandering Jew was a Christian wish-fulfilment by which the Jew was imagined to have accepted his role.[213]

To Maurras, Adams and Eliot, the Jew is no longer thought of as threatening the Body of Christ by desecrating stolen wafers or crucifying Christian children, as in medieval times; but he is still threatening the Body of Christ (i.e., the Church) by denying the value of the Sacrifice that sustains that Body in being. By inspiring humanistic movements (democracy, socialism, industrialism), by insisting on justice,[214] by embracing this world instead of regarding it as a waiting-period for the next, by embracing adulthood and maturity (what Eliot calls "old age") as positive values, and thus abandoning the beatific vision of childhood (here Eliot joins the tradition of Romanticism to that of Christianity), the Jew, in his view, is the enemy of the whole sacrificial concept, substituting for it the concept of progress and the perfectibility of man. All this can be read in that superb poem "Gerontion", which contains in embryo the whole of Eliot's literary output.[215]

Whether Eliot and his French forerunners are right in giving this important historical role to the Jews is a matter for serious consideration. Certainly Judaism is the religion that, more than any other, gives the lie to the doctrine of Sacrifice, by refusing to allow any place for the dying-and-resurrected god. What we may at least conclude, for the purposes of this study, is that antisemitism is no personal aberration of Eliot's, but an important ingredient in his total *Weltanschauung*, and thus an influence of considerable importance on his poetry.

---

[213] Editor's footnote: See Hyam Maccoby, "The Legend of the 'Wandering Jew'", in The *Jewish Quarterly*, Volume 20, Issue 1 (1972) and Hyam Maccoby, *The Sacred Executioner, op. cit.*, pp. 166-171.

[214] Editor's footnote: See Chapter 4, p. 100, footnote 219.

[215] Editor's footnote: See the next chapter (Chapter 4), *passim*.

Chapter 4: FLOWERING JUDAS: A Study of the "jew" in "Gerontion".[216]

It is interesting to note the coy way in which Eliot commentators treat the antisemitic parts of "Gerontion". Only John Harrison in *The Reactionaries*[217] pays much attention to them. Other writers (even Jews, Wolf Mankowitz for example[218]) find them of little or no significance. Even John Harrison makes no attempt to relate them to the central meaning of the poem. Yet John Harrison has pointed out that Eliot derived his antisemitism not only from Pound but from Maurras and Barrès, who had what one could call a philosophy of antisemitism, since they regarded the Jews as responsible for everything that these writers considered to be characteristically modern, such as democracy, capitalism, communism, liberalism, science, and rationalism.[219] I think it worthwhile, therefore, to consider the

---

216 Editor's footnote: Originally published in the *Jewish Quarterly*, under the title "A Study of the 'jew' in 'Gerontion'", Volume 17, No. 2 (62), Summer, 1969. Reprinted by kind permission of the Jewish Literary Trust.

217 Author's footnote: *op. cit.*, p.150.

Editor's footnote: Since John Harrison, much more attention has been made by critics to the antisemitism in "Gerontion", even before the publication of Anthony Julius's book in 1995. See Manju Jain: *A Critical Reading of the Selected Poems of T. S. Eliot*, 1991: Published in India by the Oxford University Press, 2001, p. 89: "Eliot's derogatory references to Jews have been the subject of much controversy." (Jain, as the blurb on the back of her book states, offers "comments and explanations that are informed by current critical perspectives".) Yet efforts to deny the antisemitism in "Gerontion" continue. Barry Spurr has already been mentioned in my Editor's Preface; Craig Raine argues that "squats" is "neutral" and "spawned... can be neutral" and that "spawned" suggests "poverty. I do not think the Jew who owns the '*decayed* house' and perches on its windowsill is the anti-Semitic cliché of the affluent Jewish magnate" (*T. S. Eliot, op. cit.*, pp. 166-7; emphasis in original). Also see Author's comments (p. 110) and Editor's footnote (p. 110, footnote 247) below in this chapter about critics' association of the 'jew' with Christ, because the 'jew' was born in an 'estaminet' and Christ in a stable at an inn.

218 Author's footnote: *T. S. Eliot: A Study of His Writings by Several Hands*, ed. B. Ragan, London, 1947, p. 130.

Editor's footnote: Anthony Julius also points out the phenomenon of lack of acknowledgement by Jewish critics (including Mankowitz) of the antisemitism in "Gerontion". See Julius, *op. cit.*, pp. 49-58.

219 Author's footnote: John Harrison, *op. cit.*, p.149.

Editor's footnote: Harrison writes: "The idea of metaphysical justice was abhorrent to Maurras because it was not only unnatural but essentially Jewish. He said that Jews were responsible for the egalitarian principle because it came originally from Israel and had been introduced in the sixteenth century, when the Reformation had propagated the egalitarian mysticism of the prophets by making everyone read the Bible."

See also Curtis, *op. cit.*, p. 217 on Maurras' thinking: "The invention of supernatural justice came from Judea, as did the idea of equality among men. It was from the Jew that the Protestant had received his monotheism, his belief in prophets, his anarchical thought."

For a more recent exploration of the influence of Maurras and Barrès over Eliot, see Kenneth Asher, *T. S. Eliot and Ideology*, Cambridge, 1998, especially Chapter 2, "The French Connection". In his concluding chapter, Asher

possibility that the Jew in "Gerontion" has a more important role in the poem than he has been assigned hitherto.

The main passage in question runs as follows:

My house is a decayed house,
And the jew squats on the window sill, the owner,
Spawned in some estaminet of Antwerp,
Blistered in Brussels, patched and peeled in London.[220]

The word "jew" (up till 1963) is not given the dignity of a capital letter, so that the Jew is evidently regarded as sub-human, a kind of evil animal. The Jew, in other words, is the Devil, an identification sufficiently attested by Christian teaching. The Jew is outside the window, like the ravening animal the Wolf, to whom the Devil is so often compared in the New Testament and in Christian literature. The Jew is the enemy of the House, which is Christendom. In the next poem in *Ara Vos Prec*, "Burbank with a Baedeker, Bleistein with a Cigar", we read:

The rats are underneath the piles.
The jew is underneath the lot.[221]

Again, the Jew (without a capital letter) is a kind of loathsome animal, a Super-Rat, gnawing at the foundations of Christian civilisation; or a King Rat, directing the operations of the forces of destruction. His subterranean position, moreover, reinforces the idea that he is Satan, working from his underground Hell.[222]

Yet at the same time the Jew is the "owner" of the House. This is not only because, as John Harrison writes, Eliot is saying that "the Jews are the cause of the importance of finance in the modern world".[223] It is, of course, a commonplace of antisemitism that the Jews are engaged in a secret plot to take over the world and that their power is already far greater

---

suggests that the reactionary writers by whom Eliot was influenced, who considered themselves to be "classical", were in fact Romantics: "Would we then be ... prepared to claim that the reactionary excesses of the twentieth century with which a number of modernists were to varying degrees implicated were at least *a* logical culmination of the premises of romanticism?" (*Ibid.*, p. 163; emphasis in original.)

220 Editor's footnote: T. S. Eliot, *Selected Poems*, London 1961, p. 31.
221 Editor's footnote: T. S. Eliot, *Selected Poems*, *op. cit.*, p. 35.
222 Author's footnote: There may be an echo also of the beast Geryon, in Dante's *Inferno*, Canto 17. Geryon "squats" ("bestia malvagia che cola sic orca", line 30). Geryon is the personification of Fraud and is introduced just before Dante's encounter with the Usurers.
223 Editor's footnote: *op. cit.*, p.151.

than it appears. It is certainly part of Eliot's meaning that Jewish "usuria" is the real ruler of the materialistic modern world. But there is a deeper meaning too. The Devil is called in the New Testament "the ruler of this world". This idea is part of Christianity's legacy from Gnosticism, which regarded the world as created not by the good God but by the evil Demiurge. Christianity, skating precariously near the edge of dualism, never went so far as this; but the idea that the world we know is a world of Darkness, betrayed by Adam's sin[224] into the hands of Satan, is only tenuously different from the Gnostic position. In the Jewish sacred writings, Satan, on the very rare occasions when he is mentioned, is merely a very minor angel, a kind of "agent provocateur", or prosecuting counsel, appointed by God and very much under His control.[225] The Christians awarded Satan a remarkable promotion in the scheme of things and appointed the unwitting Jew to be Satan's earthly representative ("the synagogue of Satan"[226]).

However, there is still a good deal more to be said about Eliot's squatting "jew". Though he is the owner of the house, he is outside it, peeping through the window. The House (from one aspect) is Christendom, in which the Jew is an outsider, but to which he is indissolubly tied. He is the Wandering Jew, looking, enviously and wistfully, from the outside, into the settled habitations of men, the community of the Church.

And yet, remarkably enough, the Jew is himself described in terms more appropriate to a house. He is "Blistered in Brussels, patched and peeled in London". The walls of his body, or of his soul, are those of a dilapidated house, blistered, patched and peeled. But Gerontion himself, the speaker of the monologue, is also characterized in terms of a "house". At the end of the poem, we have:

Tenants of the house,
Thoughts of a dry brain in a dry season.

Gerontion is a tenant in the Jew's house, but his thoughts are tenants in the dilapidated house of his brain, or of his body. It is difficult to avoid the conclusion that Gerontion is, in some sense, himself the Jew. For the Jew is a symbol of dilapidation, disintegration and corruption – everything that can be summed up in the phrase "old age". In so far as he is an old man, Gerontion is a Jew. This may go some way towards explaining Eliot's choice

---

[224] Editor's footnote: Grover Smith comments that the "wrath-bearing tree" in "Gerontion" is at one and the same time the Cross, the tree on which Judas hanged himself, and the Tree of the Knowledge of Good and Evil in Genesis: "the crucifixion yew tree and the death tree of the hanged traitor, a token of Christ and Iscariot, redemption and the universal fall in Eden". (*T. S. Eliot's Poetry and Plays op. cit.*, p. 61.)

[225] Editor's footnote: See Appendix 2, Note 1 for the Author's interpretation of the Fourth Tempter in *Murder in the Cathedral* as based on Satan in this Jewish form.

[226] Editor's footnote: Revelation 3: 9.

of the name "Gerontion". For the ballad[227] on which the character of Shylock is thought to have been based[228] was about a Jew called Gernutus; and this name is probably derived from an earlier play[229] in which the Jew was called Gerontus, which, of course, means "old man". Eliot merely gave the name in its more correct Greek diminutive (and therefore more belittling) form.[230]

There is also a more obvious derivation of the name from John Henry Newman's poem "The Dream of Gerontius", echoes of which can be found in "Gerontion". For example, Gerontius experiences death as disintegration into elements and descent into the abyss of Space. This is rather like the end of "Gerontion". Also, Gerontius calls his soul a "mansion"; and, floating in the wind outside this mansion, as outside Gerontion's "house", there is an evil shape.[231] This suggests another meaning in "Gerontion"'s "jew": that the Jew, or Devil, is waiting outside the window in order to claim his property when Gerontion finally "stiffens" in his "rented house". If Gerontion's soul has taken its colour from its Satan-owned habitation, the body, his soul, too, will be claimed by the ruler of this world.

But perhaps another poem by Newman is even more relevant to the theme of "Gerontion". It is Newman's poem "Judaism", which begins:

O piteous race!
Fearful to look upon,
Once standing in high place,

---

227 Editor's footnote: See https://www.bl.uk/collection-items/broadside-ballad-on-the-cruelty-of-gernutus-the-jew
228 Editor's footnote: For instance, see Stanley Wood and Rev. F. Marshall (eds.), *The Oxford and Cambridge Edition of Shakespeare's Merchant of Venice, with Introduction and Notes for Students and Preparation for the Examinations*, London, c. 1900, p. xi. One of the sources of *The Merchant of Venice* is listed here as "The Ballad of Gernutus, the Jew of Venice".
229 Editor's footnote: The play in question is *The Three Ladies of London*, a play probably written by Robert Wilson, which features a Jew called Gerontus. See F. E. Halliday, *A Shakespeare Companion 1564-1964*, London 1964, p. 530, on Wilson: "He is probably the 'R. W.' who wrote the extant *Three Ladies of London*, published 1584, a play about a generous Jewish money-lender, perhaps a reply to *The Jew*, the lost play that may have been a source of *The Merchant of Venice*". For a recent analysis of *The Three Ladies of London*, see Brett D. Hirsch, "Jewish Questions in Robert Wilson's *The Three Ladies of London*", *Early Theatre*, January 19, 2016. Hirsch argues that Gerontus is not in fact such a generous figure.
file:///C:/Users/debor/Downloads/jadmin,+ET_19-1_5_ART_Hirsch%20(2).pdf
230 Editor's footnote: Matthew Hollis, *op. cit.*, p. 104, points out another derivation, mentioned by Eliot himself: "'The title means 'little old man', he said, and was a revision of 'Gerousia', the Council of Elders in ancient Greece that had given Eliot his first title." (Also see 2015 *Poems, Vol. I, op. cit.*, p. 469.) This does not at all preclude the name's connection with Gernutus, Gerontus and Gerontius (in fact, this last is the most obvious association).
231 Editor's footnote: John Henry Newman, *Collected Poems and the Dream of Gerontius*, 1868; Sevenoaks, Kent, 1992, p. 141: "A fierce and restless fright begins to fill/The mansion of my soul. And, worse and worse,/Some bodily form of ill/Floats on the wind".

Heaven's eldest son.
O aged blind
Unvenerable![232]

To the Christian, the Jew is always an old man: "O aged blind/Unvenerable!" is a good description of Gerontion himself.[233] All Jews are old men; and, by a kind of reasoning invalid in logic but valid in poetry, all old men are Jews.

The Jews are connected with trade, especially in the eyes of the antisemite. If Gerontion (because of his old age) has become somehow a Jew, we should expect some mention of trade; and we find it in the introduction of the "Trades": "an old man driven by the Trades/ To a sleepy corner". But, when we look further into this aspect of the poem, we find more connections with the Phoenician than with the Jew. Phlebas the Phoenician appears in the fourth part of *The Waste Land* (originally, he appeared in the French poem "Dans le Restaurant", the importance of which for the understanding of Eliot's work has been adequately stressed by commentators[234]). Gerontion's "gull against the wind" is echoed by Phlebas's "cry of gulls"; Gerontion's "profit of ... chilled delirium" is echoed by Phlebas's "profit and loss"; the "Gulf" that claims Gerontion is echoed by Phlebas's "whirlpool"; Gerontion's "Trades" is echoed by "you who turn the wheel and look to windward". One commentator, George Williamson, even concluded that Gerontion "has been a merchant seaman".[235]

But I think we can assume that the Phoenician is really another form of the Jew. The Phoenicians were a Semitic nation. Their language was a form of Hebrew, and, like the Jews, they were associated with trade. It is significant that the Phoenician is given a Greek-sounding name. The modern embodiment of Phlebas in *The Waste Land* is Mr. Eugenides of Smyrna, who has the same mixture of Greek and Levantine origins. We have the suggestion of a great nation that has degenerated and become dilapidated and stained with commercialism. "Eugenides" means "well-born" – the name is ironical in view of this businessman's seedy dinginess; but the Jew is again relevant, if we remember Newman's "O piteous race!/Fearful to look upon,/Once standing in high place,/Heaven's eldest son." A Greek-Phoenician, a member of the nation of Plato and Pericles engaged in petty trade,

---

[232] Editor's footnote: *Ibid.*, p. 79.

[233] Author's footnote: For Gerontion's blindness and its source in A. C. Benson's *Edward Fitzgerald*, see F. O. Matthiessen, *The Achievement of T. S. Eliot, op. cit.*, p. 73.

[234] Editor's footnote: See, for instance, George Williamson, *A Reader's Guide to T. S. Eliot: A Poem-by-Poem Analysis*, 1953: Syracuse, 1998, pp. 115-118. Williamson writes: "It may not be going too far to regard 'Dans le Restaurant' (1918) as an earlier exploration of the vein of thought and feeling that is plumbed in *The Waste Land*" (p. 118). See also Chapter 3 for discussion of Phlebas.

[235] Author's footnote: *Ibid.*, p.112.

is a pretty good analogue for a Jew, if one accepts the antisemitic view of the Jews as a degenerate nation, who have forgotten their former greatness in petty commercialism. This conclusion is supported by the otherwise irrelevant apostrophe in "Death by Water", "Gentile or Jew".

Phlebas the Phoenician meets his death by water. The water cleanses him from the stain of trade, "the profit and loss". The old waiter in "Dans le Restaurant" is encrusted with dirt; yet he remembers a moment of ecstasy in his youth. He is offered money to have a bath; and suddenly the scene changes to Phlebas lying dead under the sea. Eliot himself, meditating on his own approaching old age in *Ash Wednesday*, writes (Part VI):

> Wavering between the profit and the loss,
> In this brief transit where the dreams cross
> The dreamcrossed twilight between birth and dying

Gerontion, too, after speaking of the "thousand small deliberations" which "protract the profit of their chilled delirium", looks forward to being claimed by the Gulf, where, presumably, like Phlebas, he will be cleansed and purified from the accumulated dirt of old age. For old age is dirtied by trade, by the Time-ridden cautious calculations of profit and loss, as opposed to the un-calculating self-surrender of youth to the eternal moment. Remarkably enough, Newman's poem "The Dream of Gerontius" also ends with a vision of Purgatory by water. An angel speaks to the soul of Gerontius:

> Softly and gently, dearly-ransom'd soul,
> In my most loving arms I now enfold thee,
> And o'er the penal waters, as they roll,
> I poise thee, and I lower thee, and hold thee.
>
> And carefully I dip thee in the lake,
> And thou, without a sob or a resistance,
> Dost through the flood thy rapid passage take,
> Sinking deep, deeper, into the dim distance.[236]

A water-Purgatory is not common in literature; a fire-Purgatory is far more usual. So this looks like more than a coincidence.

---

236 Editor's footnote: Newman, *op. cit.*, p. 169.

It may begin to appear that Eliot has a pathological obsession with old age. It is not too much to say that most of his poetry is concerned with this topic. Edmund Wilson complained about it: "'Gerontion' and 'The Waste Land' have made the young poets old before their time" and "I am made a little tired at hearing Eliot, only in his early forties, present himself as an 'aged eagle' who asks why he should make the effort to stretch his wings."[237] But Wilson fails to understand that for Eliot old age is the human condition. Old age sets in, for Eliot, at about the age of seven.[238] And here, of course, he is only continuing the Romantic tradition: "Shades of the prison-house begin to close/Upon the growing boy."[239] Eliot's poem "Animula" is his version of this sentiment. The typical scheme of an Eliot poem is as follows: *birth* (mystical, transcending time, a centre developing outwards); then *youth*, flowering in beauty, a foretaste of heaven, but the beauty is poisoned with guilt; which causes the onset of *old age* (degenerating, developing a crust of dirt and deliberation, stiffening into rigidity, all the more unhappy because of its experience of beauty in youth); finally finding release in *death*, which comes as an explosion or disintegration that may have the force of a *rebirth*. So the problem of coping with life on this earth is really the problem of coping with old age. (This indeed is the problem that Wordsworth set himself in his "Ode on Intimations of Immortality".)

Being a Greek-Phoenician, then, means being a Jew; and being a Jew means being old and encrusted with dirt and doubt; but being a Jew really means being a human being, and thus suffering from the human condition, which is old age. This might seem to mitigate very considerably Eliot's antisemitism; for it seems that his unattractive picture of the Jew is really an unattractive picture of humanity; and the Jew has been chosen (just as he was chosen by James Joyce in *Ulysses*) as a symbol of humanity. There has always been a tendency amongst Romantic writers to do this. (Eliot aspired to be a Classicist but acknowledged that he was temperamentally still a Romantic.)[240] The Wandering Jew is a symbol of humanity, because he is an alien in a hostile world, who has acquired a special wisdom because of his crime and consequent suffering. Like other Romantic figures (such as Prometheus, Cain, the Ancient Mariner, the Flying Dutchman), he is typical of humanity in so far as it is aware of itself. He is not typical of bourgeois humanity, which has no sense of alienation or guilt – consequently, though typical in one sense, he is untypical enough in another to be a Hero-figure. There is in the Romantic picture of the Wandering Jew (as a matter of fact)

---

237 Author's footnote: *Axel's Castle: A Study in the Imaginative Literature of 1870-1930*, 1931: London, 1961, p. 96 and p. 109.
238 Author's footnote: see T. S. Eliot, *Dante, op. cit.*, pp. 57-8.
239 Editor's footnote: Wordsworth, "Ode on Intimations of Immortality".
240 Editor's footnote: See Chapter 1, pp. 60-61, footnote 120.

a substratum of antisemitism. For the Wandering Jew has the romance of the criminal. He has the same glamour as Satan, who also became a hero to Byron and Shelley.[241]

But Eliot's "jew" has not even this shady glamour. He is a thoroughly degenerate figure, who, through his crime (which he is unable to acknowledge or expiate) has lost all sense of nobility and is cut off from his roots. He wallows in the slime of petty details and is wholly of this world. That he is typical of humanity is no extenuation of the antisemitism, for he is typical of humanity *at its worst* (i.e., in so far as it is unredeemed). He is the Jew of medieval legend as depicted in the "Ballad of Gernutus":

> His life was like a Barrow Hogge
>   that liveth many a day,
> But never once doth any good,
>   until men will him slay.
>
> Or like a filthy heap of dunge,
>   that lyeth in a whoard ...
> His mouth is almost full of mucke,
>   yet still he gapes for more.[242]

It should never be forgotten[243] that, in his *Criterion* articles, Eliot associated himself with Charles Maurras and Maurice Barrès, whose *Action Française* (though it failed in its objectives in France) originated the whole Fascist movement and was the inspiration of both Mussolini and Hitler. The movement with which Eliot associated himself culminated in Hitler's gas-chambers. No-one with any knowledge of cause and effect can read the antisemitic part of "Gerontion" without a shudder.[244]

In extenuation of Eliot, it must be said that he changed his attitude later, though without any public recantation, and without withdrawing his earlier poems. His later poems contain no overt anti-Jewish references; and he refused to allow the reprinting of his prose work

---

241 Editor's footnote: See Chapter 3. See also Hyam Maccoby, "The Legend of the 'Wandering Jew'", in The *Jewish Quarterly*, Volume 20, Issue 1 (1972) and Hyam Maccoby, *The Sacred Executioner, op. cit.,* pp. 166-171.
242 Editor's footnote: https://www.bl.uk/collection-items/broadside-ballad-on-the-cruelty-of-gernutus-the-jew
243 Editor's footnote: See Chapter 3.
244 Editor's footnote: I think this requires qualification. See my Memoir of Hyam Maccoby, p. 35, footnote 60 (in which I quote from Curtis, *op. cit.* and from the Author's own essay "The Antisemitism of Ezra Pound", in which the Author compares the antisemitism of Pound with that of Eliot). Clearly, there *was* a pathway from Maurras and Barrès to Hitler, but it was not the straight, direct highway implied by the Author..

After Strange Gods, probably because of its anti-Jewish content.[245] The antisemitism of the Nazi movement was clearly more than he could stomach. But there is no point to be gained by pretending (as some people have done) that the 1920 volume of poems that contains "Gerontion" is not antisemitic. The extent of the antisemitism in this volume is unsuspected even by John Harrison.[246]

The "jew" is not born; he is "spawned". Apart from the obvious antisemitic connotations of this word (the Jew is sub-human, even sub-mammalian, he is an insect or a reptile, his fertility is frightening and disgusting), there is a deeper significance. Why is the Jew's birth mentioned at all? Why is he born in an "estaminet"? Surely Eliot cannot have thought this to be a typical venue for a Jewish birth? The point is that there is another birth in the poem, the birth of Jesus – and Jesus, in the New Testament, is born in an inn. Yet the birth of Jesus in the inn is immensely different from the "spawning" of the Jew in the estaminet. One commentator, desperately trying to acquit Eliot of the charge of antisemitism, tried to argue that the "jew" is a symbol of Christ.[247] The "jew" and Christ *are* alike, but only in the sense that opposites are always alike – because they are at opposite ends of the same scale, like the minus numbers on a thermometer that echo the plus numbers. This is the kind of likeness that causes Dante to make the characteristics of Satan in Hell echo the characteristics of God in Heaven. Dante's device may even be the actual source of Eliot's procedure here. Christ, of course, was a Jew; but it does not follow that a Jew can represent Christ. *Corruptio optimi pessima*[248] -- and so the post-Christian Jew (according to Christian doctrine) is at the opposite pole to the pre-Christian Jew. Satan, too, was once an angel; and the "jew" here, as I have argued, is the representative of the Devil.

The description of the infant Jesus is a central part of "Gerontion". Eliot stresses in it the *oneness* and *centrality* of the Christ-child:

Signs are taken for wonders. "We would see a sign!"

---

245 Editor's footnote: See Chapter 3, p. 84, footnote 182, for discussion of whether this was because of the "quota" passage.

246 Author's footnote: see my "An Interpretation of 'Mr. Eliot's Sunday Morning Service'", *Critical Survey*, Jan. 1968. Editor's footnote: see next chapter (Chapter 5).

247 Editor's footnote: See Hugh Kenner, *op. cit.*, p. 111: "the Jew who was spawned in some estaminet of Antwerp cannot but prolong into the present the reputation of another who was born into a different inn". More recently, this interpretation has also been put forward by Christopher Ricks, *T. S. Eliot and Prejudice* (1988: London, 1994), p. 29: "Some of the queasy resentful feelings are bent upon a different Jew who may indeed be the owner, Christ". Still more recently, in a review of Anthony Julius's book, Jewel Spears Brooker writes: "the predator on the window sill is parodic of Christ the tiger. The landlord Jew was born in an 'estaminet' (as Julius notes, a café, but as he does not note, etymologically a barn or cowhouse) in Antwerp; the tiger Jew in a barn in Bethlehem. These characters – whether Greek, Christian or Jewish – exist in Gerontion's demented mind, and all, including himself, are represented as withered and repulsive remnants. For most readers, it would be impossible to harvest an authorial proposition from this poem." ("Eliot in the Dock" in *T. S. Eliot and Our Turning World, op. cit.*, p. 162).

248 Editor's footnote: "The corruption of the best is the worst of all".

The word within a word, unable to speak a word,
Swaddled with darkness.

It is easy to miss the point here by becoming bogged down in tracing derivations.[249] It is easy also to think one has done enough by giving prosaic explanations: "The word within a word" is the Christ-child, who is the Word (the Logos) and contains within himself the Word (the Gospel), yet cannot speak a word because he is an infant; he is "swaddled" because he is an infant, and "with darkness" because he is God, and Job says that God used darkness as a "swaddling-band" for the sea. But the real point is the contrast between the gabbling, superficial explicitness of a "sign" that gives no understanding of the thing itself, and the real "wonder", which is the inexpressible Absolute itself, existing both as an actual infant and as a kind of geometrical point of origin, like the source of the spreading ripples in a pool; as a source of energy outside space and time, surrounded by layers of meaning that emanate from it. This is the point of the images of wrappings and "within-ness" – the "word within a word" is echoed by the infant within the swaddling-clothes. These, however, are swaddling bands of darkness, because they are emanations from the light that is found in darkness and is not the light of explicitness and prosaic reality.

In *Ash Wednesday*, too (Part V), Eliot speaks of the "unspoken word" and "the light" that "shone in darkness". He speaks too of "the centre of the silent Word". The Christ-child is a "centre"; a source, which is One, but is the fountain and origin of variety. To mediate between the One and the Many was the function of the Logos in Stoic and Philonic philosophy; and this idea enters Christianity in the Gospel of St John. One of Eliot's great preoccupations (stemming from his work as a philosophical research student on Leibnitz and Bradley) is the relation between the One and the Many. He feels this problem even as a problem of poetical technique. How is he to express the Word in those awkward, sprawling, intractable things, words? It is an "intolerable wrestle"[250]; but he sees the trouble very quickly: it is a question of never losing sight of the One for the sake of achieving explicitness in some

---

[249] Author's footnote: The main source is a sermon by Lancelot Andrewes. Other sources, used by Andrewes, are Matthew 12: 38-39 (in which "certain of the scribes and the Pharisees" say to Jesus: "Master, we would see a sign from thee", to which Jesus answers: "An evil and adulterous generation seeketh after a sign") and Job 38:9: "When I made the cloud the garment thereof and thick darkness a swaddling-band for it".

Editor's footnote: The sermon was preached by Bishop Andrewes before James 1 at Whitehall on Christmas Day, 1618. The passage in question is: "Signs are taken for wonders. 'Master, we would fain see a sign,' that is a miracle. And in this sense it is a sign to wonder at. Indeed, every word here is a wonder.... an infant, *Verbum infans*, the Word without a word; the eternal Word not able to speak a word.... swaddled, and that a wonder too. 'He,' that (as in the thirty-eighth of Job he saith) 'taketh the vast body of the main sea, turns it to and fro, as a little child, and rolls it about with the swaddling-bands of darkness;' – He to come thus into clouts, Himself!" (Lancelot Andrewes, *Ninety-Six Sermons*, Vol. 1: *The Nativity, Repentance and Fasting*, 1631: Oxford 1841: reprinted Kerry, Ireland, 2018, p. 86; italics in original.)

[250] Editor's footnote: "East Coker", II.

artificially detached segment of it. This is the reason for Eliot's obscurity; he tries to achieve a texture of writing in which the full grain or pattern can be found wherever one splits the work. On the other hand, centrality must not be achieved by mere abstractness, at the expense of the concrete particulars. Graininess is the aim: a combination of universality and particularity.

If the Christ-child is the symbol of Oneness and centrality, the "jew" is the symbol of plurality and disintegration (which means flying off from connection with the centre). That is why the "jew" is not born but "spawned"; he is not a single centre, but one of a swarm. A few lines later, there is a list of miscellaneous, odd, unconnected items:

Rocks, moss, stonecrop, iron, merds.

This is the world that the "jew" inhabits. He was born in an "estaminet" because he is a wanderer who belongs nowhere. Even where he was born is not his home, because he has no roots, and moves restlessly from Antwerp to Brussels to London. (Jesus was born in an inn because his home is not in this world but in eternity.) The atomization and confusingly detailed non-relation that are the world (one might say the spiritual home) of the "jew" are expressed elsewhere in the poem; in the "cunning passages, contrived corridors" of history, in the "thousand small deliberations" and in the "fractured atoms". The winds too, which are mentioned so often, symbolize directionless, meaningless lack of relation and connectedness[251]; and, in the end, they symbolize death, the negation of life and meaning[252]. So the "jew" is the representative of Death, like the hovering creature in Newman's poem.

We may now ask the question: "How is it that Eliot's 'jew' is so utterly different from the actual Jew?" The real Jew is not rootless; he is rooted in his ancestral home, the Holy Land, from which he was forcibly ejected by the Romans[253] but which he never forgot. After two thousand years of exile in which he mentioned Jerusalem in his prayers many times a day[254], he finally returned to his land and immediately showed in its defence that he had not

---

251 Editor's footnote: For an explanation of "I have no ghosts", see the analysis in Chapter 6 (pp. 141-144, especially p. 144) of the ghosts in the rose-garden in "Burnt Norton" I.

252 Editor's footnote: But at the end of the poem, the destroying wind also becomes, as the Author writes, "revivifying", in the image of the gull battling against it, in a restoration of the "flow of the universe". See below.

253 Editor's footnote: I find it puzzling that my father wrote this, because he was always well aware that this is a myth. See his Preface to his posthumously published book, *Antisemitism and Modernity*, op. cit., p. xii: "there is still a widely-believed myth that the Jews were expelled by the Romans 2000 years ago from Palestine (a myth that has religious overtones connected with the alleged killing of Christ by the Jews). In actual fact, the Jews continued to form the majority of the Palestinian population for many centuries after that date." It seems that here my father succumbed to the power of the myth.

254 Editor's footnote: Again, my father knew perfectly well that the Jewish religious idea of a return to Jerusalem was bound up with the concept of the Messianic Age, definitely not with the idea of a secular state. My father's

lost the heroic qualities that shook the Roman Empire to its foundations.[255] As for being born or "spawned" in an "estaminet" (which suggests shallow or shifting family ties), the Jew's domestic life, throughout his exile and in the most difficult conditions, has been remarkable for its warmth, sweetness and indomitable loyalty, contrasting sharply with the frequent lovelessness and bitter family antagonisms of his non-Jewish neighbours. The rearing and education of children has been performed with unexampled labour and self-sacrifice.[256]

But the most important sense in which a person can be called "rootless" is in lacking a tradition or cultural heritage. It is almost incredible (on any ordinary reckoning of the facts) that the Jew should be chosen as an example (let alone the prime example) of this kind of person. Of all people in the world, the Jew has behind him (both in fact and in his consciousness of the fact) the longest continuous tradition. His own special culture (with its rich development of philosophy, theology, mysticism, poetry, music, history, law, science) has existed for 4,000 years, and has mixed fruitfully with every other culture of importance on its way; and yet its roots stretch back even further for another 2,000 years, into the civilisations of Mesopotamia and Egypt (Abraham was a cultured Chaldean and Moses was brought up as a cultured Egyptian).[257] 6,000 years are summed up in the mind of the Jew, the entire historical period of Man. (One wonders who is really inside the "house" and who is squatting enviously outside the window.) Yet the Jewish mind is no fossil, but alive with eager inquiry, and in the forefront of every modern topic of speculation and research. One would have thought that Eliot, with his views on the importance of Tradition and a sense of history, would have fixed on the Jew as the embodiment of his principles. But no; he fixes on the Jew as the embodiment of the very opposite: a soulless materialism rooted only in the present, grubbing about in unrelated particulars. This is something that demands an explanation.

---

own grandfather was bitterly and adamantly opposed to Herzl's political aim of a secular Jewish State in historic Palestine (see my Memoir).

255 Editor's footnote: No mention at all is made here of what is nowadays widely recognized as the ethnic cleansing of 700,000 Palestinian Arabs in order to create a Jewish-majority State. See in particular Norman G. Finkelstein, *Image and Reality of the Israel-Palestine Conflict, op. cit.,* Chapter 3, pp. 51-87. Note also Finkelstein's summing up of the conclusions reached by the mostly Israeli New Historians, who, he writes (*ibid.,* p. 51): "argue five major points: 1. the Zionist movement did not in principle support the partition of Palestine. 2. the surrounding Arab states did not unite as one to destroy the nascent Jewish State. 3. the war did not pit a relatively defenseless and weak Jewish David against a relatively strong Arab Goliath. 4. Palestine's Arabs did not take flight at the behest of Arab orders; and 5. Israel was not earnestly seeking peace at the war's end".

256 Editor's footnote: The cohesiveness of Jewish family life is well-known; but there is perhaps a touch of chauvinism here (see my Editor's Memoir of Hyam Maccoby).

257 Editor's footnote: That is, according to the Hebrew Bible. There is no archaeological evidence of the existence of either Abraham or Moses. See Israel Finkelstein and Neil Asher Silberman, *The Bible Unearthed: Archaeology's New Vision of Ancient Israel and the Origin of its Sacred Texts*, New York, 2001, Chapters 1 and 2. But of course the Israelites/Jews were deeply influenced by the ancient civilisations of Egypt and Mesopotamia.

The explanation lies in Christian doctrine. This is to the effect that the Jews, 2,000 years ago, missed the boat. They made the greatest error in all history by rejecting Jesus Christ; and, therefore, all their development after that point is not of the slightest interest or importance. This has easily led into the assumption that they *had* no development after that point, or even that they lost whatever ideals they previously had and became simply null. The true heirs of the Jewish culture (according to this theory) were the Christians. They are the true Israel; and the Old Testament, as well as the New, really belongs to them. The whole theory has been buttressed by a steadfast and complacent ignorance of every development in Judaism during the last 2,000 years. The Jews are regarded with some satisfaction as a degraded nation.[258] It is necessary for the truth of Christianity that they *should* be a degraded nation. Nothing gives a more traumatic shock to Christians than the occasional realisation of how high Jewish morale remains despite everything that has been done to lower it. The Jews do not regard themselves as having missed the boat, and indeed consider that they have been sitting firmly in the boat the whole time, waiting for the storm to subside.

In the Middle Ages, the continuing misery and exile of the Jews was regarded as a potent proof of the truth of Christianity. This was an important reason (together with the belief that the Second Coming of Jesus would be preceded by the conversion of the Jews) that the Jews were not exterminated altogether like the Albigenses. But Eliot's antisemitism is more than the traditional Christian view that the Jew was condemned to expiate his crime by a life prolonged in misery. For Eliot, as we have seen, was much influenced by modern antisemites such as Charles Maurras and Maurice Barrès, who cast the Jew in a grander and more diabolical role, as the originator of all divisive and individualistic tendencies in the modern world. Individualism, to Maurras and Barrès, was the enemy; for individualism meant pride, or holding out against God. Individualism took the form of demanding *justice*; and this led to democracy, liberalism, socialism, communism, capitalism, usury and all the other evils of modernism. Individualism, in this view, led in particular to the mass society in which each person became a kind of social atom, the member of an impersonal swarm, rather than the member of a single organism, the Body of Christ. It is this theory that is conveyed by Eliot's word "spawned", indicating the mass insect-society of the modern city, the development of which Maurras traced to Judaism. For the "jew" (as the mention of Antwerp, Brussels and London shows) is essentially a city creature. The swarm of the city

---

[258] Editor's footnote: As a result of the post-Holocaust Jewish-Christian dialogue in which my father was deeply involved (see my Editor's Memoir of Hyam Maccoby), there has been genuine Jewish-Christian reconciliation, and Christian attitudes to Judaism and Jews have changed enormously. In 1969, there was much more evidence of Christian supremacism than we find nowadays (however, there does seem to me to be a touch of paranoia here; see my Editor's Memoir of Hyam Maccoby).

lacks the personal bond that is provided by the Communion of the Church. Once again, the "jew" is the agent of disintegration, working always against One-ness.

And, of course, this is in a way a true insight; for Judaism is indeed the religion of individualism, which continually works against the desire for a mystical union with some corporate entity. Judaism is the religion that respects the status of Man and denies all attempts to confuse Man with God or God with Man. Even Jewish mysticism aims, not at union with God, but at a vision of God; and the highest variety of this vision is achieved standing up and in full consciousness.[259] But that this individualism necessarily leads to impersonality or atomism will be regarded as ludicrous by anyone who knows the community-spirit of the Jews. And if there is one feature of Jewish thinking that is typical, it is universalism – whether it is the universalism of the One God or of the Classless Society. The Jew seeks connectedness; but there must be definite things to connect. He hates vagueness and being swallowed up.

Though the "jew" is mentioned openly only once in the poem, his presence is hinted at several times later. One of these hints is the use of the words "flowering judas", which means literally a kind of flowering bush or tree. Almost the entire line in which these words occur has been traced to *The Education of Henry Adams*[260]; but, again, derivation is not explanation. Eliot would not use the word without attention to its double meaning. I think that there is even a reference to the "jew" in the strange, coined word "juvescence". Certainly, the repetition of the syllable "ju-", in two words so near together, not long after a passage about "the jew", cannot be a coincidence in a writer so careful and close-textured as Eliot.

To understand these oblique references, we have to attend to the sequence of the poem up to this point. The old man, Gerontion, after explaining his own dismal situation, suddenly conjures up a picture of the Christ-child, the dark centre, the Birth. Now he goes on to talk about youth:

---

[259] Editor's footnote: See Gershom Scholem on the difference between Catholic and Jewish mysticism in relation to the concept of "communion" with God: "Whereas in Catholic mysticism, 'communion' was not the last step on the mystical way ... in Kabbalism it is the last grade of ascent to God. It is not union, because union with God is denied to man even in that mystical upsurge of the soul, according to Kabbalistic theology." (*The Messianic Idea in Judaism and Other Essays on Jewish Spirituality*, 1971: New York, 1995, pp. 203-204.) See also Gershom Scholem, *Major Trends in Jewish Mysticism*, 1941: London, 1955, p. 56: "The Creator and His creature remain apart, and nowhere is an attempt made to bridge the gulf between them or to blur the distinction. The mystic who in his ecstasy has passed through all the gates, braved all the dangers, now stands before the throne; he sees and hears – but that is all."

[260] Editor's footnote: George Williamson, *op. cit.*, p. 109. See also Henry Adams, *The Education of Henry Adams, op. cit.*, p. 226: "Here and there a negro log cabin alone disturbed the dogwood and the judas-tree, the azalea and the laurel. The tulip and the chestnut gave no sense of struggle against a stingy nature.... No European spring had shown him the same intermixture of delicate grace and passionate depravity that marked the Maryland May."

In the juvescence of the year
Came Christ the tiger

In depraved May, dogwood and chestnut, flowering judas,
To be eaten, to be divided, to be drunk
Among whispers.

Here we have proliferation, flowering fertility. But accompanying them are fear, guilt, treachery, sin, decay, death. The "jew" is the agent of the decay that is inseparable from all growth, the maggot within the apple. "Flowering judas" expresses this; the coming to beauty of the flower brings about its own betrayal. The finest things are those that contain the most poison; and the poison, working against life where it is most vital, is the "jew". The "jew" too has a kind of vitality and fertility – this was expressed by the word "spawned". But it is the vitality and fertility of the germ or bacillus; or of a cancer, working against the principle of the organism. All this is expressed in the word "juvescence". This is a neologism (the correct word is "juvenescence"), not a mistake. Eliot has a habit of placing such a surprise-word in a strategic position; and the word usually turns out to contain the whole poem wrapped up in itself, like the Christ-child in his swaddling-clothes. "Juvescence" means primarily "youth"; but it evokes many other words too: "jew", "juice", "essence", "effervescence". It means "youth, containing the juice of reality, but fermenting with Jewish bacteria, which are the beginnings of its rottenness, though they are inseparable from its vitality". Even this does not exhaust the meaning of the word; for the ending "—escence" carries the meaning "becoming" or "growing" (as in "senescence" and "adolescence"). So "juvescence" means "growing young". The year has been old, in the winter, but it is growing young again. Though youth contains in itself the seeds of death, yet death contains in itself the seeds of rebirth. It was in the depth of winter, the death-time of the year, that the Christ-child was born.

The Devil/"jew" is in the service of Death; but he has his own horrid vitality, a kind of anti-life. This appears later in the poem in the form of the spider and the weevil:

What will the spider do,
Suspend its operations, will the weevil
Delay?

The spider and the weevil are the busy agents of disintegration. Probably the spider, like the "jew", "squats on the window-sill"; and both the spider and the weevil could be said to be "spawned". Similarly, in "Burbank", the "jew" appears as a king rat, "underneath" all the other rats, who are "underneath the piles".[261] Rats, too, are busy agents of death who are "spawned". To the Christian, the ceaseless activity of the Jew seems a fearsome thing, rather like the restless industry of a dung-beetle. To Eliot, the "jew" is one who has rejected the vision of youth and who has therefore become reconciled to being old. Old age is his way of life, which he embraces with disgusting eagerness and activity. He is thus the arch-materialist, who places all his hopes and interest in the things of this world; he is the old miser who busily accumulates and counts his unrusting pieces of gold, blind to the beauty of things that must fade because they are young. But Gerontion is, after all, despite his old age, not a "jew"; for he is "waiting for rain" – that is, for the renewal of youth.[262] He is thus unhappy and lethargic in his old age; and this is the guarantee that he is saved; the worst thing for an old man is complacency, which means that he has accepted old age and is damned:

> Do not let me hear
> Of the wisdom of old men, but rather of their folly[263]

and

> Old men ought to be explorers[264]

and

> Let me disclose the gifts reserved for age
> To set a crown upon your lifetime's effort.
> First, the cold friction of expiring sense
> Without enchantment, offering no promise
> But bitter tastelessness of shadow fruit
> As body and soul begin to fall asunder.[265]

One can almost say that for Eliot the greatest merit of Christianity is that it prevents the middle-aged and old-aged from being happy. Hell is to be an old man and immortal like Tiresias, the central figure of *The Waste Land*. Even more a figure of damnation is the

---

261 Editor's footnote: T. S. Eliot, *Selected Poems, op. cit.*, p. 35.
262 Editor's footnote: See Genesius Jones, *op. cit.*, p. 101. Jones writes of Gerontion: "while he is in a dry season, he is nonetheless waiting for rain".
263 Editor's footnote: "East Coker", II.
264 Editor's footnote: "East Coker", V.
265 Editor's footnote: "Little Gidding", II.

"jew", who does not even *want* death and rebirth. (He is thus a far more ignoble figure than the Wandering Jew of Romantic legend, who regards his immortality as a burden.) But the idea that there could be something noble in the acceptance of maturity and of the tasks of this world is an idea that is foreign to both the Romantics and Eliot. The Jewish idea of the nobility and gaiety of old age is to Eliot the worst of heresies. Jewish religious dances are performed by the old men. There is nothing ridiculous about this in Jewish eyes. For the Jew considers that there is dignity, beauty and enjoyment in maturity and limitation; in being a man as well as in being God. This is the true Classicism; Eliot's (and T. E. Hulme's) "classicism" is only a disappointed Romanticism.

Jewish energy and ability to "get on", which seem to the Christian to spring from some diabolical source of anti-life, arise not from any special talents or racial characteristics (as can be seen by comparison with those other Semites, the Arabs[266]) , but from the Jewish religion, which is the only one in the world that aims at inducing a heightening of waking consciousness, rather than a state of trance. And this is because Judaism is the only religion that promotes the idea that it is a joyful (if strenuous) thing to be an adult human being. However, to the Christian this is a betrayal. The Jewish sense of the joyousness of the "concrete particular"[267] is interpreted as a soulless materialism; a betrayal of the universality and God-consciousness of youth; a betrayal of the Young God. So the Jew becomes a "jew", who is also a "judas"; and the Jewish energy becomes the effervescence of treachery – "flowering judas". It cannot be a coincidence that the arch-traitor of the Christian myth was given the name "Judas". This noble name, full of honour in Jewish history as the name of the warrior son of Jacob, of the Royal tribe, of the heroic Maccabee, of the Rabbi Prince of the Mishnah, and of the Jewish people itself[268], was degraded by Christianity into a synonym of meanness and treachery.

There are many aspects of "Gerontion" on which I have not touched. The poem is in fact a blueprint for all Eliot's subsequent poetry. Eliot intended at first to include "Gerontion" in *The Waste Land,* as a kind of introduction. He was dissuaded from this by Ezra Pound;[269] but, instead, the poem can be read as an introduction to everything Eliot subsequently wrote,

---

266 Editor's footnote: This is a clear example of the typical triumphalism manifested by Jews in the wake of the Six-Day War. As I wrote in my Editor's Memoir of Hyam Maccoby, it is deeply ironic that, in the very same essay in which my father (in my view, justifiably) protests against Christian triumphalism and supremacism over Judaism and Jews, he exhibits Jewish triumphalism and supremacism over "the Arabs".

267 Editor's footnote: See the discussion of Eliot's concept of the One and the Many above, page 110.

268 Editor's footnote: See Maccoby, *Judas Iscariot and the Myth of Jewish Evil, op. cit.*

269 Editor's footnote: See *The Letters of T. S. Eliot, Volume 1, op. cit.,* pp. 504-505. Eliot wrote to Pound, in January 1922: "Do you advise printing Gerontion as prelude in book or pamphlet form?" Pound replied: "I do *not* advise printing Gerontion as preface. One dont [sic] miss it AT all as the thing now stands. To be more lucid still, let me say that I advise you NOT to print Gerontion as prelude." (Emphasis and capitals in original.)

including the *Quartets*. A whole essay[270] could be written on the importance of the theme of violence in "Gerontion". This is such an important theme, however, that it needs to be dealt with in relation to Eliot's poetry as a whole, including the plays.

Some points may be briefly mentioned here. "Gerontion" opens and closes with violence. Gerontion regrets, in the beginning of the poem, the fact that his 19th century youth failed to provide the experience of violent action that he would have had in the ancient world ("hot gates" – Thermopylae) or in the Renaissance world ("cutlasses"). At the end of the poem, the mood of sterility and boredom is dissipated by an explosion of violence ("fractured atoms"); and the exploded fragments find relief in the Gulf. Halfway through the poem, there is violence too – "Christ the tiger" is a violent figure who is himself the victim of violence. In general, the Romantic feeling of the boredom and stagnation of the maturing process can be relieved only by violence. He who lives to the full (i.e., youthfully) meets a violent end. Only violence can break through the hard crust of old age. (Gerontion talks of the time when his corpse will "stiffen in a rented house", but he means that the stiffening process has been under way for some time before death.) Violence is needed to re-establish the flow of the universe, so that the gull will be swept along by the destroying and vivifying wind.[271] Violence is an inseparable part of the Christian myth, with its worship of youth, and its origin in the human-sacrificial rites of the Adonis cult.

Christianity is an essentially Romantic faith; and Eliot, who is best understood as the heir of the post-Romantic movement, forged the inevitable and logical link between literary

---

270 Editor's footnote: My father did write this essay; and it is included in this book as the title essay, Chapter 1, "Christ the Tiger" (probably written about 1970).

271 Editor's footnote: In an early draft, the poem ends, after "fractured atoms": "We have saved a shilling against oblivion/Even oblivious./ Tenants of an old man's house,/Thoughts of a dry brain in a dry season." (T. S. Eliot, *Inventions of the March Hare, op. cit.*, p. 351.) "Saved" seems to have a double meaning here: the possibility of redemption, with a sense of purgation in the mention of the small coin (like the small coin the narrator gives the waiter in "Dans le Restaurant" so he can have a bath); yet "saved" also implies "profit", associating Gerontion with the "jew" (in the new version this is replaced by "the Trades"). In the new lines, the "white feathers in the snow" seem also to have contrary associations. On the one hand, the whiteness symbolizes the hope of purification in the waters of the Gulf, and the association with the white-feathered seagull suggests the hope of rebirth; in the courage, strength, resilience and beauty of the seagull (see "Cape Ann": "But resign this land at the end, resign it/ To its true owner, the tough one, the sea-gull"), the "flow of the universe", as the Author writes, is resurrected by the violent explosion. The feathers could be seen as having been blown off the seagull by the force of the wind against which it battles; or it could be that the seagull becomes a sacrificial victim; it is both given energy and destroyed by the wind. On the other hand, the white feathers and the snow seem also to symbolize the cowardice, coldness and forgetfulness of Gerontion that need to be purged -- white feathers symbolizing cowardice, as they did in Britain during the First World War; while the winter snow, which contrasts with the "warm rain" at the beginning of the poem, could be seen as representing the coldness and forgetfulness of old age -- "oblivious" is like the "forgetful snow" in *The Waste Land* I. (In the earlier version, Gerontion and the others are "saved" from "oblivion" even though they are "oblivious".) In the new version, there is also a sense of the fragmentation (feathers, snowflakes) of the "fractured atoms" which, falling from the sky in the snow, find, as the Author writes, the "relief" of unity and purgation in the Gulf.

Romanticism and Christianity (Eliot saw Baudelaire as an unconscious Christian[272]). And violence, let us remember, is also an essential ingredient in the philosophy of Fascism, which was the bastard child of the great Romantic movement. The Jew, however, has always been an anti-Romantic, denying the need for violence, and setting up peace as his ideal. The Jew is the only person in the world who can stand the strain of peace and is not continually longing for the excitement of violence. He never fights unless he is forced to; the Jews have never, in their long history, had a professional army, and all their military triumphs against the Greeks, the Romans and the Arabs, were won with amateur, civilian armies, gathered together for an emergency.[273]

If I were asked to characterise the historic role of the Jews in one sentence, I should say: "The Jews are the opponents of human sacrifice." This is a role that is even more necessary in the modern world than the ancient world; for the modern world is preparing for itself a holocaust that will make all the blood-festivals of the Phoenician Moloch-worshippers or the Aztec sun-worshippers seem insignificant.[274]

Another essay[275] that could be written about "Gerontion" would deal with its relation to the limpid *Ariel* poems "Journey of the Magi" and "A Song for Simeon", also poems about old men who, by a vision of the Christ-child, have been jolted out of the damnation of senile complacency. I will only repeat, in this connection, that I disagree profoundly with those critics who say that Gerontion's sense of sterility shows him to be a damned soul who has lost his faith.[276] On the contrary, his sense of sterility shows that he is *not* a damned soul – that his youthful vision of God is still sufficiently alive to prevent him from ever being happy and satisfied in this world.[277]

---

[272] Editor's footnote: See Eliot's essay on Baudelaire: "When Baudelaire's Satanism is dissociated from its less creditable paraphernalia, it amounts to a dim intuition of a part, but a very important part, of Christianity." (T. S Eliot, *Selected Prose*, London, 1953, p. 187.)

[273] Editor's footnote: See my Editor's Memoir of Hyam Maccoby (p. 34) for my comments on this paragraph and reference to the chapter on the Six Day War in Norman Finkelstein's book *Image and Reality of the Israel-Palestine Conflict, op. cit.*

[274] Editor's footnote: The threat of a nuclear holocaust is just as relevant nowadays – in fact, even more so – as it was in 1969. Tragically, however, the Jewish State has betrayed the Jewish tradition by becoming, in 2023-2025, a genocidal state that is a major flashpoint of escalating warfare.

[275] Editor's footnote: Unfortunately, it seems my father never wrote this essay.

[276] Editor's footnote: For instance, Grover Smith writes of Gerontion's "religious despair.... He can find neither faith through love nor love through faith." (*T. S. Eliot's Poetry and Plays, op. cit.*, pp. 63-4.)

[277] Editor's footnote: This helps to explain the lines beginning "We have not reached conclusion". Manju Jain points out (*op. cit.*, p. 93) that "the backward devils" is a reference to Dante's *Inferno* XX, in which Dante sees the souls of seers, augurs and diviners (among them Tiresias), who are condemned to walk backwards because of their doomed attempts to look forward into the future. Gerontion specifically dissociates himself from the "backward devils". Instead, he looks forward, after death, to purgatory and rebirth in Heaven. Yet Jain writes of "Gerontion's inability to believe despite the knowledge that he will thereby forgo the possibility of salvation" (*op. cit.*, p. 86).

My main object here, however, has been to discuss the "jew" in "Gerontion" and to argue that the "jew" is neither peripheral nor an aberration either in this poem or in Eliot's thought generally; that the "jew" is a central figure. Eliot ceased to make antisemitic references in his later poetry (or made them in a heavily disguised form); but that does not prove that his attitude towards the Jews changed fundamentally. He was shocked by the practical results in Germany of the Maurras-Barrès anti-Dreyfusard doctrine that appealed to him so much in his youth[278]. He did not subscribe to the "final solution". He was one of those "good" Christians who believe that it is a commendable thing not to persecute the Jews, in spite of everything. These indeed are the Christians who have often protected Jews from the worst effects of persecution; and such Christians are certainly to be preferred to the active persecutors, torturers and murderers (even though Christian forgiveness is often very hard to bear). But one must protest when these worthy people are cited, as they often are, as vindicating the Christian record. To teach that the Jews are the arch-traitors of history and then to hold up one's hands in sorrow when simple-minded people take one's teaching literally is hardly admirable. There is something seriously wrong with a civilisation in which the Jews' only protection is the principle that one ought to be kind even to the Devil.[279]

On the contrary, he remains faithful to his youthful vision of the Christ-child and to the memory of the youthful sexual drive, refusing to compromise with the world by retaining a passion that would inevitably be deteriorated and corrupted by maturity and old age: "I have lost my passion; why should I need to keep it/When what is kept must be adulterated?" Re: "I that was near your heart am removed therefrom/To lose beauty in terror, terror in inquisition", this seems to indicate that the "beauty" of his youthful sexual drive was lost in the "terror" of sin and guilt; but then the youthful "terror" was lost in the boredom of the ruminations and self-questionings of old age: the "Thoughts of a dry brain in a dry season". But the vision of the explosion at the end of the poem is one of renewed "terror", leading to the hope of renewal and rebirth. "The boredom, and the horror, and the glory" (see Chapter 2) are very much apparent in this poem.

278 Editor's footnote: See my Editor's Memoir of Hyam Maccoby, p. 35, footnote 60, (in which I quote from Curtis, *op. cit.* and from the Author's own essay "The Antisemitism of Ezra Pound", in which the Author compares the antisemitism of Pound with that of Eliot). It seems a leap too far to call the Holocaust "the practical results in Germany of the Maurras/Barrès doctrine".

279 Editor's footnote: See my comments on this paragraph in my Editor's Memoir of Hyam Maccoby, pp. 36-37.

Chapter 5: AN INTERPRETATION OF "MR. ELIOT'S SUNDAY MORNING SERVICE"[280]

Polyphiloprogenitive
The sapient sutlers of the Lord
Drift across the window-panes.
In the beginning was the Word.

Commentators (influenced by the superscription from *The Jew of Malta*) take the "sapient sutlers" to be the clergy, on whom the whole poem is generally supposed to be a satiric comment. But why are the clergy "polyphiloprogenitive"? Grover Smith[281] is reduced to saying that this is a reference to the lechery of the clergy in *The Jew of Malta.* But to be lecherous is a very different thing from desiring many children. It is difficult to understand, anyway, why the morals of some 16th century fictional friars, as reported by the villains of the play, should be made the basis of a satirical attack on the clergy generally. Also, why do the clergy "Drift across the window-panes"? Is it simply that the poet is in church, and the clergy are observed to cross the windows outside? What can be the point of this?

The name given to the Deity in this verse is "the Lord". In the next verse it is τὸ ἕν, and in the third verse, "the Baptized God". "The Lord" has an Old Testament ring. I suggest that the first verse refers to the Old Testament view of God, the second verse to that of the Greek philosophers, and the third to that of the New Testament, a compound or fusion of the previous two. The "sapient sutlers of the Lord" are the Jews. "Sutlers" means "petty traders in food and drink".[282] A strong anti-Jewish bias is to be expected of Eliot at this period of his

---

280 Editor's footnote: Originally published in The *Critical Survey*, Winter 1967, Vol 3: 3. Reprinted in *European Judaism*, Winter 1983/4, Vol. 17: 2. I have used the original text from The *Critical Survey*. Reprinted by kind permission of Berghahn Journals.

281 Author's footnote: Grover Smith, *T. S. Eliot's Poetry and Plays, op. cit.*, p. 43.

Editor's footnote:: Smith writes:"Barabas the Jew and Ithamore, his servant, themselves guilty of having just poisoned a convent of nuns, are reviling the morals of ecclesiastics. When the two friars, the 'religious caterpillars,' appear, Barabas, because they know of his crimes, offers to become a Christian, to do penance, and, what is more to their liking, to hand over his riches to them. Eliot takes from this imbroglio a double hint: that the clergy (here presbyters) are insatiate of gain and that they are immoderate in their fleshly lusts."

282 Editor's footnote: Anthony Julius (*op. cit.*, pp. 6-7; see my Editor's Preface) argues that the dictionary definition of "sutlers" is "suppliers of food and drink to an army" and that the army in question must be the members of the Christian communion. But it is a question of associations with trade, with "the profit and the loss" (*The Waste Land*

career. He would regard the Jews as chiefly traders, and their religion as being very much concerned with food and drink, both because of the Jewish dietary laws and because of the Temple sacrifices (cf. Romans, 14: 17: "for the kingdom of God is not meat and drink"). The "of" in "sutlers of the Lord" is both possessive and objective. The Jews are the people of the Lord, to whom He gives commandments about food and drink; and they also provide the Lord with food and drink in the form of animal sacrifices and drink-offerings. The Jews are called "sapient" because of their pride in the wisdom of the Law (I Corinthians 1: 20: "hath not God made foolish the wisdom of this world?"). The Jews are called "polyphiloprogenitive" because of their high estimate of fruitfulness ("Be fruitful and multiply"[283] is the first commandment in the Old Testament); because of their desire for their own increase (Genesis 22: 17: "I will multiply thy seed as the stars of heaven and as the sand which is upon the sea shore"); and also, perhaps, because of the characteristic Jewish family affection that Ezra Pound made a subject of attack in Canto XXXV.[284] ("Philoprogenitive" can mean "fond of one's children" as well as "desirous of offspring".) The stanza is saying that the Jews of the Old Testament had a materialistic religious attitude. They regarded themselves as "sutlers" providing God with food and drink and expecting in return material benefits. They failed to appreciate the non-material, spiritual nature of God, as described by Greek philosophers and expressed in John's statement: "In the beginning was the Word". Accordingly, the Jews have failed to establish their religion in the world; they "Drift across the window-panes". This is rather like a line of "Gerontion" (published in the same volume of poems): "And the jew squats on the window-sill, the owner". Eliot sees the "jew" as outside the House (European civilisation), peering in through the window, or drifting by it. The "jew" may own the House (in part, a reference to his supposed financial power), but he can never be resident in it; nor can he detach himself from it. The next line in "Gerontion" is: "Spawned in some estaminet of Antwerp". The word "spawned" expresses, like "polyphiloprogenitive",

---

IV), which are always identified by Eliot with Jews, not of dictionary definitions. If the "sutlers" are taken to be the Christian clergy, we lose the typically Eliotic ambiguity in "of" – the Jews of the Old Testament (or the Hebrew Bible, as it is known nowadays) belong to God, but also supply God with food and drink, in the form of animal sacrifices and drink-offerings in the Temple. And Julius does not explain "polyphiloprogenitive" or "Drift across the window-pane" (or indeed the rest of the poem). Even if we were to go along with Julius's insistence that "sutlers" must mean traders with an army, this does not have to mean the army of the Christian communion; it can be pointed out that a) in the Hebrew Bible, God is often called "the Lord of Hosts", meaning the army of angels; b) in 19th century America, as Eliot would probably have known, many of the sutlers who supplied the military were Jews: see an interview with David. S Koffman on the Jewish Currents website (March 7, 2019): "the Jews who worked provisioning the military – they're called sutlers –moved around and sold dry goods and foodstuffs to the military".

https://jewishcurrents.org/americas-jewish-colonizers

283 Editor's footnote: Genesis 1: 28.

284 Editor's footnote: "Tsievitz/has explained to me the warmth of affections,/the intramural, the almost intravaginal warmth of/hebrew affections, in the family, and nearly everything else", *The Cantos of Ezra Pound*, London, 1964, pp. 177-178.

but more openly, Eliot's dislike of the Jews' fertility. Another instance of the connection in Eliot's mind between Jews and windows is in "Sweeney Among the Nightingales", where a man (identifiable as a Jew by his "heavy eyes" and "golden grin", i.e. gold teeth) "Leaves the room and reappears/Outside the window, leaning in".[285]

If the above interpretation of the first stanza is correct, the superscription from Marlowe's *The Jew of Malta* acquires a new significance. It is Ithamore the Turk who speaks the words "Look, look, master, here comes two religious caterpillars" to his master, the Jew Barabas. It is, partly at least, the incomprehension shown by the non-Christians of the function of the Christian clergy to which Eliot wishes to draw attention by his superscription. If, indeed, Eliot were attacking the clergy in this poem, the villains of *The Jew of Malta* would be strange allies to call to his support.

> In the beginning was the Word.
> Superfetation of τὸ ἕν,
> And at the mensual turn of time,
> Produced enervate Origen.

The second verse deals with the opposite error to that of the Jews: namely, the error of adopting a view of God that was *too* spiritual. This was the error of the pagan philosophers who developed the idea of God as an impersonal One, which produced the Word or Logos as an emanation. This view of the Logos came into conflict, in the Christian Church, with the doctrine of the Word made Flesh, and the doctrine of the full Divinity of Christ. Origen, who was over-infected with Greek philosophy, came to despise the flesh, as his reputed self-castration showed; and he held heretical views on the status of the Incarnate God.[286]

Thus the reason for the repetition of the line "In the beginning was the Word" becomes clear. At the end of the first verse, it appears as the statement of a truth, correcting the mistake of the Jews and explaining their failure. At the beginning of the second stanza, it

---

285 Author's footnote: See John Harrison, *op. cit.*, p. 149.
   Editor's footnote: Also see Chapter 2.

286 Editor's footnote: For a summary of Origen's heretical views, see the Rev. Alexander Roberts, D. D., and James Donaldson, L. L. D. (eds.), *Ante-Nicene Christian Library, Translations of the Writings of the Fathers Down to A. D. 325, Volume X: The Writings of Origen, Volume 1, Translated by Rev. Frederick Crombie*, Edinburgh, 1869, Introductory Notice, p. vii: "The points on which it was held that he had plainly departed from the Christian faith, were the four following: -- *First*, That the souls of men had existed in a previous state, and that their imprisonment in material bodies was a punishment for sins which they had then committed. *Second*, That the human soul of Christ had also previously existed, and been united to the Divine nature before the Incarnation of the Son of God which is related in the Gospels. *Third*, That our material bodies shall be transformed into absolutely ethereal ones at the resurrection; and *fourth*, That all men, and even devils, shall be finally restored through the mediation of Christ."

appears as a proposition which itself requires further consideration and qualification if it is to escape heresy.

It may be objected that it was in fact a Jewish thinker, Philo, who first applied the Logos theory to Biblical theology. But this is just the kind of fact that is liable to be ignored or discounted by someone with an anti-Jewish axe to grind.

Why is the Word a "superfetation"? What is the point of the word "mensual"? And what is meant by saying that the Word, produced by the One, itself then produced Origen? Grover Smith introduces here some curious speculations about the sexuality of God the Father in begetting the Son[287]; but these speculations are, in my opinion, beside the point, since the stanza is referring not to Christian doctrine, but to Greek philosophy. I suggest that the image elaborated in this stanza is that the Word is an egg. The One produced an egg, the Logos (probably to be identified with the Primal Egg of mythology); and this egg "at the mensual turn of time" (that is, after the proper period of gestation), produced Origen. I would even suggest that there is here a sly pun on the Greek phrase ($\tau\grave{o}$ $\breve{\epsilon}\nu$). The Primal Egg was produced by the Primal Hen.[288] Eliot may have been given the idea of this kind of learned joke by a passage in Ezra Pound's "Hugh Selwyn Mauberley":

O bright Apollo,
τίν' ἄνδρα, τίν' ἤροα, τίνα θεόν
What god, man or hero
Shall I place a tin wreath upon![289]

That the Logos is a "superfetation" of the One can be understood by realizing that the Logos, in Stoic speculation (and in Philo) was the creative principle that mediated between the One and the Many. (John, 1: 3: "All things were made by him; and without him was not any thing made that was made"). The egg produced by the One is impregnated by the Many and can thus give rise to the full variety of life. However, for Christian doctrine (Eliot is saying), this view, if unqualified, is too intellectual and impersonal, and gives insufficient cosmic importance to the Flesh. The consequence that was hatched in the Church, therefore, was the heresy of Origen.

A painter of the Umbrian school
Designed upon a gesso ground

---

287 Editor's footnote: Grover Smith, *T. S. Eliot's Poetry and Plays, op. cit.*, pp. 43-44.
288 Author's footnote: The Primal Egg appears in Phoenician, Egyptian, Hindu, Finnish and Orphic creation myths. In some versions, the Primal Egg is laid by a Primal Bird.
289 Editor's footnote: *The Penguin Book of American Verse*, ed. Geoffrey Moore, Revised Edition, London, 1983, p. 287.

> The nimbus of the Baptized God.
> The wilderness is cracked and browned
>
> But through the water pale and thin
> Still shine the unoffending feet
> And there above the painter set
> The Father and the Paraclete.

In these next two verses, Eliot proceeds to the Christian view of the Godhead, which (he is suggesting) is free of the errors of Judaism and of pagan philosophy; yet combines and synthesizes both.[290] Eliot wants to present the Christian view not as a doctrine but as a vision – an insight simple, pictorial, and profound, like the Symbol of literary theory. Accordingly, Eliot turns not to the theologians but to the painters; and, specifically, to a painter of the Primitive School, untainted by Renaissance theory even concerning his own art. The language of these two verses is entirely different from that of the rest of the poem; the polysyllables have disappeared. The painter is a simple craftsman, apparently concerned only with the details of his craft (the "gesso ground", for example – but even here he is not entirely competent, for the materials of "the wilderness" have not stood the test of time and are "cracked and browned"), and with his commission to paint a Baptism of Christ, complete with "nimbus". Yet it is in this painting that the essential Christian vision has been expressed: the Word made Flesh, in its true relation to God the Father and to the Holy Spirit. It is the Baptized God that the painter is depicting, not the Crucified God. The Flesh is presented at its moment of apotheosis, cleansed of the stain of sin ("the unoffending feet") and so able to embody the Word.

It is now possible to understand why there is a pronounced pause or break in the poem at this point, marked by a line of dots. The poem up to this point has been a kind of Credo: an exposition of the Christian view of the Godhead, and an account of how this view was developed. The rest of the poem deals not with God but with Man. In this second part, we have an account of the nature and function of the Church; and the two parts together thus form a complete affirmation that is not inappropriately called a Sunday Morning Service. It will be objected immediately that this interpretation ignores the celebrated satirical tone

---

[290] Editor's footnote: Bryan Cheyette, *op. cit.*, p. 343, is an exception among Eliot critics in supporting this interpretation. Citing this paragraph, he agrees that "these two contrary versions of God – either Hebraically materialistic or Hellenistically ethereal – are synthesized in the painting of the 'Baptized God' in the third stanza".

However, I completely disagree with his implied suggestion (*ibid.*, p. 343) that the worker-bees in the poem's penultimate stanza are also Jews, seen negatively as "entrepreneurial middlemen". The Author argues (see below) that the worker-bees are, on the contrary, the real Christian clergy, whose role was misrepresented by the Turk and the Jew in the quotation from Marlowe's play *The Jew of Malta* that forms the poem's epigraph.

that is said to mark the poems of this period in Eliot's work. I hope to show later that this objection can be answered satisfactorily.

> The sable presbyters approach
> The avenue of penitence;
> The young are red and pustular
> Clutching piaculative pence.

The polysyllables have returned. The simple, pellucid vision of the last two stanzas, a vision of the Divine, gives way to the trivial, ugly realities of everyday life in the Church. The repeated theme in this stanza and the next is "penitence". Instead of the "unoffending feet", the purified, sinless Flesh, we have the "pustular" flesh of humans, spotted with sin. Instead of the eternal moment of union between Flesh and Word, captured in stillness by the painter, we have the painful movement of Time, in which little sins have to be expiated constantly, and a fresh start is continually being made. Instead of the eternally youthful beauty of the Baptized God (there are echoes of Adonis, Attis and Dionysus, for the Baptism is a rebirth), there is the division in the Church between the young and the old. The clergy are called "presbyters" because this means "old men"; they are black, because the fire of life has died in them. But in the young, the fire of life produces an ugly redness and an outbreak of boils. In these humans, the Flesh is corrupt in youth and impotent in age. Instead of the once-for-all Baptism, the irreversible rebirth on a supernatural plane, there are the little, continual outbreaks of sin, each requiring its expiatory penny. ("Piaculative", instead of the correct "piacular", has a diminutive effect.)

> Under the penitential gates
> Sustained by staring Seraphim
> Where the souls of the devout
> Burn invisible and dim.

The syntax of this stanza is puzzling. Should there be a comma instead of a full-stop at the end of the previous stanza? If so, it is the young who are clutching pence under the penitential gates. But what penitential gates? Is this some reference to the internal architecture of a church? If so, the details are hard to recognize. And who are the devout whose souls burn "invisible and dim"? Are they the same people as the "young" of the previous stanza? Or are they the presbyters? Or some other group? And if the souls are invisible, how can they also be dim? And why are they burning? The usual interpretation, which concentrates on the word "dim", and takes the stanza to refer to the tepid prayers of the so-called "devout",[291] does not meet these questions.

If, however, we take the full-stop at the end of the previous stanza seriously, we arrive at a different syntactical structure. The word "under" becomes an adverb, not a preposition, and the verb "are" is understood immediately after it. (A similar doubt between preposition and adverb occurs in the case of the word "above" in stanza 4. I shall consider soon whether there is a reason for this inducement of hesitation.)

The interpretation that now forces itself upon us is that the stanza refers to Purgatory. The stanza is saying: "Underneath are the penitential gates of Purgatory, guarded by awe-inspiring winged angels. Within the gates are burning the souls of those who are undergoing purgation, having gained God's grace. Some of these souls are invisible, and some are dimly visible." The stanza carries forward the idea of the previous stanza -- which deals with the Church as a community engaged in the purgation of the flesh -- and shows that this purgation must continue even after death. (Medieval doctrine insisted on the physical reality of the pains of purgatory and of its flames.) Purgatory is situated beneath the Church-worshippers (the "presbyters" and the "young") because Dante situated Purgatory in the Antipodes. The "penitential gates" are called in the *Purgatorio* "Peter's Gate", the main entrance to Purgatory. (The plural "gates" is generally used for a large double gate, except when a special name is being used.) "Peter's Gate" is penitential not only because it is the entrance to the place of penitence, but because it is approached by the Three Steps of Penitence.[292] The "staring Seraphim" who sustain the gates are the two Angels of the Valley, who guard the part of Ante-Purgatory nearest to the Gate, and the Angel of the Gate himself. The faces of all three angels are described as awe-inspiring (Canto VIII: 35 and IX: 81). That the souls in Purgatory are called "the devout" is not surprising; for these souls all embrace

---

[291] Editor's footnote: See Grover Smith, *T. S. Eliot's Poetry and Plays, op. cit.*, p. 44: "The second half of the poem returns to the 'sapient sutlers' as they tread the church aisle while the youthful members of the congregation wait to atone, their faces being as far from immaculate as the soul of Barabas, and their own souls dim like weak ghosts. The irony of the sixth stanza is heightened by the allusion to Vaughan's 'The Night'…. Eliot's poem shows darkness of a different sort." See also Jain, *op. cit.*, p. 119; she too cites the Vaughan quotation and, like Smith, sees the allusion as a satire on it: "An ironic allusion to 'The Night', a poem by Henry Vaughan (1622-95): 'O, for that Night! where I in Him/Might live invisible and dim!' Vaughan writes of the paradox of God's 'deep, but dazzling darkness', as opposed to 'this world's ill-guiding light'. This darkness is far removed from the spiritual darkness of the 'sable presbyters'. And the souls of the devout 'burn invisible and dim' in a very different sense from Vaughan's impassioned desire to 'live invisible and dim' in God's darkness." Eliot himself acknowledged the Vaughan source (see 2015 *Poems, Vol. I, op. cit.*, p. 530); but Smith and Jain do not explain why he changed "live" to "burn" and do not explain the penitential gates or the staring Seraphim; except that Jain repeats B. C. Southam's unconvincing suggestion that they refer to another painting (Southam, *op. cit.*, p. 63). Even if the lines do refer to a painting (which seems unlikely), the symbolism of the penitential gates and the seraphim would still need to be explained.

[292] Editor's footnote: *Purgatorio:* IX: 76-146.

their punishment willingly and are in God's grace.[293] Catholics call these souls "holy"; and it is even permitted to pray for their intercession. That some of the souls are invisible and some dimly visible is explained by Dante's account of the fire of the Second Cornice, where the souls are only intermittently visible to the poet. In *The Waste Land*, Eliot quotes directly from the same passage: "Poi s'ascose nel foco che gli affina".[294] Arnaut, who had come out of the centre of the fire sufficiently far to become visible, went back and became invisible again. Even when fully visible, the shades ("ombre") of Purgatory have a "corpo fittizio"[295]. A further degree of shadowiness occurs when the shade is in the process of appearing or disappearing, as when Guido (Canto XXVI: 135) "vanished through the flames, like a fish going through water to the bottom" ("come per l'acqua pesce andando al fondo").

It remains to be explained why Eliot, both in this stanza and in stanza 4, has produced in the reader a hesitation between preposition and adverb. In both cases, it is the preposition that is understood more naturally at a first reading. In stanza 4, a first reading will inevitably produce the phrase "above the painter", to be as inevitably corrected by the next line, which makes it quite clear that "above" is intended as an adverb. Yet the phrase "above the painter" still remains at the back of the mind, and the effect produced is that the painter has given such an impression of immediacy that he seems to be one of the witnessing crowd in the painting. In stanza 6, the word "under" seems to follow on so naturally as a preposition from the previous stanza that, even when we read it as an adverb (as the preceding full stop forces us to do), we still retain the impression that the people in church are somehow "under the penitential gates". And so they are, for earthly life is a kind of anteroom to Purgatory, and Peter's Gate awaits them, looming above them at the end of their earthly journey. So Peter's Gate is both below them and above them. Eliot's subtle use of punctuation to produce ambiguity was noted by William Empson in his remarks on a poem of this period, "Whispers of Immortality".[296]

It should be noted that the only part of Dante's Purgatory in which souls are purified by fire is the last or Seventh Cornice, where the sin of which they are purged is the sin of lust. This is important in view of the sexual theme in the next stanza. (In Aquinas's Purgatory,

---

293 Author's footnote: Dante calls these souls "le devote ombre" (*Purgatorio*, XIII: 82-83). See also *Purgatorio*, XXIII: 21.
294 Editor's footnote: *The Waste Land*, V, line 427. Translation: "Then he hid himself in the fire that refines them." (*Purgatorio*, XXVI: 148.) The words "Ara vos prec" (line 145) in the same passage form the title (in the London edition) of Eliot's third volume of poetry. See my Editor's Preface.
295 Editor's footnote: *Purgatorio*, XXVI:12.
296 Author's footnote: William Empson, *Seven Types of Ambiguity*, 1930: London, 1961, pp. 78-79.

on the other hand, fire was the standard instrument of punishment[297]; and the Purgatory of the Stoics was called ἐκπύρωσις[298].)

> Along the garden-wall the bees
> With hairy bellies pass between
> The staminate and pistillate,
> Blest office of the epicene.

In this stanza, we have an example of Eliot's surprise-technique, which amounts essentially to a continuation of the argument by pictorial means.[299] The sudden switch to the pre-Renaissance painting in stanza 3 was a previous example of the same technique. The parable of the bees, I suggest, is intended to throw light on the function of the Church, and on the rather depressing contrast that has been drawn between humdrum life in the Church and the moment of Divine enlightenment. The point is that life in the Church is, for all its members, and particularly for the clergy, a life of sacrifice. The true Church-member must deny the urgent claims of the flesh in order to purge his flesh of sin. Yet ultimately, in Eliot's view, the Christian religion is not a denial of the flesh, but an affirmation of it, in the central doctrine of the Incarnation. By sacrificing the desires of the flesh, the individual members of the Church contribute to the apotheosis of the flesh, which is the Body of Christ – the Flesh of God – which is the Church. The substance of the Church is the Flesh (this is the point of the poem "The Hippopotamus", in which the hippopotamus, symbolizing the flesh in all its bulky, quivering, fallible absurdity, rises superior to the Church, when the latter is

---

297 Editor's footnote: See, for instance, *Summa Theologica*, Appendix 1, Question 2, First Article, Objection 3, in *The Summa Theologica of St Thomas Aquinas, Third Part (Supplement), QQ. LXXXVII-XCIX and Appendices, Literally Translated by the Fathers of the English Dominican Province*, 1922: London, 2018, p. 225: "In Purgatory, there will be a twofold pain; one will be the pain of loss, namely the delay of the divine vision, and the pain of sense, namely punishment by corporeal fire".

298 Editor's footnote: *Ekpyrosis*, which means "cosmic conflagration". See Michael Lapidge, "Stoic Cosmology", in John M. Rist (ed.), *The Stoics*, 1978: California, 2021, p. 181: "The general outline of Zeno's and Cleanthes' theory of ἐκπύρωσις is clear: a universe turns into creative fire, whence a subsequent universe is generated from this same creative fire."

299 Editor's footnote: There is even more of a vivid word-picture in an early draft, which very much supports the Author's interpretation here of "the sexual renewal of Nature": "Salmon stretched red along the wall/Sweet peas invite to intervene/The hairy bellies of the bees/Blest office of the epicene." (*Inventions of the March Hare, op. cit.*, p. 377.) The word "salmon" makes one think not only of a bright red/pink colour but of fish as a proliferating fertility symbol (see Jessie Weston, *op. cit.*, p. 125: "the Fish is a Life symbol of immemorial antiquity"; and *ibid.*, p. 127, where Weston points out that the Fish is associated with Orpheus and Christ). By changing this vivid colour-word-picture to the Latinate, polysyllabic "the staminate and pistillate", Eliot seems to be laying more emphasis on the daily sacrifices of the clergy/worker bees and only implying the "tremendous central sexual transmission".

wrongly conceived as above the shocks that flesh is heir to).[300] So the day-to-day, humdrum penitential existence of the individual Church-members contributes to the Baptismal experience of the Godhead and keeps that experience fresh. The worker-bees renounce their sexual nature, but having done so, they bring about the sexual renewal of Nature. The experience that they have sacrificed is not lost to the universe; it becomes centralized and stored, and results in a tremendous central sexual transmission, which is identical with the descent of the Holy Spirit on the flesh of the Baptized Christ. This conception of sacrifice can be traced throughout Eliot's work and derives ultimately from the passage in Frazer's *The Golden Bough* that describes the savage sacrificial ritual by which primitive man renewed (as he believed) the powers of Nature (LII: 1)[301]. The thought behind this ritual is that we must sacrifice not what is worthless (for that would be no sacrifice), but what is supremely valuable, and that, by sacrificing it, we preserve it, not for ourselves but for the community and the Universe. This is true for every member of the Church, but particularly for the clergy. (In *The Idea of a Christian Society*, Eliot called for a renewal of the monastic orders in the Church of England.)[302] The self-denial of the ascetic is very different from the self-castration of Origen, which the word "epicene" recalls from stanza 2. Origen did not renounce sex; he eradicated it, and so denied the value and divinity of the flesh. He wanted to be a pure spirit, with no need for purgation, and so blasphemed against the Incarnation. He made things too easy for himself by a once-for-all renunciation that made the continual effort of self-sacrifice unnecessary.

The words "blest office" make us think immediately of the clergy, and this brings us back to the superscription from *The Jew of Malta*. The infidels, Ithamore and Barrabas, fail to understand the "blest office" of the clergy, but Ithamore unconsciously hits on a fruitful analogy when he calls them "caterpillars". He means, of course, "worthless parasites", as when Bolingbroke calls Bushy and Bagot "the caterpillars of the commonwealth"[303]; but the

---

300 Editor's footnote: See *The Letters of T. S. Eliot, Volume 8, 1936-1938*, edited by Valerie Eliot and John Haffenden, London, 2019, p. 11 (in a letter sent by Eliot to his brother and dated January 1, 1936): "I believe … that my abortive attempt to make myself into a professor of philosophy was due to a religious preoccupation … I think that the poems which you mistakenly call 'blasphemous' ('Hippopotamus' and 'Morning Service') point to this end." Rudolf Germer acknowledges that both poems are "fundamentally religious", but qualifies this with "paradoxically", since he also regards them as "clearly anti-clerical and possibly blasphemous". ("Eliot's Religious Development" in *T. S. Eliot and Our Turning World*, op. cit., p.19.) In a footnote to this essay, Germer writes: "I do not accept the reading of 'Mr. Eliot's Sunday Morning Service' as an expression of anti-Judaism or anti-Semitism. Cf. Hyam Maccoby's 14 June 1996 'Letter to the Editor', *TLS*." (*Ibid.*, p. 25, footnote 4.) For this 14 June 1996 letter, see Appendix 7.

301 Editor's footnote: Frazer, *The Golden Bough, Abridged Edition*, op. cit., pp. 499-500.

302 Editor's footnote: T. S. Eliot, *The Idea of a Christian Society*, London 1939, p.35: "Coleridge… quite failed to recognize the enormous value which monastic orders can and should have in the community." See also *ibid.*, p. 60: "I cannot conceive a Christian society without religious orders, even purely contemplative orders, even enclosed orders."

303 Editor's footnote: William Shakespeare, *Richard II*, Act 2, Scene 3, line 165.

metaphor from the insect world suggests to Eliot a more appropriate image from the same sphere to symbolize the clergy.

> Sweeney shifts from ham to ham
> Stirring the water in his bath.
> The masters of the subtle schools
> Are controversial, polymath.

Now we have another shock-transition, from the worker-bees to Sweeney in his bath. It is easy enough to see that, in this last stanza, we are again concerned with the Flesh and the Word. Sweeney represents the Flesh without the Word, and the "masters of the subtle schools" represent the Word without the Flesh. I suggest that, just as the opening stanzas of the poem are concerned with the pre-Christian era, the final stanza is concerned with what has been called the post-Christian era. In the paganism of the modern world (Eliot is saying), a split has taken place between the Flesh and the Word. On the one hand, we have the barbarian Sweeney, who is the Flesh personified – his body has to be described in terms of meat. On the other hand, there are the philosophers and scientists who have reached a new height of knowledge and sophistication, but whose efforts divide the world instead of uniting it. This is the same dichotomy that Eliot deplored in the literary field in his much-discussed phrase "the dissociation of sensibility".[304] There is irony in the fact that Sweeney is in his bath; he presents a picture to be put alongside that of Christ in the baptismal water -- the "unoffending feet" are juxtaposed to Sweeney's hams, and the mysterious waters of purification to the unmysterious waters of a secularized world. Both Sweeney's flesh and the water in his bath are without holiness. I think it would be a mistake to interpret "The masters of the subtle schools" as the Schoolmen of the Middle Ages[305], but I would suggest that the word "schools" is purposely chosen to relate the modern scientists to the Schoolmen, and so to the first scholastic thinker, Origen. We thus have the thought: "Modern scientists have cut off the mind from the body just as some medieval Schoolmen tended to do, and just as Origen did. Modern scientists are castrated intellects." It should be noted that the last two lines of the poem are unobtrusively related to the first two lines of the poem by the words "subtle" and "polymath", which echo "sutlers" and "polyphiloprogenitive". I think that this means that the world has come full circle; the modern scientists are another race of Jews, because of their materialism, their over-subtlety and pride of intellect,[306] and their

---

304 Editor's footnote: T. S. Eliot, *Selected Prose, op. cit.,* "The Metaphysical Poets", p. 117.

305 Editor's footnote: This interpretation is suggested by David Ward in *T. S. Eliot Between Two Worlds: A Reading of T. S. Eliot's Poetry and Plays,* 1973: London, 2016, p. 32: "Sweeney.... shifts from ham to ham in his bath, mimicking with his fleshly indolence the chop and change of the austere and abstract dialectic of the schoolmen."

306 Editor's footnote: In this interpretation, the Jews are seen as representing both Flesh without Word (in a religious sense, which differentiates them from the wholly secular Sweeney) and Word without Flesh. The two amount to

adherence to the Many rather than the One. (The Jews, it is implied, were individualists, rationalists and pluralists, who wanted to multiply their progeny rather than draw the Church together into one unitary Communion inside the Body of Christ. The Jews did not want to sink their individuality in union with God, but merely to be His privileged servants.)

Thus the "Sunday Morning Service" is complete. It contains an affirmation of faith in the Christian doctrines of both the Godhead and the Church, and a sermon against un-Christian doctrines, both pre-Christian and post-Christian.

I now come to the question: "What has happened to the satirical tone and style of the poem? If it is a pious affirmation of faith, there seems little room for the satirical qualities that have been so much admired in these sardonic quatrains. To this objection, I would answer that the poem is, in the main, not satirical, but that it is full of irony. The irony derives not from any cheap points scored against the Christian clergy, but from the conflict of the Word and the Flesh, which are always striving to meet in union, but are always failing to do so, with ridiculous and pathetic effect[307]. The pride of the Flesh and the pride of the Word are always suffering an unexpected fall, and this is productive of irony; yet, despite the ridiculousness of each in isolation, the holiness of both of them is revealed when they unite, either in the person of the Baptized God or in the day-to-day purgations of the Church. And there is another source of irony that is at least equally important. This is the irony that Eliot directs against himself. He calls the poem "Mr. Eliot's Sunday Morning Service". Eliot is often praised for the dramatic gift that enabled him to create such characters as Prufrock and Sweeney. But it is not always realized that one of the most successful of his dramatic characterizations is that of "Mr. Eliot" himself. The polysyllables of the poem convey the

---

the same thing (embodied in the phrase "sapient sutlers"), because they both mean lack of the One Communion in the Divine Incarnation that unites Word with Flesh.

[307] Editor's footnote: For instance, these lines from "Whispers of Immortality": "And even the Abstract Entities/ Circumambulate her charm". The Abstract Entities are Word without Flesh; Grishkin is Flesh without Word (a kind of female Sweeney, though more attractive). The Abstract Entities strive to unite with Grishkin, but can only "circumambulate her charm" (note the absurdity evoked by the polysyllable). In contrast to the Abstract Entities, "our lot" – by which Eliot seems to mean modern poets, would-be Donnes and Websters (see an early draft of the poem in *Inventions of the March Hare, op. cit.*, p. 370) -- do not even try to unite Word with Flesh, in contrast again to the real Donne and Webster, who united thought with feeling, Word with Flesh, in a foretaste of Heaven, as the Author points out above, referring to Eliot's famous phrase "the dissociation of sensibility". The poem seems to be saying something like: "The Christian poets Donne and Webster were 'possessed by death' not because they were merely morbid, but because they saw in the bones the longing and potential to put on flesh in heaven – 'the anguish of the marrow/The ague of the skeleton' and 'the fever of the bone' -- and become united with the Word in the Incarnation in Heaven. But modern poets are merely morbid, crawling between the 'dry ribs' of death, bones that are merely dead bones." The paradox in the poem seems to be that, because modern poets cannot look beyond the earth and earthly desires, they cannot even attempt to unite Word with Flesh in their poetry on Earth. See also Appendix 8, footnote 558.

irony and pathos of the pedantic and learned Mr. Eliot[308], whose philosophy is one of abandonment and ecstasy – an ecstasy that he can attain only in theory.

I am sorry if I have destroyed the satirical attack on the clergy that is so beloved of people who prefer those of Eliot's poems that were written before his "defection" to religion.[309] I am afraid that close inquiry would produce similar results in the case of the other "satirical" poems of this period.[310] The poem that now emerges is, in my view, a much greater poem that the one that is lost; despite the unpleasant antisemitism that (if I am right) "Mr. Eliot's Sunday Morning Service" has in common with much of Eliot's work of the same period.

---

308 Editor's footnote: See the last poem in "Five-Finger Exercises", "Lines for Cuscuscaraway and Mirza Murad Ali Beg": "How unpleasant to meet Mr. Eliot!/With his features of clerical cut,/And his brow so grim,/And his mouth so prim/And his conversation, so nicely/Restricted to What Precisely/And If and Perhaps and But."

309 Editor's footnote: See, for example, F. W. Bateson, "The Poetry of Learning", in *Eliot in Perspective, op. cit.*, p. 44: "most of us, English and American, will continue to prefer 'The Hippopotamus' and its progeny to *The Rock* and its successors". For a more recent example, see J. C. C. Mays, "The Early Poems" in *The Cambridge Companion to T. S. Eliot*, edited by A. David Moody, Cambridge, 1994, pp. 117-119; Mays writes of the *Ara Vos Prec* Quatrains: "This kind of poetry is funny, inventive and surprising, and sometimes extravagant.... It is concerned not with the rejection of the world, but with being in the world.... Eliot's way forward after *The Waste Land* was, to some extent, a narrowing."

310 Editor's footnote: For the Author's interpretation of "The Hippopotamus", see this chapter above (pp. 128-129) and Chapter 1, pp. 59-60. In addition, see Appendix 8, where I have ventured to examine "A Cooking Egg" on the lines suggested by the Author.

Chapter 6: TIME AND ETERNITY: A COMMENTARY ON "BURNT NORTON"[311]

A Commentary on "Burnt Norton" I

My general line of exegesis may conveniently be stated at once. Eliot is introducing the theme of Time; and, in some sense, he is going to say, throughout the *Quartets*, that Time is unreal. But there is also a sense, very important to him, in which Time *is* real. In this first Part, he is asserting the reality of Time, and especially the reality of *possibility*. He is opposing the sort of fatalism or necessarianism that excludes the unexpected, regards everything as already given, and thus denies Time in its aspect of richness of possibility.

Lines 1-17[312]: The poem opens with the statement that "perhaps" past, present and future are involved in one another. The force of the word "perhaps" is: "What I am now saying is true, if taken in the right sense, but...." The next two lines are:

If all time is eternally present,
All time is unredeemable.

The absence of "But" at the head of these two lines (unnecessary because of the previous "perhaps") has misled some commentators.[313] Eliot is saying: "Though we may deny the reality of Time to the extent of denying separate, discontinuous existence to past, present and future, we must not go further and deny Time altogether. This would be to assert only an eternal Present, in which case there would be no real development in history, since

---

311 Editor's footnote: "A Commentary on 'Burnt Norton' I" was originally published in *Notes and Queries*, February 1968, Vol. 15: 2. "A Commentary on 'Burnt Norton' II" was originally published in *Notes and Queries*, February 1970, Vol. 17: 2. "A Commentary on 'Burnt Norton' III, IV and V" was originally published in *Notes and Queries*, December 1970, Vol. 17: 12. All reprinted by kind permission of Oxford University Press.

312 Author's footnote: For views that have certain similarities to what follows, see Willie Schenk, "The Experience and the Meaning", *Humanitas* ii, No. 4, 1947; and J. C. Maxwell, "Reflections on Four Quartets", *Month*, N. S. iv, 1950.

313 Editor's footnote: See, for instance, B. Ragan: "The repetition, the strong stressed rhythm, the positioning of key words and the evocations of 'future' and 'past' bind together the ideas of eternity, time and presence. The taut scholastic diction held back from certainty by the donnish 'perhaps' underlines the assurance of 'unredeemable', and the emotions it evokes are reflected on the next line – 'What might have been is an abstraction'. It is not just a matter of saying with Aquinas that even God cannot undo the past. 'Abstract' used evocatively ... stresses the presence and reality of the eternal." (*T. S. Eliot: A Study of his Writings by Several Hands*, ed. B. Rajan, London, 1947, p. 81.) See also next footnote.

everything would be given and already in existence. The Christian doctrine of redemption, by which certain movements in time are all-important (something really *happens*) would then become meaningless."

The fear that the past is unredeemable must be distinguished from the very different thought (which some commentators have wrongly introduced here[314]) that the past is *irrevocable*. The latter thought is not one that Eliot would combat; in fact, the sense of the irrevocable is prominent in his work (for example, in "Eeldrop and Appleplex"[315], "Sweeney Agonistes"[316] and *The Family Reunion*[317]). There is no contradiction between a belief in contingency and a belief in the irrevocability of "what has been". Indeed, we should have no sense of the irrevocable (and thus no regret for any of our past decisions) unless we felt that something other than what actually happened "might have been". Redemption is an act in the present that puts right or makes up for something that happened in the past; but nothing can change the past itself. To realize the irrevocability of the past is for Eliot the beginning of wisdom; it means that we are facing our situation. But the *meaning* of the past can be altered by our present actions (just as each new work of art alters all the previous

---

314 Editor's footnote: *Ibid.* See also Harry Blamires: *Word Unheard, op. cit.*, p. 7: "If all time is thus eternally about us ... then all time is 'unredeemable'. It cannot be recovered, recanted, brought back." (For a review of Blamires's book by the Author, see Appendix 6.) To cite a much more recent critic: Jewel Spears Brooker points out that the opening lines of "Burnt Norton" originally appeared (they were only slightly amended in "Burnt Norton") in a draft speech (later omitted) in *Murder in the Cathedral*, in connection with the Second Tempter section: "In the play, a tempter tells Thomas: 'The Chancellorship that you resigned/When you were made Archbishop – that was a mistake/On your part – still may be regained'.... The desire to return to the past and create a different present is precisely the temptation that Eliot faced in the rose garden at Burnt Norton. In the draft of the play, Thomas rebukes his tempter, declaring 'What might have been is a conjecture/Remaining a permanent possibility/Only in a world of speculation'". (*T. S. Eliot's Dialectical Imagination*, Baltimore, 2018, pp. 153-154.) In fact, the draft lines are *not* spoken by Thomas to the Second Tempter; they are spoken by the Second Priest, after the exit of the Second Tempter (see Helen Gardner, *The Composition of Four Quartets*, 1978: London, 1980, p. 79. See also the 2015 *Poems, Vol. I, op. cit.*, p. 904). The draft lines are not a rebuke as part of a dramatic action, but a complex philosophical meditation on the nature of time, free-will and redemption. The draft lines were discarded because, as Eliot said in an interview: "the producer pointed out to me that the lines were strictly irrelevant to the action and didn't get things forward". (*Ibid.*)

315 Editor's footnote: See "Eeldrop and Appleplex I", which was first published in *Little Review* in May 1917. (The story/dialogue has been reproduced by the Dodo Press in T. S. Eliot, *Eeldrop and Appleplex and Ezra Pound: His Metric and Poetry*, Gloucester, 2007.) The relevant passage is this comment by Eeldrop: "'With the decline of orthodox theology and its admirable theory of the soul, the unique importance of events has vanished.... a man murders his mistress. The important fact is that for the man the act is eternal, and that for the brief space he has to live, he is already dead. He is already in a different world from ours.... The important fact is that something is done which can not be undone – a possibility which none of us realize until we face it ourselves." (*Ibid.*, pp. 2-3.)

316 Editor's footnote: See "Sweeney Agonistes: Fragment of an Agon": "Life is death./I knew a man once did a girl in --/.... Well he kept her there in a bath/With a gallon of lysol in a bath/.... What did he do?/.... That don't apply./Talk to live men about what they do."

317 Editor's footnote: See, for instance, Agatha's words: "everything is irrevocable,/Because the past is irremediable,/Because the future can only be built/Upon the real past". (*The Family Reunion, op. cit.*, p. 17.)

ones) and this is the essence of redemption. We cannot alter the past, but, by our present actions, we can alter the pattern of which the past forms a part and turn it from a bad pattern into a good one. It is this possibility of redemption that Eliot is defending here.[318]

Now to expound the first three lines in more detail:

Time present and time past
Are both perhaps present in time future
And time future contained in time past.

At first sight, this seems an arbitrary way of putting the matter. Why mention present, past and future in the first two lines, and only future and past in the third line? Is there any distinction between "present in" and "contained in"? Is there not, indeed, an ugly pun in the phrase "present in"? These questions might seem too carping, if we were not aware of Eliot's attention to detail, as shown in his criticism[319], and if we were not aware of his professional expertise in philosophy, which should appear, if anywhere, in such a passage as this.

Eliot is referring to the various ways in which past, present and future interpenetrate one another. The first two lines suggest one way, the way of memory, by which what is past survives into the present. If we take as our standpoint some moment in the future, we see that both what is now happening and what has already happened will then still exist as memories. This is an economical way of taking all three times together and showing how they interpenetrate one another. Moreover, the interpenetration is multiple, because the present contains memories of the past, and these memories will themselves become second-order memories in the future (we shall remember our present acts of memory). It is therefore relevant to mention all three kinds in this kind of interpenetration. Another way of interpenetration, which takes the opposite direction in time, is mentioned in the third line. It is the way of evolution or causation or potentiality, by which the seeds of the future lie hidden ("contained") in the present. Here there is a two-way relation of "before" and "after", so only two times are mentioned: future and past. The phrase "contained in" is really a spatial, not a temporal expression. Eliot is hinting that the interpenetration of times, if understood in the wrong way, can lead to the annihilation of Time altogether, leaving us

---

318 Author's footnote: The connections between this passage and *The Family Reunion* are too complex to be treated here in detail.

319 Editor's footnote: For example, see William Empson, *Seven Types of Ambiguity*, op. cit., pp. 156-159, for a report of Eliot's detailed analysis, during a discussion, of lines from two poems by Shelley. Another example is Eliot's close examination of Donne's "The Extasie", in T. S. Eliot, *The Varieties of Metaphysical Poetry*, ed. Ronald Schuchard, 1993: San Diego, 1996, pp. 108-115.

with an omnipresent Space. This is Bergson's line of attack on scientific thinking.[320] (Though Eliot preferred Bradley to Bergson, he studied Bergson carefully, and there are many points of contact between all three writers.)[321] The previous phrase "present in" is interesting, because it is an expression that can refer to either Time or Space. If the present and the past are "present" in the future in the sense in which a person is "present" in a room, then Time has been spatialized out of existence. The doubt between Time and Space that hovers over the expression "present in" is brought to the fore in the expression "contained in" and given wider significance in the next line: "If all time is eternally present". This could mean either: "Past and present have no real existence. Only the present exists" or: "Past, present and future are all there together". The pun in the word "present" is deliberate and essential to the meaning of the passage. It is not ugly, because a pun is ugly only when it is either unintentional or gratuitous.

The next lines continue to display the doctrine with which Eliot is disagreeing. If Time is declared entirely unreal, possibility is annihilated together with it. Everything is already there; and so nothing, other than what is, is possible, except as an abstract idea. But contingency is an ingredient of Eliot's world that he cannot do without; he wants to feel that what has happened might have happened otherwise; if not, nothing happens at all. This means that "what might have been" attains a kind of existence; a shadowy kind of existence, perhaps, yet one more full-bodied than an abstraction; an existence like that of ghosts; an existence (as we shall see) that gives sanction to the Imagination, to Illusion and to unsatisfied desire. The language in which Eliot talks of mere logical possibility is reminiscent of Leibnitz. The "world of speculation" reminds us of Leibnitz's possible, or compossible, worlds (which Voltaire parodied rather unfairly in *Candide*). Contingency is an important theme in Leibnitz's thought. He tries desperately to reconcile it with his mathematical vision in his doctrine of the principle of Sufficient Reason.[322] We are reminded

---

320 Editor's footnote: See Bertrand Russell's summing up, in his *History of Western Philosophy*, 1946: London, 2004, of Bergson's concept of Time and Space (p. 717): "Mathematical time, according to Bergson, is really a form of space; the time which is of the essence of life is what he calls *duration*." (Emphasis in original.) Russell's chapter on Bergson (Chapter 28) is very lucid and helpful in explaining his ideas, but highly critical of them.

321 Editor's footnote: For an interesting account of Eliot's university studies of Bergson, Bradley and Frazer, see the essay "Eliot's Philosophical Studies: Bergson, Frazer, Bradley", by Jewel Spears Brooker, in *The New Cambridge Companion to T. S. Eliot, op. cit.*, pp. 175-185.

322 Editor's footnote: See Bertrand Russell's chapter on Leibnitz (Chapter 11) in *History of Western Philosophy, op. cit.* Russell writes (p. 536) that Leibnitz "argues that every particular thing in the world is 'contingent', that is to say, it would be logically possible for it not to exist; and this is true not only of each particular thing, but of the whole universe. Even if we suppose the universe to have always existed, there is nothing within the universe to show why it exists. But everything has to have a sufficient reason, according to Leibnitz's philosophy; therefore the universe as a whole must have a sufficient reason, which must be outside the universe. This sufficient reason is God."

that Leibnitz's thought was the subject of a paper published by Eliot in a philosophical journal in the days when he was still thinking of taking up philosophy professionally.[323]

> What might have been and what has been
> Point to one end, which is always present.

Now we have another kind of interpenetration of periods of Time: that involved in desire, or purpose. In purposeful action, the future exists before it has happened; not in the way of causation, previously mentioned ("contained in"), but in the way of teleology ("pointing to"). "Point[ing] to one end" is explained more fully at the end of "Burnt Norton":

> Desire itself is movement
> Not in itself desirable;
> Love is itself unmoving,
> Only the cause and end of movement.

"Cause" here means teleological cause, not the propelling cause of science. "Love" is the unmoving object of "desire". We are reminded of Plato's doctrine of Love, and of Aristotle's First Mover; also of Augustine's view that all desire is really desire for God.[324] To Eliot, the reality of Time consists in our movement towards God. This is a real movement; but it is always frustrated by our limitations. Every movement that we make means that some other possible movement has to be given up; but that movement too would have been a movement towards God. So we are continually tormented by a sense of missed opportunities, of unsatisfied desire. Every path that we take towards God means the loss of an infinity of other paths, each in some sense valid (even the path of crime – see "Sweeney Agonistes" and *The Family Reunion*). The words "what might have been" raise, even in this quietly reflective part of the poem, the feeling of regret, the sadness of limitation, that is so important in the *Quartets* and throughout Eliot's poetry. The path we took did not lead to God; but the thought of all the other paths we might have taken keeps alive in us the feeling of dissatisfaction and striving for perfection. The acceptance of limitation is the task of middle-age; the unawareness of limitation is the glory and illusion of youth. A momentary visionary glimpse of eternity is an occasion when the limitations are dissolved, and all possibilities are actualized simultaneously. These are the themes that are explored in the rest of this section of "Burnt Norton".

---

323 Author's footnote: "The Development of Leibnitz's Monadism", *Monist*, October 1916.
324 Author's footnote: *Confessions*, III, 1.

Now the generalizations give way suddenly to imagery; but the imagery is not intensely personal, for this is something that "we" experience. The poet is talking about an aspect of the experience of all human beings; there is a kind of comradeship in this "we" that is carried on in all the subsequent uses of the word throughout Part 1. The point is that we are freer than one might have thought. We are all able to transcend to some extent the "metalled ways/Of time past and time future".[325] We do so in memory and in imagination when we imagine choices in the past that we did not make. The rose-garden may have been chosen by Eliot as a symbol because of some personal experience[326]; but he means it to be a universal symbol. It is a very complex one, which appears many times in his work. For the moment, it is important to note that the rose-garden is not, in this context, an unattainable secret garden (like the garden in H. G. Wells' story "The Green Door"). It is evident that the garden is always available for entering. (It is, in fact, in one of its aspects, the garden at Burnt Norton.) But there are many passages and doors leading into the garden; and only one passage can be used at a time; though the ones we did not take can be imagined and perhaps regretted, for one's choice of entrance affects one's experience of the garden.

The sudden change from reflective impersonality to the personal address to the reader – "My words echo/Thus, in your mind" – has been found very puzzling. Moreover, the sudden uncertainty of "I do not know" contrasts strangely with the calm assurance of the poem up to this point. Eliot seems to be claiming that his poem (which has hardly begun) has already reached deep recesses of his reader's mind. This is a claim that the reader may well resent, especially when the poet seems to add that perhaps it would have been better to have left his reader's dead and dusty mind alone. Or is it that Eliot is smitten with doubt about his own poetic mission? This stepping out of the framework of the poem in order to address the reader personally is all the stranger in view of the fact that there is no parallel to it in the rest of Eliot's work.

I think it is necessary to find a line of interpretation that gets rid of the personal address to the reader altogether. Several commentators have tried to achieve such an interpretation by suggesting that "you" refers to a woman whom the poet is addressing, and that this explains why it is "we" who go into the garden.[327] This seems to me unlikely, for reasons

---

325 Editor's footnote: The last lines of "Burnt Norton" III.

326 Editor's footnote: See next footnote.

327 Editor's footnote: See, for instance, Elizabeth Drew, *op. cit.*, p.153: "He may be addressing the reader and suggesting that such experiences are common to all, or the echoes may be in the mind of the woman in the imaginary scene". Writing to Emily Hale on January 13, 1936, Eliot describes "Burnt Norton" as "a new kind of love poem, and it is written for you, and it is fearfully obscure". https://tseliot.com/the-eliot-hale-letters/letters/l444

Lyndall Gordon describes the visit of Eliot and Emily to the actual rose-garden at Burnt Norton (*The Hyacinth Girl*, *op. cit.*, pp. 207-208); and, citing Eliot's words just quoted, writes: "In retrospect, the poet calls up the play of light on an empty pool so that it appears filled with water. This grants the visiting pair a moment of reality" (*ibid.*, p. 226). However, the Author's interpretation of this passage as impersonal seems to me to be correct;

largely connected with the general tone of the poem. This is not a "Come-into-the-garden-Maud" poem. Moreover, the word "we", when first introduced, seems uncontrovertibly impersonal; and it would be an awkward wrench to make it personal afterwards. I would suggest a different interpretation.

Eliot has just been showing that we can transcend our own individual existence in time by the use of our imagination, by which we can, in a sense, experience other lives that we might have had. He now goes on to refer to another kind of transcendence, by which we can experience the lives of other people. The "I" and "you" used in these lines are like the "I" and "you" used by philosophers in discussing the problem of Other Minds. The pronouns could almost be replaced by "A" and "B". It is in communication that our lives mingle empathetically with the lives of other people. The kind of "echo" that we experience in using our imagination can also be received in communication; and this widens our narrow existence and breaks down our limitations. "My words echo/Thus in your mind" can be paraphrased: "When A talks to B, B's mind receives an echo of A's life; and B's own life transcends its limitations". This paraphrase does not contain the whole explanation, however; for the most powerful form of communication is poetry; so Eliot is after all talking about himself, but in an impersonal way, in his poetical capacity, and as an instance of the general phenomenon of communication. This is the first introduction of the theme of communication by words and poetry that is one of the basic "musical" themes of the *Quartets*, and that is, in every instance, bound up with Eliot's view of Time and human limitations.

Having spoken of the fact of transcendence through communication, Eliot now shows the other side of the coin: the fact of human isolation. He says: "Though I (A) may enter your (B's) mind, I can never know or experience what exactly I have done there. I can never live your life with you and share in your sense of purpose and appetency." The word "purpose" touches again the theme of teleology, or movement through desire, raised in line 10 in the words "point to one end". The words "I do not know" are not an expression of hesitancy or doubt on Eliot's part, but a statement of an epistemological fact. "Disturbing the dust on a bowl of rose-leaves" suggests the activating of uncomfortable memories. Why does communication stir up long-forgotten desires, rose-leaves from the rose-garden of one's youth? Because awareness of other people's lives reminds one of the lost possibilities of one's own life. Imagination and communication are not entirely separate ways of transcendence; they involve each other (especially in poetic communication). Relevant here is a passage from *Ash Wednesday* I:

---

and his interpretation is supported by the fact that the lines were originally part of a draft speech (see footnote 314) spoken by the Second Priest in *Murder in the Cathedral*; see Gardner, *Composition, op. cit.*, p. 82 and the 2015 *Poems, Vol. 1, op. cit.*, p. 904: "Footfalls echo in the memory/Down the passage which we did not take/Into the rose-garden." Here the "we" seems entirely impersonal.

> Because I do not hope to turn
> Desiring this man's gift and that man's scope

This Shakespearean jealousy[328] is not ignoble, because it shows an awareness of possibility, a desire to transcend human limitations and broaden out the narrow path of one's own existence. The rose-garden of one's youthful aspirations may shrink to a dusty bowl of rose-leaves in adult life, but every real communication with another person disturbs the dust. Here is another relevant passage, from *Murder in the Cathedral*:

> Ambition comes when early force is spent
>
> And when we find no longer all things possible.[329]

In "Little Gidding" II, we have:

> Ash on an old man's sleeve
> Is all the ash the burnt roses leave.

Later, the same stanza refers to "The death of hope and despair". In this riddling lyric, each part of the Quartets is referred to in turn. (I believe, even, that the word "burnt" is an echo of the title "Burnt Norton".) The stanza confirms that "Burnt Norton" is concerned with "hope and despair" – the ever-narrowing circle of possibilities in life.

Despite what I have said, I do not deny that there is a faltering in the rhythm of the poem at the words "But to what purpose". This is signalized, too, by the broken lineation. But I would argue that this faltering is not because of a lapse of assurance on the poet's part as to the truth or value or utility of what he is saying. It is because of the feeling of the sadness of human isolation, which makes the power of imagination and communication so feeble – nothing more than an awareness of "echoes".

Lines 17-42: After the chill struck by his digression on human isolation, the poet returns to the opposite theme: the human power of transcendence. The return brings with it the resumption of the word "we". Despite our isolation, even because of it, all humans have a sense of comradeship. Our isolation is our common plight.

---

328 Editor's footnote: "Desiring this man's gift and that man's scope" is a quotation almost word for word from Shakespeare's Sonnet 29. The original line is: "Desiring this man's art and that man's scope".
329 Editor's footnote: Coghill, *op. cit.*, p. 53, ll. 679-680.

Another pronoun that begins to appear frequently now is "they". It occurs first in the accusative in line 19:

Quick, said the bird, find them, find them

The pronoun seems to refer to "echoes" in line 17; but it is not clear how one can find an echo; so it seems better to suppose that the reference is to some people, or beings, who have caused the echoes (unless the word "echoes" has the unusual meaning of "ghosts" – a meaning prepared by the word "inhabit"). The next use of "they" is in line 23:

There they were, dignified, invisible

This "they" has no nearby noun to refer to; so evidently "they" means some mysterious beings of the nature of spirits or ghosts. In lines 30 and 31, we have "they" again:

There they were as our guests, accepted and accepting.
So we moved, and they, in a formal pattern

The second of these two lines makes it clear that the "they" in the first line does not refer to the roses in line 28, as we might otherwise have thought. Finally, "they" appear in line 38:

And they were behind us, reflected in the pool.

Who are "they"? Are they the "children" mentioned in line 40, who are "hidden excitedly" in the leaves? If so, there would seem to be a strong link with Kipling's story "They"[330], about a garden full of ghost children. On the other hand, nothing up to this point has suggested that "they" are children. The word "dignified" suggests that they are not. I think that there *are* some connections with the story "They", one of which is the word "they" itself. In his essay on Kipling, Eliot mentions "They" as one of the stories in which Kipling shows an imaginative grasp of time.[331] Another link is that Kipling's story is partly about the function of the artist. The woman in the story can evoke the ghosts of children because she is blind and has never borne a child. At the climax of the story, the writer feels the presence of his own dead child but decides that he must not follow the villagers in accepting the blind woman's gift,[332] perhaps because he is an artist and a seer, like her. Eliot, too, had a doctrine

---

330 Author's footnote: See Helen Gardner, *The Art of T. S. Eliot, op. cit.*, p. 160.
331 Editor's footnote: *A Choice of Kipling's Verse, op. cit.*, p.32.
332 Editor's footnote: See Rudyard Kipling, *The Best Short Stories*, Ware, 2010, p. 178.

of the artist as a sacrificial figure.[333] This doctrine of sacrifice is only hinted at in the passage before us; but the poet is certainly dealing with the subject of Imagination. Though what he says applies to everyone, it is particularly relevant to the situation of the artist, who reveals Truth through Illusion. The idea of ghostly presences in a garden, in a context of meditation on Imagination, provides the real link to Kipling's story.

I think it would be best now to say distinctly what I consider to be the narrative-line of the imagery in this part of the poem. There was a garden that we first entered in childhood. The garden is still there, now that we are adults; but we now enter it by a different gate. Let us follow the invitation of the bird, and enter the garden, in imagination, by the gate of childhood, and see if we can find again the invisible spirits that used to be there when we were children. Yes, we have done it! (The verbs change to the past tense; we are back in childhood.) We can feel the presence of the invisible spirits. We cross the garden, in company with the spirits, and look into a dry, empty pool. An effect of sunlight makes the pool seem to be full of water; and this illusion becomes a mystical experience. Reflected in the illusory water, the invisible spirits suddenly become visible. But a cloud passes, and the illusion vanishes. We are left as adults in an ordinary garden. The spirits have gone; but we feel the hidden presence of children laughing at us. Our guide, the bird, tells us to resume the movement of Time; a glimpse of timeless mystical experience is all that we can expect.

If this account is correct, the question of whether there are ghost-children in the garden (as in "They"), must receive a complex answer. The adults who step back into the garden of childhood become ghost-children, in a sense -- their own past selves. But these children do not regard themselves as ghosts -- it is "they" who are the ghostly presences. When "we" return to everyday, adult reality (which is also a falling-away from Reality), the children who are our own past selves remain as hidden presences to taunt us. "They" are not at first children at all. To the children, "they" appear as dignified, adult presences. It is only when the children return to adulthood that the hidden presences turn into children. Children's ghosts are adults; adults' ghosts are children. The shifts in standpoint are like those that occur in dreams.

The meaning must be something like this. The garden is the world. But the world that we experience is sensed, at certain moments and especially in childhood, to be part of a wider world that is Reality. (Eliot always followed F. H. Bradley in regarding Appearance not as unreal, but as a limited aspect of Reality.) This wider world can be sensed when,

---

333 Editor's footnote: See Eliot's essay "Tradition and the Individual Talent": "The progress of an artist is a continual self-sacrifice, a continual extinction of personality." (*The Sacred Wood*, op. cit., p. 53.) Eliot's second wife, Valerie, said that he had told her that "he felt he had paid too high a price to be a poet". (Interview with Timothy Wilson, The *Observer*, February 20, 1972; quoted in Moody, *Thomas Stearns Eliot, Poet*, op. cit., p. 285.) See also Chapter 2, pp. 68-69, on the poet and the Nine Muses, the thrice-Triune Goddess.

for a moment, the limitations of Time and individual isolation melt away. But these very limitations define what we normally call reality. The faculty by which we break down the barriers is Imagination; and Imagination tells us not what is, but what might be and what might have been. So it is through Illusion that we approach the broader Reality ("the deception of the thrush"). It is an optical illusion ("water out of sunlight") that gives the glimpse into Reality.

The guide to the realm of Imagination is a bird, the thrush; because a bird soars away from mundane reality, and because a bird is "quick". (See "Cape Ann": "O quick quick quick, quick hear the song-sparrow".) To be "quick" means to be alive; but it also means to be able to catch the present moment, and thus to escape from "the enchainment of past and future"[334]. Children too are "quick". (See the end of "Burnt Norton":

There rises the hidden laughter
Of children in the foliage
Quick now, here, now, always –

The present moment is our experience of eternity, but it is always escaping from us.)

The Rose-Garden is the world; but it is also the world as it might be, the world for which we all yearn, the "end" towards which everything "points". In *Ash Wednesday* II, the Garden is identified with the Virgin Mary and with the Church, which is a pattern of the ideal world:

The single Rose
Is now the Garden
Where all loves end

("End" because desire is satisfied and because they reach their "end" or purpose, as in "point to one end".) The Garden is the "one end, which is always present". It is a sexual symbol, too, as in the *Roman de la Rose*, because sexual yearning is the supreme symbol of yearning for God (though a psychoanalyst might put the matter the other way round). At any rate, the Garden is clearly a feminine symbol. So is the Rose, and so is the Lotus, the mystical feminine symbol of Hinduism and Buddhism that appears in line 36.[335]

---

[334] Editor's footnote: See "Burnt Norton" II.
[335] Author's footnote: Some commentators, surprisingly, regard the Lotus as a phallic symbol; but in Sanskrit poetry it represents female beauty.

Editor's footnote: See, for instance, C. L. Barber: "the lotus ... carries an obvious phallic significance". (Unger, *op. cit.*, p. 440.)

In childhood, we are nearest to the unseen world, so that the mystic must return to childhood. The spirits that are sensed by the child (or by the adult who has become a child) are the possibilities that our narrow world shuts out – everything that might be or might have been, including what we ourselves might be or might have been. The child is at home in this wider world. The roses have the look of flowers that are looked at, because it seems natural to the child that there should be spirits in the garden who look at the roses when he is not there, and whose invisible eye-beams cross his own when he *is* there. These spirits are not alien to the child but are friendly guests. The spirits seem adult and "dignified" to the child, because his own life is opening out into adulthood, and his sense of possibility is directed to the future, to the possible selves that lie before him. That is why the old man in "Gerontion" says: "I have no ghosts". He has lost all sense of unfulfilled possibility, whether of the past or the future. Eliot's use of "ghosts", in the sense of unsatisfied desires, has more in common with Freudian theory than with the symbolism of Ibsen.

The mystical vision itself draws on the child's power of imagination and illusion, by which objects leap out of their conventional categories. There is one aspect of the vision, however, that applies more to the mystic or artist than to the child himself. The vision of wetness that arises from dryness is a symbol of the way of renunciation: "In order to possess what you do not possess/You must go by the way of dispossession." (East Coker, III.) Emphasis is laid on the dryness of the pool that is soon to seem full of water:

Dry the pool, dry concrete, brown-edged

A similar image recurs in "Little Gidding" I, when "The brief sun flames the ice". The "pentecostal fire" arises "In the dark time of the year". The adult can regain the vision of childhood only by the path of sacrifice and non-attachment. The vision itself is a complex one. The appearance of the spirits in visible form, reflected in the non-existent water, is a powerful image for the widening of perception, the actualization of all possibilities in the moment of expanded vision. The rising of the lotus derives from Eliot's interest in Hindu and Buddhist mysticism. The glittering of light has often been a focus for mystical experience.[336] Water, in Eliot, often represents the flow that relieves spiritual aridity. Another ingredient

---

336 Author's footnote: "Jehudah the Hasid relates to his pupil Eleazar how, when he was once standing in the synagogue with his father and there was a bowl of water and oil before them, his father drew his attention to the incomparable radiance which the light of the sun produced on the surface of the liquid, and said to him: 'Fix your attention on this radiance, because it is the radiance of the Hashmal' (one of the personified objects of Ezekiel's Merkaba vision)." (Gershom Scholem, *Major Trends in Jewish Mysticism, op. cit.*, p. 103.)

Editor's footnote: "Ezekiel's Merkaba vision" is explained by Scholem as "the vision of God's throne-chariot" in the first chapter of Ezekiel (*ibid.*, p. 42; see also Ezekiel 1: 26).

in the vision, as Grover Smith points out[337], is the idea of the "centre", which is gradually approached "in a formal pattern", as in the image of the dance.

When the cloud passes and the vision disintegrates, the adults ("we") return to everyday reality. It would seem more natural here, perhaps, for the poet to return to the present tense, which he dropped in line 23. But the retention of the past tense has the effect of the completion of a dream or trance, in which the poet has become immersed, and from which he cannot shake himself free. It is like the Grail story of Percival, in which the knight's vision disintegrates, leaving him dazedly facing a desolate scene.[338] The bird who has been the guide to the Garden tells the awakened dreamer (it is hard to think of more than one *dramatis persona* at this point, and the "we" has been dropped) to resume his life; but there still remains a mysterious supernatural element in the scene – the leaves are "full of children/ Hidden excitedly, containing laughter". There are many reverberations of meaning in these words. The word "containing" has a typical Eliotic ambivalence. The children are holding in their laughter, which suggests a feeling of kindly ridicule. Alternatively, "containing" echoes "full of" in the previous line – the children are full of joy and merriment. The idea of children's ridicule is taken up again at the end of "Burnt Norton":

> There rises the hidden laughter
> Of children in the foliage
> Quick now, here, now, always --
> Ridiculous the waste sad time
> Stretching before and after.

The word "ridiculous" amplifies and explains the "laughter". The children laugh at the adults because of their absurd enchainment in time. This reminds us of Bergson's theory of laughter in *Le Rire*, by which humour is an attacking device for jolting people out of their rigidity.[339] On the other hand, there is the laughter of pure joy. When the leaves are full of children, this means that the garden itself is full of joyous fruitfulness, just as the children are full of laughter. The children are "hidden excitedly" because life is full of exciting hidden

---

[337] Author's footnote: Grover Smith, *T. S. Eliot's Poetry and Plays, op. cit.*, p. 256 and p. 260. Grover Smith's exposition of "Burnt Norton" is the most helpful that I have seen.

[338] Author's footnote: See Tennyson's "The Holy Grail".

[339] Editor's footnote: See Bergson, *Laughter: An Essay on the Meaning of the Comic*, 1900: Glasgow, 2022, p. 36: "The comic is that side of a person which reveals his likeness to a thing, that aspect of human events which, through its peculiar inelasticity, conveys the impression of pure mechanism, of automatism, of movement without life. Consequently it expresses an individual or collective imperfection which calls for an immediate corrective. This corrective is laughter, a social gesture that singles out and represses a special kind of absentmindedness in men and in events."

potentialities, of things that are going to happen, not just wearily unfold. The adult, however, must "go", because the garden has become for him something in the past, something that belongs to the children, not to him, for the children can bear more Reality than he can. On the other hand, the adult's vision has not been in vain, for his faith in the potentialities of the garden has been restored. When he first entered the garden, he found there "dead leaves" (line 24), but now the leaves are "full of children". They are alive and brimming, teaming with possibilities.[340] The feminine aspect of the Garden has been reinforced; it is fecund and creative, like a woman with children. Both the reality and the unreality of Time are here summed up; the reality of the creativeness, potentiality, and novelty that we find in our experience of Time, and (in the ridicule of the children) the unreality of the restrictions that limit that experience. The word "containing" has a further significance. It points back to the line "And time future contained in time past". Eliot had used the word "contained" in that line to express the causal or deterministic sense in which the past holds the future within it. But there is another way in which the past may "contain" the future; the way in which the children "contain" laughter – a way that is brimming over with new life, not a way that is a mere unrolling or evolution of what is already there. The future comes out of the past like water bubbling from a fountain. This final interpretation of "containing" combines the two meanings of the word; the children are full of laughter that is spilling over despite themselves (not proceeding into existence in predictable fashion). By a characteristic Eliotic stroke, the whole passage is condensed into one strategically placed word.

The poet now brings back the words he has already used, turning back from imagery to statement; but the statement has now acquired new meaning and immediacy because of the imagery. The poet has "felt his thought". At the opening of his long poem about Time, Eliot has now defined his attitude towards Time. It is an attitude that may be summarized in the words of the philosopher whom Eliot most respected: F. H. Bradley[341]:

> The Absolute is timeless, but it possesses time, as an isolated aspect, an aspect which, in ceasing to be isolated, loses its special character. It is there, but blended into a whole which we cannot realize.[342]

---

340 Author's footnote: The image of children in a garden is found a little earlier in "New Hampshire" (published 1934), one of the purely descriptive "Landscapes". Editor's footnote: The image occurs first in "Ode" (published 1920; see Chapter 2, footnote 127).
341 Author's footnote: For an interesting study of Eliot's debt to Bradley, see Hugh Kenner, *op. cit.*, pp. 35-59.
342 Editor's footnote: F. H. Bradley, *Appearance and Reality: A Metaphysical Essay*, London, 1893, p. 210.

Part II

Helen Gardner says about the lyrical passage that opens "Burnt Norton" II: "This passage is not susceptible of too close analysis."[343] I agree with this if what is meant by "too close analysis" is "immediate line-by-line analysis". The lines are not sufficiently detachable from each other for this to be attempted in the first instance. However, a loose thematic analysis can be undertaken, which can be gradually focused and integrated until it finally amounts to a close analysis. The realization that the first two lines of the passage are derived from Mallarmé has perhaps proved misleading to commentators.[344] For, though Eliot's poetic method includes the kind of "word music" effect aimed at by Mallarmé, this method is based on a solid core of precise philosophical thinking. The word-melodies of the lyrical passages of the *Quartets* create, in the first instance, an atmosphere of feeling; but they can tolerate philosophical probing too. (I do not overlook the possibility that this is true of Mallarmé also.)

I propose, therefore, to begin by isolating certain themes, with the reservation that, in the last resort, the themes so detached are not really separable from each other.

1. *Motion and stillness.* The theme of motion is the most pervasive in the passage. The rapid, almost hectic movement of the verse contrasts strongly with the slow, measured rhythm of the succeeding reflective section. Everything moves, sometimes vertically, sometimes horizontally, sometimes with linear motion, sometimes with circular motion, sometimes with a mass indeterminate motion ("drift" and "lymph"). One might say that the lyrical passage is about motion, while the succeeding passage is about stillness. But

---

343 Author's footnote: *The Art of T. S. Eliot, op. cit.*, p. 160.

344 Editor's footnote: Helen Gardner continues: "Its opening line: 'Garlic and sapphires in the mud', inspired by Mallarme's jewel imagery, is an image of the variety contained in a single sense-impression: the soft and the hard, vegetable and mineral, the living and growing and the petrified and glittering, the common and the precious, the scented and the scentless." (*Ibid.*, pp. 160-161.)

Eliot took the line "Tonnerre et rubis aux moyeux" ("Thunder and rubies up to the wheel-hubs", in Eliot's own translation; see the 2015 *Poems, Vol I, op. cit.*, p. 913), from Mallarmé's sonnet "M'introduire dans ton histoire" (the line evokes the poet's triumph at his conquest of his frigid mistress). Eliot combined this line with another phrase from a Mallarmé poem: "bavant boue et rubis" ("slobbering mud and rubies") from "Le Tombeau de Charles Baudelaire". See Helen Gardner, *The Art of T. S. Eliot, op. cit.*, p. 160, n.1, and, in more detail, Helen Gardner, *Composition, op. cit.*, pp. 80-81. The Author's analysis of Part II sheds light on the puzzling 1935 minor poem "Lines for an Old Man", drafts of which ended with the first two lines of Part II (*ibid.*, pp. 79-80). The Old Man is hellish (see Genesius Jones, *op. cit.*, pp. 228-229 and Moody, *Thomas Stearns Eliot Poet, op. cit.*, p. 183), yet his hellish aspects are heavenly at the same time.

this is not quite true; the theme of stillness is in the lyrical passage too. But the lyrical passage *celebrates* motion; and the stillness here is, on the whole, something clogging and obstructive – the "fixity" decried also in the reflective passage's celebration of stillness. Thus, the whirling axle-tree is bedded in the mud; the flow of blood is arrested by the coagulation of scars; the rooted tree is contrasted with the mobility of the animals. Motion is something alive and active, constantly threatened by immobility, degeneration, and death. On the other hand, there are also contrary suggestions: that the clogging mud is rich in vegetable and mineral treasure; that there is something frenzied and mechanical in vital motion ("trilling wire"); that the tree is after all a "moving tree"; that the motions of the animals may be a fixed routine ("as before").

2. *Pattern and formlessness.* Line 57 speaks of "the figured leaf" and later "the boarhound and the boar/Pursue their pattern". These references to pattern clearly have some relation to the theme of pattern in other sections of the *Quartets*, especially Part V of "Burnt Norton": "Only by the form, the pattern/Can words or music reach/The stillness" and "The detail of the pattern is movement". Also, in Part 1 of "Burnt Norton", in the vision of the garden, we have "So we moved, and they, in a formal pattern". The notion of dancing is related to formal pattern, especially in "East Coker I", so we must include as contributing to this theme "the dance along the artery". The word "figured" in line 54 ("Are figured in the drift of stars") is interestingly ambiguous. It can refer to pattern in the geometrical sense, as in "the figured leaf", or to symbolization, which itself points to a hidden pattern in phenomena. Again, the idea of pattern is two-sided; pattern can be regarded as dynamic harmony and beauty, or as boring, static repetition. Its opposite, formlessness, is hinted at in the word "drift", and in the chaotic richness of the first line – "Garlic and sapphires in the mud" – in which formlessness is, on the one hand, a drag on creative activity and, on the other hand, a womb of creativity, the source of uncategorized variety.[345] Pattern and motion are variously related; motion may be patterned, as in the movements of "the boarhound and the boar", or the circular motion of the blood, or un-patterned, as in the "drift" of the stars. Stillness, too, can be un-patterned like the mud or patterned like the leaf (or the Chinese jar in Part V of "Burnt Norton").

---

[345] Editor's footnote: Eliot wrote to Emily Hale (March 19, 1936): "The first lines of that passage [ie the lyrical passage] are intended to convey a momentary sense of triumph and glory, after pain and mutilation (inveterate scars)". https://tseliot.com/the-eliot-hale-letters/letters/l468

The sense of "chaotic richness" described by the Author seems to be part of this "momentary sense of triumph and glory", as is the sense of "healing and peace" implied by the scars and the word "clot" (see end of next paragraph in main text).

3. *War and Peace.* The theme of war or aggression is raised by the mention of "long-forgotten wars" and their resultant scars. This suggests that the "axle-tree" of line 48 is that of a broken war-chariot; and this conjecture is supported by the mention, in the closely related corresponding lyric in "East Coker", of "triumphal cars/Deployed in constellated wars". The theme of aggression, allied to headlong motion, appears again with "the boarhound and the boar", who seem to pursue each other in a circle (cf. Chorus I from *The Rock*: "The Hunter with his dogs pursues his circuit"). On the other hand, the opposite theme of peace appears in the words "appeasing" and "reconciled". The scars, or blood-clotting, that impede the flow of blood (as the contents of the mud "clot" the motion of the chariot-wheel) bring, nevertheless, healing and peace. But motion, too, can be associated with peace; for the frantic aggressive motion of the animals has its heavenly harmonious counterpart.

4. *Animal, vegetable and mineral.* The word "tree" appears three times, each time at the end of a line, so that the repetition has an insistent effect, especially as the last two appearances are at the end of successive lines. This is partly what has led commentators to read a great deal into the "axle-tree" of line 48, seeing a reference to the Cross, regarded as the "still centre" of the wheel of life.[346] This interpretation has value; but there is a simpler symbolism, underlying the symbolism of the Cross itself (and of the Tree of Life with which Christian legend identified the Cross); namely, that a tree symbolizes the life of faith and sinlessness, because of its rootedness, its fruitfulness and its ability to draw sustenance from earth, water and sun, without requiring the cunning, mobility and aggression of the animal. (See, for example, Psalms 1, 3, 13, 92.) If the axle-tree, a product of human aggression (though made originally of peaceful wood) becomes "bedded" in the mud, it is returning to its original vegetable condition of sleep and rootedness – a condition that has both bad and good aspects. Our mobility has enabled us to develop consciousness, so that we "move above the moving tree/In light"; but we cannot escape from the animal aggressiveness ("the boarhound and the boar") that our evolution towards consciousness entailed. The thought here may have been derived from Bergson's discussion of the relation of the animal to the plant and the connections between mobility, aggression and consciousness.[347] A similar thought is expressed in Frederic Prokosch's poem "The Campaign": "They sought, in this career of killing/Escape from the hushed and paralysed career of the plants."[348] (In the double meaning of "career", there is even a parallel to Eliot's "moving tree".)

---

346 Author's footnote: Elizabeth Drew, *op. cit.*, p. 155, n. 12.

347 Author's footnote: *Creative Evolution*, Chapter II.

    Editor's footnote: *Creative Evolution*, 1907: Kansas, 2011, pp. 56-98 (authorized translation by Arthur Mitchell).

348 Editor's footnote: Frederic Prokosch, *Chosen Poems*, London 1944, p. 52.

The passage contains references to mineral (inorganic) substances, as well as to animal and vegetable substance. The mud of line 41 contains "sapphires" as well as "garlic" – here mineral substance is precious and unchanging, a symbol of eternity. But the mud itself (later "the sodden floor") stands for everything earthy, base and unbeautiful. The "wire in the blood" in line 49 is a telegraph wire, a mere mechanism in the service of hurry and fear, "trilling" like an alarm bell. Yet the wire "sings": a double-barrelled word that can signify either joy[349] or mechanical vibration. Later the stars, which are also mineral objects, are mentioned; and the fact that their motion is likened to that of the blood makes the word "sings", in retrospect, have some reference to the music of the spheres. Moreover, when we find the stars in line 61 as objects of superlunary perfection, in which earthly imperfections are "reconciled", we are reminded of medieval notions of the crystalline substance of the heavenly spheres; and so we are brought back to the "sapphire" of the beginning. (Sapphires, being blue and transparent, are especially associated with the heavens. In Ezekiel 1: 26, the Lord's throne is made of sapphire.) Yet even the stars have their mud-like aspect, for they "drift".

5. *Earth, Water, Air, Fire.* The second prefatory quotation from Heraclitus -- ὁδὸς ἄνω κάτω μία καὶ ὡυτή[350] -- expressing, in its straightforward interpretation, Heraclitus's cyclic theory of the elements, prepares us for references to the Four Elements. In the lyrical passage in "Little Gidding" corresponding to the passage before us, there is explicit reference to the doctrine of the Four Elements in its Heraclitan form. Here, too, we can discern this theme. Lines 47-51 deal with Earth (mud and scars). Lines 52-55 deal with Water, as it appears in organic matter (blood, lymph and sap). In line 56, we hover in Air above the tree; and the mention of "light" hints at the Fire of the sun; but we then return, in cyclic motion, to Water and Earth ("sodden floor") -- with a final hint at their kinship with the stars (Fire). We complete the circuit of the Elements; but the sense of their kinship, and common origin, in Fire makes us feel that "the way up and the way down is one and the same" – that all cyclic transformations of Matter, from the gross to the rarefied and back again, reveal a fundamental Oneness, though all four Elements retain an obstinate individuality.

In Heraclitus's system, the whole Universe, including the sun and stars, consists of the Four Elements, with Fire as the highest and most important, to which the others return cyclically by an "upward and downward path".[351] In Aristotle's system, the Four Elements hold sway only in the sublunary world, and the superlunary world is unchanging and crystalline.

---

349 Editor's footnote: See footnote above about Eliot's comments to Emily Hale in a letter dated March 19, 1936. Eliot seems to have intended the trilling wire to be singing with "a momentary sense of triumph and glory". (But "trilling" does sound mechanical as well; and the "triumph and glory" are only "momentary".).

350 Editor's footnote: fr.69 Bywater, translated by Bertrand Russell as "the way up and the way down is one and the same", in *History of Western Philosophy, op. cit.,* p. 51.

351 Author's footnote: fr.69 Bywater.

Both these systems have their influence here. The doctrine of the Four Elements, indeed, as commentators have pointed out, has influenced the whole structure of the *Quartets*, since each Quartet centres a different Element (though it may be doubted whether Eliot had this general scheme in mind at the time when he wrote "Burnt Norton"[352]). However, though the Aristotelian distinction between the sublunary and the superlunary worlds is used by Eliot, his use of the Four Elements is Heraclitan, not Aristotelian. He is attracted by Heraclitus's subtle conception of the Elements constituting "a harmony of opposing tensions"[353] – the idea that the very contradictions and conflicts of experience are the stuff of an underlying Unity, and that the Unity is to be sought *through* the contradictions, rather than by denying them as illusory.

We now have the thematic materials for a closer understanding of this very rich and complex passage, and of its place in the structure of "Burnt Norton". I suggest that the basic theme, from which all the other themes radiate, is that of *motion*. Just as Part I of "Burnt Norton" is a meditation on Time, Part II is a meditation on the allied philosophical theme of Motion. Part I takes the well-worn philosophical and religious thesis that Time is unreal, and, while agreeing with this thesis, salvages for Reality whatever is positive in our experience of Time; thus asserting that Reality is more, not less, than Time, which it includes. Similarly, Part II, while allowing the thesis that Motion is metaphysically unreal (Part V: "Love is itself unmoving,/Only the cause and end of movement,/Timeless, and undesiring"), nevertheless attributes to Reality whatever is positive in Motion, since it is just as mistaken to say that Reality (or God) is inert and motionless as to say that it is in motion. Finally, the image of the "still point" is reached. It is at rest, yet it is a centre of motion (like the centre of a whirlpool) and is full of motion. It is without spatial dimensions, yet, as a centre, it implies and generates Space. The contradictions of Motion and Rest, of Time and Space, of the One and the Many, are resolved in it; for Motion means change of position of Rest in the multiplicity of Space over a period of Time. The reconciliation is reflected in the word "still", which has the double meaning of "motionless" and "continuingly". (Eliot underlines the pun in Part IV: "the light is still/At the still point of the turning world", and in *Ash Wednesday* V.[354])

Accordingly, the chief strategy of the passage is to swing from an expression of Motion to an expression of Rest and back again, each time finding something to accept and something

---

352 Editor's footnote: See the 2015 *Poems, Vol. I, op. cit.*, p. 899, quoting Eliot: "It was after writing the first two [*Quartets*] that I saw that the pattern required four in all. I associated them with the four elements: air, earth, water and fire, in that order."

353 Author's footnote: fr.45 Bywater: Cyril Bailey's translation in *The Greek Atomists and Epicurus*, Oxford, 1928, p. 19.

354 Editor's footnote: "Still is the unspoken word, the Word unheard/.... Against the Word the unstilled world still whirled/About the centre of the silent Word." See also "Burnt Norton" V: "as a Chinese jar still/Moves perpetually in its stillness".

to reject; until finally, after these pendulum-like oscillations, "the still point" is reached that combines Rest and Motion. It may be observed further that the alternation of movement and rest is almost the definition of *rhythm*; so that the passage (which is itself strongly rhythmic) is, in its very structure of meaning, an expression of the concept of Rhythm. So the "still point", when it is reached, is a rhythmic or pulsating point; except that the experience of rhythm can be achieved by us only through Time, by successive experience of alternate Motion and Rest, while the "still point" combines both simultaneously and without succession. Rhythm is thus one of the ways in which, through Time, we transcend Time and experience a synthesis of Motion and Rest. "Only through time time is conquered."

Yet, despite the alternation of Motion and Rest, there is in the passage as a whole a spiralling *upward* motion (as in the *Purgatorio* and in *Ash Wednesday* III), from the mud to the stars, from Earth to Fire, from mineral substance to vegetable, animal and human life. This upward tendency too is contained in the "still point", for "*Erhebung*[355] without motion" is ascribed to it. Also, the higher in the scale of being an entity is, the more motion it contains. Earth, water, air and fire are progressively more flowing, mobile and volatile. Mineral, vegetable, animal and human is a progression that increases in mobility. God, we extrapolate, is the most mobile of all. Yet, as we rise from stage to stage and increase in mobility at each stage, the lower stages are not left behind. For at every stage something is lost, something too precious to be abandoned -- such as the sapphires in the mud – something to which we must return in cyclic motion if we are to grasp Reality. The immobile mud is just as real as the dancing fire. As we pursue our upward and downward cycle, we are pursuing the perfection of God, who is mud and fire, flesh and spirit, at the same time. This circular motion – a progression in Time and Space that describes a single complete figure, returning on itself – is a symbol of completion and eternity; and, like the Hindu snake with its tail in its mouth, it is a symbol also of human yearning for the completion, continually returning to what it has left behind. In Heraclitus's system, the upward and downward paths provided the equilibrium of the Universe: "If the upward path were to gain the victory over the downward, all would end in a great conflagration."[356] In other words, the principle of Motion would gain the victory over the principle of Inertia. It is in the mutual tension of opposites that equilibrium and peace consist. So, while the progress towards God and spirituality is correctly described as an upward motion, it must contain a downward tendency too (see Part III: "Descend lower"). And in God, or Reality, there is "neither ascent nor decline", but a combination or synthesis of both.

This leads us to reconsider the theme of Strife or War in the lyrical passage before us. Motion and Strife are linked concepts; Heraclitus's insight that all is flux (Motion) leads to

---

355 Editor's footnote: Meaning: "elevation".
356 Author's footnote: Cyril Bailey (describing Heraclitus's system), *op. cit.*, p. 22.

his insight that "war is the father of all and king of all".[357] This is true both on the material or biological plane (animals fighting for life and territory) and on the conceptual plane (each concept generates its opposite, which fights against it for survival – "Words strain/Crack and sometimes break, under the burden,/Under the tension, slip, slide, perish", Part V). This vision of a Universe of flux and strife can be a vision of Hell, as in the Chorus in *Murder in the Cathedral* beginning "I have smelt them, the death-bringers"[358]. Yet even this ghastly vision of continual motion, in which all beings eat each other, is transformed in the end into a vision of calm and peace:

> We praise thee, O God, for thy glory displayed in all the
>   creatures of the earth,
> In the snow, in the rain, in the wind in the storm; in all of
>   Thy creatures, both the hunters and the hunted....
> They affirm Thee in living; all things affirm Thee in living;
>   the bird in the air, both the hawk and the finch; the
>   beast on the earth, both the wolf and the lamb; the
>   worm in the soil and the worm in the belly.[359]

The ingredients of reconciliation, of peace, of Heaven, are the ingredients of Hell, "the hunters and the hunted" (here, in the lyrical section of "Burnt Norton" II, represented by "the boarhound and the boar"). Christ is usually represented as a Lamb; but Eliot calls him, in "Gerontion", "Christ the tiger". Heaven and Hell are the same universe, seen from different angles. This is Heraclitus's vision of a world of Unity and Peace, of which the ingredients are endless motion and strife: "Homer was wrong in saying 'Would that strife might perish from among gods and men'; if his prayer were heard, all things would pass away."[360]

In the conceptual sphere, the kingship of War means that each concept is locked in combat with its opposite; every formulation of the mind has its aspect of Heaven and Hell. This is the dialectical philosophy of Thesis and Antithesis that Eliot derived from Bradley and Hegel. Hell is limitation; every concept is heavenly as long as its limitations and incompleteness are acknowledged, but hellish in so far as it is worshipped and regarded as complete. A concept that points beyond itself is a glimpse of heaven; but a concept that

---

357 Author's footnote: fr.44 Bywater.
358 Editor's footnote: Coghill, *op. cit.*, p.74, l. 233.
359 Editor's footnote: *Ibid.*, p. 90, l. 623.
360 Author's footnote: fr.43 Bywater.
    Editor's footnote: Author's translation.

claims finality is, by its acceptance of limitation, a trap or prison that is hell. In other words, all concepts must be kept in motion; a static concept is false. Here Eliot's view of poetry as continually self-renewing and fighting against ossification links up with his philosophy of Motion and Time.

Thus every concept or formulation mentioned in these lines has its heavenly and hellish aspect. The mud signifies slowing down and death, the disintegration of purpose and pattern into chaos; but the mud also signifies peace and fecundity. Pattern itself signifies harmony and beauty, but also the horror of boring repetitiousness; the opposite of pattern, chaos, also enters into the synthesis that is Reality. The circle, the essence of geometrical pattern, signifies, as often in Eliot, eternity and peace; but the circle also signifies futility, especially when combined with motion in the concept of the Wheel, or in the mutual chase of the boarhound and the boar, or in "the crowds of people, walking round in a ring" in *The Waste Land* I, who remind us of the circles of Dante's Hell. (See also Chorus I from *The Rock*: "O perpetual revolution of configured stars" and *The Family Reunion*: "shrieking forms in a circular desert"[361].) The tree, the blood, the scars, all have their aspects of heaven and hell. Each, one may say, is a specialization, a realization of one of the possibilities of the plenitude of Reality; each therefore represents an isolation from all the other possibilities of Reality. To feel the pain of this isolation is also to feel the infinity of the universe; not to feel the pain is to be complacent and damned.[362] But the incompleteness of concepts, the fact that none of them ever rules out the validity of its opposite, is the guarantee of the inexhaustibility of the universe. Also, a vision of Hell is necessary in order to be saved; one must feel the full horror of a world uncompleted and unreconciled – a world that needs redemption (see lines 77-82).[363]

An interesting technical point that requires comment is the breakdown in punctuation in line 55: "Ascend to summer in the tree". Eliot frequently omits punctuation, but not often

---

361 Editor's footnote: *op. cit.*, p. 100.

362 Author's footnote: The condemnation of this complacency is one of the meanings of the first prefatory quotation from Heraclitus.

Editor's footnote: This quotation (fr.92 Bywater) is translated by Helen Gardner as "Although the Word is common to all, most men live as if each had a private wisdom of his own." (*The Art of T. S. Eliot, op. cit.*, p. 59 and p. 61.) For Eliot's own translation, see the 2015 *Poems, Vol. I, op. cit.*, p. 907: "Although the Logos is common the majority of men live as if they had an individual understanding."

363 Editor's footnote: Eliot summarized the whole lyrical passage to Emily Hale (in the letter – already mentioned in footnotes above -- dated March 19, 1936) as "an attempt to convey a sense of two beings together in an almost disembodied state in which the world appears as a pattern in sunlight full of beauty, although the abominations such as war (the boarhound and the boar) are there nevertheless". https://tseliot.com/the-eliot-hale-letters/letters/1468

This explanation of "a pattern in sunlight full of beauty" yet including all the "abominations" as well, is very close to the Author's analysis of this passage.

in a way that makes the syntax puzzling. Empson pointed out some interesting examples of ambiguous punctuation in Eliot[364]; and these remarks point the way to a possible solution here. The line "Ascend to summer in the tree" is purposely placed so that it can act either as the last clause of one sentence or the first clause in another. If we take the first alternative, the subject of the verb "ascend" is "the dance" and "the circulation"; which makes "ascend" coordinate with "are". The sense, therefore, is: "The blood and the lymph are similar to the drifting stars and the sap rising in the tree in response to the rhythm of the seasons." If we take the second alternative, the verb "Ascend" is a rather abrupt imperative, telling "us" to rise in the tree in order to reach the sunlight and finally float free in the air above the tree. This is perhaps a figure for the return to the vegetative life in meditation: "This is the one way, and the other/Is the same, not in movement/But abstention from movement." (Part III.) The absence of the full stop tells us to take the line both ways; or combine them in one thought: "The sap rising rhythmically in the tree is more like the process of meditation than the external movement and aggression of animals." This explains why the tree is a "moving tree". Its outer immobility contributes to a profounder internal motion.

Lines 62-89. The lyrical expression of the lines so far discussed (which give, in their pulsating movement, the feeling of Eliot's vision of the rhythm of being) now gives way to more prosaic, external, informative or reflective statement. The alternation between lyrical expression and contemplative statement is an important feature of the *Quartets*. This alternation requires extended discussion; but here it suffices to note that this, too, is, among other things, a rhythmical feature. Since the general meaning of the passage has been utilized in the previous discussion, I confine myself to notes on various points.

Line 62: "neither flesh nor fleshless". This does not mean that the "still point" is some third thing that is neither flesh nor fleshless. It means that the "still point" is both flesh and fleshless at the same time (just as it is both in motion and at rest at the same time, and both spatial and non-spatial at the same time). Thus we have a clear reference to the doctrine of the Incarnation, by which God is both flesh and fleshless.

Does this mean that the "still point" is God? In the first instance, the answer, I think, is "No". The "still point" is the moment of illumination, which was described in Part I, and is further described in these lines. It is the "point of intersection of the timeless/With time ("The Dry Salvages", V). The "still point" is a moment in Time, and also, as the word "point" suggests, an infinitesimally small tract of Space ("*there* we have been"). But in that moment all Time is somehow included, and also all Space; the "point" is infinitely small and also infinitely large (cf. the mathematical conception of a point as a *limit* that defines and, in a sense, creates the line leading to it). One might say that the "still point" is a tiny peephole

---

364 Author's footnote: *Seven Types of Ambiguity, op. cit.*, pp.78-79.

through which one receives a vision of the whole of Reality; except that the peephole is also the Reality. In a more prosaic sense, the "still point" is simply the present moment. But the present moment, when one reflects on it, is not at all prosaic, because it is in time and yet out of time, it is life itself, and yet it is nothing. The "still point" is the world when it is seen as a unity of Motion and Rest, of the One and the Many, of the Actual and the Possible. But the world, in this sense, is Reality; it is therefore God. The moment of illumination is an experience of God. The individual, when he opens out in vision, is irradiated by God. So, in the last analysis, the "still point" *is* God, and the hint of the Incarnation in "neither flesh nor fleshless" is relevant. The hint is not wholly unprepared for in the preceding lyrical passage. For the progress of the "upward path" from mud to light is also a progress from flesh to spirit. The Heraclitan reference reminds us that the "downward path" is just as important: "the way up and the way down are one and the same". The development of the spirit does not mean that the flesh is rejected. The "boarhound and the boar" – the animal flesh – are a perennial part of the "pattern" and are "reconciled among the stars". The wheel has a centre, but the centre has a wheel. "Except for the point, the still point,/There would be no dance, and there is only the dance."

Line 74: "concentration without elimination". This phrase has relevance to the "still point", since a point (in our human experience of Space), even if it is a point where desirable qualities are concentrated, can be reached only by traversing and rejecting the space surrounding it; but the "still point" includes the space surrounding it. Yet in our world concentration that involves elimination is necessary; this is the path of sacrifice. The attempt to avoid elimination, not to miss anything in life, leads to the empty life of those who are "Distracted from distraction by distraction" (Part III).

Lines 85 and 89: "only in time can the moment in the rose-garden ... /Be remembered; involved with past and future". Memory is the faculty that is in Time; and yet, through it, "time is conquered". Memory transcends Time, in the sense that Memory enables the mind to hold together past and present; a creature with no memory is entirely at the mercy of Time. Yet memory is temporal, while the moment of vision is not. If it were not for memory, the moment of vision would remain unrelated to the development of the life of the individual. By the agency of memory, the moment of vision, instead of remaining unrelated, becomes "involved with past and future". (Grover Smith[365] takes "involved with past and future" to be a denigrating description of the human mind, which can retain the moment of vision only in an imperfect way. I think rather that Eliot's point is that it is desirable that the moment should be involved in the past and future of the individual by the operation of the memory.)

---

365 Author's footnote: *T. S. Eliot: Poetry and Plays*, op. cit., p. 263.

    Editor's footnote: To quote Grover Smith here: "Memory, which is consciousness not transcending time, allows the mind, though 'involved with past and future', to apprehend the simultaneous point corresponding to the eternal."

The moment of vision, by being remembered, gives past and future a meaning – just as the apprehension of a melody gives meaning to a series of musical notes held together in the memory. To say that "only through time time is conquered" is therefore to assert the validity of our ordinary life; to deny that our life is worthless apart from the occasional flashes of vision. On the contrary, the flashes of vision would be worthless if they remained uninvolved with past and future. The musical notes are important, as well as the melody. The flesh, despite its "weakness", is as important as the spirit.

The theme of memory has already been raised in the lyrical passage in the lines:

The trilling wire in the blood
Sings below inveterate scars
Appeasing long forgotten wars.

Here memory is regarded as something clogging and impeding the free flow of communication and life. I think that Eliot is referring here to what psychologists call "trauma", or psychological wounds, which form "scars" in the shape of neurotic fixations, setting the character in certain fixed moulds, or at least causing a certain area of the personality to become "compulsive" or rigidly determined. These "inveterate scars" are "appeasing long forgotten wars" because the original conflict has become repressed, and the memory of the trauma has become unconscious.[366] In the context, it is the process of forgetting that is being stigmatized as impeding the flow of life; because to remember is too painful, and to be alive in the flux of being means to be exposed to the "War" that Heraclitus declared to be King of all. To forget is to achieve peace, but at the cost of dynamic power. On the other hand, of course, peace is good and is an attribute of the Divine. It is interesting that in early versions the line reads: "And reconciles forgotten wars".[367] In this version, the subject of "reconciles" is "the trilling wire". The meaning, therefore, is that the flow of life gradually heals and brings back into the flux the scarred and hardened tissue that old conflicts have engendered. The flow itself, as well as being the ground of Strife, is the ground of Peace. Eliot changed the line to "Appeasing long forgotten wars", and the participle "appeasing" goes more naturally with the adjacent noun "scars" than with "wire". Nevertheless, it can be taken with either or both, so the alteration produces a more subtle complex of meanings

---

[366] Author's footnote: Grover Smith (*T. S. Eliot's Poetry and Plays*, op. cit., p. 261) points out that "inveterate scars" comes from Chapman's translation of the second "Penitential Psalm" of Petrarch: "Rage, Lord, my sin's inveterate scars". This derivation reinforces my point that the scars are psychological.

[367] Editor's footnote: See Helen Gardner, *The Composition of Four Quartets*, op. cit., p. 84, footnote: "And reconciles forgotten.... The reading 'Appeasing long-forgotten wars' appeared first in *Four Quartets* [1944]. The change was presumably made to avoid anticipating 'reconciled' in line 61. Editions of CP [*Collected Poems*] after 1944 read with *Four Quartets*."

(peace in both its good and its bad sense – the word "appeasing" could be pejorative even before Munich). However, by altering "reconciles" to "appeasing", Eliot sacrificed something too, namely the echo in line 61: "But reconciled among the stars". The original version of the lyrical passage has an attractive echoing of the peace inherent in Motion.

The above remarks show that the lyrical passage has already raised tangentially the subject of memory as the agent of active involvement in life.

Part II has advanced Eliot's study of the significance of the moments of illumination:

the moment in the rose-garden,
The moment in the arbour where the rain beat,
The moment in the draughty church at smokefall

A contrast is drawn here between the moment of vision and the fortuitous or dingy surroundings in which it is experienced. This contrast is between the unitary vision of Reality, in which there is "plenitude" and "pattern", and the haphazardness of life as we normally know it. Yet both Part I and Part II stress also the other side of the matter: that Reality is the world we know transfigured, not a Never-Never Land separated from us by a metaphysical gulf. Time (Part I) and Motion (Part II) are ingredients of the world; and they are also ingredients of Reality. Everything we know, from "mud" to "light", is a symbol of the Divine, just as, from another point of view, it is a symbol of Hell. But this does not reduce the world to a mere system of symbols, with everything standing for something other than itself. The mud is a symbol of the Divine because it forms substantially part of the Divine; it is the Divine, viewed under certain limitations, which enable it to be what it is. The Divine is One, but it also comprehends the limitless variety of the Universe. The Wheel of life is also the "great Ring of pure and endless light".[368]

---

368 Editor's footnote: Henry Vaughan, "The World", which begins: "I saw Eternity the other night,/Like a great ring of pure and endless light".

Part III

In Parts I and II, Eliot has explored the moments of illumination in which the "still point" is apprehended. The "still point" has been shown to reconcile Time with Eternity and Motion with Stillness. In this way, a kind of defence of both Time and Motion, as ingredients in the Divine or Real, has been achieved.

However, near the end of Part II, Eliot has referred to "the enchainment of past and future". The implications of this phrase are explored in Part III, which is in fact the expected but postponed attack on Time and Motion. To the religious metaphysician, the categories of this world are illusory; but Eliot has dissociated himself, in Parts I and II, from the cheaper kind of "other-worldliness" in which the repudiation of this-worldly categories is a form of escape from responsibility, engagement and love – an inability to appreciate this world or to see it as the Divine "in the aspect of time" (l.166).

In Part II, Eliot has said:

Yet the enchainment of past and future
Woven in the weakness of the changing body,
Protects mankind from heaven and damnation
Which flesh cannot endure.

Here we are very close to *Murder in the Cathedral*, with its people who are "living and partly living"[369], able to survive only because they avoid the extremes of experience and insight. "Go, go, go, said the bird: human kind/Cannot bear very much reality" ("Burnt Norton" I). In Part III, the people who are "living and partly living" are described and are displayed particularly as people who are immersed in the flux of Time, or "time-ridden".

It is a widely accepted idea that the scene described in Part III is that of an Underground train journey. This idea was first put forward by F. O. Matthiessen[370], and has been followed unquestioningly by most commentators since. The indications of an Underground journey

---
369 Editot's footnote: Coghill, *op. cit.*, p. 30, l. 168, and p. 51, l. 648.
370 Author's footnote: *The Achievement of T. S. Eliot, op. cit.*, p. 181.
   Editor's footnote: Though Matthiessen's book was first published in 1935, two chapters on Eliot's later work, including the *Quartets*, were added in the second edition, published in 1947. Matthiessen writes (*op. cit.*, p. x) that his chapter on the *Quartets* "first appeared in *The Kenyon Review* (Spring 1943)".

are in fact slight. Perhaps the strongest is "Descend lower", which may be held to imply that a descent has already taken place. The expression "metalled ways" is certainly a reference to railway lines, but this single metaphor is hardly conclusive about the scene as a whole. Another consideration probably has been the fact that the corresponding section of "East Coker" refers explicitly to the Underground: "Or as, when an underground train, in the tube, stops too long between stations". But this could be held to be an argument *against* an Underground scene here, since such a repetition would be rather clumsy, especially as the Underground reference in "East Coker" is introduced with an air of novelty. Other considerations are the "dim light" and the "cold wind", neither of which is conclusive. The "cold wind" seems too elemental to be a platform draught, and surely ought to be identified with "the wind that sweeps the gloomy hills of London".[371] Perhaps the expression "time-ridden" has prompted the idea of riding in a vehicle; but this association is either invalid or tenuous.[372] "Eructation of unhealthy souls/Into the faded air" has been explained as referring to the emergence of commuters from the Underground into the street[373]; but it is much more likely to refer to the exhalation of breath mentioned in the previous lines. The place-names of London hills – "Hampstead and Clerkenwell, Campden and Putney,/ Highgate, Primrose and Ludgate" -- are not a list of Underground stations. The list of seven hills is clearly intended to recall the seven hills of Rome, and so to extend the idea of London into that of the City in general (cf. *The Waste Land*: "Jerusalem Athens Alexandria/Vienna London").

On the whole, we may conclude that the "Underground" theory has been accepted on very little evidence.[374] The scene of Part III is in fact purposely left vague. The impression

---

371 Editor's footnote: However, Ricks and McCue, the editors of the 2015 edition of Eliot's *Poems*, point out in their Commentary (*Vol. I, op. cit.*, p. 918), in relation to the line "Men and bits of paper, whirled by the cold wind", that, in the margin of his copy of Genesius Jones's book *Approach to the Purpose*, Eliot wrote "tube-station, of course, as the train approaches". If this is meant seriously (see following footnotes), there is no "of course" about it; Eliot has not made this at all clear. Fr. Jones (*op. cit.*, p. 211), calls the wind "Infernal" and writes that the vision of the wind "looks back to the early poetry and the 'draughty church' of *The Waste Land*" — a description that seems to me to be closer to the effect of the "cold wind" than Eliot's own explanation.

372 Editor's footnote: It could also perhaps be argued that the word "strained" includes the word "train" and so is a hint on the part of Eliot that the scene is taking place on the tube; but there is something tenuous about these associations, as the Author writes; and this kind of word-play is not characteristic of the *Quartets;* moreover, even if it is meant as a hint, Eliot should surely have made the locality clear (see later footnotes), instead of just hinting.

373 Editor's footnote: See Grover Smith, *Poetry and Plays, op. cit.*, p. 264: "And then the outdoor scene into which the 'unhealthy souls' drift like bats from the underworld."

374 Author's footnote: Hugh Kenner (*The Invisible Poet, op. cit.*, pp. 256-257) summarises a letter written by Eliot to his brother, elaborating the "Underground" theory humorously. This letter, written after the theory had become current, seems intended to be a parody on the theory, rather than (as Kenner thinks) a confirmation of it.

Editor's footnote: Kenner writes, in relation to "Burnt Norton" III, that "its locale, Eliot noted, sharing a private joke with his brother in Massachusetts, is specifically the Gloucester Road Station, near the poet's South Kensington headquarters, the point of intersection of the Circle Line with the Piccadilly tube to Russell Square. Whoever would leave the endless circle and entrain for the offices of Faber & Faber must 'descend lower' and by spiral stairs if he chooses to walk. 'This is the one way, and the other is the same'; the other, adjacent to the stairs, is a lift, which he negotiates 'not in movement but abstention from movement.'" (*Op. cit.*, pp. 256-257.)

Neither Kenner nor the Author provide a reference or date for this letter. Helen Gardner, in *The Composition of Four Quartets, op. cit.*, writes (p. 86; she leaves out the humour): "The setting of Section III is the London Tube. Eliot travelled daily from Gloucester Road Station, whose two means of descent, by the stairs or by the lift, suggested to him the movement down and the 'abstention from movement' while being carried down…. He gave this information in a letter to his brother." But she too provides no reference or date for the letter. Ricks and McCue, the editors of the 2015 *Poems*, quote from the Kenner and Gardner passages, but again give no reference or date for the letter (*Vol. I, op. cit.*, p. 917).

The Author asserts that the letter was "written after the theory had become current"; so he must have had access to the letter or at least have obtained information about its date. It must have been written between 1943 (when Matthiessen's theory first appeared in print) and 1947, the year when Eliot's brother, Henry Ware Eliot, died. T. S. Eliot's letters after 1941 have not yet been published; the letter will probably be included in a later volume. The letter does not appear in Vols. 7, 8, 9 or 10 (just published), which cover the years 1935-1944. This supports the Author's claim that the letter was written after Matthiessen's theory became current.

However, it is clear that Eliot *did* associate "Burnt Norton" III with the Gloucester Road tube station, long before Matthiessen's theory appeared in print. Eliot's widow, Valerie Eliot, wrote, in a letter to the *Times Literary Supplement* (July 16, 1971): "'Burnt Norton' and 'East Coker' were written in the Royal Borough [of Kensington] in Grenville Place and Emperor's Gate, respectively, and contain local allusions – for example, 'a place of disaffection' is Gloucester Road Underground Station". And Eliot himself wrote to Emily Hale about "Burnt Norton", on January 16, 1936, when he had only just finished the poem: "There is the reference to Heraclitus, and there are passages from St John of the Cross and a reference to Flaubert's Tentation de S. Antoine and a passage in the underground station at Gloucester Road; and besides that a good deal that you and no-one else will identify." https://tseliot.com/the-eliot-hale-letters/letters/l446

Of course, this does not rule out a primary association with the passage in *The Waste Land* I, with its connection to Dante's *Inferno*, Canto III. Helen Gardner argues that "Burnt Norton" III is about both: "The first paragraph reminds us of *The Waste Land*'s vision of the crowd flowing over London Bridge, the slaves of time, each one imprisoned in his own solitude. Here we are in the twilight world of the London Tube." (*The Art of T. S. Eliot, op. cit.*, p. 161.)

Yet the Author's distinction between obscurity and vagueness in Eliot's poetry seems to me to be a valuable one; and this passage is indeed uncharacteristically vague (in contrast, the crowd scene in *The Waste Land* I takes place both in Dante's *Inferno* and specifically on London Bridge, "down King William Street" and to where "Saint Mary Woolnoth kept the hours"); and the Author's argument that the passage is deliberately vague is convincing. The Gloucester Road tube reference was told by Eliot only to family and close friends – Kenner calls it a "private joke" shared with his brother -- and it is an entirely personal reference, not a generalized London Underground scene, which would seem more impersonal and associated with artistic purposes. So the Gloucester Road tube association was perhaps not meant too seriously. The part about the stairs and the lift is clearly a joke.

Eliot wanted to call *Four Quartets* by the unifying name *The Kensington Quartets;* but was dissuaded by his friend John Hayward; see Helen Gardner, *The Composition of Four Quartets, op. cit.*, pp. 26-27. This discarded title appears to have been intended as a kind of disguise or camouflage, and also to have had an ironic effect (irony against himself), like the title of "Mr. Eliot's Sunday Morning Service" (see Chapter 5): Eliot's persona of the prim and pedantic Mr. Eliot, living in genteel Kensington, yet putting forward a "philosophy of abandonment and ecstasy" (as the Author puts it in Chapter 5). In a letter to Frank Morley, a co-director of Faber and Faber and another close friend of Eliot, Hayward argued against the title (on the grounds that it was likely to suggest to readers "a private joke of some kind or an allusive jibe at all that 'Kensington' is commonly thought to stand for – the decaying rentier, frayed respectability and the keeping up of outmoded conventions"), but wrote in the same letter, evoking the image of camouflage: "I can understand Tom's [i.e., Eliot's] wanting to associate the tetralogy

given is of a sort of featureless region, vaguely situated in a City. It is only in the last four lines of the scene (ll.110-113) that any real indication of locality is vouchsafed; and these lines point to a London street-scene on a windy evening or morning in late autumn or winter.

The "Underground" theory, indeed, has arisen out of a dissatisfaction with the vagueness of Eliot's topography in this passage. The theory is false to the deliberate topographical imprecision of the writing. If the scene is indeed the Underground, Eliot ought to be censured for not making this more ascertainable.[375] Eliot is often obscure, but he is rarely vague, except when he has some special point in being vague. Here, he has such a point. He wishes to express the homelessness of the City crowd, which, "living and partly living", has no rooted sense of belonging to a clearly-defined and culturally-rooted area. Those who are "time-ridden" have no moorings.

The scene has been connected with the Underworld scene of *Odyssey* XXIV[376] (because of the word "twittering"[377]). But there seems a much stronger connection with Dante's *Inferno*, Canto III. Here are described those "who lived without blame and without praise", who "were never alive", and who live in an indeterminate, featureless place, dimly-lit ("buia campagna") outside the confines of the city of Hell, in air that "eddies in a whirlwind" ("a turba spira"). This passage in the *Inferno* has strong connections with the crowd-scene in

---

with the Gloucester Road Period, as anyone must who knows how thoroughly he took on its protective colouring." (Helen Gardner, *The Composition of Four Quartets, op. cit.*, pp. 26-27.) Hayward was surely right to dissuade Eliot from giving the four poems the confusing collective title *The Kensington Quartets* – and the Gloucester Road tube station association may have been a reflection of the camouflage frame of mind that suggested this title to Eliot. Kenner calls the Gloucester Road tube station association "the Possum's whimsey" (*op. cit.*, p. 257); and Eliot was nicknamed "the Possum" because the possum plays dead.

375 Editor's footnote: See previous footnote. If the Gloucester Road tube station connection is meant seriously, then it could be argued that Eliot's artistic purpose in keeping the passage deliberately vague conflicts with the deterministic imagery of a tube station (which is why there are no specific references to a tube station context); and this results in an artistic flaw in this passage -- a contradiction, rather than complexity. The Author argues below that, if it is meant seriously that we are in the Gloucester Road tube station both at the beginning and end of Part III, we lose the contrast between the vagueness at the beginning and the "metalled ways" at the end of Part III: Time as random and arbitrary and Time as fixed and determinate. It is true that the Author writes that Eliot's point at the end of Part III is that waywardness and arbitrariness are, in fact, the same as the deterministic "metalled ways" – as the Author puts it, "Aimless people are the most predictable" – but the reconciling paradox at the end only has an impact if we are first presented with the contrast. It is indeed difficult to see how Eliot, for all his powers of complexity, could have presented Time as simultaneously indeterminate and determinate; but, as the Author points out, there is no attempt at ambiguity; the first part of Part III is one-sided and unambiguous. The whole point of this first passage in Part III is to convey a sense of indeterminacy that militates against the evocation of the fixed, determinate "metalled ways" of a tube station.

376 Editor's footnote: See Grover Smith, *T. S. Eliot's Poetry and Plays, op. cit.*, p. 264.

377 Editor's footnote: The word is strangely prophetic of 21st century social media.

The Waste Land I – a passage that, I suggest, has stronger affinities that any other part of Eliot's work with the present passage.[378]

I do not wish to deny, however, that there is a hint of the Underground, and of suburban trains too, in the phrase "metalled ways". In a generalized picture of London, a glimpse of the trains is to be expected, though their deterministic symbolism needs to be reconciled with the images found elsewhere in the passage that symbolize the arbitrary and haphazard.

If the connection between this passage and *The Waste Land* I is as strong as I have suggested, then the "dim light" (once the Underground lighting has been abandoned) may be no other than "the brown fog of a winter dawn".[379] On the other hand, it may be the evening twilight -- an alternative that I prefer, because of the twilight theme of the succeeding Part IV. In either case, the dimness of the light symbolizes the indeterminate quality of the lives of those who live "without blame and without praise". More positively, the light symbolizes the transitional quality of life in this world. In "The Hollow Men", this world is called "death's twilight kingdom"; and in *Ash Wednesday* VI, "The dreamcrossed twilight between birth and dying". "Twilight" is positive when the mind becomes aware of transience and so senses the possibility of permanence. This embracing of transience is what Eliot calls "waiting":

> Those who are torn on the horn between season and season, time and
> > time, between
> Hour and hour, word and word, power and power, those who wait
> In darkness (*Ash Wednesday* V)

Here "twilight" has become the quality of all earthly life, caught "between un-being and being" ("Burnt Norton" V). But, in the passage before us, the twilight creatures are unaware of transience and are simply carried along with it unresistingly. In *The Waste Land* III, the tension between the positive and negative aspects of twilight is expressed in the ironic beauty of "the violet hour", introducing the typist-clerk scene.

Even in this passage, the possibility of the fruitful use of transience is shown in the lines:

---

378 Editor's footnote: There is also a strong resemblance to "The Hollow Men" I; the "hollow men" live underground in a vaguely described "dry cellar". They too "lived without blame and without praise". The wind is evoked here too; their whispering voices are "Quiet and meaningless/As wind in dry grass". See the references to "The Hollow Men" in the text in the next paragraph but one and on page 164.

379 Editor's footnote: From the cited passage in *The Waste Land* I: "Unreal City,/Under the brown fog of a winter dawn,/A crowd flowed over London Bridge, so many,/I had not thought death had undone so many." Eliot's note is: "Cf. Inferno III, 55-57."

Turning shadow into transient beauty
With slow rotation suggesting permanence.

But this possibility depends on an awareness of contrast between light and darkness, and between motion and stillness. Those who always live in twilight, and are never still, cannot grasp the possibility of transcendence suggested by an awareness of polarity. They are too greedy to give up anything and must always half-grasp at everything at once; an awareness of polarity would force them to acknowledge the essential contradictoriness and incompleteness of experience. The paradox is that those who are full are really empty, since they have nothing that they really want ("tumid apathy" – compare with "tumid" the word "stuffed" in "The Hollow Men" I), while those who are empty, and are most keenly aware of the transitory, unsatisfying quality of life, at least preserve the ideal of fulfilment, and so in a sense are satisfied; they possess at least the idea of the infinite. The "rotation" between polar opposites (here the circular motion of the Heraclitan Part II is recalled) suggests permanence, because in God polar opposites are reconciled, and all possibilities are realized simultaneously. This is very different from the human attempt to grasp everything at once by reducing everything to a grey twilight sameness.

Now for some specific comments on the first paragraph of Part III.

Here is a place of disaffection. The word "disaffection" is one of Eliot's surprise words (like "dissembled" in *Ash Wednesday* II[380] or "prevents" in "East Coker" IV). One is forced to give it an unusual meaning, yet the normal meaning lingers and reverberates in the background. The main meaning of "disaffection" is "lack of affection" or "lack of love"; and the word is meant to convey the state of those who "were never alive" and have never applied their emotions passionately enough to acquire either salvation or damnation (compare "indifference" in "Little Gidding" III). But another meaning is "misapplied affection" -- a meaning taken up in l. 98: "Cleansing affection from the temporal". Behind this meaning lies Dante's doctrine that all wrong conduct springs from the misdirection of love (*Purgatorio* XVII, 103-105). The sinful do not really lack love; they merely divert it from its true object: God. But, if we take the two meanings of "disaffection" together, we arrive at the further meaning: those who avoid life deal with their feelings by suppressing them. They are too aware of the terribleness of love to allow themselves to feel it (as both the sinful and the saintly do); for, if they felt love in the true intensity, this would lead to "concentration", and therefore to sacrifice of other objects of love, and (even harder to face) to the admission that earthly love always falls short of its object.

---

380 Editor's footnote: See Appendix 1(b).

But still further in the background is the original meaning of the word "disaffection", which is "feeling of disloyalty or discontent". Lack of love, the refusal to engage with life, is a disloyalty. We are reminded of the fact that, mingled with those on the "buia campagna", were the angels who "were not rebellious, nor were faithful to God". "Disaffection" is a good expression for this lukewarm disloyalty.

Distracted from distraction by distraction. Here "distraction" is used entirely pejoratively, as the opposite of "concentration", and to express the "many-ness" of the time-ridden life. Yet even "distraction" has its positive side, for later, in "The Dry Salvages" V, a visionary moment is described as "the distraction fit". It is typical of the deliberate one-sidedness of this section of the poem that the element of spontaneity and self-surrender in "distraction" is left uncelebrated, just as the "wind" is here a symbol for mere meaninglessness; not, as elsewhere in Eliot, an ambivalent symbol.

the cold wind/That blows before and after time. The variation from "Time before and time after" (l. 90 and l.107) is interesting. Here "before" and "after" can be read either as prepositions or as adjectives. If we read them as prepositions, the wind blows before Time begins and after it ceases to exist. We have the impression of a cold, indifferent Universe, in which man and even God are merely incidents. Time appears as a warm island in the indifferent ocean of the Universe. Such a random Universe is timeless – for "lived" time, in Bergson's sense,[381] cannot exist in a lifeless Universe. But those who surrender to the flux of Time surrender also to this elemental wind, which abolishes Time together with Life. This reading, however, is secondary. The primary reading takes "before" and "after" as adjectives describing "Time". Even in this reading, however, it is the wind that creates Time, rather than existing in Time (since "blows" now becomes a transitive verb with the object "time"). The wind is still elemental and impersonal, the symbol of a Godless Universe.

The second paragraph of Part III describes a way of escape from the ceaseless, meaningless movement of Time, with its unrelated "many-ness" ("men and bits of paper"). The method is that of certain Christian and Eastern mystics[382]: an attempt to achieve an experience of Nothingness. By stripping away all qualities, whether of sense, imagination or activity, a condition of blankness is reached in which the One is given ground to assert itself. (The word "property" in l. 118 is used in its philosophical sense of "quality", though there is probably a hinted reference to the monastic vow of poverty in both "property" and

---

381 Editor's footnote: See Bergson, *Creative Evolution*, op. cit., p. 31: "We do not *think* real time. But we *live* it, because life transcends intellect" (emphasis in original).

382 Editor's footnote: Lyndall Gordon writes (*The Hyacinth Girl*, op. cit., p. 227) that Eliot "mailed the whole poem in proof" to Emily Hale: "Next to the line 'darkness to purify the soul', Eliot gives Hale a clue in ink: 'The Ascent of Mount Carmel'. And next to the passage beginning 'Descend lower' he writes, again in ink, 'The Dark Night of the Soul'. These sixteenth-century treatises by the Spanish monk St John of the Cross preach a solitary discipline: to divest oneself of natural human affections so as to arrive at the love of God."

"destitution".) The point of the word "solitude" is the One-ness achieved by detachment from everything multifarious. (We are reminded of the method of a philosopher such as Descartes, who, on the purely intellectual plane, strips away all qualities by "doubting", hoping to arrive at a basic unity from which he can reconstitute reality.)[383] The method is not really a denial of the world, but rather an attempt to arrive finally at the real world that is hidden from us by the ceaseless motion and distraction of Time – it is like looking away from something in order to turn back and see it afresh. The "other" way, referred to in l.122, is one in which the sense-impressions themselves flower into unity, and their meaninglessness vanishes. This is the spontaneous unbidden way described in Part I. The "negative" way is more deliberately undertaken. It is the way of "concentration"; and to some extent it is employed whenever anyone concentrates on anything.

There is a tension here between two kinds of Nothingness. One kind was hinted at in "the cold wind/That blows before and after time". This is the kind of Nothingness that is a denial of the richness of Time altogether – it is a vision of utter meaninglessness and absence of all value and purpose. Ceaseless activity and motion can act as a means of avoiding this chilling vision. To cease activity means to be forced to face the vision, as in the Underground train that stops in "East Coker" III:

And you see behind every face the mental emptiness deepen
Leaving only the growing terror of nothing to think about.

But the way to face this "emptiness" (or, as Eliot calls it elsewhere, "the desert") is to go to meet it by the "negative" way of emptiness or "evacuation". One can only conquer the Desert by entering it, not by pretending it is not there. In this way, the Desert can be made to flower, for the Desert is only our suppressed knowledge of the inadequacy of all our satisfactions; a knowledge that is in fact the most hopeful thing in our being. Far better to yearn than to pretend to be happy – this is almost a summing-up of Eliot's message.

In the last lines of this section, we come across the image of Time as "metalled ways". This image is in strong contrast with what has gone before. The representation of Time up to now in Part III has been one of *randomness*, the chief symbol of which is the wind. Words like "flicker" and "twitter" bring out the theme of waywardness, unpredictability, and arbitrariness; but now we have an image that stresses Time's predictability and quality

---

[383] Editor's footnote: See René Descartes, *A Discourse on Method*, 1637: London, 1912, p. 23: "as I made it my business in each matter to reflect particularly upon what might fairly be doubted and prove a source of error, I gradually rooted out from my mind all the errors which had hitherto crept into it. Not that in this way I imitated the sceptics who doubt only that they may doubt, and seek nothing beyond uncertainty itself; for, on the contrary, my design was singly to find ground of assurance, and cast aside the loose earth and sand, that I might reach the rock or the clay."

of predestination. (The "Underground" theory, if applied to the whole of Part III, does away with this contrast.)[384] The point is that "appetency", or the pursuit of ends suggested by isolated desires, seems to itself to be boundlessly free; yet this very freedom is a form of slavery. One is reminded of Bradley's discussion of Indeterminism:

> In short, the irrational connection that the Free-Will doctrine fled from,
> in the shape of external necessity, it has succeeded only in reasserting in
> the shape of "chance".[385]

Those whose actions are bound by no law, because they are "Distracted from distraction by distraction" are actually bound by the iron laws of Chance. Aimless people are the most predictable.

It is worthy of note that the time-expression at this point has changed from "time before and time after" to "time past and time future". The words "before" and "after" are more immediate; they express the sensation of the passing of time from the point of view of the person experiencing it. "Past" and "future", however, are more public words. They carry us back to the discussion of determinism at the very beginning of "Burnt Norton". The image "metalled ways" reminds us of another point in that discussion: the way in which (as Bergson pointed out) determinism transforms Time into Space.[386] "The world moves ... on its metalled ways"; but the "metalled ways" themselves are static and unmoving, while the whole course of the journey is mapped out and can be seen simultaneously. Those who live immersed in Time lose all real movement, despite all their scurrying, while those who can achieve "abstention from movement" will achieve true movement, like the "moving tree" in Part II.

---

384 Editor's footnote: See my footnotes above about the Gloucester Road tube station association.
385 Author's footnote: *Ethical Studies*, 1876: Oxford, 1962, p. 12.
386 Editor's footnote: See the Author's comments in Part 1 above (pp. 135-136) on the opening lines of "Burnt Norton": "Eliot is hinting that the interpenetration of times, if understood in the wrong way, can lead to the annihilation of Time altogether, leaving us with an omnipresent Space. This is Bergson's line of attack on scientific thinking."

Part IV

It would be easy to take this graceful little lyric, with its charming deployment of alliteration and internal rhyme, as merely an elegy on the inevitability of death, with perhaps the linking meaning that the "darkness" spoken of in Part III will one day come to each individual (so that the "negative" way is seen in retrospect as "dying to this world" – an anticipation of death). But the surprising return of "the still point" in the last line demands an interpretation of the lyric that gives it an even stronger relationship to the thought of the reflective sections.

I suggest that the key phrase is "Will the sunflower turn to us …?" The sunflower turns always to the Sun. The disappearance of the Sun brings a desolating awareness of man's dependent status. The whole world of Nature yearns towards the Sun, not towards man. But the city crowd of Part III are too cut off from Nature to know this; they have a kind of tepid self-sufficiency. The rich natural imagery of this lyric, strongly visualized, is in contrast to the artificiality and vagueness[387] of the previous city-scene. This lyric is concerned with the "primitive terror" mentioned in "The Dry Salvages" II – the savage's sense of insufficiency, which is the beginning of religion. Thus the previous section about the "negative" way is seen as the deliberate effort to become aware of insufficiency, of emptiness that needs to be filled, a self-emptying in preparation for love.

The resonances of sound in this lyric, used with luxuriance unusual in Eliot, have an effect of hothouse growth, of the richness of tangled plants pressing upon one another, but all questing ultimately for the Sun. The words "clutch" and "cling", expressive of this desire for intimate contact, are illustrated phonetically by words that reach out for each other by alliteration and assonance. In the biological world, the motive force is love. Even the word "Chill", which comes as an icy shock, echoes the plaintively stressed "Will". Even the fingers of the death-tree curl in sensual contact. It is only the death-tree, in fact, that loves us as the other plants love the Sun. Only through death or "darkness" can we yearn for the "still point", or God, as the sunflower yearns through the night for the Sun. The whole lyric expresses the paradox of a world full of colour, tender love or "affection", in which, however, the road to fulfilment is through detachment or self-deprivation.

---

387 Editor's footnote: If meant seriously, the Gloucester Road tube station association would be appropriate to convey a sense of artificiality, but not appropriate to convey a sense of vagueness (see discussion of Part III above).

Part V

In this Part, the themes of the whole of "Burnt Norton" are brought together in a meditation on art and poetry. The basic concept of Part V, I suggest, is that of form or pattern. Through the paradoxes inherent in the concept of form, the themes of Time, Motion and Multiplicity are further illuminated.

We may note an immediate paradox. Form is something creative; yet it is also something limiting. It points beyond itself to infinity ("Only by the form, the pattern/Can words or music reach/The stillness"); yet it is reached by a process of strict elimination, and it is essentially finite and limited (l. 67: "the form of limitation"). Here Eliot is facing the problem of "inscape" that fascinated Gerard Manley Hopkins. How can we bridge the gap between the finite and the infinite? The answer given by both Eliot and Hopkins is that infinity must be sharply distinguished from *vagueness*. We do not reach the infinite by blurring the edges of the finite (as in the cheaper kind of mysticism), but by making them more distinct. It is through awareness of individuality that the infinite can be glimpsed. Eliot sees artistic creation as a continual struggle against "imprecision", against the tendency of ideas and words to "slip, slide" into vagueness. Poetry is the attempt to impose upon words the "stillness", unity, and individuality of form. The infinite cannot be just a grey, formless mass. It must contain more individuality, not less, than finite things. For us, individuality is bound up with finiteness; the sculptor hacks out the finite form of his sculpture from an indeterminate mass of stone. So our way to the infinite is through the finite, by the way of "elimination" or Sacrifice. But this means that the infinite must contain within itself the positive aspects of finiteness – just as it must contain the positive aspects of Time, Motion and Multiplicity.

Yet there is another side to this matter. Though a work of art, by its very wholeness and individuality, is finite and isolated (because it has a "beginning" and an "end"), yet, in another sense, it is not isolated at all. For every work of art is organically related to every other work of art. Each poem, for example, arises out of the whole literature of which it is part, and modifies, or is modified by, that literature. A work of art, just *because* it is so individual, extends the meaning of a whole culture; it is the realization of a possibility inherent in that culture. Similarly, in the realm of biology, all the strange and individual varieties of species are realizations of the inherent possibilities of life. Such varieties of individuality are impossible without a background of meaning, which is being worked out in infinite ways. It is through the concept of *tradition* that Eliot mediates the paradox of the finite and the infinite, as far as human culture is concerned. He sees tradition not as an inhibiting force but as a releasing force, enabling infinite variety to take place, because it provides a background of meaning and possibility. A piece of wood, sawn off from a plank, never achieves the isolation of a work of art; on the other hand, it never achieves such connectedness either, even before it is sawn off. Isolation and connectedness do not contradict each other; they even imply each other. That is why Eliot is able to recommend "solitude" and yet to value the community (e. g. in "East Coker" V).

The foregoing considerations apply to Part V as a whole; but here are some comments on individual points.

> Words move, music moves
> Only in time; but that which is only living
> Can only die.

There is an interesting ambiguity here in the word "only", an ambiguity that is continued in the use of the word in ll. 140-143: "Only by the form, the pattern/Can words or music reach/The stillness". The word "only" can carry either the meaning "merely" or the meaning "exclusively"; the two meanings are almost opposite in effect. Here both meanings operate together to express Eliot's ambivalent attitude towards Time and towards Form. Even subtler is the ambivalence of "that which is only living/Can only die". The primary meaning is: "that which is merely alive can do no more than die" (i.e., that which is so immersed in time that it does not point to a life beyond time is doomed to extinction – a judgment on worldly or popular poetry and art). Even without introducing the second meaning of "only", there are reverberations here; for the opposite of "that which is only living" may be "that which is both living and dying" – i.e., the life of the Negative way, which "dies to this world". Such a life does not "only die" but is reborn. But the ambiguity of "only" suggests the further meaning, "only that which is truly living can die", a thought that contains the essence of tragedy, and has many echoes in Eliot's work, especially in *Murder in the Cathedral*.

> as a Chinese jar still
> Moves perpetually in its stillness.

There is a deliberate illogicality here, since the form of the sentence suggests that the Chinese jar is to be introduced as an example of stillness; yet in the outcome it is proffered as an example of movement. "The form, the pattern" enable words or music to "reach the stillness"; but the form is not static. An artistic composition is a kind of stillness, by which unrelated objects become "composed" and are made to "stay still"; yet a composition can be praised as "full of movement". The beginning and the end are part of a pattern that exists in a perpetual "now", but it is not a static "now". The matter is taken further in "East Coker", where the theme of the "end and the beginning" is resumed immediately. At first, the pattern is a cyclic one, a pagan vision of Nature; but this vision is brutally contradicted in "East Coker" Part II by the attack on the cyclic pattern of knowledge: "The knowledge imposes a pattern and falsifies/For the pattern is new in every moment". We are to think of a pattern that, despite its "stillness", is full of change; every moment produces a new pattern. "Little Gidding" V says: "Every phrase and every sentence is an end and a beginning,/Every poem an epitaph". The past becomes dead not because it is wiped out, but because it is constantly being subsumed into a new whole, or pattern. (This is Eliot's version of Heraclitus's "You never step into the same river twice".[388] This view must not be confused with Hume's superficially similar view that atomic periods of time are discontinuous, and that time starts afresh with every moment.) This again is what Eliot means by saying ("The Dry Salvages" III) "the time of death is every moment". Just because there is so much new life continually bursting into being, there is also continual death of what has become outmoded. This vision of Life-and-Death is expressed here in l.157 in the phrase "funeral dance":

The Word in the desert

Is most attacked by voices of temptation,

The crying shadow in the funeral dance,

The loud lament of the disconsolate chimera.

These last "voices of temptation" seem to represent the temptation to *regret*. The "crying shadow in the funeral dance" is the impulse to weep over the many deaths that occur throughout one's life, the doors that close, the possibilities that remain unfulfilled.[389]

---

388 Editor's footnote: fr.41 Bywater (Author's translation).

389 Editor's footnote: In his letter to Emily Hale dated March 19, 1936, Eliot wrote: "One of the best lines in the poem occurs near the end: 'The crying shadow in the funeral dance'. The passage refers to the Temptation of Our Lord in the wilderness and by extension to the temptations besetting hermits in the desert of the Thebaid in Egypt in early Christian times; and principally the Temptation of Despair. Thus 'the crying shadow in the funeral dance' is intended to evoke some image of a barbaric or savage funeral ceremony (non-Christian of course): *savage* because the funeral ceremony is described as a 'dance'; and the 'crying shadow' may be thought of in terms of some person appointed to make lamentation, in some ritual costume in which the body is covered with a black robe and the face hooded or masked (hence 'shadow')."
https://tseliot.com/the-eliot-hale-letters/letters/l468 (italics in original).
It seems Eliot saw the "funeral dance" as a pagan, primitive, "barbaric or savage" rite, not the Christian "pattern" of Life-and-Death that appears in East Coker II or "Little Gidding" V (the 'funeral dance' also seems very different from the harmonious but boring pagan dance of "East Coker" I). But Eliot's "the Temptation of Despair" is very similar to the Author's "regret". Feelings of regret can lead to a sense of despair over irrevocably lost opportunities – "the doors that close, the possibilities that remain unfulfilled", as the Author puts it.

The "chimera" is the ambition that proved illusory.[390] The motto "Fare forward" of "The Dry Salvages" III is relevant here. Life is a continual narrowing of possibilities, a continual closing in of the "Desert". *Ash Wednesday* explores the fruitful consequences of the willing acceptance of this narrowing. The Negative Way is in any case the way we all have to travel, simply through growing old. The question is whether we travel it affirmatively, by an attitude of "sacrifice", or whether we try to avoid it, either by complacency or regret. Here "Burnt Norton" returns to the theme of possibility with which the poem started. To regret is to feel that somehow the past can be altered or that somehow one could have fulfilled all possibilities; it is a rebellion against human finitude, just as much as complacency.

Paragraph 2: The poem ends with a philosophical statement that modulates daringly into a vision. God, or Love, is timeless and unmoving, yet the still pattern of reality has time and movement as ingredients.[391] Time is an aspect of the timeless; the Infinite is caught in a framework of finiteness and is half in and out of the framework, "Between un-being and being".

Finally comes the vision (recalling that of Part I) in which the true, positive nature of Time is expressed. The vision, like all visions, is a return to childhood: the time when nothing seems impossible. It is a vision of an eternal present, a perpetual "now", which is, however, not static, but brimming with creative life and laughter. Time, in this picture, is not a straight line, as mathematicians picture it, but, as Bergson said, the crest of an advancing wave[392]; so that past and future are merely potential time (not, as mathematicians picture, the real body of time, the present being an empty, dimensionless mathematical point). Infinity is timeless, but it contains the creativeness and newness of our experience of the present moment.

---

390 In the same letter, Eliot continues: "The Chimera (with the more general French meaning of chimere) appears in Flaubert's 'Temptation of St. Anthony.'" https://tseliot.com/the-eliot-hale-letters/letters/l468

In Flaubert's novel, the Chimera says: "I offer to the eyes of men dazzling perspectives with Paradise in the clouds above and unspeakable felicities. Into their souls I pour the eternal madnesses; prospects of happiness, plans for the future, dreams of glory, vows of love, and all virtuous resolutions." (1874: Translated by Lafcadio Hearn, New York, 1992, p. 181.) So the "chimera" is indeed "the ambition that proved illusory".

391 Editor's footnote: For an explanation of "the ten stairs" in the lines that begin paragraph 2 – "The detail of the pattern is movement,/As in the figure of the ten stairs." -- see Moody, *Thomas Stearns Eliot Poet, op. cit.*, p. 240: "'the figure of the ten stairs' is an allusion to John of the Cross's *Dark Night of the Soul*, in which, in Chapters 19 and 20 of Book II, he explains 'the ten steps of the mystic ladder of Divine love, according to St Bernard and St Thomas'. The first five are the Dark Night of Faith, the *via negativa*; the next five are the stages of the illuminative way, by which the soul mounts upward toward the Beatific Vision." (Emphases in original.) Moody goes on (*ibid.*) to quote from Chapter 20 of Book II: "The tenth and last step of this secret ladder of love causes the soul to become wholly assimilated to God".

392 Editor's footnote: see *Creative Evolution, op. cit.*, p.135: "From our point of view, life appears in its entirety as an immense wave which, starting from a centre, spreads outwards, and which on almost the whole of its circumference is stopped and converted into oscillation: at one single point the obstacle has been forced, the impulsion has passed freely."

This vision comes "Sudden in a shaft of sunlight/Even while the dust moves". The dust is that of memories (as in "the dust on a bowl of rose-leaves") and of the detritus of generations of civilisation ("Dust inbreathed was a house" ["Little Gidding" II]). The dust is the symbol of lived Time, with its continual deaths and crumblings. But the dust "moves" and gives rise to the vision of the vital present; this vision must be integrated somehow even with the dust. We must supplement the condemnation of stretched-out, lived Time by other pronouncements in the corresponding movement of "East Coker":

Not the intense moment
Isolated, with no before and after,
But a lifetime burning in every moment

and

Love is most nearly itself
When here and now cease to matter.

Eliot's Puritan vision combines a conviction of the loss of Paradise with a determination to tread valiantly the path of the Desert, knowing that this path is the only one that will lead back somehow to the lost happiness. "Only through time, time is conquered." The way of discipline is the way of order, form and pattern. Though Eliot is able to see that form and pattern "reach/Into the silence", his most characteristic attitude is to connect them with renunciation and the "desert". In *Ash Wednesday,* when he spoke of the "desert", he added: "This is the land which ye/Shall divide by lot." But the land spoken of in the Bible[393] was the Promised Land, not the Desert. The true Classical ideal of "rejoicing in the Law" is a note not often struck by Eliot (though sometimes it is, as in "Little Gidding" V[394]). The "regret" that he tried to exorcise in *Ash Wednesday* never quite disappeared from his work. His Puritanism, as he himself recognized[395], is rooted in a fundamental Romanticism.

---

393 Editor's footnote: Ezekiel 48:29.

394 Editor's footnote: In the celebration of form and pattern without a sense of "regret": "And every phrase/And sentence that is right (where every word is at home,/ ... The complete consort dancing together)".

395 Editor's footnote: See Chapter 1, p. 60, footnote 120.

APPENDIX 1: TWO NOTES ON *ASH WEDNESDAY*[396]

(a) "Nothing again" (Part 1).

Because I cannot drink
There where trees flower and springs flow, for there is nothing again.

What is the meaning of the words "there is nothing again"? E. E. Duncan-Jones comments[397]: "the mirage recedes". Evidently, she takes the words to mean: "nothingness returns". Hugh Kenner[398] takes the same view; for he suggests, as the source, a passage from Tennyson's "The Holy Grail" in which a mirage vanishes.

Eliot is here saying farewell to youth. The springs at which he can no longer drink are the springs of youth. It is at the youthful time of the year that "trees flower"; and the springs, as well as symbolizing the sap of youth, as opposed to the dryness of old age, are themselves youthful, since they are sources and suggest, by subdued puns, vigour and springtime.

There is a closely analogous passage in *Murder in the Cathedral,* where the same imagery of flowering trees and water is used to evoke youth, when the First Tempter is trying to evoke in Thomas an interest in his early pleasures:

Laughter and apple-blossom floating on the water[399]

Thomas replies to the Tempter:

We do not know very much of the future
Except that from generation to generation
The same things happen again and again.
Men learn little from others' experience.

---

396 Editor's footnote: Originally published in *Notes and Queries,* November, 1966. Reprinted by kind permission of Oxford University Press (OUP).
397 Author's footnote: B. Rajan (ed.), *T. S. Eliot, op. cit.*, p. 42.
398 Author's footnote: *The Invisible Poet, op. cit.*, pp. 230-1.
399 Editor's footnote: Coghill, *op. cit.*, p. 34, l. 269.

> But, in the life of one man, never
> The same time returns.[400]

These lines give the clue to the passage in *Ash Wednesday*. "There is nothing again" means "Nothing happens twice" (in "the life of one man"). Youth occurs only once and cannot be revived.

There may be a hint here, too[401], of the deeper thought expressed by Heraclitus in the saying: "You cannot step into the same river twice".[402] Eliot, from his simple insistence that the stages of life are never repeated, later developed the theme that *nothing* is ever repeated; that it makes no sense to talk of *one* person, for example, persisting through time. This theme (common to Heraclitus and Hume) can be elaborated in very different ways.[403] Eliot's fullest treatment of it is in "The Dry Salvages" III.

b) "Dissembled" (Part II)

> And I who am here dissembled
> Proffer my deeds to oblivion and my love
> To the posterity of the desert and the fruit of the gourd.

Helen Gardner[404] comments on the word "dissembled": "the verb 'dissemble'... seems to be employed primarily in a special sense as the opposite of 'assemble'". Anne Ridler[405] praises the word, without saying what it means, as a "coining of meaning which keeps in mind the origin of the word". However, "assemble" is derived from the Latin "simul"; while "dissemble" is derived from the Latin "similis". If the origin of the word is being kept in mind, "dissembled" should mean "made dissimilar" or "changed". Since the poet is in fact being changed, it seems preferable to take this as the primary meaning of the word, with the meaning "dismembered" as a secondary, punning meaning. In general, I would argue that the meaning nearest to the normal use of the word should be taken as primary; unless (as in the case of "prevents" in "East Coker" IV) another meaning with strong historical or etymological claims (or both) is being thrust upon us (in the case of "prevents", it is the

---

400 Editor's footnote: *Ibid.*, pp. 34-35, ll. 282-287.
401 Author's footnote: I owe this suggestion to Mr. J. C. Maxwell.
   Editor's footnote: The literary critic Professor James Coutts Maxwell (1916-1976), a Fellow of Balliol College, Oxford, was the Editor of *Notes and Queries* at the time.
402 Editor's footnote: Bywater fr.41.
403 Editor's footnote: See the Author's reference to the different views of Heraclitus and Hume, Chapter 6, p. 171.
404 Author's footnote: *The Art of T. S. Eliot, op. cit.*, p. 116.
405 Author's footnote: *T. S. Eliot: A Study of his Writings by Several Hands, op. cit.*, p. 112n.

normal use that acts as an undercurrent). I am not arguing that Eliot's coinages are always etymologically sound ("juvescence" in "Gerontion" is an example to the contrary[406]). But I think he would not attempt to nullify or subordinate the strong pressure of the normal use of an existent word in favour of a coined meaning depending entirely on a pun. The meaning "changed" is not the normal meaning of "dissembled", but it is fairly near to it and has etymological justification. Elizabeth Drew's gloss[407] "changed and scattered" supports this analysis.

But perhaps it is possible to rescue even more of the normal associations of the word. What is it that is being changed? Does Eliot mean merely that he has been changed by the loss of his legs, heart, liver etc.? This would be to ignore the associations of the word "dissembled", which suggests disguise, or the assumption of an unrecognizable form. I suggest that the change referred to is the transformation of the portions of the poet eaten by the leopards.

The lines leading up to the passage under discussion are:

Lady, three white leopards sat under a juniper-tree
In the cool of the day, having fed to satiety
On my legs my heart my liver and that which had been contained
In the hollow round of my skull. And God said
Shall these bones live? shall these
Bones live? And that which had been contained
In the bones (which were already dry) said chirping:
Because of the goodness of this Lady
And because of her loveliness, and because
She honours the Virgin in meditation,
We shine with brightness.

What does the chirping here and what shines with brightness? Not the bones, as all commentators[408] assume (misled perhaps by the fact that the bones do chirp later on), but

---

406 Editor's footnote: See Chapter 4.
407 Author's footnote: *T. S. Eliot: The Design of his Poetry*, op. cit., p. 107.
408 Editor's footnote: Even Grover Smith, one of the most illuminating of Eliot critics, makes this misreading: "The bones, despite their dryness, are able to emit a sound of life, thin and sad, because of the Lady's loveliness and devotion" (*Poetry and Plays*, op. cit., p. 145; in the context, he is clearly referring to this passage, rather than to the later passages in which the bones do sing). The only partial exceptions I have found are a) Leonard Unger, in

"that which had been contained/In the bones". This refers back to "that which had been contained/In the hollow round of my skull". It is the parts that have been devoured by the leopards that chirp and shine with brightness. They shine with brightness because they are now part of the leopards, which are "white", and thus the parts are not only changed but transformed.

My view of the general symbolism of the passage is that Eliot is referring to the mystery by which sacrifice and renunciation keep the eternal sap flowing in the Body of the Church. The leopards, symbolizing both the three stages of renunciation[409] and the Body of Christ (cf. "Christ the tiger" in "Gerontion"), live and remain eternally youthful because of the renunciation of youth by members of the Church. (The Lady, a Beatrice figure, represents the sublimation of sexual desire, another form of renunciation by which what is naturally

---

T. S. Eliot: A Selected Critique, op. cit., p. 361; he recognizes the distinction, but connects "that which had been contained/In the bones" to "the anguish of the marrow" in "Whispers of Immortality" and argues that the words are in some way spoken by the departed marrow, "as a symptom of intensity". I find this unconvincing; and b) a much more recent critic, Jewel Spears Brooker, who also notes the distinction, but writes (*T. S. Eliot's Dialectical Imagination, op. cit.*, p. 137): "In the first stanza, it is the first-person narrator who laments the desiccation of 'my legs my heart my liver and that which had been contained/In the hollow round of my skull' (3-4)." It is the *bones* here that are "desiccated" ("which were already dry").

409 Editor's footnote: The Three Stages of Renunciation are a crucial part of the Baptism Service of the Church of England. To quote from the Book of Common Prayer (1662 Version): "*Question*. Dost thou renounce the devil and all his works, the vain pomp and glory of the world, with all covetous desires of the same, and the carnal desires of the flesh, so that thou wilt not follow or be led by them? *Answer*. I renounce them all" (1662: Cambridge, 2004, p. 284; emphases in original). The Three Stages of Renunciation are thus the renunciation of the Devil, the World, and the Flesh. In several letters to correspondents, Eliot explained that the three leopards symbolize the World, the Flesh and the Devil (see 2015 *Poems, Vol. I, op. cit.*, pp. 741-742 and next footnote). It has become a generally accepted critical interpretation that the three leopards represent the World, the Flesh and the Devil. But why are the leopards white, the colour of purification? Why do the soft parts of the poet's body that have been eaten by the leopards "shine with brightness"? And why, as the Author puts it, do the leopards convey a sense of "calm, bright dignity"? Spurr (*op. cit.*, p. 220), writes of "the dire process of being devoured by death-dealing sin – represented by the three white leopards, symbolising the world, the flesh and the devil – who have all but consumed him", but also points out that "the various manifestations of whiteness tell of a rite of purification". Grover Smith (*Poetry and Plays, op. cit.*, p. 144) suggests that the leopards represent the World, the Flesh and the Devil, but points out that they are also "agents of purgation". Spurr and Smith do not mention the Baptism Service (Smith only refers to St John of the Cross); but the Baptism Service is surely the key to reconciling the two elements. Not one critic that I have read, apart from the Author, has related the World, the Flesh and the Devil to the Three Stages of Renunciation at Baptism: this link is the basis of the Author's interpretation that the leopards represent the *renunciation* of the World, the Flesh and the Devil – i.e., the sacrifice of sinful desires, and yet, at the same time (on the principle, it seems, that we are what we eat), the mystery of their preservation in a transmuted, purified form, which also represents the Incarnation – the union of the Flesh with the Word to create the Body of Christ, which is a term for the Church. In the Commentary to the 2015 *Poems, Vol. I, op. cit.* (a Commentary that sums up recent critical thinking on this passage), the editors, Ricks and McCue, quote (p. 741) from the Church of England Litany: "Good lord, deliver us. From fornication and all other deadly sins; and from all the deceits of the world, the flesh and the devil"; and from St John of the Cross: "the three enemies of the soul, which are world, devil and flesh". The editors make no mention of the Baptism Service. But, after all, *Ash Wednesday* is Eliot's "conversion" poem, written to celebrate his recent Baptism into the Church of England!

crude and transient becomes refined and fixed.[410]) Thus, the soft parts of the poet's body[411] (representing his youthful desires), by being renounced, become transformed and transmuted into the eternally youthful and beautiful Body of the Church. The "posterity of the desert" are the leopards themselves, to whom the poet offers, as a sacrifice, his "love" – that is, his emotional juiciness.[412] (The desert too is a symbol of the renunciation that feeds the leopards.) The "indigestible portions/Which the leopards reject" are the shrivelled sinews of old age, deprived of the sap of youth, but achieving their own kind of life because of the willingness of their sacrifice.[413]

It may seem a bizarre suggestion that the soft portions chirp from inside the leopards; but I think we are to consider the leopards as being nourished entirely by the soft parts (or sacrificed desires) of members of the Church, and thus the chirping is representative of the leopards themselves (or of the Church in relation to the individuals who compose it). Moreover, the whole imagery of the passage is intentionally grotesque. The combination

---

410 Editor's footnote: Eliot referred three correspondents, in connection with the leopards, to Dante's *Vita Nuova*, which is all about the sublimation of sexual desire. On July 20, 1930, Eliot wrote to the Church of England Bishop George Bell: "The three leopards ... are deliberately the World, the Flesh and the Devil; and the whole thing aims to be a modern *Vita Nuova*, on the same plane of hallucination, and treating a similar problem of 'sublimation' (horrid word).'" (*The Letters of T. S. Eliot, Volume 5, op. cit.*, p. 258.) On May 22, 1930, Eliot wrote to the novelist Charles Williams, with specific reference to the three leopards: "if one can explain *obscurus* by *obscurior*, and the less by the greater, the *Vita Nuova* may help" (*ibid.*, p. 197). On May 17, 1930, Eliot wrote to Philip Parker, of St. John's College, Oxford, specifically about the leopards: "The *Vita Nuova* might give you some help; but on the other hand it is much more obscure than I have the talent to be. If you call the three leopards the World, the Flesh and the Devil, you will get as near as one can, but even that is uncertain." (*Ibid.*, p. 187.) These three quotations (particularly the last) seem to point to the complexity of Eliot's use of the World, the Flesh and the Devil (despite Eliot's explanation, in a letter of February 10, 1937, to Gregor Ziemer, Headmaster of the American School in Berlin, who had written to him with many questions on behalf of a Professor Schirmer and his class of 25 students: "my leopards represent simply the world, the flesh and the devil"). (*Letters, Volume 8, op. cit.*, p. 491.)

411 Author's footnote: "Legs", I think, is a euphemism for genitals. See Baudelaire's "Un Voyage à Cythère". Editor's footnote: See my footnote in Chapter 1 (page 45, footnote 79) on this Baudelaire source, which no other critic has identified.

412 Editor's footnote: This helps to explain the juniper tree – the poet sacrifices his youthful desires also to the juniper tree (which grows in the desert but is an evergreen), so that it can remain always green and fresh (the same with the gourd). Juniper berries are also used for purification: see Frazer, *Abridged Edition, op. cit.*, p. 560, on exorcism of witches in Central Europe: "On the last three days of April all the houses are cleansed and fumigated with juniper berries." The juniper tree, like the white leopards, seems to represent both the sacrifice of youthful desires and the preservation of those desires in purified form.

413 Editor's footnote: Similarly, the bones have their own limited brightness -- "scattered and shining" -- and their own dry, thin (though beautiful), "chirping" song, later in Part II. In their Commentary, the editors of the 2015 *Poems, (Vol. I, op. cit.,* p. 744) point out the pun on "burden" in "with the burden of the grasshopper"; on the one hand, it refers to Ecclesiastes 12:5: "and the grasshopper shall be a burden and desire shall fail", but on the other hand it means the refrain of a song. For the Author's interpretation of the lines "The single Rose/Is now the Garden/Where all loves end" see, the commentary, in Chapter 6 (p. 143), on Part 1 of "Burnt Norton". The bones (while remaining scattered) also have their own kind of unity: "united/In the quiet of the desert". See the end of Chapter 6 (p. 173) for a reference to the last lines of *Ash Wednesday* II.

of gruesomeness, comic invention and calm, bright dignity is very like the combination of qualities in a Surrealist painting. The kind of analysis required is not far removed from Freudian dream-analysis.

The whole passage expresses Eliot's conviction that sacrifice is not waste; that sacrifice is a positive thing; that what is sacrificed somehow survives in a purer form and nourishes the community. The ferocity of the imagery relates Christian sacrifice to pagan sacrificial rites. Frazer's *The Golden Bough* has its influence on Eliot's later, as well as on his earlier, poetry.[414]

I have admitted that the word "dissembled" also acts, in a supplementary fashion, as an expression for "dismembered". Eliot, of all poets, responds to Empsonian treatment. I would even add that the derogatory force of the normal meaning of "dissembled" is also faintly present; a residual feeling of resentment thus achieves expression. The "I" of the poet has not been completely transformed, for there remains an element of pretence. Eliot never ceases to count the cost of the spiritual life.

---

414 Author's footnote: See *The Golden Bough*, Ch. LII: 1, for the connection between youth and sacrifice.
Editor's footnote: *The Golden Bough, Abridged Edition, op. cit.,* pp. 499-500.

APPPENDIX 2: TWO NOTES ON *MURDER IN THE CATHEDRAL*[415]

(a): THE FOURTH TEMPTER: DEVIL OR ANGEL?[416]

[Editor's note: In Chapter 1 (p. 57), the Author writes: "In Eliot's poetry ... it is the mystery-cult inheritance of Christianity that is really significant." Yet here the Author argues that, in his depiction of the Fourth Tempter, Eliot is drawing on Christianity's Jewish heritage.]

Why does the Fourth Tempter end his Temptation by repeating to Thomas his own words: "You know and do not know, what it is to act or suffer"[417]? Commentators seem to agree that this is some kind of taunt or sneer. The Fourth Tempter "flings" the words "back at him" (D. E. Jones)[418]; "the advice he has given is turned against him" (Nevill Coghill)[419]. On this interpretation, the whole speech is to be delivered in tones of savage irony. Thomas's analysis of action has been refuted by the revelation that disinterested action is impossible; even to give one's wholehearted and disinterested assent to God's preordained pattern is beyond the capacity of a human being, whose aspirations towards saintliness are only a particularly deadly form of self-regard. Alternatively, the Tempter is taunting Thomas about his failure to understand and live up to his own words (D. E. Jones). This, according to Jones, is the final "turn of the screw".[420]

These interpretations seem to me implausible. It would be very difficult, perhaps impossible, for the actor to deliver the speech effectively in the way described. The rhythms are too calm and measured to be given the required ironic twist; and in any case, the speech is too long for such a tone to be sustained. A receptive reading of the whole passage in the play leaves the conviction that, on the contrary, the repetition of this profound and central

---

[415] Editor's footnote: Originally published in *Notes and Queries*, July 1967. Reprinted by kind permission of Oxford University Press.

[416] Editor's footnote: Note (a) was reprinted in *Twentieth Century Interpretations of Murder in the Cathedral*, ed. David R Clark, New Jersey, 1971.

[417] Editor's footnote: Coghill, *op. cit.*, p. 49, l. 591. For Thomas's "own words", see *ibid.*, p. 32, l. 208.

[418] Author's footnote: *The Plays of T. S. Eliot,* 1960: London, 1963, p. 64.

[419] Author's footnote: Coghill, *op. cit.*, p. 17.

[420] Editor's footnote: Jones, *op. cit.*, p. 64.

speech is intended as a kind of summing-up of the lesson of the Fourth Temptation. The Tempter is not taunting, but teaching; not sneering, but comforting; just as Thomas was comforting the women of Canterbury when he first spoke the same words. This is not to deny that there is a touch of irony in the situation; for the Tempter is teaching Thomas something that he thought he knew already. The irony is not an expression of vindictiveness, nor does it lie in any allegation of falsehood in the words themselves. It arises simply from the fact that Thomas, the teacher, is now the pupil. There is especial irony in the phrase "You know and do not know". When Thomas had applied similar words to the women of Canterbury, there had been a little condescension in his assertion that the women had an instinctive grasp of profundities that they were unable to put into articulate form. Now it has become clear that Thomas has been able to put into articulate form something of which, so far, he has had no instinctive grasp. He too "knows and does not know"; but he knows what the women of Canterbury do not know; and does not know what they know.

What kind of person does this make the Fourth Tempter? There are several indications that he is not a mere seducer from virtue; but has a deeper role. This role is to make Thomas face his own repressed motives in all their ugliness; and so achieve purification from them. The Tempter speaks not as one putting before Thomas seductive pleasure and glory, but as one laying bare to the horrified Thomas the vulgarity of his own desires. Does the Fourth Tempter really think that he is *tempting* Thomas by offering him the pleasure of seeing "far off below you, where the gulf is fixed,/Your persecutors, in timeless torment"[421]? Or is he not rather forcing Thomas to realize the baseness of his own secret vision of glory? (This particular pleasure, as Eliot undoubtedly knew, was one much prized by Tertullian[422] and other authorities; and the historical Thomas would perhaps not have found it disreputable.) The essence of the kind of vainglorious, sadistic daydreaming exposed in the Fourth Temptation is that it should not be admitted to full consciousness. Once it is so admitted, and the critical light of the adult moral consciousness allowed to play on it, it immediately loses its force. If the Fourth Tempter had really wished Thomas to be damned in this particular way, it would have served the Tempter's demonic purposes far better

---

421 Editor's footnote: *Ibid.*, p. 48, ll. 571-572.

422 Editor's footnote: See Tertullian, *De Spectaculis*, 30: "Which sight gives me joy? which rouses me to exultation? – as I see so many illustrious monarchs, whose reception into the heavens was publicly announced, groaning now in the lowest darkness with great Jove himself ... governors of provinces too, who persecuted the Christian name, in fires more fierce than those with which in the days of their pride they raged against the followers of Christ! What world's wise men besides.... Poets also, trembling not before the judgment-seat of Rhadamanthus or Minos, but of the unexpected Christ! I shall have a better opportunity then of viewing the play-actors ... in the dissolving flame ... the charioteer, all glowing in his chariot of fire; of witnessing the wrestlers, not in their gymnasia but tossing in the fiery billows; unless even then I shall not care to attend to such ministers of sin, in my eager wish rather to fix a gaze insatiable on those whose fury vented itself against the Lord." (*Ante-Nicene Christian Library: Translations of the Writings of the Fathers Down to A. D. 325, Vol. XI, the Writings of Tertullian, Vol. 1, op. cit.*, pp. 34-35.)

not to have approached Thomas at all. The approach of the Fourth Tempter is, in fact, the beginning of Thomas's salvation.

Yet there is also enough in the presentation of the Fourth Tempter to make him appear to be, after all, the Evil One, Satan himself. The Tempter says: "I offer what you desire. I ask/ What you have to give."[423] Here he speaks the language of Mephistopheles to Faust. While the first three Tempters are solid human beings, individually characterized, the Fourth Tempter is a supernatural being, bringing with him an aura of dread and fascination. (It is, of course, possible to regard all four Tempters as embodiments of aspects of Thomas's own mind; but, once they have been so embodied, we must take them on their own dramatic terms. Eliot's first conception of the first three Tempters was even more solidly characterized.[424] He toned down the realism of their presentation, but still left them recognizable human beings.)

The solution to the paradox, I suggest, is that Eliot has hit on a conception of the Tempter as the servant of God. This is a Jewish rather than a Christian notion. It would be interesting to know how far Eliot had studied the idea in the Jewish sources.[425] No other conception, I think, can do justice to the extraordinary interest and subtlety of the Fourth Tempter's role. He forces upon Thomas a loathing that reveals itself as self-loathing. He tempts him with his own thoughts, which he has been unwilling to avow for what they are, and which only have to be avowed to be rejected. The Fourth Tempter has a grasp of the total situation far beyond that of the other Tempters, who naively expect that Thomas will be seduced. It is thus not at all inappropriate that, when Thomas, convinced of his own worthlessness, sinks into despair and doubts the possibility of human justification ("Can I neither act nor suffer/Without perdition?"[426]), the Tempter reminds him of the analysis previously made by Thomas himself of the meaning of action and justification. The conviction of sin must precede salvation; and Thomas's despair here corresponds to the despair of the Chorus later in the play that breaks through their complacency and prepares them for purification. Self-regard, the Tempter is saying, rests ultimately on an overestimation of the power of human action. Thomas is ambitious because he still thinks that his fate is in his own hands; that he can manipulate his promotion in the Court of the Heavenly King. The conviction

---

423 Editor's footnote: *Ibid.*, p. 48, ll. 578-579.

424 Editor's footnote: In a prefatory note to the 1937 edition of *Murder in the Cathedral*, Eliot wrote: "When, as originally intended, the parts of the Tempters are doubled with those of the Knights" (London, 1937), p. 7. For his reason for the change from this original intention – a reason that strongly supports the Author's interpretation of the Fourth Tempter -- see footnote 427 in this Appendix (2a).

425 Author's footnote: In the Babylonian Talmud (Baba Bathra 16a), R. Achar bar Jacob expounds Satan's good intentions in the Job affair; and Satan comes and kisses the Rabbi's knees in gratitude. In the Hebrew Bible, Satan appears in heaven among the "sons of God" (Job, 1). The idea that Satan was responsible for the Fall is not found in the Hebrew Bible. Nor is the story of Satan's rebellion against God.

426 Editor's footnote: Coghill, *op. cit.*, p. 49, ll. 589-590.

of helplessness accompanies the conviction of sin; and this helplessness is the essential basis for a true exercise of free-will in consenting to God's inevitable plan. This is the point of the Tempter's reminder; and, when he makes it, he is revealed as a messenger of God, a comforter and angel, rather than a devil; or, more accurately, he is a devil who is the servant of God, using temptation to awaken men to the knowledge of their own souls.[427]

APPENDIX 2(b): THE FLESH AND THE SPIRIT

I have smelt them, the death-bringers; now it is too late
For action, too soon for contrition.
Nothing is possible but the shamed swoon
Of those consenting to the last humiliation.
I have consented, Lord Archbishop, have consented.
Am torn away, subdued, violated,
United to the spiritual flesh of nature,
Mastered by the animal powers of spirit,
Dominated by the lust of self-demolition,
By the final utter uttermost death of spirit,
By the final ecstasy of waste and shame,
O Lord Archbishop, O Thomas Archbishop, forgive us, forgive us,
pray for us, that we may pray for you, out of our shame.[428]

The intensely charged Chorus passage beginning "I have smelt them, the death-bringers; now is too late/For action, too soon for contrition" has met with various interpretations. The paradoxical phrases "spiritual flesh" and "animal powers of spirit" have led commentators to say that these lines express primarily the Chorus's sense of chaos; the sense that all due

---

[427] Author's footnote: For a similar ambiguity of role in *The Cocktail Party*, see D. E. Jones, *The Plays of T. S. Eliot, op. cit.*, p. 153. Reilly is the "devil" who is really an angel. [Added in Clark, *op. cit.*, p. 96] The Eumenides, too, in *The Family Reunion*, have a devil-angel role.

Editor's footnote: Martin Browne, in *The Making of T. S. Eliot's Plays,* Cambridge, 1969, published two years after this essay appeared in *Notes and Queries*, cites (p. 58) a personal letter, written to him by Eliot on 20 September 1956, that strongly supports the Author's interpretation of the Fourth Tempter: "'I am by no means now sure that it is not better to have the knights played by different actors from the tempters. I like to leave questions for the audience to resolve for themselves, and one question which is left for them if the knights and tempters are different actors, is whether the fourth tempter is an evil angel or possibly a good angel. After all, the fourth tempter is gradually leading Becket on to his sudden resolution and simplification of his difficulties.'"

[428] Editor's footnote: Coghill, pp. 74-75, ll. 233-244.

boundaries have been broken down by the Knights' surrender to evil. D. E. Jones[429] speaks of "disorder of evil", L. L. Martz[430] of "the vision of a universe without order". Nevill Coghill[431] (citing Donne and C. S. Lewis) sees in the lines "United to the spiritual flesh of nature/ Mastered by the animal powers of spirit" a reference to a medieval three-tier doctrine of "spirit", "flesh" and "soul", the "spirit" acting as an intermediary substance between soul and body (the doctrine actually derives from Porphyry[432]). The arrangement, apparently, has broken down, and the "hierarchy of things is going into reverse".[433] It seems to me much more likely that Eliot intended by "spirit and flesh" what any modern playgoer would take them to mean – expressions more or less synonymous with "soul" and "body". Many New Testament passages (including the one about the spirit being willing but the flesh weak[434]) can be adduced in support of this straightforward interpretation.

Moreover, I cannot agree that the idea of chaos, or disruption of a hierarchy of substances, is the main idea to be stressed in the interpretation of this passage. The phrases "spiritual flesh" and "animal powers of spirit" should be taken as paradoxes, not as mere jarring contradictions. Eliot is bringing out the fact that, in human beings, "flesh" and "spirit" are not two neatly divided categories, but interpenetrating aspects of an indivisible whole. The interpenetration of "spirit" and "flesh" is no less important than the distinction between them that pervades the play. The paradox is a fundamental one in Eliot's thought; it enters into the meaning of the Incarnation for him.

---

429 Editor's footnote: *The Plays of T. S. Eliot, op. cit.*, p. 77.

430 Author's footnote: Unger (ed.), *op. cit.*, p. 457.

431 Editor's footnote: Coghill, *op. cit.*, p. 129. Coghill quotes Donne's poem "The Ecstasie": "As our blood labours to beget/Spirits as like souls as it can,/ Because such fingers need to knit/The subtile knot which makes us man"; and comments that "the allusion to 'the spiritual flesh of nature, mastered by the animal powers of the spirit' refer[s] to the 'spirits' here mentioned in Donne's poem. The nature of *spirit*, as understood by Donne and the middle ages, is a kind of emanation within us from our animal bodies and bloods; they are 'just sufficiently material for them to act upon the body but so very fine and attenuated that they could be acted upon by the wholly immaterial soul' (C. S. Lewis, *The Discarded Image*, [Cambridge] 1964, p. 167)." (Emphases in original.)

432 Editor's footnote: Neoplatonist philosopher (c. 234-c. 305 CE); disciple, editor and biographer of Plotinus. See Thomas Taylor (editor and translator), *Select Works of Porphyry*, 1823: Westbury, Wiltshire (Prometheus Trust, 2nd edition), 1999, p. 169, from "Auxiliaries to the Perception of Intelligible Natures", Section 1: 4: "Things essentially incorporeal, are not present with bodies, by hypostasis and essence; for they are not mingled with bodies. But they impart a certain power which is proximate to bodies, through verging towards them. For tendency constitutes a certain secondary power proximate to bodies."

433 Editor's footnote: Coghill, *op. cit.*, p. 129: "The lines under discussion ... mean that a reversal of the natural order is taking place, and the *spirit* that should be acted on by the soul, and so act upon the body, is in fact being acted on by bodily lust and so the soul is unable to act upon it. The hierarchy of things is going into reverse." (Emphasis in original.)

434 Author's footnote: Matt., 26: 41.

Yet the greater part of the Chorus so far has been an evocation of the flesh at its most fleshy. The kinship of man with the animals ("the horror of the ape"[435] is that it is a caricature of man) has been stressed with a combination of sensuality and disgust. The utter concreteness of the flesh, and ceaseless mutual incorporation of all animals – man eating animals and being eaten by the worm – has been brought out with a wealth of tastes, smells, and textures. The Chorus is overwhelmed by the sense of its own fleshy animality; and this is accompanied by the consciousness of death; for it is the flesh that is susceptible to death, not the soul. And this horrified awareness of the flesh is the accompaniment and effect of shame, which is aroused by the spectacle of the Knights, "men/Who would damn themselves to beasts".[436]

The shame crystallizes into an image of impending rape; and the mindless animal fury of the Knights becomes identified with blind lust, the triumph of the flesh. The Chorus-woman, identifying herself with Thomas, sees herself as a victim of rape ("the last humiliation"), to which she must "consent" and so be reduced to mere body. (This "consenting" of the victim of violence is a way of yielding one's will to God's pattern "to which all must consent"[437]. Thomas, too, calls his decision to die one "To which my whole being gives entire consent"[438]. At the same time, there is the guilt of having allowed things to develop in this way, and at the body's involuntary cooperation and participation in the lust by which it is violated. To accept fully and with agonized shame the consequences of one's sins is a preliminary to salvation.)

It is at this point that Eliot brings in the consideration that it is only a human being, a creature with a soul, that is capable of "damning itself to a beast". To allow supremacy to the animal, the flesh, is itself a spiritual decision. Only a creature with a soul can bring about the "final utter uttermost death of spirit". The "spirit" has "animal powers" by which it is capable of self-annihilation. (The Shakespeare allusion[439] hints at this too, for the original sonnet has the phrase "the expense of spirit", and the word "of" can be taken as either an objective or a possessive genitive.[440]) The sinful man regards his "self-demolition"[441] as an assertion of his freedom against God, though in fact the result is slavery to the flesh. The corollary of this is that nature has a "spiritual flesh", capable of redemption, and the

---

435 Editor's footnote: Coghill, *op. cit.*, p. 74, l. 222.
436 Editor's footnote: Coghill, *op. cit.*, p. 79, l. 330.
437 Editor's footnote: Coghill, *op. cit.*, p. 32, l. 213.
438 Editor's footnote; Coghill, *op. cit.*, p. 79, l. 342.
439 Editor's footnote: The allusion is to Sonnet 129, which begins "The expense of spirit in a waste of shame/Is lust in action".
440 Editor's footnote: In other words, spirit is either being expended (objective) or is expending itself (possessive).
441 Author's footnote: The later reading (1949) "self-domination" is more pointed in view of "dominated" in the same sentence; but the earlier reading connects more with the "death of spirit".

subject-matter of redemption. Animals themselves, the beasts of the field, having no souls, are incapable of either redemption or damnation. It is man's fleshly nature combined with his possession of spirit that makes him capable of both.

Since redemption consists of a reconciliation between "flesh" and "spirit", Eliot does not finally condemn the flesh. Though in most of the play animal imagery is used as a symbol of sin and corruption, the final image of the play is one of reconciliation between man and the animals, joining to praise God. Even the "living worms/In the guts of the women of Canterbury"[442] receive their baptism in the line "All things affirm Thee in living; the bird in the air ... and the worm in the belly"[443]. The right relation between man's own animal nature and his spiritual nature is embodied in a new joyous animal imagery, free of disgust.

Since the function of the State is to look after the interests of the body ("flesh"), while the function of the Church is to look after the interests of the soul ("spirit"), a right relation between flesh and spirit will lead to a right relation between Church and State. In such a relation, the State is no longer despised as the rule of "a wolf among wolves"[444]. The Church is reconciled with the State, and forms with it a unity that reflects the unity of "spirit" and "flesh". The passage under discussion is thus very relevant to the dramatic theme of the play.

To sum up: while I do not deny that the passage is in a sense about chaos and disorder, what I wish to emphasize is that this disorder is not a confusion and intermingling of two elements that ought to be kept tidily apart. The two elements "flesh" and "spirit" are aspects of a single whole, and thoroughly interpenetrate each other. It is the attempt to expel one of these elements, "spirit", from the unity of the organism (an attempt that can only be made by an exercise of the spirit) that is being described.

---

[442] Editor's footnote: Coghill, op. cit., p. 74, ll. 231-232.
[443] Editor's footnote: Coghill, *op. cit.*, p. 90, l. 623.
[444] Editor's footnote: Coghill, *op. cit.*, p. 44, l.464.

APPENDIX 3:

DIFFICULTIES IN THE PLOT OF *THE FAMILY REUNION*[445]

The plot of *The Family Reunion* had to be a complicated one, because the theme of a family curse must involve at least two generations. (Eliot, in early drafts, tried to make the play involve three, but gave this up as a bad job.)[446] As Eliot finally worked it out, the plot covers a period of 37 years (on the lowest reckoning)[447] from the marriage of Harry's parents to the day of the Family Reunion; though the action of the play itself takes place in the course of one day. Eliot worked for three years on the play; and the project gave him more trouble than any other that he undertook. A considerable part of this trouble can be attributed to complications of the plot. Yet, after all the labour spent on it, the plot still exhibits a number of difficulties and contradictions. No doubt, with the kind of ingenuity employed by Sherlock Holmes addicts, these difficulties can be reconciled. Some of them may even be intentional subtleties, contributing to the meaning of the play. Some of them, however, give a definite impression of bad workmanship. Perhaps the very fact that Eliot wrote five separate versions of the play tended to multiply contradictions in the plot. The typescript drafts of the play preserved at Harvard (which have not yet been published[448], and which I have not had an opportunity of examining) probably throw light on the matter. A further possibility is that Eliot's need to write version after version of the play may have been due to a fundamental dissatisfaction with his theme; and that the residual defects of the plot indicate that this dissatisfaction was never finally overcome. Later Eliot came to say of this play: "I soon saw that I had given my attention to versification at the expense of

---

445 Editor's footnote; Originally published in *Notes and Queries*, August 1968. Reprinted by kind permission of Oxford University Press.

446 Author's footnote: Grover Smith, *T. S. Eliot's Poetry and Plays, op. cit.*, p. 202.

447 Editor's footnote: If we adopt the Author's hypothetical chronological table (see below in the text), the marriage of Amy and Harry's father took place in the *winter* of 1898; the day of the Family Reunion is in the *spring* of 1936; so the time-span is 37 years and a few months.

448 Editor's footnote: A year after the publication of this article, E. Martin Browne, who directed all Eliot's plays, published *The Making of T. S. Eliot's Plays, op. cit.*, which includes long extracts from the early drafts. The Editor's footnotes in this Appendix refer to Browne's book as *Browne*. On the whole, the extracts from *Browne* bear out the argument put forward in this Appendix that the difficulties are the result partly of Eliot's trying to do too much, partly of the number of drafts; but are also partly intentional. These matters may seem trivial, but an examination of them greatly increases our understanding of the play and our appreciation of it as, in my view, and that of the Author, "a major work of art" (to quote *Browne*, p. 148).

plot and character".[449] However, there is a sense of confusion in the play that goes beyond any mere carelessness or lack of attention, and on which a close analysis of the plot may throw some light.

The inconsistencies and problems in the plot are these:

(1) On p. 19[450], Ivy says that Harry's wife was "Swept off the deck in the middle of a storm". But Harry himself says (p. 28) that the night on which he "pushed her over" was "cloudless". Downing, too, in his account on pp. 35-39, makes no mention of a storm; and it is unlikely that he would have taken "a bit of air" before going to bed if a storm had been raging. Perhaps Ivy got it wrong; or perhaps a false story was given to the newspapers in order to avoid the scandal of suicide or of a drunken accident (not of murder, which was not suspected). Or perhaps Eliot simply forgot about the storm.[451]

(2) On p. 72, Harry says that his aunt Agatha never visited Wishwood after the separation of his parents ("Agatha never came then").[452] But Amy says later (p. 109):

I even asked you back, for visits, after he was gone,
So that there might be no ugly rumours.

Perhaps Amy asked Agatha, but Agatha did not come? A natural interpretation of her words does not support this theory. Further, Mary says to Agatha (p. 45): "Why do *you* so seldom come here?" This suggests that visits took place fairly regularly, but infrequently.

---

449 Author's footnote: *Poetry and Drama*, London, 1951, p. 27.
450 Editor's footnote: All page numbers for the play are taken from the Faber Paper-Covered Edition of *The Family Reunion*, London, 1963.
451 Editor's footnote: In a 1938 letter (*Browne*, p. 107), Eliot writes that the question of whether or not Harry killed his wife is "meant to be left in doubt"; but Eliot goes on to suggest that, in a moment of hysterical play-acting, the wife fell overboard and drowned, while Harry just watched, without trying to help or to raise the alarm: a scenario – though it is only a suggestion -- that seems to be supported by Downing's evidence (p. 39). The issue of whether the night was calm or whether there was a storm -- the storm features in all the early drafts; see the earliest draft scenario (*Browne*, p. 91) and *Browne*, p. 112: "The opening scene remains almost unaltered from the first draft to the final text" -- seems to be part of this deliberately created sense of doubt. Another instance of discrepancy is that Downing says: "there wasn't a moon" (p. 39) – which seems to mean that the moon was obscured by clouds -- whereas Harry says the night was "cloudless". These multiple contradictions do suggest intentional obfuscation on this point.
452 Editor's footnote: A letter from a close friend of Eliot, Frank Morley, is included by Browne in his book; at one point Morley asks (in 1938, before the opening lines of the quarrel scene were added; see next footnote): "Another trivium: Agatha *never* came? Is that so?" (*Browne*, p. 110.) But Eliot seems to have paid no attention to this brief question. Either he was too preoccupied with all the other problems with the play; or this was part of a creation (conscious or not) of an inner core of chaos.

Perhaps Agatha's visits were resumed only after Harry grew up? But, on p. 108, we find Amy saying to Agatha:

> I was a fool, to ask you again to Wishwood;
> But, I thought, thirty-five years is long, and death is an end,
> And I thought that time might have made a change in Agatha[453]

The most natural interpretation of this is that Agatha had not been to Wishwood for thirty-five years. This is inconsistent with visits either shortly after Harry's father's departure, or at a later date. A further complication is that Harry (p. 30) alludes to Agatha's explanations, during his childhood, of "the sobbing in the chimney/The evil in the dark closet". This, too, could not have happened if Agatha had not visited Wishwood for 35 years, since Harry is 34 (as will soon be shown). On the whole, we must adopt the interpretation that Agatha's visits ceased on the departure of Harry's father, and were resumed, but infrequently, after Harry grew up. This makes it possible for her to have reassured Harry's childhood fears, and also to have made sufficient impression on his adult mind to account for the expressions of esteem that he makes to her (e. g., p. 94: "I have thought of you as the completely strong,/The liberated from the human wheel.") Amy's reference to "visits" shortly after her husband's departure remains inexplicable, unless one interprets (unnaturally) "after he was gone" to mean "long after he was gone", or (even more unnaturally) "long after his death". Amy's difficult remark "thirty-five years is long" can be interpreted (with some forcing perhaps) to mean "the events that might have induced me not to invite you *this time* took place a long time ago".

(3) On p. 62, Warburton, the doctor, says to Harry:

> I haven't a patient left at Wishwood.
> Wishwood was always a cold place, but healthy.
> It's only when I get an invitation to dinner
> That I ever see your mother.

Soon, however, Dr Warburton is telling Harry (p. 74) that his mother is very ill: "A sudden shock/Might send her off at any moment." Presumably, such a patient would require frequent attention. Indeed, on p. 81, Warburton tells Amy:

---

[453] Editor's footnote: Browne writes that these three lines were only added in the final text: "I now proceed with the comparison between the drafts and the final text. The quarrel scene is strengthened in the latter by the addition of the opening lines". (*Browne*, p. 137.) Both Browne and Eliot seem to have forgotten about the earlier passages that these opening lines contradict.

> I repeat, Lady Monchensey, that you must not go out.
> If you do, I must decline to continue to treat you.

Perhaps Warburton did not want to alarm Harry about his mother's condition at first. But his remark was made in front of the whole Chorus of uncles and aunts, who must have known that Amy was receiving medical attention. This is a strange lapse on Eliot's part, in view of the importance of Amy's illness in the story; it is by neglecting this illness that Harry brings about her death and fulfils his fate as the counterpart of Orestes.[454]

(4) When Charles says to Downing (p. 35): "You've looked after his Lordship for over ten years", Downing replies: "Eleven years, Sir, next Lady Day." Lady Day is March 25 (it is the day of the Annunciation, nine months before Christmas). The day on which Downing is speaking (according to the title page of Part I) is "An afternoon in late March". Late March begins, I should think, about March 20. When Downing says: "next Lady Day", one is entitled to expect that Lady Day is two or three months off. If Lady Day is only a few days off, one would expect Downing to say: "on Lady Day". This is a tiny point, but it may be a revealing one. For part of Eliot's difficulty in plot-making was that he was trying to combine so many stories in one: the story of Orestes; the story of Adam; the story of Jesus; the story embedded in Kipling's short story "The House Surgeon"[455]; and the modern story that is the surface for

---

[454] Editor's footnote: In an earlier draft extract (*Browne*, p. 126), Amy suddenly enters, after Charles has read out a newspaper item about Arthur's motor smash; she says "I have been listening" and goes on to say: "I might die at any moment,/But not of this sort of news, you may be sure." (It is the departure of Harry that kills her.) This intervention by Amy was removed in the final draft. Unfortunately, Browne does not provide any early draft extracts for the scene between Warburton and Harry; but it is possible that, in the final draft, after taking out Amy's "I might die at any moment", Eliot transferred the warning about Amy's health – which prepares us for her death -- to Warburton -- "A sudden shock/Might send her off at any moment" (p. 74) -- but forgot to take out the lines in a previous draft about "I haven't a patient left at Wishwood" (pp.62-3). It could be called yet another discrepancy in the final play that the family decides in Part 1 to call on Warburton to talk to Harry about his wife's death (pp. 30-2); but in the scene between Harry and Warburton that opens Part II, Warburton doesn't mention Harry's wife at all, but talks mainly about Amy's health and personality, warning Harry against giving her "A sudden shock". In the earliest draft synopsis, the conversation is only about Harry's wife's death; the doctor believes Harry is deluded in believing he killed his wife: "Doctor more and more convinced that the loss of A's wife has upset his mind, and brought out some latent sense of guilt from early years, which he has materialised in this way." (*Browne*, p. 92.) The changes from this original draft synopsis seem to be mainly the effect of what Browne calls the "increased power" of Amy, who, in the original draft scenario, is a "bewildered person" dependent on Agatha, who, in this earliest version, is the eldest of Amy's three sisters, later becoming the youngest (*Browne*, p. 93). The changes seem to bring out the idea – linked to "the latent sense of guilt from early years" -- that Harry's real crime is the Orestes-like murder of his mother (in the original draft synopsis, there is no mention of the death of Amy).

[455] Author's footnote: See "*The Family Reunion* and Kipling's 'The House Surgeon'", published in *Notes and Queries*, July 1967. Editor's footnote: See Appendix 4.

them all. Downing is Pylades, the friend of Orestes; later Downing is Apollo[456]; and also, as Downing's connection with Lady Day suggests, he is the Archangel Gabriel. It is no wonder that the dates got a little mixed. A part of the confusion in *The Family Reunion* (but only a part) can be attributed to the fact that Eliot was trying to do too much.

(5) Another small difficulty occurs on p. 45. Mary, speaking of her position as housekeeper for Amy, says:

> She didn't need me:
> She would have done just as well with a hired servant
> Or with none. She only wanted me for Harry....
> Even when he married, she still held on to me
> Because she couldn't bear to let any project go

The natural interpretation of this is that Amy appointed Mary as housekeeper in the hope that Harry would marry her; but continued to employ her in that capacity even after Harry's marriage. But only a little enquiry is needed to show that Mary was not appointed housekeeper until a full year *after* Harry's marriage. This marriage took place eight years before this conversation; and Mary has been housekeeper for the last seven years, before which she was an undergraduate at Agatha's college. It may be said that Amy, even while Mary was an undergraduate, had intended to appoint her eventually as housekeeper, and continued with this plan even though its object had apparently ceased to be attainable. It would have been very easy for Eliot to have made this plain. As the matter stands, there appears to be a mistake.[457]

(6) I now come to a very puzzling problem of chronology that arises in Harry's speech on p. 99. Harry says to Agatha:

---

[456] Editor's footnote: Apollo -- who, as the sun-god, was often depicted riding in a chariot -- appears in *The Eumenides*, to provide support for Orestes against the Furies.

[457] Editor's footnote: In an extract from an early draft that is provided by Browne, the quarrel scene takes place between Amy, Agatha and Mary. Amy says to Agatha: "You take him from me, you take him from Wishwood,/You take him from Mary." Mary replies to her: "I am very much obliged to you, Cousin Amy,/It would have been most useful for your designs/To have a tame daughter-in-law with no money,/A housekeeper-companion for you and Harry". (*Browne*, p. 138.) In earlier drafts, Mary is only 22 and has only been down from Oxford since the previous summer (*Browne*, pp. 92, 118). In the earliest draft scenario, Harry's wife dies after only "a year or so" of marriage, about six years previously (*Browne*, p. 91); Harry has been wandering ever since. Amy, therefore, it seems, planned to bring Mary to Wishwood, after she left Oxford, to marry Harry on his return after his wanderings. Eliot incorporated some of this speech by Amy in the final version – but the seam shows. This seems to be an example of a small puzzlement caused by so many drafts.

> Family affection
> Was a kind of formal obligation, a duty
> Only noticed by its neglect. One had that part to play.
> After such training, I could endure, these ten years,
> Playing a part that had been imposed upon me;
> And I returned to find another one made ready –
> The book laid out, lines underscored, and the costume
> Ready to be put on.

Why does Harry say "these ten years? Up to this point in the play, the last main period in Harry's life has always been referred to as one of eight years. It was eight years before that he had left Wishwood and married his ill-fated wife (see pp. 16, 20, 35). His wife's death took place one year before the Family Reunion (see p. 18); so his marriage lasted seven years. Only a few pages before, in the same scene, Harry says (p. 95): "At the beginning, eight years ago". Significance has been found in this eight-year period of wandering, which corresponds to a variant in the period of wandering in the lives of ancient heroes.[458] Surely Eliot could not have been so careless as to forget that Harry's wanderings were for eight years, not ten? An instance like this makes one suspect that some at least of the inconsistencies in the plot may be deliberate; that Eliot had some artistic point in having a core of bafflement within the apparently solid structure of his story. One can, of course, patch up the matter by some expedient. One could say, for example, that Harry met his future wife two years before he left Wishwood to marry her; and that the ten-year period consists of these two years plus the eight years of his wanderings. All this requires far too much work from the reader. (On a more prosaic level of explanation, it would be interesting to know whether, in one of the early drafts, Eliot made the period of wandering ten years throughout the play, and, in the final draft, forgot to alter Harry's speech here.[459])

Also, it is not very easy to understand what was the "part" that Harry was compelled to play during these ten years. Perhaps he means that, in his wife's circle, he had to act in a way that was unnatural to him. Amy has already suggested this (p. 20):

---

458 Author's footnote: Grover Smith, *T. S. Eliot's Poetry and Plays, op cit.*, p. 203.

459 Editor's footnote: We learn from the typescript extracts provided by Browne that, in early drafts, Harry was away from home for *seven* years (*Browne*, p. 118). In an earlier draft, he says, in this very speech: "those *seven* years". (*Browne*, p. 133; my emphasis.) But instead of changing "seven" to "eight" in the final play, Eliot changed it to "these *ten* years". (*The Family Reunion, op. cit.*, p. 99; my emphasis.) Significantly, in the final play, Eliot took out, at the beginning of Harry's speech cited here, these lines in the earlier draft: "One cannot rearrange the past, that would mean going/Back to the beginning of time, the original chaos." (*Browne*, p. 133.) Eliot perhaps left these lines out because they were too explicit. It could be that it was to provide a concrete example of "the original chaos" beneath the surface of his play that he changed "seven", not to "eight", but to "ten".

> She never wanted
> Harry's relations or Harry's old friends;
> She never wanted to fit herself to Harry,
> But only to bring Harry down to her own level.

Still, in that case, it seems rather unfair of Harry to complain that the part "had been imposed" upon him. After all, he had married his wife quite voluntarily and had known her way of life, especially if he had had the opportunity to observe it for two years before the marriage. Moreover, in view of his unhappiness at home, he would hardly agree with Amy that he had been forced away from congenial relations and surroundings. Also, how can he say that he could "endure" playing a part, when in fact he was driven (or at least he thinks that he was driven) to the point of murder? Again, during the last of the ten years, he was not in his wife's circle but wandering alone. What part was he playing then? Or is Harry simply supposed to be in an unreasonable mood here? The context suggests, on the contrary, a return to sanity and understanding of other people.

The only other explanation that occurs to me is that the period of ten years was not the previous ten years, as I have assumed, but an earlier period of ten years of residence at Wishwood, after Harry's childhood "training". This, I am afraid, is a very forced interpretation, for the natural interpretation of the phrase "these ten years" is "the ten years that have just gone by". In fact, the phrase occurs elsewhere in the play with exactly this meaning, when Winchell the policeman says (p. 77) that his mother has been "dead these ten years".

(7) We now arrive at some questions that are vital for an understanding of the main chronology of the play. These questions arise in the quarrel scene between Amy and Agatha (Part II, scene III). Amy says to Agatha (p. 108):

> Thirty-five years ago
> You took my husband from me. Now you take my son.

This precise dating seems at first sight to give us a clear idea of the main time-structure of the story. According to the account given to Harry by Agatha (pp. 95 ff.) Harry's father and mother were childless for three years. In the summer before Harry's birth, the love-affair between Agatha and Harry's father began. In the autumn, when Harry was "due in three months' time", Harry's father planned to murder his wife. (If we take "autumn" to be the end of September, then Harry could have been born at Christmas, which would support the identification of Harry with Jesus suggested at several points in the play.) So the period from the time of the marriage of Harry's parents to the Family Reunion is thirty-seven and a half years (thirty-five plus the two and a half years before the adulterous love-affair).

This means that Harry is 34 at the time of the action of the play. Mary is 29 (Charles says she is "getting on for thirty" -- p. 15 -- and, for a reason that will soon be mentioned, it is best to take the highest possible age for her). We learn on p. 109 that Harry's father left Wishwood after seven years ("Seven years I kept him"). So it appears that we are well on the way to constructing a complete chronological table of the events of the play, helped by the unusually precise dating provided by the author.

However, we immediately strike difficulties.

From what year are we to reckon the thirty-five years mentioned by Amy? Are we to assume that Amy knew the exact time when the love-affair between her husband and Agatha began? She does indeed say to Agatha (p. 109; emphasis in original):

You thought I did not know!
You may be close, but I always saw through *him*.

This suggests that she knew all that there was to know. But she betrays no knowledge of the worst thing of all – that her husband, at one stage, planned to murder her. If her knowledge is defective in this respect, it is perhaps defective in other respects too; so her claim to full knowledge does not compel us to think that she knew accurately when the love affair began. But any considerable error on her part in this matter affects the chronology of the play, for she dates the thirty-five years from the start of the love-affair. Indeed, it could be argued that she makes an error of as much as six months in her reckoning. For she says about Harry (p. 110) that she has spent "Thirty-five years designing his life". This suggests that Harry is thirty-five years old; and, since she dates the love-affair thirty-five years before the Family Reunion, this means that, on her reckoning, the love-affair began at the time of Harry's birth. This is a possible solution of our difficulty (which is: "When did Amy *think* the love-affair began?"). Unfortunately, however, this makes Harry uncomfortably old. For we have to bear in mind that Harry and Mary were childhood playmates; and Mary is, at the most, twenty-nine years old. An age gap of six years seems too great for childhood playmates.

I think it best, therefore, to suppose that Amy's knowledge of the start of the love-affair *was* accurate. After all, it is quite possible that, looking back, she realized that the beginning of her husband's involvement with Agatha had been in the Long Vacation visit that Agatha made during Amy's pregnancy. That Amy says she has spent thirty-five years designing Harry's life does not prove that the thirty-five years began with Harry's birth; she might very well have begun designing her son's life as soon as she knew she was pregnant. If this is so, Harry is only thirty-four. It is just about possible, therefore, for him to have had

Mary as a childhood playmate. (Note that an error of six months, from June to December, in Amy's reckoning of the love-affair would make a difference of a whole year to Harry's age. The explanation of this curious fact is that the Family Reunion takes place in March; so that an approximate thirty-five-year period starting in December would be an actual period of thirty-five and a quarter years, whereas an approximate thirty-five-year period starting in June would be an actual period of thirty-four and a quarter years. So we gain six months from the approximation change as well as six months from the date-change.)[460]

However, it is not so easy to decide how to reckon the seven years that Amy "kept" her husband. Does she mean that she kept him for seven years altogether, or for seven years after the beginning of his love-affair with Agatha? Arguments can be adduced for both sides of this question. In favour of the solution that Amy kept her husband for seven years after her marriage is Agatha's remark (p. 108) that she herself had "thirty years of solitude". Agatha's years of solitude, "alone, among women, in a women's college", are likely to have begun when her lover, Harry's father, left Wishwood and went abroad. If Harry's father went abroad seven and a half years after his marriage, this would mean that Agatha had the opportunity of seeing him at Wishwood for exactly five years after the commencement of their love-affair, leaving the correct number of thirty years until the time of the Family Reunion. Apart from the negligible discrepancy of half a year (which, by a judicious selection of dates, can be distributed among the periods concerned), this scheme dovetails the datings so well that one must seriously consider it. The fact that Agatha reckons her thirty years in pointed distinction from Agatha's thirty-five is a strong argument in favour of this solution.

But there are also strong arguments in favour of the other solution. Amy's actual words to Agatha are (pp. 108-9):

> You knew that you took everything
> Except the walls, the furniture, the acres;
> Leaving nothing -- but what I could breed for myself,
> What I could plant here. Seven years I kept him,
> For the sake of the future, a discontented ghost,
> In his own house.

---

460 Editor's footnote: Put differently: Let us adopt the hypothetical date of March 1936 for the Family Reunion (see timeline in text below). If Amy believes the love-affair started in December, at the time of Harry's birth, then, in saying "thirty-five years ago", in terms of approximation, she is going *back* three months, from March 1936 to December 1935. This means that Harry was born thirty-five years previously, in December 1900; i. e. Harry is 35. If, however, she believes the love-affair began in June, when she was pregnant with Harry, then, in saying "thirty-five years ago", in terms of approximation, she is going *forward* three months to June 1936. "Thirty-five years ago" thus means June 1901, six months before Harry's birth in December 1901; so Harry is 34.

The natural interpretation of this is that Amy kept her husband against his will for seven years after he had transferred his affections to Agatha. Before he met Agatha, Harry's father had not actively hated his wife, so she had no need to keep him against his will. "There was no ecstasy" (p. 95); but there had not been hate. (This means that Helen Gardner is wrong in saying that Harry "was conceived and brought forth in hatred not in love".[461] This is true of his younger brothers but not of him. This is a material point in connection with the theme of Original Sin in the play.)

Moreover, if Harry's father left Wishwood seven and a half years after his marriage, then Harry was only four and a half years old at the time. This would mean that Harry would have to have a phenomenally good memory; for he has some clear recollections of the time before his father's departure. For example, though he does not remember his father well, he remembers that he was "kept apart" from his father, "till he went away" (p. 72). He also remembers that Agatha used to explain "the sobbing in the chimney/The evil in the dark closet" (p. 30); and this must have been before his father's departure, because afterwards she "never came" (p. 72). If Harry was six and a half when his father went abroad, these recollections would not be surprising. Further, there is an impression that Harry is several years older than his brothers. He must be about five years older than Mary, who talks of herself (p. 49) as of about the same age as Harry's brothers -- "you seemed so much older. We were rather in awe of you". If Harry's father left after only seven and a half years of marriage, the three brothers must be very close in age, since they must all have been born within a space of four and a half years.

So, on the whole, I think it a more plausible theory that Harry's father left Wishwood after nine and a half years of marriage, not seven and a half. If so, why does Agatha speak (p. 108) of her "thirty years of solitude"? The explanation must be that Agatha and Harry's father broke off their illicit relationship two years before the father's departure from Wishwood; though Agatha continued to visit Wishwood until her former lover's departure. This is not very satisfactory, but it is the best that can be done. This has the advantage, if it is an advantage, of making it possible to suppose that the births of Arthur and John took place after the end of the love-affair between their father and Agatha.

The important thing to notice is that Eliot could have avoided this kind of enquiry by not being so specific in his reckoning of intervals of time. Throughout the play, we have a surface impression of extreme precision that melts into bafflement when we follow out the details.[462]

---

461 Author's footnote: Helen Gardner, *The Art of T. S. Eliot, op. cit.*, p. 154.

462 Author's footnote: I have not gone into the question: "When did Mary see the Eumenides?", because she might have seen them at any time. But it is certainly curious that the incident is so casually introduced (p. 112). That she

Before going into possible reasons for this, I offer the following chronological table, summing up my necessarily tentative conclusions. I have taken the year of the Family Reunion (somewhat arbitrarily) as 1936, the year that Eliot began work on the play.

1896: Warburton begins his practice (see p. 61).

1898 (Winter): Marriage of Amy and Harry's father.

1901 (Summer): Agatha, an undergraduate at Oxford, visits Wishwood. Her love-affair with Harry's father begins.

(September): Harry's father plans to murder Amy. Agatha dissuades him.

(December 25): Birth of Harry.

1906: Love-affair between Agatha and Harry's father ends.

1906-8: Births of Arthur and John.

1907: Birth of Mary.

1908 (Summer): Harry's father leaves Wishwood and goes abroad. Agatha's visits to Wishwood cease.

c. 1910 (Summer): Death of Harry's father.

c. 1915: Destruction of the "wilderness" (p. 51).

c. 1920: Agatha's visits to Wishwood are resumed.

---

saw them during her scene with Harry, and pretended not to see them, seems to me implausible (see D. E. Jones, *The Plays of T. S. Eliot, op. cit.*, p. 94: "Thinking to help him, Mary pretends that the Eumenides are not there").

Editor's footnote: The Author seems here mistaken in suggesting that Mary did not see the Eumenides during her scene alone with Harry. Browne (who worked very closely with Eliot, as the director of all his plays, and must have known his intentions) writes (*Browne*, p. 137): "When the Eumenides appear in Part I, they are seen by Harry through the window; we see nothing except a change of lighting, and Mary who is looking at Harry does not see them when he does. She *does* of course see them (as she reveals later to Agatha); but only at the moment when she makes the supreme effort of drawing the curtains and denying their existence." (Emphasis in original.) So Mary sees them at this point; but it is not really the case that she is pretending not to see them, as Jones suggests. She says "Harry! There is no one here" (p. 58), then goes to the window to draw the curtains; and this is when she suddenly sees the Eumenides; they have come to warn Harry against the "evasion" of marriage with her; see Eliot's letter to Browne of March 19, 1938: "This is the first time since his marriage ... that he has been attracted towards any woman. This attraction glimmers for a moment in his mind, half-consciously as a possible 'way of escape'; and the Furies (for the Furies are *divine* instruments, not simple hell-hounds), come in the nick of time to warn him away from this evasion – though at that moment he misunderstands their function." (*Browne*, p. 107; emphasis in original.) From then on, in this scene, Mary is struck dumb (apart from her anguished cry "Oh Harry!", on p.58) by "shock" and a sense of "defeat" (*Browne*, p. 122), until she exits with the almost monosyllabic words (p. 60): "I must go and change. I came in very late." This comment seems to carry the double meaning that she knows it is too late now for her to marry Harry. Unlike Agatha, however, she regards the Eumenides as a great danger to Harry; Agatha has to reassure her (p. 112) that they are divine guides, not demons. However, it is not too late for Mary to leave Wishwood, by applying, with Agatha's help, for an Oxford fellowship (p. 113).

1925 (March 25): Downing becomes Harry's servant.

1926: Harry meets his future wife.

1928: Marriage of Harry. He leaves Wishwood.

1929: Mary leaves Oxford. Decides not to apply for Fellowship. Takes up duties as housekeeper for Amy.

1935: Death of Harry's wife.

1936 (March 20): The Family Reunion. Death of Amy.

Notes

(1) 1910 seems a reasonable date for the death of Harry's father. Harry was "only a boy" (p. 72); Arthur and John were "too young" to remember (*ibid*.). It was a summer day of unusual heat" (*ibid.*) when Harry received the news. (This recalls the "summer day of unusual heat" – p. 96 -- when the love-affair with Agatha began. Why both days are given the same characterization is an interesting subject of conjecture.)

(2) I have put the destruction of the "wilderness" (p. 51) at a date when Harry was fourteen and the other children about nine.

(3) How old are Agatha and Amy? Agatha must have been about twenty when her love-affair began, which makes her fifty-five now. Amy says to Dr Warburton (p. 63): "I think we are very much the oldest present". Dr Warburton has been in practice for forty years (p. 61); which suggests he is about sixty-five. Amy's remark to him, just quoted, carries a strong suggestion that she and Dr Warburton are about the same age. If we put Amy's age at 67, we arrive at a plausible age for her marriage (29) and for the birth of her youngest child (39), while still allowing her to be eight years older than Ivy, the next sister (if Agatha is fifty-five, then Violet could be fifty-seven and Ivy fifty-nine). Eight years seems an age-gap between the two eldest sisters appropriate to Amy's comment about herself and Dr Warburton: "I think we are very much the oldest present" (p. 63) —a remark uttered in the presence of Ivy.[463]

---

[463] Editor's footnote: Browne (p. 143) quotes from the Harvard typescripts a page in which Eliot "sums up the conclusions reached about ages". Here Mary is 29, Violet is 58 and Ivy is 62. Amy is 65-70, Harry is 32-35, and Agatha is 50-55. The Author's suggestions are all in accordance with these conclusions. But it is odd that Eliot is so specific about Mary, Violet, and Ivy, but so unspecific about Harry, Amy, and Agatha (the three most important characters, while Ivy and Violet are very minor characters). Harry cannot be 32 or 33; he must, for the reasons given in this Appendix, be 34 or 35 (and is more likely to be 34). It is very unlikely that Agatha was 15, 16 or 17 as an Oxford undergraduate; she must have been 18-20, so must be 53-55. In order to be eight years (i.e., "very much") older than Ivy, Amy would have to be 70 on this birthday (but it is possible for her to have given birth to her youngest child at the age of 42).

What conclusions can we reach from this investigation? It is clear that it is only with a good deal of patching up that *The Family Reunion* can be made to yield a coherent story. Eliot has evidently not taken much trouble to make the time-sequence of his story watertight. If he had worked with a chronological table (as most authors do, when they have a complicated story to manage), he could not have failed to notice the difficulties. Yet this would perhaps have been all right; the surface appearance of the play is convincing enough; and most members of an audience, even most readers, do not enquire too closely. But what makes the matter an intriguing puzzle is that Eliot takes such pains to give an impression of extreme exactitude. There can be very few plays that are so full of exact figures. Even Winchell the policeman cannot mention his mother without giving the exact number of years she has been dead (p. 77). A typical example is provided by Downing's length of service. Charles puts it at "over ten years", which would be exact enough for most people; but Eliot seems dissatisfied and makes Downing provide a punctilious correction (p. 35): "Eleven years, Sir, next Lady Day." But, as we have seen, this very precision gives rise to trouble when the matter is checked.

I have suggested two possible sources of the trouble: the number of drafts that Eliot made; and the problem of dovetailing so many stories together. But this does not explain why Eliot went out of his way to invite trouble. There remains the possibility that Eliot's very carelessness (whether by his conscious intention or not) served an artistic purpose. A central theme in the play is Time. From one point of view, the subject of the play could be summed up as follows: under the façade of regularity symbolized by the ticking of the clock, the reality of life is chaos. Harry says at one point (pp. 69-70):

O God, man, the things that are going to happen
Have already happened.

Harry is the person who has seen that the passage of time, as ordinarily understood, is a sham. The very sequence of cause and effect is a sham. Even a sin is not necessarily followed in time by remorse; in Harry's case, he suffers all his agonies of remorse *before* he commits his only real crime: the killing of his mother. Even the obtuse Chorus, in their terror, say (p. 63):

And the past is about to happen, and the future was long since settled.

This dissolution of Time forms a much more difficult subject of enquiry than that attempted here. But the façade of regularity in Eliot's time-sequence, with its inner core of shifting ambiguity, certainly contributes to the deeper theme.

APPENDIX 4: *THE FAMILY REUNION* AND KIPLING'S "THE HOUSE SURGEON"[464]

The influence of Kipling's short stories on Eliot's work has often been noticed. For example, "Burnt Norton" I probably owes something to Kipling's *They*[465]; and images in "The Hollow Men" and *The Family Reunion* have been traced to Kipling's "The End of the Passage"[466]. The depth of Eliot's interest in Kipling's short stories is confirmed in his essay on Kipling.[467]

An instance that appears to have escaped notice is the influence on *The Family Reunion* of Kipling's "The House Surgeon".[468] A snatch of conversation at the beginning of Kipling's story gives a tantalizing glimpse of another story that was never written:

"'I didn't quite catch the end of that last story about the Curse on the family's first born.'

'It turned out to be drains,' I explained. 'As soon as new ones were put into the house, the Curse was lifted, I believe.'"[469]

The Family Reunion is about a Curse on a family's first-born; and at one point Harry, the first-born, says:

> You do not know
> The noxious smell untraceable in the drains,
> Inaccessible to the plumbers, that has its hour of the night; you do not
> know

---

464 Editor's footnote: Originally published in *Notes and Queries*, February 1968. Reprinted by kind permission of Oxford University Press.
465 Author's footnote: Helen Gardner, *The Art of T. S. Eliot, op. cit.*, p. 160.
   Editor's footnote: See Chapter 6, pp. 141-142.
466 Author's footnote: Grover Smith, *T. S. Eliot's Poetry and Plays, op. cit.*, pp. 101, 105, 201.
467 Author's footnote: *A Choice of Kipling's Verse, op. cit.*
468 Author's footnote: *Actions and Reactions*, London, 1909. All page numbers are taken from this edition.
469 Editor's footnote: *Ibid.*, p. 263.

The unspoken voice of sorrow in the ancient bedroom
At three o'clock in the morning.... I am the old house
With the noxious smell and the sorrow before morning[470]

In Kipling's story, a house afflicts its inhabitants, the M'Leods, with a deep feeling of depression. Mr. M'Leod tries changing the drains, with no success.[471] The feeling of depression is described as an "aching helpless grief"[472]; and it is in a bedroom that the narrator first feels it. Later he feels it during the night: "I lay awake till dawn, breathing quickly and sweating lightly, beneath what De Quincey inadequately describes as 'the oppression of inexpiable guilt'."[473]

Eliot seems to have combined the story of which Kipling gives a glimpse with elements of the story that Kipling actually wrote: "The House Surgeon". From the first, he takes the Curse on the family's first-born and the "noxious smell", while from the second he takes "the sorrow before morning" and the fact that the trouble was "untraceable in the drains".

Further scrutiny of "The House Surgeon" reveals many more parallels with *The Family Reunion*. The central one is that both stories deal with an event of which it is doubted whether it is a crime or an accident, and with the guilt and sorrow attendant on this doubt. In the case of *The Family Reunion*, the "crime" is murder, and in "The House Surgeon" it is suicide; but both incidents involve a fall. (Murder is actually mentioned in "The House Surgeon" when Baxter says: "'Things that seem on the face of 'em like murder, or say suicide, may appear different to God.'"[474]) Moreover, in both stories, the chief character feels guilt that rightly belongs to someone else.[475]

Another important parallel is that both stories have unobtrusive reference to Greek myth. *The Family Reunion* is the story of Orestes, and "The House Surgeon" is the story of Perseus. In *The Family Reunion*, the only direct reference to the underlying myth comes when the Chorus say:

---

470 Author's footnote: p. 27.

    Editor's footnote: Again, all page numbers for the play are taken from the Faber Paper-Covered Edition of *The Family Reunion*, London, 1963.

471 Editor's footnote: p. 263.

472 Author's footnote: p. 272. Actually, there are two different feelings, felt at different times, one of horror and one of grief.

473 Author's footnote: p. 273.

474 Author's footnote: p. 279.

475 Editor's footnote: Although guilt does seem to be attributed to Harry in relation to the deaths of both his wife and his mother, he also suffers for his father's guilt in plotting to kill Amy.

There is no avoiding these things
And we know nothing of exorcism
And whether in Argos or England
There are certain inflexible laws[476]

There is a passage similar to this in "The House Surgeon", where Thea says: "'What do you think it is – bewitchment? In Greece, where I was a little girl, it might have been; but not in England, do you think? Or *do* you?'"[477] The fact that Thea is Greek-born intensifies the identification of her with Andromeda. A further parallel is that both *The Family Reunion* and "The House Surgeon" begin with the arrival of the hero by steamship; and this coincidence in turn derives from the fact that both Orestes and Perseus arrive at their scenes of action by sea. Another parallel between the two myths is reflected in the two stories. The three Eumenides whom Orestes faces are paralleled by the three female Gorgons whom Perseus overcomes. Just as, in *The Family Reunion*, the Eumenides gradually reveal their psychological identity with the hero's mother, Amy[478], so in "The House Surgeon" the Gorgons, who are at first located in the horror of the haunted house[479], are later revealed as three old maids, and particularly the most fearsome one, Mary (Medusa).

Here we arrive at another parallel: the similarity in character between Amy of *The Family Reunion* and Mary of "The House Surgeon". Both are women of great will power who exercise excessive influence on their respective families. Amy, by managing and planning the lives of her family, arrogates to herself the position of God. She acquires such baleful power that it is suggested at one point that she killed Harry's wife from a distance by her will.[480] Similarly, Mary in "The House Surgeon" has arrogated to herself the divine right of judgment; and has thus poisoned from a distance the lives of the inhabitants of the House, and prevented her dead sister from attaining repose. This is perhaps the point of the song[481] that Thea sings at the end of the story about the discontented bird who wants to be a human; it is an allegory of the human who wants to be God.

Another parallel between the two stories is the attitude towards death of some of the characters. Amy and her sisters and brothers-in-law in *The Family Reunion* are avoiding the

---

476 Author's footnote: p. 91.

477 Author's footnote: p. 270 (emphasis in original).

478 Author's footnote: See Grover Smith, *T. S. Eliot's Poetry and Plays, op. cit.*, p. 206.
   Editor's footnote: See Chapter 2, p. 78, footnote 167.

479 Aurhor's footnote: p. 274.

480 Author's footnote: p. 46.
   Editor's footnote: Mary says: "I believed that Cousin Amy -- /I almost believed it -- had killed her by willing".

481 Editor's footnote: pp. 298-299.

thought of death. In "The House Surgeon", the House is sold to M'Leod with an assurance (for which he pays an extra one thousand pounds) that no death has taken place in it.[482] Finally, the death has to be faced; and only then happiness is restored. A minor parallel connected with facing the unpleasant can be observed in the bright lights that appear in both stories. Harry objects to the "blaze of light"[483] by which his relatives cut themselves off from contact with the dark things ("the evil in the dark closet"[484]). Similarly, the M'Leods switch on over-bright lights all over the house in a vain attempt to combat the lurking evil.[485]

A parallel can be found in "The House Surgeon" for the preoccupation with Time that pervades "The Family Reunion". After Mr. Perseus has felt the extremity of guilt, he falls asleep and dreams

> the most terrible of dreams – that joyous one in which all past evil has
> not only been wiped out of our lives, but has never been committed;
> and in the very bliss of our assured innocence, before our loves
> shriek and change countenance, we wake to the day we have earned.[486]

This highly charged passage expresses the irrevocability of time that Harry feels so strongly when, for example, he speaks of

> the sorrow before morning,
> In which all past is present, all degradation
> Is unredeemable.[487]

Both stories are concerned with salvation. Eliot's story is clearly so; but Kipling's strange story has very serious intentions too. Mr. Perseus, the House Surgeon, is the Saviour who cures the ills of the House. The owner of the House is a Jew with a Scottish surname; and he is married to a Greek. Does this mean that the House is Western Christian civilisation, with its Jewish and Greek origins? (That the Jewish aspect is taken seriously is shown by the poem that Kipling appended to the story, "The Rabbi's Song", which stresses the mercifulness of God and the need to restrain gloomy thoughts.) The opening snatch of story is not irrelevant; it represents the attitude of Western materialism, which attempts

---

482 Editor's footnote: pp. 263-264.
483 Author's footnote: p.23.
484 Author's footnote: p. 30.
485 Author's footnote: pp. 270, 271, 273 ("blaze of electric light"), 296.
486 Author's footnote: p. 273.
487 Author's footnote: p. 27.

to exorcise its guilt by attributing all evil to the state of the drains. But later the narrator says of this tale: "It wasn't true"[488]. The guilt remains. Perhaps Kipling thought that a pagan Saviour was needed to rescue the House from its sense of condemnation. (In *The Family Reunion* too, the House is a symbol of the community, though it has other values as well.)

Mary, the condemning Evangelical, disapproves of prayers for the dead, quoting "As the tree falls".[489] Harry uses the same phrase:

> Everything tends towards reconciliation
> As the stone falls, as the tree falls.[490]

The reference is to Ecclesiastes 11: 3: "and if the tree fall toward the south, or toward the north, in the place where the tree falleth, there it shall be". That this is the text that Kipling had in mind is put out of doubt (despite the difference in wording) by the fact that the old-time Protestants often used this Ecclesiastes verse in their arguments against the doctrine of Purgatory and the institution of prayers for the dead.[491] It is a very suitable text in the mouth of Mary. Kipling, however, misquotes the text; and it is interesting circumstantial evidence of Eliot's debt to Kipling's story that Eliot repeats the misquotation. The difference is that Kipling's Mary uses the quotation to show the impossibility of forgiveness, while Eliot's Harry uses it to express the idea of reconciliation through ruin:

> in the end
> That is the completion which at the beginning
> Would have seemed the ruin.[492]

Both stories, it seems, are concerned with forgiveness. Both approach their subject by a conflict between the pagan and Christian points of view. But Eliot gives the healing power to the Christian, while Kipling gives it to the pagan.[493]

I wish to thank Mr. J. C. Maxwell[494] for substantial help in the development of this article.

---

488 Author's footnote: p. 265.
489 Author's footnote: p. 292.
490 Author's footnote: p. 97.
491 Author's footnote: *Catholic Encyclopaedia*, article: "Dead, Prayers for the"; section "Objections Alleged".
492 Editor's footnote: p. 97.
493 Author's footnote: Eliot, in his essay on Kipling, writes of the "pagan vision" of Kipling's later short stories.
   Editor's footnote: See *A Choice of Kipling's Verse, op. cit.*, p. 33: "It is not a Christian vision, but it is at least a pagan vision – a contradiction of the materialistic view: it is the insight into a harmony with nature which must be re-established if the truly Christian imagination is to be recovered by Christians."
494 Editor's footnote: See p. 175, footnote 401.

APPENDIX 5:

Review[495] by Hyam Maccoby of *T. S. Eliot, Anti-Semitism and Literary Form*, by Anthony Julius (Cambridge, 1995: republished London, 2003).

Was T. S. Eliot an antisemite? If he was, how much ought this to matter to those who read and enjoy his poetry? Should they stop reading him, or simply regard the antisemitic passages (e. g. "The rats are underneath the piles./The jew is underneath the lot"[496]) as lamentable but inessential lapses?

Anthony Julius robustly and convincingly dismisses all the usual excuses: that Eliot was only echoing the pervasive antisemitism of his time (what about E. M. Forster, who combated antisemitism when it most mattered, in the 1930s?); that, Eliot's poems being dramatic monologues, the antisemitism should be attributed to his characters, such as Gerontion, not to him; that poetry in general does not state anything, so the antisemitism is merely an element in an abstract pattern of words.

More important, Julius argues that the antisemitic passages (all belonging to one particular period of Eliot's work, that of the *Ara Vos Prec* volume of 1920) are not mere aberrations; but form an important part of Eliot's poetic output. Eliot made poetry out of antisemitism; a fact that has repercussions in the general theory of what poetry is and does.

I have argued the same point (the genuine poetic quality of Eliot's antisemitism) in many publications, so I am delighted to claim Julius as a disciple. It is an important point, because it means that antisemitism (though it usually gives rise to material of wretched literary quality) is so deeply embedded in western culture that it can function as an archetype or symbol. The evil is not in the artist (Shakespeare, for example, with *The Merchant of Venice*) but in the culture; and the function of the artist is not to present the true and the good, but to reflect the culture.

Julius, however, does not fully appreciate the complexity and individuality of Eliot's personal involvement in the western background of antisemitism. Eliot (in the light of his reading of anthropology) saw and accepted the kinship between the Cross and the dying-and-resurrected young gods of ancient mystery religions; and he connected these themes with the Romantic cult of youth. All this entered into his contempt for the Jews

---

495 Editor's footnote: Originally published in The London *Evening Standard*, September 18, 1995, under the title "Shock of the Jew". Reprinted by kind permission of Evening Standard Ltd.
496 Editor's footnote: T. S. Eliot, *Selected Poems, op. cit.*, p. 35.

as opponents of the Young God and un-Romantic devotees of earthbound values and "liberalism" (here the influence of the unspeakable French fascist[497] Charles Maurras comes into play). Unawareness of these dimensions vitiates Julius's attempt to analyze Eliot's greatest antisemitic poem, "Gerontion". Julius provides useful analyses, however, of those stunning masterpieces of antisemitic art "Burbank with a Baedeker, Bleistein with a Cigar", and "Sweeney Among the Nightingales". Another antisemitic tour de force, "Mr. Eliot's Sunday Morning Service", Julius totally fails to understand; it contains a lapidary conspectus of the history of religion: Judaism, Hellenism, Christianity, and secularism. The poem "Dirge" (omitted, on Ezra Pound's advice, from *The Waste Land*) is an artistic failure; yet it is a good deal more subtle than Julius's crude analysis allows.

Julius is at his strongest in analysing Eliot's prose, and in assembling material to illustrate Eliot's attempts to excuse or deny his antisemitism, after the Holocaust had put an end to the era of unabashed Jew-hatred in literature. Julius also provides an excellently argued critique of Christopher Ricks's half-apologia for Eliot in his *T. S. Eliot and Prejudice*. Above all, one is grateful for a book that avoids the current jargon of literary "theory" and has the courage to say that a poem is not necessarily "self-referential" but can be treated as a statement.

---

[497] Editor's footnote: See p. 35, footnote 60 (in which I quote from Curtis, *op. cit.* and from the Author's own essay "The Antisemitism of Ezra Pound", in which the Author compares the antisemitism of Pound with that of Eliot). In Curtis's view, to call Maurras a "fascist", deeply reactionary and antisemitic though he was, is "unfair and unrealistic". (Curtis, *op. cit.*, p. 8.)

APPENDIX 6:

Review[498] by Hyam Maccoby of *Word Unheard: A Guide through Eliot's Four Quartets*, by Harry Blamires (1969: London, 2016).

Mr. Blamires tells us in his Introductory Note that he was prompted to write his Guide by his disagreement with a critic "who observed that *Four Quartets* is a poem which only a highly trained philosopher could understand". Convinced that the work of a poet "richly nourished on literary and theological orthodoxies" must be intended not for "learned specialists" but for "the general reading public"[499], Mr. Blamires has provided a line-by-line elucidation, designed to clear away difficulties and to inculcate an awareness of "echoes".[500]

Much of this commentary is indeed likely to be helpful to the general reader, and Mr. Blamires has many insights that will be new to the Eliot specialist also. Clearly Mr. Blamires is not in any sense "writing down" to the general reader but is intending to give him everything that it is in the nature of a commentary to offer. It must be said, then, that the book as a whole is less than a distinguished performance, mainly for the reason that the philosophical dimension of the poem is only thinly present. Bradley and Bergson are not even mentioned. This is rather like discussing Dante without mentioning Aquinas. *Four Quartets* is not a philosophical treatise, but it *is* a philosophical poem, produced in the midst of ideas (philosophical and scientific) about Time. No doubt the "general reading public" can gain much from the poem without philosophical knowledge; but, once the need for a Guide has been granted, Eliot's use of technical philosophy must be acknowledged to be an important part of the terrain.

Mr. Blamires contends (p. 5 and p. 140) that the thought of the poem cannot be schematized, and that far more important than a knowledge of the technical philosophical background is an awareness of "thematic cross-references" (p. 140), as in the appreciation of music. But the analogy with music can be carried too far. Even the distinction between philosophical prose and philosophical verse can be carried too far. (Bertrand Russell

---

[498] Editor's footnote: Originally published in *Notes and Queries*, September 1972. Reprinted by kind permission of Oxford University Press.

[499] Editor's footnote: p. 1. All quotations are taken from the 1969 edition.

[500] Editor's footnote: p. 3: "The poem is *about* echoes; the poem *utilizes* echoes; the poem *is* echoes." (Emphases in original.)

attacked Bergson's philosophy as "poetry".)[501] Mr. Blamires seems to think that an awareness of thematic cross-references is valuable in itself, and that an ineffable message is mystically conveyed by such patterning alone. The relation between word-music and thought in Eliot is more complex than this; and, consequently, the task of a Guide is more exacting than Mr. Blamires is prepared to concede.

Moreover, the phrase "literary and theological orthodoxies" (p. 1) does little justice to the originality of Eliot's religious position. His journey to faith took a most unorthodox route, through Baudelaire and Frazer, and there is nothing comfortable about any of his views. One too often feels, in Mr. Blamires's exposition, that the mountain has brought forth a mouse; that, when all the obscurity of allusion and cross-reference has been cleared away, we are left with the kind of platitude that would appeal to the average churchgoer, who, I am convinced, would be most disconcerted by a real glimpse into Eliot's mind. There is a savagery in that mind that is lost in the blandness of Mr. Blamires's exposition. "Christ the tiger", "the boredom, and the horror", have almost disappeared from view.

In another respect, Mr. Blamires is only too original. In his search for undertones of meaning, he not infrequently falls into a kind of tasteless ingenuity. An example is the comment (pp. 12-13) on "Burnt Norton", I, line 28: "the words 'unseen eyebeam' remind us that fallen man queers the pitch in the created world by failing to see the beam in his own eye (St. Luke, VI, 41-2)". This, of course, like all Mr. Blamires's less felicitous comments, is offered merely as a possible secondary nuance hovering around the main meaning; but it shows a crossword type of ingenuity that is far from characteristic of Eliot. Perhaps the most extraordinary of these lapses is the suggestion (p. 85) that, among the connotations of "It tosses up our losses" ("The Dry Salvages", I, line 22), there is a reference to masturbation; but closely rivalling this is the suggestion (p. 153) that "And the fullfed beast shall kick the empty pail" ("Little Gidding", II, line 64) has some reference to the killing of the fatted calf in the parable of the Prodigal Son – since the calf "kicks the bucket"! Perhaps the trouble is that Mr. Blamires, a student of Joyce, is over-convinced of affinities between Eliot and Joyce. High-spirited, jokey verbal acrobatics are a congruous part of Joyce's style but not of Eliot's.

I am afraid that those parts of Mr. Blamires's work in which he seems most conscious of his originality all have something of the strained ingenuity shown in the above examples. I find his discovery (pp. 6, 112, 194-195) of references to the Titanic and Tay Bridge disasters most unconvincing. But the general level of his commentary is much higher than this. An example is his exposition of "Little Gidding" I, showing the relation of "midwinter spring" (line 1) to "frigid purgatorial fires" ("East Coker", IV, line 19) and to the revelation in "Burnt Norton" I. The whole passage (p. 125) shows Mr. Blamires at his best. His reverence for the

---

501 Editor's footnote: See Bertrand Russell, *History of Western Philosophy, op. cit.*, p. 714, on Bergson: "His imaginative picture of the world, regarded as a poetic effort, is in the main not capable of either proof or disproof".

text is expressed in patient attention to detail and alertness for "echoes", both within the *Quartets* and in the rest of Eliot's work, both verse and prose. Good are the treatment of the "November ... disturbance" ("East Coker", II) (pp. 54-55); of "humility is endless" ("East Coker" II) (p. 58); of "disowning the past" ("The Dry Salvages", II) (p. 97); of "disfigured" ("Little Gidding", II) and "transfigured" ("Little Gidding" III) (p. 160) ; of "discharge" ("Little Gidding", IV) (p. 170); and of the relation between form and content in the fourth movements (pp. 170-171).

The ideal *Quartets* commentator needs, perhaps, a dash of unease about Eliot's prophetic message, but he certainly needs both Mr. Blamires's conviction of the rightness of that message's expression and his understanding of the unity of all Eliot's work and thought. This book is not in the first rank of commentaries on the *Quartets*, but it is a useful addition to a subject of study that even now, is in its early stages.

APPENDIX 7:
Three letters by Hyam Maccoby

a) The *Times Literary Supplement*, February 9, 1990

    Sir, Craig Raine's article on T. S. Eliot's imagery ("NB", February 2-8[502]) has at least the merit that he assumes that some rational process is going on, rather than, as so many others have argued, a process of free association or meaningless word-patterning. However, it is hard to accept Mr. Raine's suggestion that an important element in Eliot's imagery is the revivification of clichés. Of the examples he gives, only the first[503] carries any conviction. The others (and he presumably cites the best candidates he can find) require a very different kind of comment. An example is the line in "Mr. Apollinax": "I heard the beat of the centaur's hoofs over the hard turf", which Raine explains as an extension of the cliché "flogging a dead horse". It would be hard to imagine a more insensitive reaction to Eliot's evocation of Bertrand Russell's "dry and passionate talk". In view of the earlier references in the poem to Fragilion[504] and Priapus, the centaur recalls a Greek combination of intellect and sensuality; Cheiron was a consummate teacher, to whom Socrates was compared, but could not escape the centaurs' reputation for lechery. What we know of Russell's life makes the comparison not inapposite. To sacrifice the rich associations of "centaur" in favour of the connotation "dead horse" is hardly a gain, quite apart from the clumsy inappropriateness by which Russell himself becomes the dead horse which he is allegedly flogging.

---

502 Editor's footnote: Republished, under the title "To Purify the Dialect of the Tribe", in Craig Raine, *Haydn and the Valve Trumpet*, 1990: London 2013, pp. 58-64.

503 Editor's footnote: At the beginning of his list of examples, Raine applies the word "self-conscious" to the lines from "Portrait of a Lady": "I feel like one who smiles and turning shall remark/Suddenly his expression in a glass". But Raine says this is "not exactly a cliché", so the example cited by the Author is probably "whichever way the wind blows", the cliché that Raine applies to the opening lines of "The Boston Evening Transcript": "The readers of the Boston Evening Transcript/Sway in the wind like a field of ripe corn".

504 Editor's footnote: "Fragilion" sounds like an ancient Greek name but is yet another of Eliot's made-up names. For a convincing explanation of it, see Stephen Medcalf, "Points of View, Objects and Half-Objects: T. S. Eliot's Poetry at Merton College, 1914-15", in *T. S Eliot and Our Turning World, op. cit.*, pp. 73-74: "This is a dream-world apparently deriving from the paintings of Fragonard in the Wallace Collection (where Eliot 'made notes!!!" in April 1911) (*Letters* 1, 19), especially from *The Lady in the Swing* displaying her legs for the delight of men and statues among the shrubbery.... Fragonard's name blends with 'fragile' to fit this artificial, sensual, decadent, delightful but eery eighteenth century world. No doubt Bertrand Russell's combination of sexual and mental energy with aristocratic Whiggishness partly called this imagery out (the clerical-looking gentleman in Fragonard's painting, according to gossip a bishop, who pushes the lady in the swing, actually resembles Russell)." (Emphases in original.)

Similarly trivial and inappropriate is his comment on the lines:

His laughter was submarine and profound
Like the old man of the sea's
Hidden under coral islands
Where worried bodies of drowned men drift down in the green silence,
Dropping from fingers of surf.

To Raine, this means that Russell's hearers were "out of their depth", his conversation being "over their heads". But it is not Russell's hearers who are pictured as under the sea, but Russell himself, who is being compared to the old man of the sea. The point is that Russell's laughter derives not from levity, but from the standpoint of eternity, from which the lives and worries of ordinary people appear ludicrous; yet there are also indications of trickiness and mischief, deriving from stories of Proteus and of the Arabian Nights. Eliot's use of sea-imagery throughout his work is far more relevant here than Craig Raine's crossword-clue associations.

b) The *Times Literary Supplement*, June 14, 1996.

Stephen Medcalf writes, in his review of three books on T. S. Eliot (June 7), "Anthony Julius rightly castigates Hyam Maccoby for finding anti-Semitism in 'Mr. Eliot's Sunday Morning Service', where the target of the nastiness is precisely what the title implies: the Christian Church". Others, more plausibly, have seen the Christian clergy as targeted in the first lines:

Polyphiloprogenitive
The sapient sutlers of the Lord
Drift across the window-panes.
In the beginning was the Word.

But how can the Christian clergy be called "polyphiloprogenitive", which means "desirous of, or fond of, many children"? Grover Smith is reduced to saying that this is a reference to the lechery of the clergy[505] in *The Jew of Malta*, from which the superscription of the poem is taken.

But being lecherous is very different from being desirous of many children, perhaps even the opposite. The Jews, on the other hand, certainly qualify for this adjective ("I will

---

505 Editor's footnote: *Poetry and Plays, op. cit.*, p. 43. See Chapter 5.

multiply thy seed as the stars of heaven"[506]). They also qualify for the description of "sapient sutlers of the Lord", at least in the mind of one steeped in Christian anti-Judaism. "Sutlers" means "petty traders in food and drink". Hinted at are the Jewish dietary laws, the image of the Jews as essentially traders, the Jewish sacrificial system (of which a Christian text says "the kingdom of God is not meat and drink"[507]); none of these reverberations has any relevance to the Christian clergy. The word "sapient" too has many such reverberations; it points to the Jewish pride in "wisdom" that Paul denounced.[508]

Thus, the stanza is saying that the Jews of the Old Testament had a materialistic religious attitude, concerned with food and drink and with worldly wisdom. They failed to appreciate the dimension of spirituality expressed in John's statement, "In the beginning was the Word". Accordingly, as religious failures, the Jews "drift across the window-panes", an expression unmistakably recalling the "jew" in "Gerontion" who "squats on the window-sill" – i.e., remains the eternal outsider in Christian society. The word "polyphiloprogenitive" also finds its echo in "Gerontion", in the word "spawned".

With this clue, the whole poem falls into place. The second stanza deals with the over-spiritualized conception of Origen and of the Greek philosophers, the third and fourth point to the mediating conceptions of the New Testament, combining the Word with the Flesh.

Stanzas 5, 6 and 7, so far from satirizing the Christian clergy, give a sympathetic picture of their practical function in an imperfect world, ministering in a piecemeal way to a fallible humanity, but functioning as useful and fertilizing "bees", though themselves abjuring sex. There are echoes of Dante in these stanzas. The final stanza, about Sweeney, describes the secularization of modern life, where the Word and the Flesh have been divided. Sweeney in his bath is ironically contrasted with Christ in the water of baptism, and modern scientists are criticized as castrated intellects perpetuating both the error of Origen and the pluralism of the Jews.

The superscription from *The Jew of Malta* has formed an important part of the case that the poem satirizes the Christian clergy. But we should see the superscription in the context of the play. The criticism of the Christian clergy as "caterpillars" is voiced by a Muslim Turk in conversation with a Jew. Eliot has turned Ithamore's pejorative "caterpillars" into non-pejorative "bees".

---

506 Editor's footnote: Genesis 22: 17.
507 Editor's footnote: Romans 14: 17.
508 Editor's footnote: Corinthians 1: 20: "hath not God made foolish the wisdom of this world?"

The poem expresses anti-Judaism rather than anti-Semitism, but the distinction is generally hard to maintain. Eliot's undoubted anti-Semitism is rooted in traditional Christian anti-Judaism and is thus ultimately theological rather than racialist. The poem gives a survey of the development of religion, from materialism and over-intellectualism to communion within the Body of Christ. The irony of the title is directed not against the clergy but against Eliot himself, who is able to express his philosophy of ecstasy only in pedantic polysyllables.

I would refer your readers to my full argument (see *Critical Survey*, 3: 3, 1967); also, *European Judaism*, 17: 2, 1983).[509]

c) The *Jewish Chronicle*, October 11, 1996 (see Editor's Preface for background details).

Professor Gabriel Josipovici (*JC*, September 20, 1996), thinks that, because he derives pleasure from T. S. Eliot's poetry, this proves that Eliot is not antisemitic. He misses the point.

Aesthetics should not be confused with morality. It is quite possible to derive great aesthetic pleasure from Eliot's poetry – as I do myself – even at its most antisemitic. The artistry of Eliot's early poetry is not in conflict with his antisemitism but is actually stimulated by it. Eliot is never so sinuously witty and deftly assured as when he is being antisemitic. This is because Eliot's antisemitism, as expressed in his poetry, is an expression of a philosophy – though, on a personal level, he was capable of the vulgar kind of antisemitism too.

To him, the Jews represent the antithesis of the view of life which he found both in Christianity and in the mystery religions he studied, in which a young divine figure suffers a terrible sacrificial death.

The Jews represent, for Eliot, the acceptance of the values of this world and of old age and are the archetypal anti-Romantics. (I refer your readers to my articles, "A Study of the 'jew' in 'Gerontion'" in the *Jewish Quarterly*, Volume 17, number 2, 1969[510]; and "The Antisemitism of T. S. Eliot" in *Midstream,* Volume 19, number 5, 1973.[511]) Since the Jews represent all that is calculating and worldly, they also represent whatever is sordid in the poet's own nature. This is the "identification" of Eliot with his "jew", wrongly regarded by Professor Josipovici as excusing the antisemitism[512]; to regard the Jews as the yardstick of evil is undoubtedly antisemitic.

---

509 Editor's footnote: see Chapter 5 for the full article.
510 Editor's footnote: See Chapter 4.
511 Editor's footnote: See Chapter 3.
512 Editor's footnote: Josipovici had written in his September 20 1996 letter: "Why Eliot's poems are so moving is that he identifies with the outsiders in all of them – wounded Prufrock, empty Gerontion, mad Hieronimo, and the Jew who squats upon the windowsill. That is why the tone is different from that of Pound and Wyndham Lewis,

Anthony Julius (*JC, Literary Supplement*, August 30) fails to distinguish between vulgar and philosophical antisemitism, and therefore cannot explain how Eliot's antisemitism is compatible with great poetry. He thus lays himself open to Professor Josipovici's criticism.

---

for whom the Jew is always one of them, as opposed to us." The Author had in fact made a similar comparison between Eliot and Pound in his essay "The Antisemitism of Ezra Pound": "to Eliot the Jew is symbolic of humanity itself; in criticizing the Jew, he was criticizing himself: the part of himself that he most disliked". (*Antisemitism and Modernity, op. cit.*, p. 123; for a longer extract see p. 35, footnote 60.) But, as the Author points out, it is antisemitic to identify the Jew with all the worst aspects of humanity.

APPENDIX 8:

An Examination, by the Editor, of "A Cooking Egg", on the lines suggested in *Christ the Tiger*.

Introduction

The July 1953 issue of the literary quarterly *Essays in Criticism* featured a long and heated debate (spilling over into the October 1953 and January 1954 issues) among eminent literary critics over the meaning of Eliot's *Ara Vos Prec* poem "A Cooking Egg". Gilbert F. Cunningham complained that many critics of T. S. Eliot's poems

> are content with safe generalities, contriving to suggest at the same time that they have no difficulty in penetrating the profundities whose surface they skim. The few bold spirits who venture to commit themselves to a definite and specific reading are very vulnerable.[513]

A "definite and specific reading" of the poem seems impossible to me, in view of the ambiguous, shifting nature of Eliot's poetry, with its myriad of meanings and associations: a quality nowhere more apparent than in "A Cooking Egg". Eliot himself warned against "assuming that there must be one interpretation" of a poem "that must be right", adding "the meaning is what the poem means to different sensitive readers".[514] Indeed, a static "definite and specific reading" goes against Eliot's philosophy of poetry. Explaining this philosophy, and also Eliot's obscurity, the Author writes, in Chapter 6 of *Christ the Tiger*:

> Hell is limitation; every concept is heavenly as long as its limitations and incompleteness are acknowledged, but hellish in so far as it is worshipped and regarded as complete. A concept that points beyond itself is a glimpse of heaven; but a concept that claims finality is, by its acceptance of limitation, a trap or prison that is hell. In other words, all concepts must be kept in motion; a static concept is false. Here Eliot's view of poetry as continually self-renewing and fighting against ossification links up with his philosophy of Motion and Time. (Pages 153-154.)

---

513 *Essays in Criticism*, July 1953, "The Critical Forum", p. 350.
514 "The Frontiers of Criticism", in *On Poetry and Poets, op. cit.*, p. 126.

Nonetheless, I was struck by the omission, in the whole debate in *Essays in Criticism*, and in almost all the later interpretations of "A Cooking Egg" that I have read, of the possibility that this is a religious poem that takes the concept of Heaven seriously[515] (and indeed, as the above quotation makes clear, Eliot's very idea of poetry involves taking the concept of Heaven seriously). It seems to me that a detailed examination of "A Cooking Egg" on the lines suggested in *Christ the Tiger* might at least shed some light on the poem.

To help me in this venture (which, though it does not aim at a "definite and specific reading" still makes me "very vulnerable"), I am armed, not only with the lines of interpretation put forward in *Christ the Tiger*, but with early drafts of the poem that are included in the collection of Eliot's early notebook writings - plus loose leaves -- that was published in 1996 under the notebook's title, *Inventions of the March Hare*.[516] Even though the variants and additional verses were discarded, they provide valuable indications of Eliot's thought processes while he was writing the poem. And I think the connection between "A Cooking Egg" and Eliot's unfinished long poem "Coriolan" will also prove very helpful. Even though the first was published in 1919[517], and the second was written in 1931, there are close verbal links that I believe throw light on Eliot's intentions in "A Cooking Egg".

The question most wrangled over by the *Essays in Criticism* critics was: who is Pipit?[518] The debate began in the January 1953 issue, in which F. W. Bateson took issue[519] with I. A. Richards's theory that Pipit is the narrator's old childhood nurse or nanny (to whom,

---

515 An exception is A. David Moody, who writes of the narrator: "His testamentary dispositions, if that is what we have in the middle section, renounce the earthly goods which he expects to find in heaven in their ideal forms." (*Thomas Stearns Eliot Poet, op. cit.*, p. 61.) But Moody does not expand on this intriguing suggestion. Also, it seems to me that it is not so much a question of "ideal forms", as in the philosophy of Plato, but of the deification of the Flesh in the Incarnation, a concept that has something primitive about it, as in the mystery-religions and the totem cults. My main problem with Moody's major book is what seems to me to be an over-emphasis on Eliot as an "anti-Romantic" (e. g. *ibid.*, p. xiv) and an "idealist" (e. g. *ibid.*, p. 297). I find this over-emphasis puzzling, in view of Moody's emphasis on the influence of Frazer, Jane Harrison (Moody calls *Prolegomena* and *Themis* "pioneering and still indispensable", *ibid.*, p. 372, n. 33) and Freud on Eliot – i.e., Eliot's fascination with the primitive. Like Anthony Julius, Barry Spurr, Genesius Jones and Harry Blamires (see Editor's Preface and Appendix 6), Moody, it seems to me, shows insufficient awareness of "Christ the tiger".

516 T. S. Eliot, *Inventions of the March Hare, op cit.* The notebook was sold by Eliot, in 1922, to John Quinn, who died in 1924. Unknown to Eliot, who never learned what had happened to the notebook, it was bought in 1958 by the New York Public Library and included in its Berg Collection. Inside the notebook are loose leaves, which include drafts of the 1920 *Ara Vos Prec* poems. These *Ara Vos Prec* drafts are published in *Inventions of the March Hare* as Appendix C.

517 Critics disagree on when it was written. Ricks and McCue point out that the typescripts of the poem are undated, but also write that Eliot himself wrote the date of 1917 against the poem in two copies, owned by friends, of published collections of his poetry. (See 2015 *Poems, Vol. 1, op. cit.*, p. 507.) Lyndall Gordon argues that "A Cooking Egg" was written in 1919. (*The Hyacinth Girl, op. cit.*, p. 410.)

518 For the identification of Pipit with Emily Hale, see the discussion of Section 1 below.

519 *Essays in Criticism*, January 1953, "The Function of Criticism", pp. 4-5 and p. 13.

Richards argued, the 30-year-old narrator had sent the book *Views of Oxford Colleges* ten years earlier, in his first term at Oxford). Richards explained the two lines that begin the third section: "But where is the penny world I bought/To eat with Pipit behind the screen?" as a flashback to the narrator's childhood, with Pipit as his nanny or nurse.

In the July 1953 issue, some critics agreed with Bateson that Pipit in Section 1 wasn't an old nanny but a young woman about the same age as the 30-year-old narrator; others agreed with Richards. But the most helpful was Elizabeth Drew, who wrote that Richards had told her that "Eliot had corrected him about the interpretation of Pipit as an old nurse and had said that the clue was in 'Dans le Restaurant'". As we have seen in *Christ the Tiger*, in "Dans le Restaurant" (written in French), a waiter, old, soiled and decrepit, remembers a visionary moment of sexual ecstasy – "un instant de puissance et de délire" ("a moment of power and delirium") that he experienced at the age of seven, when he was alone with a little girl a year or so younger. Drew goes on to interpret "A Cooking Egg" as follows:

> But it is surely obvious, as Richards saw from the first, that there are two Pipits and two "I"s in the poem, those of the present and those of the past, the two periods being indicated by the dots between the stanzas. It would indeed be rather staggering if an *adult* were having these childish daydreams about heaven. Following the clue given by Eliot, perhaps we may say that the "I" of the poem remembers "un instant de puissance et de délire" he had on an occasion when he and Pipit (a childish nickname) were children together. Now they have met again when he is thirty and she a prim spinster or whatever. It has all proved a sterile cooking egg, and the whole world of actuality in the present is so dreary and disillusioning compared with the "penny world" of glorious thoughts.[520]

I agree with Drew that, in the first section of the poem, we have a meeting of the narrator and his childhood playmate, Pipit, at a time when they are grown up; he is thirty and she is a year or two younger. (This view of the two Pipits, one grown up in the first section, the second a child in the flashback of the first two lines of the third section, is also argued by Grover Smith[521].) I agree also with Drew that, at the beginning of the third section, the "penny world" is the world of childhood. B. C. Southam explains that the term "penny world" "has long been used in the confectionary and baking trades for various kinds

---

520 *Essays in Criticism*, July 1953, "The Critical Forum", p. 353. Emphasis in original.
521 *T. S. Eliot's Poetry and Plays, op. cit.*, pp. 48-49.

of cakes and sweets"[522]. In the January 1954 issue of *Essays in Criticism,* I. A. Richards wrote: "I take the speaker to be looking back a long way to a time when something a penny could buy could be all the world to him".[523] In relation to "behind the screen", Southam explains that "in some households, (particularly in the nineteenth century), it was customary for the children to have some meals with the rest of the family, but at their own table and separated from the adults by a screen".[524] This confirms the idea of childhood; but "behind the screen" also means Reality, or the Divine, or the Rose-Garden. The name "Pipit" means a small song-thrush, providing a link to the thrush in "Burnt Norton" I who is the guide into the Rose-Garden of childhood and Reality (see Chapter 6 of *Christ the Tiger*). The narrator, like the waiter in "Dans le Restaurant", experienced, as a child of about seven, a moment of sexual ecstasy, when he was alone with the child Pipit, a year or two younger, like the little girl in "Dans le Restaurant" – a moment of vision that was a foreshadowing of the Divine (but that seems to have been interrupted, just like the beatific moment in "Dans le Restaurant").

But I disagree with Drew about the middle section, which she sees in terms of "childish daydreams about heaven". If we abandon the idea that Eliot is satirizing the Christian concept of heaven, a very different picture emerges. But to start with section 1.

> Pipit sate upright in her chair
> Some distance from where I was sitting;
> *Views of Oxford Colleges*
> Lay on the table, with the knitting.
>
> Daguerreotypes and silhouettes,
> Her grandfather and great great aunts,
> Supported on the mantlepiece
> An *Invitation to the Dance.*

A "cooking egg" means an egg that is no longer fresh; it is stale and cannot be eaten on its own; but must be cooked in a dish along with other ingredients. This appears to describe the narrator at the age of thirty. The epigraph to the poem is: "En l'an trentiesme de mon aage/Que toutes mes hontes m'ay beues", from "The Testament" by the 15th century French poet Francois Villon: "In the thirtieth year of my life/When I had drunk up all my shames". Villon's "Testament", like "A Cooking Egg", is a mixture of ironic tone and religious feeling. See Eliot's comments in his essay "Religion and Literature", in which he writes of

---

[522] *A Student's Guide, op. cit.,* p. 57.
[523] *Essays in Criticism,* January 1954, "The Critical Forum", p. 105.
[524] *A Student's Guide, op. cit.,* pp. 57-58.

"the sense in which Villon and Baudelaire, with all their imperfections and delinquencies, are Christian poets".[525]

The narrator is worn-out and debilitated at the age of thirty, like Villon at the same age – and Pipit seems to be a "cooking egg" as well, in her own way. She, it seems, has become drearily respectable, associated with a past, traditional society – "Oxford Colleges", her "grandfather and great great aunts". The archaic wording "sate" increases this idea of the old-fashioned, decaying past (and also suggests "sedate"). She is "upright", which could imply moral integrity but seems in this context to mean rigid respectability. They are estranged from each other – she sits "Some distance from where I was sitting". She has taken to the spinsterish activity of knitting. The photographs of her ancestors are like shadows or ghosts. She is herself a kind of ghost of the child Pipit, who is also a ghost, since she no longer exists. The first section implies some positive qualities – order, pattern (the knitting, the dance), the coherence of tradition; but it is all cold and dead (Eliot wrote in a letter: "Oxford is very pretty, but I don't like to be dead."[526]). In her guardianship of tradition, the adult Pipit is reminiscent of Amy in *The Family Reunion* (see Chapter 2 of *Christ the Tiger*); but the grown-up Pipit also resembles Mary in the same play; they are about the same age (nearly thirty); each has been the childhood playmate of the hero and experienced with him in childhood an ecstatic vision that was a foreshadowing of Heaven (in the case of Mary and Harry, this was in "the wilderness"[527]); the hero in both cases finds himself unable in their adulthood to marry his childhood playmate.

In her 2022 book *The Hyacinth Girl,* Lyndall Gordon cites a letter written by Eliot, on November 3, 1930, to Emily Hale (one of the letters embargoed until 2020):

> I want to ask you please, to re-read the hyacinth lines in <Part 1.> The Waste Land, and the lines toward the very end beginning 'friend, blood shaking my heart' (where *we* means privately of course *I*) and compare them with Pipit on the one hand and Ash Wednesday on the other, and see if they do not convince you that my love for you has steadily grown into something finer and finer.[528]

525　T. S. Eliot, *Selected Essays, op. cit.*, p. 391.
526　*The Letters of T. S. Eliot, Volume 1, op. cit.*, p. 74.
527　*The Family Reunion, op. cit.*, p. 50.
528　https://tseliot.com/the-eliot-hale-letters/letters/l4
　　　(Emphases and arrows in original.) See also Lyndall Gordon, *The Hyacinth Girl: T. S. Eliot's Hidden Muse, op. cit.*, pp. 85 and 135.

As a matter of biographical fact, Eliot and Emily Hale were *not* childhood playmates; they first met briefly in 1905, when she was 14 and he was 17, but Eliot did not fall in love with her until 1912, when she was 21 and he was 24[529]. Nonetheless, in "A Cooking Egg" it seems that Eliot imagined Emily as a playmate of his early childhood, a little girl of five or six (as in "Dans le Restaurant"), with whom, as a little boy of about seven, he had experienced a moment of sexual ecstasy – beatific but tinged with sin and guilt. The vision of "the hyacinth girl" in *The Waste Land* is more mystical and spiritualized – "seeing into the heart of light, the silence" – and in *Ash Wednesday* I Eliot renounces the love of his youth (clearly Emily): "I renounce the blessed face" (in the letter of November 3, 1930, he refers to her "blessed face") and Emily seems to become subsumed into the image of the "Lady" (who is also the Church, Dante's Beatrice and the Virgin Mary).

In a statement that Eliot wrote about his relationship with Emily – a statement that he embargoed until the date on which the embargo on his letters to her was to be lifted, to ensure that the statement would be read alongside the letters – he explained why in 1915 he had married Vivienne, his first wife, instead of Emily, and had stayed in England (after spending a year at Merton College, Oxford, on a travelling scholarship). He wrote that to return to America and marry Emily would have necessitated completing his Doctorate in Philosophy at Harvard and then finding "a post somewhere in a college or university". Yet

> my heart was not in this study, nor had I any confidence in my ability to distinguish myself in this profession. I must still have yearned to write poetry…. Emily Hale would have killed the poet in me; Vivienne nearly was the death of me ["me" is underlined], but she kept the poet alive. In retrospect, the nightmare agony of my seventeen years with Vivienne seems to me preferable to the dull misery of the mediocre teacher of philosophy which would have been the alternative.[530]

Clearly, the ambivalence of Eliot's attitude towards Emily – on the one hand, she was to him the beatific Muse in her different guises; on the other hand, the stifling, unpoetic guardian of tradition and family expectations (like his family and especially his mother, she was an upper-class, high-minded Boston Unitarian) – is very relevant to "A Cooking Egg", with its two contrasting Pipits, the beatific child and the prim, dull, respectable adult. (There is a similar biographical relevance to *The Family Reunion*, in which Harry's dead

---

[529] *Ibid.*, p. 32.
[530] https://tseliot.com/foundation/statement-by-t-s-eliot-on-the-opening-of-the-emily-hale-letters-at-princeton/

wife is clearly based on Vivienne, while Mary is based on Emily). Nonetheless, it seems to me that Lyndall Gordon over-emphasizes the biographical element of the poem, ignoring the extent to which Eliot universalizes his personal experiences and emotions (for Gordon's interpretation of section 2, see below). Eliot himself makes a clear distinction between "me" and "the poet". As the Author writes in Chapter 6 of *Christ the Tiger* (p. 138), in the Commentary on "Burnt Norton" I: "The rose-garden may have been chosen by Eliot as a symbol because of some personal experience; but he means it to be a universal symbol." (The Rose-Garden in "Burnt Norton" too is linked biographically to Emily Hale.) Pipit is not just an individual woman; she is Woman in different aspects (according to Eliot's view of Woman).

To return, then, to the poem: there is something incongruous and stultifying about the book of "*Views of Oxford Colleges*" being on the table next to "the knitting"; intellect and beautiful architecture juxtaposed to dull domesticity. In relation to "Daguerreotypes and silhouettes,/Her grandfather and great great aunts": in the second part of "Coriolan", we find:

Here is the row of family portraits, dingy busts, all looking remarkably
                                                                                                        Roman,
Remarkably like each other, lit up successively by the flare
Of a sweaty torchbearer, yawning.

The "sweaty torchbearer" is reminiscent of the beginning of Part V of *The Waste Land*: "After the torchlight red on sweaty faces" – which seems to mean the torches and faces of the Roman soldiers who have come to arrest Jesus (a few lines earlier, in "Coriolan", we find "the guards shake dice"). In "Coriolan", it seems that the decaying traditional society of Rome needs to be revived by the sacrifice of Christ. There could be a similar idea underlying this first part of "A Cooking Egg" (see the discussion of Section 2 below for consideration of the meaning of Coriolanus to Eliot).

The "*Invitation to the Dance*" could imply an invitation to marriage on Pipit's part (see "East Coker" I: "dauncing signifying matrimonie"), but one that the narrator rejects, because the support from the shadowy photographs of her grandfather and great great aunts rob the invitation of all excitement. There is a somewhat acerbic argument in the *Essays in Criticism* correspondence as to whether "An *Invitation to the Dance*" is an invitation card *on* the mantlepiece[531] or a sentimental Victorian painting *above* the mantlepiece[532] (another suggestion has been that it is a piece of sheet music[533] – but surely sheet music wouldn't be on the mantlepiece; it would be on the piano). The first interpretation seems to me to be the most likely, because, although it is possible to argue that the photographs are morally supporting the painting *from* their position *on* the mantlepiece, we would then lose the typically Eliotic double meaning of "supported" (implying at the same time both moral and physical support). The *"Invitation to the Dance"* is, in my view, probably a large, formal invitation card – the only one the grown-up Pipit has recently received – displayed, somewhat pathetically, propped up by family photographs, on her mantlepiece.[534]

There is something very disturbing about the complete immobility of the man and woman in this first section; they seem to sit silent and motionless, at a distance from each other and only described in terms of the inanimate objects around them. In an addendum to the "Cooking Egg" controversy, the Editor of *Essays in Criticism*, in the October 1953 issue, cites a note by Constance I. Smith, who comments illuminatingly on the adult Pipit's

> petrified immobility (the knitting is on the table and not in Pipit's hands),
>
> which is contrasted with the living physical 'penny world' of the
>
> childhood romance (sitting as against eating).[535]

The main impression is of coldness, deadness, rigidity, boredom and estrangement between the sexes. The adult Pipit lives in the past, which seems to be why the two verses, even though they are set in the present, are in the past tense.

---

[531] F. W. Bateson, Essays in Criticism, July, 1953, pp. 354-355. I agree with Bateson that "the preposition on ... cannot mean 'over the mantlepiece'". In *The Waste Land* II (which bears some resemblance to the first section of "A Cooking Egg"; there is the chair, the sitting woman, the table, the mantlepiece, the estrangement between the sexes, even though the woman in question is based on Vivienne), we find "*Above* the ancient mantle was displayed/...The change of Philomel". (My emphasis.) Eliot tends to be precise about such matters.

[532] E. M. W. Tillyard, *Essays in Criticism*, July 1953, p. 346.

[533] B. C. Southam, *op. cit.*, p. 56.

[534] Lyndall Gordon claims – in my view unconvincingly – that, in the form of a picture on the mantlepiece, it "has to be a scene from the ballet" *Le Spectre de la Rose*, produced by Sergei Diaghilev (*The Hyacinth Girl, op. cit.*, p. 86). Earlier in her book *(ibid.,* pp. 23-24), Gordon points out convincingly that Eliot was likely to have seen the ballet in Paris, during the year of study that he spent there in 1910-1911; she argues, again convincingly, that he based his early poem "Suppressed Complex" (*Inventions of the March Hare, op. cit.*, p. 54) on *Le Spectre de la Rose*. She also points out (*The Hyacinth Girl, op. cit.*, p. 24) that Diaghilev used Carl-Maria von Weber's *Invitation to the Dance* as music for the ballet. In her discussion of "A Cooking Egg" she concedes that "An *Invitation to the Dance*" cannot be von Weber's score: "It can't be the score: Pipit is not a musician and you don't keep a score on the mantlepiece." (*Ibid.*, p. 86.) Instead, Gordon insists: "it has to be a scene from the ballet that provided a template for exhilarating love". (*Ibid.)* This idea seems to me to be too complicated and far-fetched; certainly, it is not the case that it "has to be" a picture of a scene from the ballet.

[535] *Essays in Criticism*, October 1953, p.477.

The complexity of the tenses in the poem – in the first section, the present time is written in the past tense; the second section has the narrator still in the present but looking far ahead, after death and purgation, to a future in Eternity in Heaven; the third section is back to the present, in the modern secular "Waste Land", but this present time includes a flashback to the past of childhood – surely has a link to the complex meditation on Time and Eternity in the *Quartets* (see Chapter 6 of *Christ the Tiger*).

In early drafts of the poem, two very different verses appear directly after the first two verses. These two discarded verses verge on nonsense poetry and also on erotic poetry; the verses seem to refer to the narrator and Pipit when they were children – he about seven ("when I was strong and young"), and she five or six:

When Pipit's slipper once fell off,
It interfered with my repose;
My self-esteem was somewhat strained
Because her stockings had white toes.

I wanted Pipit [in another version "Peace"] here on earth,
While I was still strong and young;
And Peace was to have been extended
From the tip of Pipit's tongue.[536]

It is possible, in view of Eliot's reference in the early poem "Mr Apollinax" to Fragonard's painting *The Swing* -- see Appendix 7(a) -- that he may be thinking here of that same painting, which he would have seen in the Wallace Collection in London -- see footnote 504, p. 210, on the name "Fragilion". In *The Swing*, the focal point is the lady's pink satin slipper, which has dropped off her foot and is flying in the air; we see her "white toes" at the end of her white-stockinged foot; far from being "upright" in a chair in "frozen immobility", she is reclining, full of life and motion, in her swing. The painting conveys a sense of playful, frivolous joyousness and sensuality; and so does Pipit in these verses. She is a world away from the sedate, prim Pipit of the first two verses. The verse form, too, is very much freer, lighter and looser. The image of Pipit losing her slipper also makes us think of Cinderella, which links with "An *Invitation to the Dance*" in Section 1. Rick de Villiers, commenting on the next draft verse, points out: "The 'tip of Pipit's tongue' is sexually suggestive, but also intimates her capacity for intimate communication."[537] Again, this is in stark contrast to

---

536 *Inventions of the March Hare, op. cit.*, p.358 and p. 360.
537 "Eliot's Quatrain Poems and 'Gerontion'", in *The New Cambridge Companion to T. S. Eliot, op. cit.*, p. 60.

the silent adult Pipit of the poem's first two verses (the words "the tip of Pipit's tongue" themselves make a playful tongue-twister). But these two verses were probably discarded because they are too "sexually suggestive".

Section 2

I shall not want Honour in Heaven
For I shall meet Sir Philip Sidney
And have talk with Coriolanus
And other heroes of that kidney.

I shall not want Capital in Heaven
For I shall meet Sir Alfred Mond.
We two shall lie together, lapt
In a five per cent. Exchequer Bond.

It is true that a first, superficial reading does seem to support the "satirical" interpretation. F. O. Matthiessen (who argues that Pipit is a child all the way through the poem) pointed out a connection between "A Cooking Egg" and a letter that John Ruskin wrote to a friend, Susan Beever, about a young woman called Rose La Touche, with whom he had fallen deeply in love when he was a middle-aged man and she was about 12; her death at the age of 27 strongly affected him. He wrote to Susan Beever, in relation to the death of a young girl who had been a close friend of hers:

> But, Susie, you expect to see your Margaret again, and you will be happy with her in heaven. I wanted my Rosie *here.* In heaven I mean to go and talk to Pythagoras and Socrates and Valerius Publicola. I shan't care a bit for Rosie there, she needn't think it.[538]

There is a clear echo of "I wanted my Rosie *here*" in "I wanted Pipit here on earth/ When I was still strong and young" But the meaning of "When I was still strong and young" is "when I was seven years old". As the Author points out in Chapter 4 (p. 106): "Old age sets in, for Eliot, at about the age of seven." At thirty, the narrator regards himself as stale, weak and old; so, the thought-process seems to go, he now no longer wants Pipit (herself a deteriorated "cooking egg") on earth. Instead, his thoughts of the future turn to Heaven.

---

538 Quoted in The *Achievement of T. S. Eliot, op. cit.,* p. 92. (Ruskin's emphasis.)

The superficial meaning of Section 2 does seem to be: "In heaven I want to talk to famous people, and I shan't care a bit for Pipit there." The tone comes over as sardonic, supercilious, name-dropping. But the people in Eliot's Christian Heaven are very different from the ancient Greek and Roman philosophers in Ruskin's pagan Heaven. Yet Eliot's Christian Heaven seems highly unorthodox, to say the least. If we take Eliot's Christian concept of Heaven seriously, what are such people as the Jewish industrialist and financier Sir Alfred Mond, the Renaissance *femme fatale* Lucretia Borgia, and the modern theosophist Madame Blavatsky (evidently regarded by Eliot as a fraud) doing in his Heaven?

We can, perhaps, find an opening to resolving the puzzlements in the second section by looking first at the two lines that begin the third section – "But where is the penny world I bought/To eat with Pipit behind the screen?". In their sudden seriousness and anguish after the sardonic, superior, name-dropping tone, these two lines point us back to the second section, as though its ironic tone is itself a screen through which we can catch glimpses of the Divine Reality of Heaven. We are only allowed glimpses, because "human kind/Cannot bear very much reality". (See Chapter 6 of *Christ the Tiger*, p. 146, on "Burnt Norton" I.) The two lines are a sudden irruption of Reality into the poem and seem to form its core – the opening through which we can perhaps gain some inkling of the poem's meaning, because childhood is the link between adulthood and the Reality of Heaven.

If we go back to Eliot's words "the clue is in 'Dans le Restaurant'", we remember that the second section of that poem was about the drowning/purging/baptism of Phlebas the Phoenician, who, it is argued in Chapter 4 of *Christ the Tiger* (pp. 104-105), is a muted form of a Jew, symbolizing the degraded aspects of humanity. So I suggest that the people in Eliot's Christian Heaven have also been through Purgatory (with the exception of Piccarda de Donati, from Dante's *Paradiso*, who is already in Heaven; she is a former nun who was forced into marriage against her will, so was allowed to go straight to Heaven, though only to its lowest circle[539]). The narrator is a "cooking egg", who, perhaps, has been "cooked" in a fire with other souls in Purgatory to make him palatable to God.

One indication of a hidden meaning in this second section is the word "Bond" in the second verse of this section:

I shall not want Capital in Heaven
For I shall meet Sir Alfred Mond.
We too shall lie together, lapt

---

539 *Paradiso*, Canto III, ll. 46-57.

In a five per cent. Exchequer Bond.[540]

The ironic tone (including the bathos of the "Sidney/kidney" rhyme in the first verse, a rhyme that corresponds to "trumpets/crumpets" in Section 3) seems to derive from a sense of the irreconcilability of these elements on Earth and of the triumph on Earth of "Capital" over "Honour". Anthony Julius usefully points out the relevance here of Eliot's comment in *The Idea of a Christian Society*: "a people feels at least more dignified if its hero is the statesman however unscrupulous, or the warrior however brutal, rather than the financier".[541] But the false knight Sir Alfred Mond (reminiscent at first of Sir Ferdinand Klein in "Burbank"), having been purged and purified in Purgatory, is now at one with the true knight Sir Philip Sidney and the ancient hero Coriolanus ("the words "I shall not want" and "For I shall meet" are identical in both verses) and also with the "cooked" and purified narrator; they are all one in the unifying Bond of Heaven. Mond seems to represent one aspect of the narrator – an aspect that he had despised on Earth. Mond represents degraded Jewish materialism – "Capital" – which can be accepted in Heaven and united with spiritual "Honour", after materialism has been purged and purified. Sidney/Coriolanus and Sir Alfred Mond seem to symbolise contradictory aspects of the narrator himself that can only be reconciled in Heaven.

It is worth briefly considering here the importance to Eliot of the figure of Coriolanus. In Shakespeare's tragedy, Coriolanus is a Christ-figure, a sacrificial victim who spares and saves Rome, in response to the pleas of his mother and wife, at the price of his own life. He is thus linked to this comment in Chapter 2 of *Christ the Tiger*: "Eliot derived from his study of Frazer the knowledge that it was as a sacrifice to the Mother Goddess or the female principle that the Young God always died."[542] Coriolanus also appears in *The Waste Land*, in precisely the section in Part V in which, Eliot tells Emily Hale, he was thinking of her: "the lines toward the very end beginning 'friend, blood shaking my heart'". This passage

---

540 Grover Smith, *Poems and Plays*, op. cit., p. 50, points out a parody here of Dante Gabriel Rossetti's "The Blessed Damozel", verse XIV: "We two will lie i'the shadow of/That living mystic tree,/Within whose sacred growth the Dove/Sometimes is felt to be."

541 *The Idea of a Christian Society*, London, 1939, p. 42. Julius, op. cit., p. 137.

542 P. 68. It is significant that Eliot wrote of *Coriolanus* and *Antony and Cleopatra*: "*Coriolanus* may not be as 'interesting' as *Hamlet*, but it is, with *Antony and Cleopatra*, Shakespeare's most assured artistic success." (*Selected Prose*, op cit., p. 107.) Antony too is a Christ-like victim of Cleopatra, the representative of the Mother Goddess; and in "Burbank", Antony is contrasted with Bleistein, the ignoble Jewish opponent of the noble sacrificial view of life. On Coriolanus, see also *The Letters of T. S. Eliot, Vol. 5*, op cit., p. 368: Eliot wrote to G. Wilson Knight, on October 30, 1930: "I have been re-reading *Coriolanus*. I wonder if you will agree with me – it is rather important – I feel now that the political criticism, so much mentioned, is a very surface pattern; and that the real motive of the play is the astonishing study of the mother-son relation: 'he did it to please his mother...' I think of writing a poem on this and on Beethoven's version *Coriolan*." (Ellipsis and italics in original.)

ends: "Only at nightfall, aethereal rumours/Revive for a moment a broken Coriolanus." Here memories of Emily as an ethereal, beatific Muse resurrect (if only for a moment) the "broken Coriolanus" Eliot, who has been sacrificed to Vivienne as the cruel, vengeful Mother-Goddess (see Chapter 2 of *Christ the Tiger*). (Vivienne, however, who "kept the poet alive" is also a Muse and indeed a more effective one than Emily, who, in one aspect, "would have killed the poet in me".)

> I shall not want Society in Heaven,
> Lucretia Borgia shall be my Bride;
> Her anecdotes will be more amusing
> Than Pipit's experience could provide.
>
> I shall not want Pipit in Heaven:
> Madame Blavatsky will instruct me
> In the Seven Sacred Trances;
> Piccarda de Donati will conduct me.

What about the three new female characters in the next two verses? Lyndall Gordon interprets "Lucretia Borgia will be my Bride" as Eliot's Henry Jamesian admission of his mistake in marrying "vamp"-like, sophisticated Vivienne in "corrupt old Europe", in contrast with the remembered innocence of Pipit (Emily Hale in unsophisticated, prelapsarian America):

> To go on with this false marriage is to banish faith in goodness,
> specifically the comfort of the twenty-third Psalm, 'The Lord is my
> shepherd, I shall not want'. That balm is lost not only for a lifetime but
> for the afterlife as well, in what the poem ironically calls 'heaven'. It's
> to Pipit's credit that she has no place in the fake 'heaven' of
> celebrities: 'I shall not want Pipit in Heaven', says the bridegroom, who
> is locked to the likes of Lucretia Borgia. Lucretia, not to be relied on for
> fidelity, is allied with others on the make, Alfred Mond and 'red-eyed
> scavengers'. The message is to pity the speaker his Fall into a
> licentious and greedy world where innocence remains no more than
> a distant memory.[543]

---

543 *The Hyacinth Girl, op. cit.*, pp. 86-87.

To repeat my comments in the discussion of Section 1 above: it seems to me that – even though Pipit appears to be based on Emily Hale, and there are autobiographical elements of Vivienne and Emily in *The Waste Land* and *The Family Reunion* -- Lyndall Gordon over-emphasizes the biographical element, ignoring the extent to which Eliot universalizes and transmutes into art his personal experiences and emotions.[544] I also disagree strongly with her adoption of the usual view that Eliot's "Heaven" is nothing more than a satirical "fake 'heaven' of celebrities". It seems to me that, just as Sidney, Coriolanus and Mond are all aspects of the narrator, so these three women are all aspects of Pipit.

To start with Lucretia Borgia: beatific though the childhood sexual ecstasy was, it was infused with sin and guilt. The "penny" in the "penny world" of childhood seems to have a double meaning. The penny doesn't just mean childhood; it is also linked to the expiatory "piaculative pence" clutched by the "red and pustular" young people of "Mr. Eliot's Sunday Morning Service" (see Chapter 5 of *Christ the Tiger*) and to the small coin that the narrator in "Dans le Restaurant" gives the dirty waiter, so that he can have a purgative bath. Lucretia Borgia seems to represent dangerous female sexuality – alive in the child Pipit, repressed in the adult Pipit – purged and purified and united with the beatific, Beatrice-like purity of Piccarda de Donati. Lucretia also seems to represent the cruel Goddess to whom the Young God is sacrificed; she is a Cleopatra or Clytemnestra figure. I don't think "Society" refers only to high birth; in the earlier drafts, Eliot first wrote "Conversation" and then "Company"[545], which seems to indicate that he is thinking of Lucretia as (like Cleopatra)

---

[544] Gordon is also, in my view, far too personal and biographical in her interpretation of the end of *Ode* -- an ending that depicts the sea-monster of the Perseus and Andromeda myth as a male "dragon": "Indignant/At the cheap extinction of his taking-off./Now lies he there/Tip to tip washed beneath Charles' Wagon." (*Inventions of the March Hare, op. cit.*, p. 383.) Gordon's interpretation of these final lines is that they describe "a premature ejaculation, some way below the stars". (*The Hyacinth Girl, op. cit.*, p. 51.) Certainly the poem (originally published in *Ara Vos Prec*, but never subsequently reprinted by Eliot), does seem to have a very personal, autobiographical connection with what appears to have been the disastrous wedding night of Eliot and Vivienne; and this is probably why Eliot never allowed it to be republished. But the end of *Ode* surely repeats Eliot's constant theme, emphasized by the Author, of drowning/baptism/sacrifice/purgation leading to rebirth of transfigured, divinized Flesh in the Incarnation in Heaven (hence the reference to the stars). Grover Smith points out (*Poetry and Plays, op. cit.*, p. 37) that the "concluding section" of *Ode* is modelled on Laforgue's prose-poem *Persée et Andromède*. This story combines the Perseus and Andromeda myth with the fairy-tale of Beauty and the Beast; the male sea-monster is killed by the effete, petulant Perseus in an unfair, unheroic way – "the cheap extinction of his taking-off"; Perseus decamps; and Andromeda realizes that she loves the now-dead monster and kisses him. He then changes into a handsome young prince, who had been laid under a spell, from which the kiss releases him. At the end of Eliot's poem, the lines just before "Indignant/At the cheap extinction of his taking-off" are: "Sailing before the wind at dawn./Golden apocalypse." This seems to represent the Heavenly Marriage of the monster and Andromeda in reborn, transfigured, apotheosized Flesh. Earlier in the poem, Vivienne/the bride seems to be not Andromeda but the sea-monster (female in the original Greek myth), who is killed by the bridegroom/Eliot/Perseus: "There was blood upon the bed.... /Succuba eviscerate." The lines of interpretation suggested by the Author again throw a great deal of light upon this poem.

[545] *Inventions of the March Hare, op. cit.*, p.360.

alive, amusing and entertaining, which is like the child Pipit in the two discarded verses – and very different from the dull adult Pipit, with whom the narrator sits in cold, motionless silence in the first section, and marriage with whom he rejects.

In trying to understand why Sir Alfred Mond, Lucretia Borgia and Madame Blavatsky appear in Eliot's Heaven, we need to remember the interpretation in *Christ the Tiger* of another *Ara Vos Prec* poem: "The Hippopotamus", which, the Author writes "has been misread as a satire on the Church". To quote from Chapter 1 of *Christ the Tiger* (p. 59-60):

> Christianity ... in Eliot's view, while deriving its world-weariness from the mystery cults, did not really reject the body. In fact, Christianity deified and apotheosized the body in the doctrine of the Incarnation, a doctrine central in all Eliot's thought.... The beauty and blessedness of the body could not be realized on earth, but it should be realized after death. This is the meaning of Eliot's profound early poem "The Hippopotamus", which has been misread as a satire on the Church, but is really about the deification of the body, which, in all its apparent bulkiness and ridiculousness (as symbolized by the Hippopotamus), is the substance of the Incarnate God and of the Church, which is called the Body of Christ.

Again, in Chapter 5 of *Christ the Tiger* (pp. 128-129), we find: "the hippopotamus, symbolizing the flesh in all its bulky, quivering, fallible absurdity, rises superior to the Church, when the latter is wrongly conceived as above the shocks that flesh is heir to". The Flesh that is united in Heaven with the Word and is therefore deified, becoming one with the Incarnate God, must be the Flesh in all its grossness, errors, sins and absurdities, which have been purified and purged in Purgatory. Thus the body achieves its sexual flowering in Heaven, after sexuality has been purged and purified of sin. This is why Lucretia Borgia becomes in Heaven the narrator's "Bride".

What about Madame Blavatsky, the famous Russian theosophist? She is clearly regarded by Eliot as an absurd charlatan. Though she was not Jewish, she seems to be one of Eliot's mutedly Jewish characters, non-Jews who are really Jewish, like Phlebas the Phoenician and Mr. Eugenides in *The Waste Land* (see Chapter 4 of *Christ the Tiger*, pp. 104-105). She is the female equivalent of the explicitly Jewish Sir Alfred Mond (the only other modern character), the fake knight. Section 2 is very symmetrical in form; and, just as Mond is contrasted with two heroic male figures from the past, so Blavatsky is contrasted with two heroic female figures from the past; in her case, two Renaissance figures, in his case one

Renaissance figure, the other from the ancient world. Like Sir Alfred, Blavatsky is a modern materialist pretending to be spiritual; she is degraded Flesh posing as Word. Blavatsky also seems to represent the corruption of an ancient tradition that has degenerated into mere witch-like magic – just as Mr. Eugenides (the name means "well-born") represents a noble tradition that has become debased (see Chapter 4 of *Christ the Tiger*, pp. 104-105). Blavatsky is a forerunner of the Egyptian/Semitic-sounding Madame Sosostris, the "famous clairvoyante" in *The Waste Land* I who is associated with the purgation of Phlebas the Phoenician -- "Here, said she,/Is your card, the drowned Phoenician Sailor". Blavatsky seems to represent everything that is deceptive, degraded and materialistic in the stale "cooking egg" that is the adult Pipit, with her dubious claims to being "upright", intellectual, and spiritual.

But Madame Blavatsky's fake, witch-like, materialistic spiritualism could be seen as having become transfigured in Heaven, after her purgation and purification in Purgatory, into the true spirituality of Christianity. She, the false spiritual guide, shares a verse with the true spiritual guide, Piccarda de Donati. Madame Blavatsky's "Seven Sacred Trances" have, perhaps, become transmuted into the Seven Sacraments of Christianity -- one of which is Marriage.

Indeed, the two last verses of Section 2 seem to contain, as a hidden meaning, the idea of marriage: Lucretia Borgia had four husbands; Piccarda broke her vow of chastity as a nun because she was forced into marriage. Hidden in the second section seems to be a third Pipit: Heavenly Pipit, the reborn and transfigured Pipit after the death, purgation and purification of the adult Pipit. The heavenly marriage with this Pipit seems to represent the overcoming of the adult estrangement between the sexes that we saw in Section 1. As critics have pointed out, the word "want" is highly ambiguous; it can mean "need", "desire" or "lack"[546]. In all the other verses in Section 2, it means "lack" (and, as Lyndall Gordon writes, seems to be based on Psalm 23: "The Lord is my shepherd; I shall not want.") In the overt, ironic meaning, "I shall not want Pipit in Heaven" appears to signify "I shan't need, desire or care about Pipit in Heaven", echoing Ruskin's words about Rosie. But the hidden, contrary meaning seems to be: "I shall not lack Pipit in Heaven; Pipit and I (with all our contradictory aspects purified and integrated within ourselves) will be entirely united in a heavenly, sinless marriage of flesh and spirit, of which the ecstatic moment in our childhood was only a foreshadowing." Pipit, in the surface reading a Cinderella excluded from the Heavenly Ball (this idea takes us back to the *Invitation to the Dance* in Section 1)

---

546 See, for instance, *Essays in Criticism*, October 1953, p. 477: "Miss Constance I. Smith.... explores the ambiguity of *want* in the four-times repeated 'I shall not want'." (Emphasis in original.)

is invited to the Divine "dance" (see Chapter 6, p. 156, on the "dance" in "Burnt Norton" II) and becomes the Bride, the Rose, the Queen of Heaven.

The last line of the second section – "Piccarda de Donati will conduct me" prompts in the reader's mind the question: "To where will Piccarda conduct the narrator?" In an earlier draft, the question is answered in a verse that immediately follows:

> To the communion of the Lord,
> With bread and wine the tables drest;
> I hope the potables will be
> Such as my stomach can digest.[547]

Here we have explicitly the Heavenly Incarnation of Christ – the ultimate fusion of Word and Flesh -- the Sacrifice, and a memory of the original Totem Meal, in which the communicants are united by feeding on the flesh and blood of the sacrificed totem animal. The narrator is "cooked" as a palatable meal for God; but he also eats God. (The reason that this verse was left out in the final version was probably that the verse gives too explicit a glimpse into the Divine Reality of Heaven, which has something very savage about it.) The narrator, still on Earth, in his weak, decrepit adult state, wonders ironically whether he will be able to stomach such powerful fare (this is irony against himself).

But he goes on to remember the Divine meal that he came close to eating in his childhood, a time when his stomach would have been strong enough for the Divine sacrificial "potables". With these lines coming straight after the discarded last verse of Section 2, we now seem to see what he and Pipit had been about to eat:

> But where is the penny world I bought
> To eat with Pipit behind the screen?

The killing and eating of the sacrificed god and the visionary moment of sexual ecstasy are clearly very closely associated, indeed here they seem identical.[548] So, at the end of the second section, in the discarded last verse, it could be that the Heavenly Communion Meal is also a Heavenly Marriage-Feast[549] to celebrate the Heavenly Marriage-Union of the purged and purified narrator and the purged and purified Pipit – Flesh united with Word, the estrangement of the sexes finally overcome.

---

547 *Inventions of the March Hare, op. cit.,* p.359.

548 A Frazerian anthropologist would see this identity as the sacrifice leading to the regeneration of nature and human sexuality; a Freudian psychoanalyst would see the identity in terms of the Oedipus complex.

549 In a Catholic wedding-ceremony, the bride and groom and guests often take Communion.

Section 3

The crucial question "But where is the penny world I bought/To eat with Pipit behind the screen?" not only looks back to Section 2; it also looks forward to Section 3, asking: "Where on Earth, in the modern world, is there any equivalent to the foretaste of Heaven that I experienced as a child, when alone with the child Pipit?" In this third section we are in the post-Christian, secular world of the Waste Land:

The red-eyed scavengers are creeping
From Kentish Town and Golder's Green.

Anthony Julius writes usefully:

Golders Green after the [1914-1918] war was already an area where Jews were settling; furthermore, there is a precedent in 'Burbank' for the pairing of low and elevated Jews: Mond and the scavengers meet Klein and Bleistein.[550]

Moreover, "red-eyed scavengers" make one think of rats, just as, in "Burbank", Bleistein is seen in terms of rats: "The rats are underneath the piles./The jew is underneath the lot."[551] The scavengers are "red-eyed" because their eyes are bright with the fire of life, because they alone are alive in the Hell of the Waste Land, their spiritual home. But because the modern secular world is seen as a world of Death, the scavengers are really dead, whereas the ironic, diffident narrator is really alive. The word "scavengers" has two meanings: feeders on dead flesh and pickers-up of stray odds and ends. The Jews are seen as feeding on the dead world of modern Western civilisation; and perhaps also they are eating the flesh of Christ and drinking his blood in the same furtive, Judas-like, treacherous sense in which figures like Mr. Silvero and Madame de Tornquist (who resembles Mesdames Blavatsky and Sosostris) do so in "Gerontion" (see Chapter 4, p. 114).[552] In the meaning of pickers-up of stray odds and ends, the scavengers represent the Many as opposed to the One; they are feeders on miscellaneous scraps. Except when in Heaven, after being purged and purified, like Sir Alfred Mond and the honorary Jewess Madame Blavatsky, the Jews deny the efficacy of the Oneness, the Sacrifice and the Incarnation. They create, flourish within and feed off the modern secular Waste Land, in which the ancient glory and heroism of the now-decaying civilisation (a glory and heroism symbolized in English civilisation by Sir Philip Sidney and in Roman civilisation by Coriolanus in his warrior aspect) are dead

---

550 *op. cit.*, p. 138.
551 T. S. Eliot, *Selected Poems, op. cit.*, p. 35.
552 In an early draft, "creeping" is "feeding" (*Inventions of the March Hare, op. cit.*, p. 359).

and deep buried, underneath Alps that, as Grover Smith writes, are "mountains of snow that cannot melt away".[553] The evocation of the Alps' rigid coldness makes us think of the frozen "upright" Pipit of Section 1:

Where are the eagles and the trumpets?

Buried beneath some snow-deep Alps.
Over buttered scones and crumpets
Weeping, weeping multitudes
Droop in a hundred A.B.C.'s.

Here again we have a very significant connection with "Coriolan". At the end of Part I of "Coriolan", we find:

But how many eagles! and how many trumpets![554]
(And Easter Day, we didn't get to the country,
So we took young Cyril to church. And they rang a bell
And he said right out loud, *crumpets*.)

Barry Spurr comments on this passage:

It is a classic example, in his poetry, of how we need to be aware of
Eliot's Anglo-Catholicism in order to understand what is being
said. The bell is the consecration (or sacring or Sanctus) bell.... But for
young Cyril - and possibly his cross-grained parents too, wishing they
were heading off to Maidenhead, rather [than] being reduced to
church-going to fill up the holiday – the sound of the bell and the sight
of the Host, a doughy, dull-white circular disk in the distance, reminds
him of the crumpet-man, ringing his bell as he does his rounds and

---

[553] *T. S Eliot's Poetry and Plays*, op. cit., p. 49. As Smith implies, the snow seems to have been suggested to Eliot by Villon's famous refrain in his "Testament": "Mais ou sont les neiges d'antan?", translated by Dante Gabriel Rossetti as "But where are the snows of yester-year?" As Smith points out (*ibid.*), this is part of "the whole *ubi sunt* tradition".

[554] In contrast to "A Cooking Egg", the eagles and the trumpets are very much present here – but they are seen ironically, as part of the deterioration of modern warfare into mechanization; they become hollow symbols of a former Romantic conception of warfare, now discredited by the First World War. But "A Cooking Egg" was written either during or after the First World War, so this could be one meaning of "Where are the eagles and the trumpets?"; following the First World War, the heroic European Romantic conception of war is now dead and buried "beneath some snow-deep Alps".

dispensing his wafer-like wares.[555]

To return to the last lines of "A Cooking Egg": the deeply unhappy, atomized multitudes of the secular modern world no longer experience the Holy Communion that is a foreshadowing of the Incarnation in Heaven; instead of eating the wafer that is the Host, the Divine Body of the Sacrificed Christ, they feed on meaningless "buttered scones and crumpets" in cheap, mass-market teashops.[556]

The first section of the poem has a rigid, deliberately boring tum-tum rhythm. The second section is much more flexible in rhythm, but creates a sense of unification, signifying the Oneness of Heaven (each verse begins with the words "I shall not want"). But the third section is broken up; and even the rhyme-scheme breaks down in the end.

The religious interpretation of this poem is backed up by words that Ezra Pound wrote in the margin of an early draft, against the last two lines. The Editor of *Inventions of the March Hare* tells us: "Pound wrote: 'Other manner intruded on the purely religious' and glossed 'other manner' as 'the modern or joltographic.'"[557]

It is interesting that one of the early drafts of "Whispers of Immortality" (another *Ara Vos Prec* poem) ends with a verse that brings in Pipit:

As long as Pipit is alive,

One can be mischievous and brave;

But where there is no more misbehaviour

I would like my bones flung into her grave.[558]

By "where there is no more misbehaviour", the narrator seems to mean either "when Pipit is literally dead" or "when Pipit is grown up" – ie spiritually dead. "As long as Pipit is alive" – i. e. a mischievous child – the narrator too can be happy to be alive on Earth; if Pipit is no longer a mischievous child, he looks forward only to Heaven, wanting their bones to be together in Pipit's grave (either the grave of the child Pipit or the eventual grave of the adult Pipit, who is herself the grave of the child Pipit), so that their bones can be resurrected

---

555 *Op. cit.*, p. 130.

556 Eliot acknowledged as a source for "weeping, weeping" two lines from Blake's "Jerusalem" I, describing a vision of a golden Jerusalem being built amid the misery of London: "What are those golden Builders doing/Near mournful ever-weeping Paddington". (See 2015 *Poems, Vol. I, op. cit.*, p. 514.)

557 *Inventions of the March Hare, op. cit.*, p. 360.

558 *Ibid.*, p. 365. In another early draft of this poem, Eliot ends with the verse: "And when the Female Soul departs/ The Sons of Men turn up their eyes./The Sons of God embrace the Grave – / The Sons of God are very wise." (*Ibid*, p. 368.) In other words, the Sons of Men look towards a mere disembodied spirit (see "the vanishd shade" in the previous verse); the Sons of God "embrace the Grave" because the grave contains the bones of the dead woman – bones that have the desire and potential to put on Flesh and be united with Word in the Incarnation in Heaven.

together in Heaven, putting on transfigured sinless Flesh and being united in a Heavenly Marriage.

To conclude: as stated at the beginning, this interpretation of "A Cooking Egg" is not offered as "definite or specific"; but it does seem to me that the main themes put forward in *Christ the Tiger* – themes of childhood, of the visionary moment, of rejection of adult sexuality and earthly marriage, of Sacrifice, of the Incarnation, of the One versus the Many, of the antisemitism that is a "natural concomitant" of these themes – shed some light on this much-debated poem and show that it is a far deeper and greater poem than is conveyed by the interpretation of it as "satirical".

APPENDIX 9:

THE *LISTENER* CORRESPONDENCE

Editor's Introduction

In March 1971, George Steiner delivered four T. S. Eliot Memorial Lectures at the University of Kent, in Canterbury. The lectures, collectively entitled *In Bluebeard's Castle: Some Notes Towards the Re-definition of Culture*, were published later in the same year in book form by Faber and Faber. They were also serialized, between March 18 and April 15, 1971, in the now defunct, but at that time very influential BBC magazine The *Listener*. The lectures gave rise to a voluminous correspondence, lasting from April 15 to July 1, 1971, that came to focus for weeks on one paragraph in Lecture 2 (published in The *Listener* on March 25). Writing about the Holocaust, Steiner touched (but only touched) on the issue of Eliot's antisemitism:

> The failure of Eliot's *Notes Towards [sic] a [sic] Definition of Culture* to face the issue, indeed to allude to it in anything but an oddly condescending footnote [see *Notes towards the Definition of Culture, op. cit.,* p. 70n, and Julius, op. cit., pp.163-167], is acutely disturbing. How, only three years after the event, after the publication to the world of facts and pictures that have, surely, altered our sense of the limits of human behaviour, was it possible to write a book on culture and say nothing? How was it possible to detail and plead for a Christian order when the holocaust had put in question the very nature of Christianity and of its role in European history? Long-standing ambiguities on the theme of the Jew in Eliot's poetry and thought provide an explanation. But one is not left the less uncomfortable. (George Steiner, *In Bluebeard's Castle: Some Notes Towards the Re-definition of Culture*, London, 1971, p. 34.)

In a letter printed in The *Listener* on April 29, Steiner, replying to the correspondence so far (which included one letter on Eliot's antisemitism, published on April 15, from Piers Burton-Page -- who later became well-known as a BBC Radio 3 music producer -- accusing Steiner of a "vicious smear that is unworthy of its perpetrator"), identified the crux of the debate about Eliot's antisemitism: "The obstinate puzzle is that Eliot's uglier touches tend to occur at the heart of very good poetry".

On May 13, another letter on Eliot's antisemitism, by Anne Ridler, was published (see below). Hyam Maccoby contributed to the correspondence three letters, published a) on May 27 (in reply to Ridler's letter); b) June 10, and c) June 24. From May 27 to June 24, the correspondence (apart from a long letter on June 24 from George Steiner that was concerned chiefly with his theory about the main cause of antisemitism and only briefly touched on Eliot) was confined to the issue of Eliot's antisemitism and became an increasingly acrimonious debate between Hyam Maccoby and various eminent opponents.

a) LETTER OF MAY 27, 1971, FROM HYAM MACCOBY

Editor's introduction: The first letter was written in response to the May 13 letter, referring to "the young man carbuncular" in *The Waste Land* III, from the eminent poet and literary critic Anne Ridler. See Chapter 3 of *Christ the Tiger*, p. 85, where this letter is quoted.

SIR: Anne Ridler (*Listener*, 13 May) asks: "Is a poet to be labelled 'antisemitic' because he describes unpleasant people who are Jews?" The answer is: "Certainly not." But Eliot's case is quite different. When Eliot writes (in earlier editions):

The rats are underneath the piles.
The jew is underneath the lot.

it is not a particular Jew who is being described but a generalized "jew" without even the individuality conferred by a capital letter. Eliot was certainly above the vulgarity of personal animosity towards particular Jews. His antisemitism was of a much profounder kind. He was antagonistic towards what he conceived to be the Jewish role in history. Following the line of Charles Maurras, Maurice Barrès and Henry Adams, he regarded Judaism or Jewishness as being, in essence, divisive and atomistic, and as being responsible for the lack of integration of the modern world. A close study of "Gerontion" shows the "jew" (again without a capital letter) as central to the meaning of the poem, the opposite extreme to the Christ-child.

Even Eliot's individualized Jews, like Bleistein, are not without symbolic significance. After all, as Mrs. Ridler well knows, even the "young man carbuncular" is not introduced for the sheer interest of his personality. It would be odd if Eliot's characteristic reverberations of meaning were to desert him just when he is writing about Jews.

b) LETTER OF JUNE 10, 1971, FROM HYAM MACCOBY

Editor's Introduction: The second letter was written in reply to two letters, published on June 3 in reply to Hyam Maccoby's letter of May 27: one by the eminent poet and literary critic Bernard Bergonzi and one by the eminent academic Murray Biggs (he wrote at this time from New College, Oxford and later became a Professor at Yale University). The June 3 letter from Biggs, describing the "jew" in "Gerontion" as a "historical type", is quoted on p. 86 of *Christ the Tiger* (see also my footnote 185 on p. 86).

SIR: Mr. Bergonzi agrees that Eliot was antisemitic in "the Twenties and early Thirties", but claims that he ceased to be antisemitic later (*Listener*, 3 June). Eliot's claim in conversation after the war that he had never been antisemitic [see *Christ the Tiger*, p. 84; this claim was quoted by Bergonzi in his letter] was thus false, on Mr. Bergonzi's own showing, and displays the depth of Eliot's self-deception on this subject. Eliot was clearly dismayed by the Hitler persecution, but he never admitted that he or Charles Maurras had been wrong. All that happened was that, six million murdered Jews later, he surreptitiously changed his small "j"s into capitals, added a mildly pro-Jewish footnote, remarkable not for what it says, but for what it omits, and refrained from further overt antisemitism. There is no reason to suppose that his ideas on the Jews changed fundamentally. All we can say is that Eliot did not believe that antisemitism ought to issue in mass murder. His attitude may be contrasted with that of E. M. Forster, for example, who spoke out trenchantly in the Twenties and Thirties against antisemitism, at the time when such declarations were really needed.

Mr. Murray Biggs cannot see anything antisemitic in the "jew" in "Gerontion", who is merely a "historical type". The "jew" in "Gerontion" is a rootless cosmopolitan, who moves from Antwerp to Brussels to London, and was "spawned", not born, in an "estaminet", not a home. He is the "owner" of Gerontion's house, but "squats" outside on the "window-sill": i.e., his financial power rules society, to which, however, he does not belong, and over which he hovers as an evil presence.

When one understands the references to Newman's "Dream of Gerontius", the "jew" is seen also as the "prince of this world" who owns the body but not the soul: in other words, he is the Devil. This picture corresponds not with any "historical type" but with the medieval Christian Jew-devil and with the Nazi stereotype of the Jewish capitalist. (See my "The 'jew' in 'Gerontion', The *Jewish Quarterly*, Summer 1969.) But Mr. Biggs, no doubt, in his no-nonsense, literal way, thinks that there just happens to be one kind of "historical" Jew who is spawned in an estaminet, travels frequently about Europe and makes a regrettable practice of squatting on the window-sills of houses which he owns; and that Eliot just happened to feel like writing about this particular unrepresentative type of Jew.

Mr. Biggs thinks that an antisemite would have to "disown Christ and his earliest disciples as well". Christian antisemitism is not racialist. It depends on the theory that the Jews, after their rejection of Jesus as the Divine Saviour, became an accursed, instead of blessed, people. Christian antisemitism, therefore, does not involve antagonism towards pre-Christian Jews or Christian Jews, many of whom were taken over into the pantheon of Christian saints. Mr. Biggs seems to suggest that a Christian antisemitism is impossible, whereas it is historically the most virulent and far-reaching of all. (I am using the term "antisemitism", according to common usage, to mean every kind of Jew-phobia, not merely the 19th century post-Christian rationalization based on pseudo-scientific notions of "race".)

As one who regards Eliot as the greatest writer of modern times in the English language, I think that his antisemitism should not be glossed over. For those seeking a re-definition of culture and an assessment of Western civilization, it is a most important *datum*. It is quite true, as Mr. Bergonzi points out, that Eliot was not alone in his antisemitism. In fact, he was representative, and this makes it all the more important not to hide or excuse the facts.

c) LETTER OF JUNE 24, 1971, FROM HYAM MACCOBY

Editor's Introduction: The third letter was written in response to three letters published on June 17 in reply to Hyam Maccoby's letter of June 10. Murray Biggs seems almost incoherent with indignation. He claims, despite the evident irony of Hyam Maccoby's second letter, that "he cannot make up his mind if the 'Gerontion' figure [of the 'jew'] is an idiosyncratic sill-squatter or someone more representative". Biggs adds that Hyam Maccoby's "latest inspiration, that this Jew is the Devil, takes my prosaic breath away". Biggs has read the *Jewish Quarterly* article (Chapter 4 of *Christ the Tiger*) and describes it as "even more extravagant and, by the way, hotly anti-Christian as well. There the Jew is identified with, among other things, Death, Gerontion himself and – holiest of smoke – the whole human race." Biggs insists that his own "literalness ... is needed to keep this thing down to size". He ends his letter by asking what Hyam Maccoby means "by saying that Eliot changed small 'j's to large 'surreptitiously'? Did the poet go sneaking round Fabers' after hours upcasing the letter with his own fair Aryan hand?"

Anne Ridler comments that "no doubt this argument has gone on long enough, but I do not think Mr Maccoby should have the last word on 'Gerontion'". She argues that "it is Gerontion in his apathy and despair, not the Jew, who is the antithesis of Christ in the poem, and it is his fear of Christ's disturbing power that Eliot condemns, in himself as in us all". She also refers to *The Waste Land* IV, in which Jews (capitalized) do not squat but, it is implied, are "handsome and tall": "Gentile or Jew/... Consider Phlebas, who was once handsome and tall as you."

But the angriest June 17 correspondent is a new one: the eminent poet and literary critic Geoffrey Grigson. He describes himself as "someone who doesn't, as it happens, bend double at Eliot's name, and who has long thought that in the end he will have the kind of position now given to Abraham Cowley". Nonetheless, Grigson is outraged by Hyam Maccoby's "loftily smearing letter". Grigson defines antisemitism (as opposed, he writes, to "dislike of Jews or simple bias against Jews") as "wholesale condemnation of Jews, encouragement of persecution, and the Final Solution; and Streicher" and calls it "obscene" to label Eliot an antisemite. He ends his brief letter with the pronouncement that "in making these statements, with Eliot's nature and writing before us, Hyam Maccoby is an ass – in a company of asses".

The *Listener* issue of June 24 carried, under the heading "In Bluebeard's Castle", two letters, one by George Steiner and one by Hyam Maccoby. Steiner's long letter (as pointed out above) only touches briefly on Eliot's antisemitism. Steiner comments that "the issue is only marginally relevant to the argument of my lectures", adding: "It is surprising that so voluminous a correspondence should ensue." His conclusion on the subject is that "the facts stand and anyone interested can readily interpret them himself". The rest of his letter concerns his theory on the main cause of antisemitism.

Despite Anne Ridler's wish that Hyam Maccoby should "not have the last word on 'Gerontion'", he was allowed in this letter the last word on "Gerontion" and on Eliot's antisemitism in general.

SIR: Mr. Grigson arbitrarily defines "antisemite" in such a way that only a full-blown paid-up Nazi will qualify and then declares that it is "obscene" and asinine to call Eliot an antisemite. Consequently, Mr. Grigson does not deign even to mention the evidence. Eliot's support for the violently antisemitic *Action Française*, and his antagonistic references to Jews, are presumably just "simple bias", not antisemitism.

Open persecutions, such as that by the Nazis, do not spring into being *ex nihilo*. The ground is prepared by all kinds of minor forms of antisemitism, including the literary and theoretical type exemplified by Eliot and Pound. I suggest that Mr. Grigson acquire a more sensible working definition of antisemitism by reading an elementary history of the subject, such as Poliakov's. Meanwhile, shouting "Ass!" is no substitute for thought or argument, and an olympian *ex cathedra* pose is no substitute for genuine moral concern. The real obscenity is antisemitism itself, to which, on the evidence of Mr. Grigson's letter, he has given little serious attention.

I cannot make much sense of Mr. Biggs's new letter. I used the word "surreptitious" about Eliot's changing of the small "j"s to capitals, because this and other changes were not accompanied by any public explanation or retraction, as they ought to have been.

Anne Ridler's interpretation of "Gerontion" assigns no role to the "jew" at all. I wonder what she thinks he is there for. I have the impression that she hopes he will go away. I agree with her that there is one friendly reference to a Jew in Eliot's poems, in the Phlebas episode, but I would remind her that this episode is concerned with the ancient world, and that the Old Testament Jew, in Christian theory, is noble. It is to the ancient Jew alone that Eliot grants a capital letter.

I am amazed that your correspondents cannot see anything belittling in spelling "Jew" with a small "j". It is surely obvious in the lines,

> The rats are underneath the piles.
> The jew is underneath the lot.

that the small "j" dehumanizes the Jew and assimilates him to the rats. However, even without this device, the meaning of the above lines is clear enough: that the Jews are gnawing like rats at the foundations of society. This is part of the "writing" which, in Mr. Grigson's indignant words, is "before us". Would he please read it?

I should like to emphasize, finally, that, unlike Mr. Grigson, I regard Eliot as a great and profound poet. He is by no means the only great poet to have been antisemitic. Chaucer's "The Prioress's Tale" was a contribution to the vicious blood-libel campaign. Marlowe's *The Jew of Malta* and Shakespeare's *The Merchant of Venice* both take for granted that the Jews are an accursed and wicked people. These facts are not "smears" on individual writers: they are comments on a civilization.

BIBLIOGRAPHY

Ackroyd, Peter: *T. S. Eliot*, London, 1985.

Adams, Henry: *The Education of Henry Adams*, 1918: Oxford, 1999.

Adams, Henry: *Letters of Henry Adams, Volume 2 (1892-1918)*, ed. Worthington Chauncey Ford, Boston, 1938.

Alderman, Geoffrey: *British Jewry Since Emancipation*, Buckingham, 2014.

Andrewes, Lancelot, *Ninety-Six Sermons, Volume 1: The Nativity, Repentance and Fasting,* Second Edition, 1631: Reprinted Oxford, 1841 (collated with editions of 1641 and 1661): Reprinted Kerry, Ireland, 2018 (CrossReach Publications).

Asher, Kenneth, *T. S. Eliot and Ideology*, Cambridge, 1998.

Bailey, Cyril: *The Greek Atomists and Epicurus,* Oxford, 1928.

Bergson, Henri: *Creative Evolution,* 1907: Kansas, 2011.

Laughter: An Essay on the Meaning of the Comic, 1900: Glasgow, 2022.

Blamires, Harry: *Word Unheard: A Guide through Eliot's Four Quartets*, 1969: London, 2016.

Bradley, F. H.: *Appearance and Reality: A Metaphysical Essay*, 1893, London, 1897.

Ethical Studies, 1876: Oxford, 1962.

Brooker, Jewel Spears: *T. S. Eliot's Dialectical Imagination,* Baltimore, 2018.

(ed.): *T. S Eliot and Our Turning World,* New York, 2018.

Browne, E. Martin: *The Making of T. S. Eliot's Plays,* Cambridge, 1969.

Bywater, Ingram: *Heracliti Ephesii Reliquiae by Heraclitus of Ephesus,* Oxford, 1877.

Chinitz, David E.: *T. S. Eliot and the Cultural Divide,* Chicago, 2003.

Chinitz, David E. (ed.): *A Companion to T. S. Eliot,* Chichester, 2014.

Clark, David R. (ed.): *Twentieth Century Interpretations of Murder in the Cathedral: A Collection of Critical Essays,* New Jersey, 1971.

Cox, C. B. and Hinchliffe, Arnold P. (ed.): *T. S. Eliot: The Waste Land: A Selection of Critical Essays,* London, 1968.

Crawford, Robert: *Eliot After the Waste Land,* London, 2022.

Curtis, Michael: *Three Against the Third Republic: Sorel, Barrès and Maurras,* 1959: Princeton, 2015.

Drew, Elizabeth: *T. S. Eliot: The Design of His Poetry,* New York, 1949.

Eliot, T. S.: Poetry and Plays:

The Complete Poems and Plays, London, 1969.

The Family Reunion: A Play, 1939: London, 1963.

Inventions of the March Hare: Poems 1909-1917, edited by Christopher Ricks, New York, 1996.

Murder in the Cathedral, 3rd Edition, London, 1937.

Murder in the Cathedral, with an Introduction and Notes by Nevill Coghill, London, 1965.

The Poems of T. S. Eliot, edited by Christopher Ricks and Jim McCue,

Volume 1: Collected and Uncollected Poems, London, 2015.

Volume 2: Practical Cats and Further Verses, London, 2015.

Selected Poems, London, 1961.

The Waste Land: A Facsimile and Transcript of the Original Drafts, edited by Valerie Eliot, London, 1971.

Prose Works:

After Strange Gods, London, 1934: reprinted Maroussi, Athens, 2020 (Alpha Editions).

Dante, 1929: London, 1965.

Eeldrop and Appleplex, and Ezra Pound: His Metric and Poetry, 1917 and 1918: Gloucester, 2007.

The Idea of a Christian Society, London, 1939.

Notes towards the Definition of Culture, London, 1948.

On Poetry and Poets, 1943: New York, 2009.

Poetry and Drama: The Theodor Spencer Memorial Lecture, Harvard University, November 21, 1950, London, 1951.

The Sacred Wood: Essays on Poetry and Criticism, 1920: London, 1932.

Selected Essays, 1932: London, 1999.

Selected Prose, edited by John Hayward, London, 1953.

The Use of Poetry and the Use of Criticism: Studies in the Relation of Criticism to Poetry in England, 1933: London, 1964.

The Varieties of Metaphysical Poetry: The Clark Lectures at Trinity College, Cambridge, 1926, and the Turnbull Lectures at the Johns Hopkins University, 1933, Edited and Introduced by Ronald Schuchard, 1993: San Diego, 1996.

Letters:

The Letters of T. S. Eliot:

Volume 1 (1898-1922), edited by Valerie Eliot, New York, 1988.

Volume 5 (1930-1931), edited by Valerie Eliot and John Haffenden, London, 2014.

Volume 8 (1936-1938), edited by Valerie Eliot and John Haffenden, London, 2019.

Volume 9 (1939-1941), edited by Valerie Eliot and John Haffenden, London, 2021.

The Letters of T. S. Eliot to Emily Hale (online only): https://tseliot.com/the-eliot-hale-letters

Editorial:

(ed.): *A Choice of Kipling's Verse: Selected, with an Essay on Rudyard Kipling,* 1941: London 1963.

Ellis, Marc: *Israel and Palestine: Out of the Ashes – The Search for Jewish Identity in the Twenty-First Century,* London, 2003. *Judaism Does not Equal Israel,* New York, 2009.

Empson, William: *Seven Types of Ambiguity,* 1930: London, 1961.

Finkelstein, Norman: *Beyond Chutzpah: On the Misuse of Anti-Semitism and the Abuse of History,* 2005: New York, 2008. *Image and Reality of the Israel-Palestine Conflict,* 1995: Second Edition, New York, 2003.

Frankl, George: *The Failure of the Sexual Revolution,* London, 1974. *Foundations of Morality: An Investigation into the Origin and Purpose of Moral Concepts,* London, 2000.

The Social History of the Unconscious, London, 1989.

The Three Faces of Monotheism: Judaism, Christianity, Islam, London, 2004.

Frazer, Sir James: *The Golden Bough: A Study in Magic and Religion, Abridged Edition*, 1922: London, 1950.

The Golden Bough: A Study in Magic and Religion: Part VI, The Scapegoat, London, 1913.

Freud, Sigmund: *The Penguin Freud Library, Volume 13:: The Origins of Religion,* London, 1990.

Gardner, Helen: *The Art of T. S. Eliot,* 1949: London, 1968.

The Composition of Four Quartets, London, 1980.

Gordon, Lyndall: *Eliot's New Life,* New York, 1988.

The Hyacinth Girl: T. S. Eliot's Hidden Muse, London, 2022.

Harding, Jason: *The New Cambridge Companion to T. S. Eliot,* Cambridge, 2017.

Harrison, Jane: *Prolegomena to the Study of Greek Religion,* 1903: London, 1962.

Themis: A Study of the Social Origins of Greek Religion, 1912, revised 1927: London, 1963.

Harrison, John: *The Reactionaries,* London, 1966.

Hirst, David: *The Gun and the Olive Branch: The Roots of Violence in the Middle East,* 1977: London, 2003.

Hollis, Matthew: *The Waste Land: A Biography of a Poem,* London, 2022.

Jain, Manju: *A Critical Reading of the Selected Poems of T. S. Eliot,* 1991: India, 2001.

Jones, David: *The Plays of T. S. Eliot,* 1960: London, 1963.

Jones, Genesius: *Approach to the Purpose: A Study of the Poetry of T. S.*

Eliot, London, 1964.

Julius, Anthony: *T. S. Eliot, Anti-Semitism and Literary Form*, 1995: Second Edition, London, 2003.

Jung, Julius: *Champions of Orthodoxy*, London, 1974.

Kahl, Joachim: *The Misery of Christianity or A Plea for a Humanity without God*: English translation (by N. D. Smith) of *Das Elend des Christentums,* Hamburg, 1968: London, 1971.

Kenner, Hugh: *The Invisible Poet: T. S. Eliot,* 1960: London, 1965.

Kipling, Rudyard: *Actions and Reactions,* London, 1909
The Best Short Stories, Ware, 2010.

Kojecky, Roger: *T. S. Eliot's Social Criticism,* London, 1971.

Laity, Cassandra and Nancy K. Gish: *Gender, Desire and Sexuality in T. S. Eliot*, Cambridge, 2004.

Lerman, Antony: Whatever Happened to Antisemitism?: Redefinition and the Myth of the 'Collective Jew', London, 2022.

Levy, William Turner, and Victor Scherle: *Affectionately, T. S. Eliot: The Story of a Friendship 1947-1965,* London, 1968.

Maccoby, Hyam: *Antisemitism and Modernity: Innovation and Continuity,* London, 2006.
The Disputation, London, 2001.
Judaism on Trial: Jewish-Christian Disputations in the Middle Ages, New Jersey, 1982.
Judas Iscariot and the Myth of Jewish Evil, New York, 1992.
The Mythmaker: Paul and the Invention of Christianity, New York, 1986.
Revolution in Judaea: Jesus and the Jewish Resistance, 1973: New York, 1980.

The Sacred Executioner: Human Sacrifice and the Legacy of Guilt, London, 1982.

Martin, Graham (ed): *Eliot in Perspective: A Symposium,* London, 1970

Matthiessen, F. O.: *The Achievement of T. S. Eliot: An Essay on the Nature of Poetry,* 1935: Second Edition, New York, 1947.

Moody, A. David: *Thomas Stearns Eliot Poet,* 1979: Second Edition, Cambridge, 1994.

(ed.) *The Cambridge Companion to T. S. Eliot,* Cambridge, 1994.

Morris, Benny: *The Birth of the Palestinian Refugee Problem Revisited,* Second Edition of *The Birth of the Palestinian Refugee Problem,* 1998: Cambridge, 2004.

Murray, Gilbert: *Aeschylus: The Creator of Tragedy,* Oxford, 1940.

Five Stages of Greek Religion, 1925: London, 1935.

Newman, John Henry: *Collected Poems and the Dream of Gerontius,* 1868: Sevenoaks, Kent, 1992.

Praz, Mario: *The Romantic Agony,* first published in English 1933, translated from the Italian by Angus Davidson, Second Edition, Oxford, 1970.

Prokosch, Frederick, *Chosen Poems,* London, 1944.

Raine, Craig: *Haydn and the Valve Trumpet: Literary Essays,* 1990: London, 2013.

T. S. Eliot, Oxford, 2006.

Rajan, B. (ed.): *T. S. Eliot: A Study of his Writings by Several Hands,* London, 1947.

Ricks, Christopher: *T. S. Eliot and Prejudice,* 1988: London, 1994.

Rosenbaum, Ron: *Explaining Hitler: The Search for the Origins of his Evil,* London, 1998.

Russell, Bertrand: *History of Western Philosophy*, 1946: London, 2004.

Scholem, Gershom G.: *Major Trends in Jewish Mysticism,* 1941: Third Edition, London, 1955.

The Messianic Idea in Judaism and Other Essays on Jewish Spirituality, 1971: New York, 1995.

Smith, Grover: *T. S. Eliot's Poetry and Plays: A Study in Sources and Meaning,* 1956: Chicago, 1960.

(ed.): *Josiah Royce's Seminar 1913-1914, as recorded in the Notebooks of Harry T. Costello,* New Brunswick, 1963.

Southam, B. C.: *A Student's Guide to the Selected Poems of T. S. Eliot,* London, 1968.

Spender, Stephen: *Eliot,* London, 1975.

Spurr, Barry: "*Anglo-Catholic in Religion*": *T. S. Eliot and Christianity,* Cambridge, 2010.

Steiner, George: *In Bluebeard's Castle: Some Notes Towards the Re-definition of Culture,* London, 1971.

Unger, Leonard (ed.): *T. S. Eliot: A Selected Critique,* New York, 1948.

Ward, David: *T. S. Eliot Between Two Worlds: A Reading of T. S. Eliot's Poetry and Plays,* 1973: London, 2016.

Weston, Jessie L.: *From Ritual to Romance,* 1920: New York, 1957.

Wilson, Edmund: *Axel's Castle: A Study in the Imaginative Literature of 1870-1930,* 1931: London, 1961.

Williamson, George: *A Reader's Guide to T. S. Eliot: A Poem-by-Poem Analysis,* 1953: New York, 1998.

ACKNOWLEDGEMENTS

I am grateful to Evening Standard Ltd. for its kind permission to include in the book (as Appendix 5) my father's review of Anthony Julius's book *T. S. Eliot, Antisemitism and Literary Form*. This review was originally published as "The Shock of the Jew", in The London *Evening Standard*, September 18, 1995.

I acknowledge with gratitude the gracious permission of the Jewish Literary Trust to republish, as Chapter 4 in this book, my father's article "A Study of the 'jew' in 'Gerontion'". This essay was originally published in The *Jewish Quarterly* in its issue of Summer 1969, Volume 17, No 2 (62).

I understand, from the Berghahn Journals website, that permission is granted by Berghahn Journals to publish articles from The *Critical Survey*, so long as the original publication is fully acknowledged. Chapter 5, "An Interpretation of 'Mr. Eliot's Sunday Morning Service'" was originally published in the Winter 1967 (Volume Three, Number Three) issue of The *Critical Survey*. I am grateful to Berghahn Journals for its kind permission to republish this article.

I understand, from an email communication from Oxford University Press (OUP) that permission is granted for me to republish eight pieces contributed by my father to *Notes and Queries*, provided that the origin of each article is fully acknowledged. Appendix 1, "Two Notes on 'Ash Wednesday'", was published in the November 1966 issue. Appendix 2, "Two Notes on *Murder in the Cathedral*", was published in the July 1967 issue. Appendix 3, "Difficulties in the Plot of *The Family Reunion*", was published in the August 1968 issue. Appendix 4, "*The Family Reunion* and Kipling's 'The House Surgeon'", was published in the February 1968 issue. Appendix 6, "Review of *Word Unheard: A Guide Through Eliot's Four Quartets*, by Harry Blamires", was published in the September 1972 issue. Chapter 6 is composed of three *Notes and Queries* pieces. They are: "A Commentary on 'Burnt Norton', I", which was published in the February 1968 issue; "A Commentary on 'Burnt Norton', II", which was published in the February 1970 issue; and "A Commentary on 'Burnt Norton, III, IV and V", which was published in the December 1970 issue. I acknowledge with gratitude OUP's gracious permission to reprint these eight pieces.

Midstream magazine ceased publication in 2013. It was published by the Theodor Herzl Foundation Inc., which is now basically defunct, but which remains a legal entity. Its remaining affairs are managed by the American Zionist Movement (AZM). I acknowledge here the original publication of Chapter 3, under the title "The Antisemitism of T. S. Eliot", in the *Midstream* issue of May 1973, Volume XIX, No. 5. I am grateful to Mr. Herbert Block, the Executive Director of the AZM, for his kind permission to reprint this article.

Extracts from "Mr. Eliot's Sunday Morning Service" and "A Cooking Egg" that exceed Faber and Faber's "fair use" Guidelines are published in *Christ the Tiger* by permission of Faber and Faber.

I would like to thank the renowned American Jewish scholar Dr. Norman Finkelstein for his advice, help and encouragement, particularly in relation to my Preface and Memoir. My editing of his brilliant and hilarious book *I'll Burn That Bridge When I Get to It* gave me the experience and confidence to embark on editing *Christ the Tiger*. I would also like to thank my dear friends Abe and Ros Hayeem for their encouragement with all my projects, including this one. I am also grateful to my brother, David Maccoby, for his help, encouragement and advice. I would also like to thank my sister and brother-in-law, Melanie Craig and Dr. Alan Craig, who are my father's Literary Executors, for giving me permission to publish these essays, and in general for their help and encouragement. They are of course not responsible for the personal political views I have expressed in my Memoir and footnotes. All errors in the editing of this book are entirely mine.

Above all, my thanks go to my mother, Cynthia Maccoby, to whom this book is dedicated. She worked on *Christ the Tiger* until she became too ill to continue; it was the discovery of a folder in which she had begun to collect printouts of the articles that made me decide to complete the project, because it seemed to me that, put together, they would make a coherent, original and illuminating book. And, of course, my final acknowledgement must go to the author of these essays: Hyam Maccoby, my father and teacher, *zichrono livracha* (may his memory be for a blessing).

ABOUT THE AUTHOR AND EDITOR

The Author: Hyam Maccoby (1924-2004) was Emeritus Fellow of the Leo Baeck College, London and Research Professor at the Centre for Jewish Studies, University of Leeds. He published many books and articles, and they include: *Revolution in Judaea: Jesus and the Jewish Resistance* (Taplinger, 1980); *Judaism on Trial: Jewish-Christian Disputations in the Middle Ages* (The Littman Library of Jewish Civilization, 1982); *The Sacred Executioner: Human Sacrifice and the Legacy of Guilt (*Thames and Hudson, 1982); *The Mythmaker: Paul and the Invention of Christianity (*Harper and Row, 1986); *Judas Iscariot and the Myth of Jewish Evil (*Macmillan, 1992); and *Antisemitism and Modernity: Innovation and Continuity* (published posthumously by Routledge, 2006). His play *The Disputation* (Calder Publications, 2001), a dramatization of the 1263 Barcelona Disputation, was made into a Channel 4 film in 1986 and has been performed on stage in London (New End Theatre, 2001) and widely performed in the United States.

The Editor: Deborah Maccoby (the Author's daughter) holds an M.A and M. Litt (for a thesis on the poetry of Emily Brontë) from the University of Oxford. Her literary biography of the Anglo-Jewish First World War poet Isaac Rosenberg -- *God Made Blind: Isaac Rosenberg: His Life and Poetry* -- was published in 2000 by the Symposium Press. She worked as a Production Assistant at the BBC World Service before taking early retirement in 2008. She has written book reviews for The *Jewish Chronicle*, The *Jewish Quarterly* and the BBC Arabic Service and has also written talks on literary anniversaries for the BBC World Service Talks and Features Department. She is currently a regular book reviewer for the Jewish Voice for Labour website. She has recently been the General Editor of the first edition of a book by the renowned American-Jewish scholar Norman Finkelstein: *I'll Burn that Bridge When I Get to It: Heretical Thoughts on Cancel Culture, Identity Politics and Academic Freedom* (2nd edition, Or Books, 2025). She now lives in Leeds.

INDEX

Ackroyd, Peter, 12n, 68n

Adam, 19, 102, 190

Adams, Henry, 83, 89-90, 91, 91n, 113, 113n

Adonis, 7, 43, 43nn, 49, 68, 68nn, 78, 78n, 96-97, 97n, 117, 125

Aeschylus, 48, 48n, 73, 74n, 74n-75n

Agamemnon, 65-69, 73-74

Andrewes, Lancelot, 15n, 109n

Andromeda, 202, 228n

Antisemitism, 13-16, 28, 32, 35-37, 35n, 36n, 37n, 57n, 80-82, 80n, 81n, 82n, 83-119, 120-123, 120n, 121n, 132, 205-206, 211-214, 236-241

Antony, 226n

Aphrodite, 68n

Apollo, 74n, 191, 191n

Aquinas, Thomas (St.), 128, 128n, 133n, 207

Argos, 75n, 202

Aristotle, 137, 150-151

Arnold, Matthew, 66n

Asher, Kenneth, 60n, 100n-101n

Athens, 74n-75n, 160

Attis, 7, 43, 43nnn, 49, 68, 68n, 78, 78n, 125

Augustine (St.), 32, 137

Bailey, Cyril, 151n, 152, 152n

Barber, C. L., 79, 79n, 143n

Barrès, Maurice, 35, 35n, 91, 92n, 107, 107n, 112

Bateson, F. W., 132, 216-217, 222n

Baudelaire, Charles, 7, 41, 45, 45n, 60n, 70, 79n, 118, 118n, 178n, 208, 219

Beatrice, 70, 82n, 220, 228

Bergonzi, Bernard, 237-238

Bergson, Henri, 136. 136nn, 145, 145n, 149, 165, 165n, 167, 167n, 172, 172n, 207, 208, 208n

Berlin, Isaiah (Sir), 84n

Biggs, Murray, 86, 86n, 237, 238-241

Blamires, Harry, 8n, 134n, 207-209

Blavatsky, Madame, 82n, 225, 229-230

Bradley, F. W., 109, 136, 136n, 142, 146, 146n, 153, 167, 207

Brooker, Jewel Spears, 83n, 108n, 134n, 177n

Brooks, Cleanth, 42n

Browne, Martin, 183n, 187n, 188nn, 189n, 190n, 191n, 192n, 197n, 198n

Buchan, John, 90

Buddhism, 143, 144

Burton-Page, Piers, 236

Byron, George Gordon (Lord), 60n, 107

Calvinism, 11-12, 19, 60-61, 60n, 204

Carthage, 72, 94

Chaucer, Geoffrey, 6, 81n, 98, 241

Cheyette, Bryan, 82n, 124n
Chicago, 88-90, 89n
Chinitz, David, 38n, 41n, 82n
Clarke, David R., 6n
Cleopatra, 226n, 228
Clytemnestra, 67, 70, 81, 228
Coghill, Nevill, 46n, 47n, 180, 184, 184nn
Coleridge, Samuel Taylor, 57n, 129n
Cooper, John Xiros, 57n
Coriolanus, 226-227, 226n, 228, 232
Cox, C. B., 42n
Crawford, Robert, 5, 36n, 60n, 84n-85n
Cunningham, Gilbert F., 215
Curtis, Michael, 35n, 92n, 119n, 206n
Cybele, 68n

Daniel, Arnaut, 12n, 127, 127n
Dante (Alighieri), 12n, 39, 45n, 58, 59, 62n, 101n, 106n, 108, 118n, 126-127, 152, 161n, 162, 163n, 164, 207, 212, 220, 225, 227, 230-231
Davie, Donald, 41n, 42nn, 87
De Villiers, Rick, 223
Descartes, René, 166, 166n
Dionysus, 48, 48nn, 125
Donne, John, 131n, 135n, 184, 184n
Drew, Elizabeth, 65n, 69n, 138n, 149, 149n, 176, 217
Drumont, Édouard, 88, 92
Duncan-Jones, E. E., 174
Durkheim, Émile, 49, 49n, 51

Eliot, Andrew, 11
Eliot, Charlotte Champe, 11, 220
Eliot, Henry Ware, 160n-161n
Eliot, Thomas Stearns,
Poetry
"Animula", 63, 106
Ara Vos Prec, 12-13, 12n, 64n, 67n, 101, 108, 127n, 205, 215, 216n, 229, 234
Ariel, 118
Ash Wednesday, 39, 44-46, 59, 70, 96, 105, 109, 139-140, 143, 151, 151n, 152, 163, 164, 172, 174-179, 219, 220
"Boston Evening Transcript", 210n
"Burbank with a Baedeker, Bleistein with a Cigar", 13, 14, 80, 85, 88-93, 94, 98, 101, 114-115, 206, 226, 226n, 232, 237, 241
"Burnt Norton", 8
I, 110, 133-146, 200, 208, 209, 218, 225
II, 39, 147-158, 231
III, 62n, 159-167, 168n
IV, 168
V, 169-173
"Cape Ann", 117n, 143
"Conversation Galante", 70
"A Cooking Egg", 6-7, 12n, 132n, 215-235
"Coriolan", 216, 221, 233
"Dans le Restaurant", 59, 70, 95, 105, 217, 225, 228
"Dirge", 14, 59n, 93-98, 206

"The Dry Salvages", 51, 155, 165, 168, 171, 172, 175, 208, 209

"East Coker", 11, 16n, 54, 55, 57, 63, 70, 76, 109n, 144, 148, 149, 160, 164, 166, 170, 171, 171n, 173, 175-176, 209, 221

Four Quartets, 58, 59, 82n, 117, 147, 148, 151, 151n, 161n-162n

"Gerontion", 13, 15, 16n, 32, 44, 58, 62-63, 80, 81, 82n, 85-88, 86n, 89-90, 90n, 91, 95, 97, 100-119, 144, 153, 176, 177, 206, 212, 213, 213n, 232, 237-240

"The Hippopotamus", 13, 59-60, 128-129, 129n, 132n, 229

"The Hollow Men", 62n-63n, 163, 163n, 164, 200

Inventions of the March Hare, 60n, 68n, 81n-82n, 117n, 128n, 216, 216n, 223-224, 228n, 231, 234

"Journey of the Magi", 118

"King Bolo", 82n

"Landscapes", 146n

"Lines for Cuscuscaraway and Mirza Murad Ali Beg", 132n

"Lines for an Old Man", 147n

"Little Gidding", 59, 59n, 72, 82n, 115, 140, 144, 150, 164, 171, 171n, 173, 208, 209

"The Love-Song of J. Alfred Prufrock", 70, 131, 213n

"Mr. Apollinax", 210, 210n, 223

"Mr. Eliot's Sunday Morning Service", 12, 14, 81, 96, 108n, 120-132, 161n, 206, 211-213, 228

"Ode", 64n, 68n, 228n

Old Possum's Book of Practical Cats, 82n

"Portrait of a Lady", 210n

"Prufrock": See "The Love-Song of J. Alfred Prufrock"

"A Song for Simeon", 118

"Sweeney Agonistes", 69, 70, 73, 134, 134n, 137

"Sweeney Among the Nightingales", 7, 13, 14n-15n, 65-69, 70, 80, 94, 98, 206

"Sweeney Erect", 64n, 69, 70

The Waste Land, 42, 42n, 43-44, 43n, 44n, 46, 50, 54, 57, 57n, 59, 59n, 66, 69-70, 76, 85, 87, 93-97, 104-105, 104n, 106, 115, 116, 116n, 120n-121n, 127, 127n, 154, 160, 160n, 161n, 163, 163n, 206, 213n, 219, 220, 222n, 226-227, 228, 230, 232, 237, 240

"Whispers of Immortality", 127, 131n, 234, 234n

Plays

The Cocktail Party, 59, 61, 63, 70, 72, 183n

The Confidential Clerk, 61, 61n, 62n, 70n

The Elder Statesman, 61n-62n, 70n

The Family Reunion, 7, 48, 54, 59, 69, 70, 72, 73-79, 134, 134n, 135n, 137, 154, 183n, 187-204, 219, 228

Murder in the Cathedral, 46-48, 134n, 139n, 140, 153, 159, 170, 174-175, 180-186

The Rock, 53, 149, 154

Prose

After Strange Gods, 57n, 80n, 83, 83n, 84, 84n, 107-108, 108n

A Choice of Kipling's Verse (Introductory Essay), 54, 54n, 76, 141-142, 200, 204n

Dante, 39, 58, 58n, 106, 106n

"Eeldrop and Appleplex", 134, 134n

For Lancelot Andrewes, 15, 15n

The Idea of a Christian Society, 129, 129n, 226

Notes towards the Definition of Culture, 57n, 236

On Poetry and Poets, 42n, 60n, 215, 215n

Poetry and Drama, 187-188, 188n

The Sacred Wood, 6, 68, 68n-69n, 142n

Selected Essays, 57n, 218-219, 219n

Selected Prose, 60n, 130, 130n, 118, 118n, 226n

The Use of Poetry and the Use of Criticism, 57n, 66n

Eliot, Valerie, 10, 45n, 59n, 61n-62n, 66n, 82n, 84n, 129n, 142n, 161n

Eliot, Vivienne, 63 ("encounter with the 'primitive terror'"), 69 ("purely personal unhappiness"), 220-221, 222n, 227, 228

Eliot, William Greenleaf, 89n

Empson, William, 127, 135n, 155, 179

Erinyes: See Furies

Eumenides, 48, 70, 74, 74n-75n, 78nn, 79, 196n-197n

Eumenides, The (play; last of the *Oresteia* trilogy), 74n-75n

Euripides, 61n

Finkelstein, Israel, 111n

Finkelstein, Norman, 34, 34n, 37n, 111n, 118n

Flaubert, Gustave, 7-8, 72, 94, 161n, 171n, 172n

Fragonard, Jean-Honoré, 210n, 223

Frankl, George, 27-28, 27n, 49n, 75n

Frazer, Sir James, 16, 41, 42, 43, 43nnn, 44, 44n, 46, 48n, 51, 67, 68, 68nn, 69n, 73, 97n, 129, 178n, 179, 179n, 208, 216n, 231n

Freud, Sigmund, 44n, 49n, 90, 144, 179, 216n, 231n

Furies, 67, 67n, 68, 73, 74, 74n-75n, 81, 197n

Gardner, Helen, 10, 65, 65n, 73, 134n, 147, 147n, 157n, 161n-162n, 175, 196, 200, 200n

Germer, Rudolf, 129n

Gish, Nancy K., 5n

Gloucester Road Underground Station, 160n-162n, 168n

Gordon, Lyndall, 5, 138n, 165n, 216n, 219, 221, 222n, 227-228, 228n, 230

Gorgons, 202

Gospels, The, 29-30, 97-98, 109, 109n, 121-123, 208, 212

Grasser, Erich, 97

Grigson, Geoffrey, 239-241

Gruber, Patricia, 84n

Haffenden, John, 45n, 84n, 129n

Hale, Emily, 5, 36n, 161n, 148n, 150n, 154n, 161n, 165n, 171n, 172n, 216n, 219-221, 226-228

Hamilton, Ian, 64n

Harari, Yuval Noah, 71n

Harding, Jason, 42n, 57n

Harrison, Jane, 41, 48n, 49, 51, 56n, 67, 74n-75n, 216n

Harrison, John, 92n, 94, 100, 100n, 101, 108

Hayward, John, 60n, 161n-162n

Hegel, G. W. F., 153

Heraclitus, 72, 72n, 150-151, 150n, 151n, 152, 152n, 153, 154n, 156, 161n, 164, 171, 171n, 175

Hinduism, 143, 143n, 144, 152

Hinchcliffe, Arnold P., 42n

Hitler, Adolf, 90, 92, 107, 107n

Hollis, Matthew, 5, 103n

Holocaust, see Hitler and Nazis

Homer, 153, 162

Hopkins, Gerard Manley, 169

Hulme, T. E., 116

Hume, David, 171, 175, 175n

Ibsen, Henrik, 144

Incarnation, 11, 13, 21, 39, 59-60, 124, 128-129, 155, 156, 184, 229, 231

Iphigenia, 67

Israel, State of, 31, 32, 33, 34-35, 34nn, 37n, 110-111, 110n-111n, 111n, 116, 116n, 118, 118n

Jain, Manju, 100n, 118n, 126n

James, Henry, 89, 227

James, William, 88

John of the Cross, St., 161n, 165n, 172n, 177n

Jones, David, 61n, 180, 183n, 184, 197n

Jones, Genesius, Fr., 15n-16n, 62n, 92n, 96n, 115n, 160n, 216n

Josipovici, Gabriel, 14-15, 14n-15n, 213-214, 213n-214n

Joyce, James, 14n, 29n, 42n, 98, 106, 208

Judaism, 17-39, 56, 120-122, 130-131, 212-213

Judas, 113-114, 116, 116n, 232

Julius, Anthony, 13-15, 14n, 14n-15n, 29n, 57n, 84n, 100nn, 108n, 120n-121n, 211, 214, 216n, 226, 232

Justin Martyr, 50

Kahl, Joachim, 97-98

Keats, John, 50, 51

Kenner, Hugh, 42n, 108n, 146n, 160n-162n, 174

Kensington, 160n-162n

Kingsley, Charles, 95

Kipling, Rudyard, 54, 54n, 76-77, 77n, 141-142, 190, 190n, 200-204

Knight, G. Wilson, 226n

Kojecky, Roger, 57n

Laforgue, Jules, 68n, 70, 228n

Laity, Cassandra, 5n

Lang, Andrew, 49

Lapidge, Michael, 128n

Lawrence, D. H., 64, 71, 72

Leibnitz, Gottfried Wilhelm, 109, 136n, 136-137, 137n

Levy, William Turner, 84n

Lévy-Bruhl, Lucien, 49, 49n
Lewis, C. S., 184, 184n
Lewis, Wyndham, 63n, 213n
Longenbach, James, 41n-42n

Maccoby, Chaim Zundel (The Kamenitzer Maggid), 17, 17n, 18n, 110n-111n
Mallarmé, Stéphane, 147, 147n
Mankowitz, Wolf, 100, 100n
Marlowe, Christopher, 120, 120n, 211, 212, 241
Martin, Graham, 41n
Martz, L.L., 184
Mary, The Virgin, 10, 68n, 70, 81, 81n, 82n, 143, 220
Matthiessen, F. O., 66n, 104n, 159, 159n, 161n, 224, 224n
Maurras, Charles, 35, 35n, 83, 91, 92, 92n, 100, 100n-101n, 107, 112, 206, 206n
Maxwell, J. C., 133n, 175n, 204, 204n
Mayes, J. C. C., 132n
McCue, Jim, 40n, 160n, 161n, 177n, 216n
McDonald, Gail, 64n
Medcalf, Stephen, 14n, 210, 211
Medusa, 202
Michelangelo, 68n
Moody, A. David, 44n, 60n, 61n, 73nn, 132n, 142n, 172n, 216n
Morley, Frank, 161n, 188n
Müller, Max, 49
Murray, Gilbert, 48n, 52, 52n, 56, 56n, 74n

Muses, 68-69, 68-69n, 142n
Mystery-religions, 7, 15, 49-50, 55-56, 56n, 59, 68n, 78n, 213

Naasenes, 50, 50n
Nazis, 27, 33n, 35n, 81, 236, 238-240
Newman, John Henry (Cardinal): 103-105, 103n, 110
Oedipus, 49n, 61n, 67n, 231n
Oldham, J. H., 84n
Oresteia, The (trilogy), 48, 73, 73n, 74, 74n-75n
Orestes, 48, 59, 67, 73, 190, 190n, 201-202
Origen, 122, 122n, 123, 129, 130, 212
Orpheus/Orphism, 56n, 68n-69n, 123n
Osiris, 7, 43, 43nn, 49, 68n

Parker, Philip, 178n
Paul, St., 30, 96n, 212
Parkes, James, 84n
Pausanias, 68n-69n
Pearson, Gabriel, 89, 89n
Perseus, 201-204, 228n
Philo, 109, 123
Philomela, 67, 67n, 69, 222n
Phoenicians, 72, 94, 104-106, 123n, 230
Plato, 104, 137, 216n
Plotinus, 184n
Pondrom, Cyrena, 64n
Porphyry, 184, 184n

Pound, Ezra, 6, 35, 81n, 83, 116, 116n, 119n, 121, 121n, 123, 206, 206n, 213n, 214n, 234

Praz, Mario (*The Romantic Agony*), 7, 41, 52

Prokosch, Frederic, 149

Quinn, John, 216n

Ragan, B., 100n, 133n

Raine, Craig, 83n, 100n, 210-211

Rainey, Lawrence, 42n

Ricks, Christopher, 40n, 108n, 160n, 161n, 177n, 206, 216n, 234

Richards, I. A., 216-218

Ridler, Anne, 85, 85n, 175, 237, 239-241

Rist, John M., 128n

Roman de la Rose, 143

Rossetti, Dante Gabriel, 226n, 233n

Ruskin, John, 224, 224n, 230

Russell, Bertrand, 136nn, 150n, 208, 208n, 210-211, 210n

Sade, Marquis de, 52

Santayana, George, 88

Schenk, Willie, 133n

Scherle, Victor, 84n

Scholem, Gershom, 113n, 144n

Schuchard, Ronald, 135n

Scott, Sir Walter, 18, 80n

Semnae, 74n-75n

Set, 68n

Shakespeare, William, 18,

Antony and Cleopatra, 226n

Coriolanus 226, 226n

Hamlet, 72n, 74

The Merchant of Venice, 8-10, 28-30, 37n, 90-92, 92n, 98, 103, 103n, 205, 241

Richard II, 129n

Sonnets, 140, 140n, 185, 185n

Tempest, The, 93, 98

Shaw, George Bernard, 71

Shelley, Percy Bysshe, 50, 107, 135n

Silberman, Neil Asher, 111n

Smith, Constance I., 222, 230n

Smith, Grover, 49n, 60n, 62n-63n, 64n, 67nn, 68n, 73, 75, 78, 78n, 102n, 118n, 120, 120n, 123, 126n, 145, 145n, 156-157, 156n, 157n, 160n, 162, 162n, 176n-177n, 177n, 187n, 192, 192n, 200, 200n, 202n, 211, 217, 233, 233n

Sophocles, 61n, 67n

Sorel, Georges, 35n

Southam, B. C., 12n, 126n, 217-218, 222, 222n

Spender, Stephen, 39

Spurr, Barry, 10-15, 14n, 37n, 38n,100n, 177n, 216n, 233-234

St. Louis (city), 89, 89n

Steiner, George, 57n, 236-237, 240

Stoics, 109, 123, 128, 128n

Strindberg, August, 71

Talmud, 17, 18n, 19, 22, 24, 182n

Tammuz, 49

Tennyson, Alfred Lord, 52, 139, 145, 174
Tertullian, 181, 181n
Thaventhiran, Helen, 5, 85n
Thompson, David M., 83n
Thurber, James, 71, 71n
Tillyard, E. M. W., 222, 222n
Tiresias, 115, 118n
Totemism, 44, 44n, 48, 231
Tradition, 37-38, 111, 169-170
Tylor, Edward Burnett, 49

Unitarianism, 11, 15, 220
Unger, Leonard, 65n, 177n

Vaughan, Henry, 56, 56n, 126n, 158, 158n
Vienna, 88, 90-91, 160
Voltaire, 136
Villon, François, 218-219, 233n
Wandering Jew, The, 99, 99n, 106-107, 116
Webster, John, 131n
Wells, H. G., 138
Weston, Jessie, 42-43, 42n, 43nn, 50n, 128n
Williams, Charles, 45n, 178n
Williamson, George, 104n, 113
Wilson, Edmund, 65n, 106
Wilson, Robert, 103n
Wolheim, Richard, 71
Wordsworth, William, 50, 51, 57n, 106

Yeats, William Butler, 82n

Zeus, 74n
Ziemer, Gregor, 178n
Zionism, see Israel

www.ingramcontent.com/pod-product-compliance
Lightning Source LLC
Chambersburg PA
CBHW051402070526
44584CB00023B/3262